Age of Emergency

*Living with Violence at the
End of the British Empire*

ERIK LINSTRUM

OXFORD
UNIVERSITY PRESS

OXFORD
UNIVERSITY PRESS

Oxford University Press is a department of the University of Oxford. It furthers the University's objective of excellence in research, scholarship, and education by publishing worldwide. Oxford is a registered trade mark of Oxford University Press in the UK and certain other countries.

Published in the United States of America by Oxford University Press
198 Madison Avenue, New York, NY 10016, United States of America.

© Oxford University Press 2023

Library of Congress Cataloging-in-Publication Data
Names: Linstrum, Erik, 1983– author.
Title: Age of emergency / Erik Linstrum.
Description: New York, NY : Oxford University Press, [2023] |
Includes bibliographical references and index. |
Identifiers: LCCN 2022053522 (print) | LCCN 2022053523 (ebook) |
ISBN 9780197572030 (hardback) | ISBN 9780197572054 (epub) | ISBN 9780197572061
Subjects: LCSH: Great Britain—Colonies—Administration—History—20th century. |
State-sponsored terrorism—Great Britain—History—20th century. |
Punishment—Great Britain—History—20th century. | Imperialism.
Classification: LCC JV1060.L56 2023 (print) | LCC JV1060 (ebook) |
DDC 325/.320941—dc23/eng/20221220
LC record available at https://lccn.loc.gov/2022053522
LC ebook record available at https://lccn.loc.gov/2022053523

DOI: 10.1093/oso/9780197572030.001.0001

1 3 5 7 9 8 6 4 2

Printed and bound in Great Britain by Clays Ltd, Elcograf S.p.A.

Portions of Chapter 5 are adapted from Erik Linstrum,
"Facts about Atrocity: Reporting Colonial Violence in Postwar Britain,"
History Workshop Journal, Volume 84, Autumn 2017, Pages 108–127.
Used by permission of Oxford University Press.

For my parents

Contents

Acknowledgments

IT IS A great pleasure to acknowledge the programs and institutions that remain committed to research in the humanities and made this book possible with their generous support: the Kluge Fellowship and the Kluge Center at the Library of Congress, the Frederick Burkhardt Fellowship of the American Council of Learned Societies, and the Berlin Prize of the American Academy in Berlin. I thank Mary Lou Reker and Travis Hensley at the Kluge Center and Rachel Bernard and Tami Shaloum at ACLS for facilitating these opportunities. The staff of the American Academy at Berlin managed to create an idyllic residential experience in the midst of a pandemic. My thanks to René Albhorn, Daniel Benjamin, Mathias Buhrow, Berit Ebert, Caitlin Hahn, Reinold Kegel, Ilya Poskonin, Carol Scherer, my illustrious fellow fellows, and everyone else there for a memorable stay.

The University of Virginia has nurtured this book from the early days of exploratory research to the final preparation of the manuscript. I am grateful to the College of Arts and Sciences, the Department of History, the Institute of the Humanities and Global Culture, and the Center for Global Inquiry and Innovation for funding support, release from teaching obligations, and most of all, a congenial scholarly home. I would like to collectively thank my colleagues in the Department of History and to particularly acknowledge two department chairs, Karen Parshall and Claudrena Harold, for their support. I am grateful to the department staff who helped in ways large and small: Ashley Herring, Pamela Pack, and Kelly Robeson. My thanks also to Rob Smith and his team in the Digital Production Group at the University of Virginia Library for assistance with illustrations.

The many librarians and archivists who fielded queries, arranged visits, and copied documents made this book possible. Sophie Bridges at the Churchill Archives Centre and Samantha Blake and Matthew Chipping at the BBC Written Archives went beyond the call of duty. I owe another debt of gratitude to the research assistants who helped to gather materials across long distances and pandemic restrictions: Hannah Briscoe, Francesca Edgerton, Alex Hird, Matthew Kidd, Andrew Lewis, Adonis Li, Tashi Namgyal, Karolina Ondruskova, Chris Perry, Nikita Shepard, and Marita Vyrgioti.

I had the privilege of rehearsing arguments and presenting research from this book at Birkbeck College London, Cambridge University, the Central Virginia British Studies Seminar, Harvard University, Northwestern University, Ohio State University, the University of Chicago, the University of Potsdam, and the University of Warwick. My thanks to Daniel Pick, Helen McCarthy, Chris Bischof, Caroline Elkins, Deborah Cohen, Christopher Lane, Bruno Cabanes, Julian Go, Steven Pincus, Sönke Neitzel, and Callie Wilkinson for the invitations and the fruitful discussions that followed. Those conversations are among the exchanges with other scholars who generated ideas, asked questions, shared research, suggested leads, and otherwise made this book much richer than it would otherwise be. My thanks to David Anderson, David Armitage, Emily Baughan, Huw Bennett, Ellen Boucher, Robin Bunce, Lucy Delap, Brian Drohan, Jordanna Bailkin, David Edgerton, Geoff Eley, Freddy Foks, Aidan Forth, Niamh Gallagher, Susan Grayzel, Dagmar Herzog, Chris Hilliard, Dane Kennedy, Krishan Kumar, Fred Leventhal, Danny Loss, Margaret Macmillan, Erin Mosely, Sam Moyn, Vanessa Ogle, Tehila Sasson, Carol Summers, and Luise White. For reading a draft of the manuscript in its entirety and offering immensely perceptive comments, I am grateful to Peter Mandler, Stuart Ward, and two anonymous readers for Oxford University Press. They, too, made this a better book. Maya Jasanoff, as always, offered tireless support and sage advice. I am glad to thank Susan Ferber for her sharp editorial eye and for championing the book at every stage. It has been a pleasure to work with her and with everyone at Oxford.

Since I began working on this book in 2015, the world has changed more than I could have expected. Some things, happily, have changed for the better. To my daughter Nina, my son Max, and my wife Sheela, I love you more than I can say. This book is dedicated to my parents, who have given me so much for thirty-nine years and counting.

Age of Emergency

Introduction

THE WARS WERE LIKE A MIST

FOR ONE YORKSHIRE woman in the 1950s, the violent end of the British Empire was never entirely out of mind. A January day in 1953 began with breakfast in bed. "Then got up and pottered around," Mary Towler noted in her diary. "Things in Kenya seem very grim." On another winter's day five years later, she "spent some time in the garden. Cyprus seems to have quieted down for the moment. One miniature daffodil in bloom." Nine months after that, she watched her husband go off to London on the early train, then wondered whether "there is some truth in the stories of Cypriot suspects not being treated well. You've only to listen to ordinary people saying what they would do to the Cypriots." The banality of the everyday—domestic chores, blooming flowers, the comings and goings of friends and relations—mingled with fleeting but uneasy acknowledgments of war in the colonies.[1]

If every diary is a performance, Mary Towler's was no exception. The Mass Observation project that invited Towler to chronicle her thoughts was itself designed to produce a certain idea of everyday life: a collective identity forged through the reception and reworking of mass media.[2] For that reason, her diary can provide few definite answers about the experience of decolonization in Britain. It can, however, can raise questions. How did she learn about the distant colonial wars whose twists and turns she recorded? Was it lack of information or lack of interest that marked the limits of her knowledge? If anything troubled her for more than a moment, was it the seeming endlessness of war, the brutality committed in Britain's name, or the long, slow retreat of empire itself?

Colonial violence was a fact of life in postwar Britain. For most people, it demanded only occasional attention amid the press of more immediate concerns. But it was never altogether absent. When the Second World War ended in 1945, another era of conflict began. It lasted for almost two decades as uprisings threatened British rule in colonies across the world, in Palestine, Malaya, Kenya, Cyprus, and Aden. Tens of thousands of British soldiers, conscripts as well as career soldiers, were dispatched to one trouble spot after another. New wars began before their predecessors were finished. The same grim tactics were tried again and again with uncertain results. Lurking behind it all was the suspicion that the fighting dramatized Britain's decline as a global power rather than reversing it. For the British people, colonial war was not a series of events so much as an atmosphere: geographically diffuse, morally problematic, impervious to neat endings or declarations of victory. What novelist Graham Greene wrote from Malaya in 1950 could stand as an epitaph for the age: "The war was like a mist; it pervaded everything; it sapped the spirits; it wouldn't clear."[3]

There were other threats to peace in those years, including the Korean War and the nuclear rivalry of the Cold War. But the seeming endlessness of war in the colonies solidified a sense that the stability promised in 1945 had proven illusory. As a Lancashire woman asked her diary in 1948, after hearing the latest news from Palestine: "Another lot of youngsters growing up—for what? To go through all war's danger & agony again?" She could not help thinking that "the war is not yet over, it's only a lull."[4] When a University of London sociologist carried out a study of English teenagers in 1956, she asked them to write essays from the perspective of their older selves, "to look back over your life and say what has happened to you." Several responses referred to colonial war. One envisioned a thrilling though treacherous spell as a soldier in Cyprus, chasing "bomb-throwing terrorists" through "the winding back streets of Nicosia" and narrowly missing an assassin's bullet. Another darkly predicted that the effort to maintain imperial power by force would be futile. "By now Britain had loss [sic] nearly all her Empire," the student wrote. "I am glad my days are to an end [sic] because this world is full of fear and trouble."[5]

For some, imperial decline was synonymous with racial decline. Visiting the common room at Nuffield College, Oxford, in 1953, business leader Raymond Streat noted "a sense of foreboding" shortly after the outbreak of the Mau Mau rebellion in Kenya. Streat and his hosts shuddered at the thought of "millions of primitive uneducated Africans" on the march and worried that "once the tide was blown up by a heavy wind, it could sweep all defenses aside."[6] Newspaper magnate Lord Beaverbrook, tipsy at a country house party four years later, was gripped by racial melancholy after noticing a First World War–era atlas on his bookshelf. "Red everywhere," he exclaimed.

"Britain ruled the world!" Then he turned the page to an image of stereotypically primitive-looking Africans. "Savages!" Beaverbrook shouted. "We've given it all to them."[7]

The question was whether the waning of British power should be accepted with fatalism or resisted with force. Public opinion reports from Conservative Party agents across the country showed broad support for military action to prop up imperial power. The muscular language favored by Tory operatives hinted at the political dividends they sensed in an ongoing war for empire. They saw "firm action" in Malaya as a popularity booster for the new Churchill government in 1952, "tough policy" in Kenya as a safe position later that year, and "strong action" in Cyprus as a political winner in 1955.[8] On the other end of the political spectrum, *Daily Mirror* editor Hugh Cudlipp thought that his predominantly left-leaning and working-class readers disliked military interventions in theory but rallied to the flag in practice. Once British troops were in the field, he observed, they "were all for bashing the Wogs."[9]

Electoral history seemed to confirm those judgments. The governing Conservative Party won easy victories in 1955 and 1959 despite efforts by some Labour campaigners to portray them as callous warmongers. The 1959 election—which took place just seven months after colonial guards beat eleven African prisoners to death at a detention camp in Hola, Kenya—dealt an especially harsh blow to hopes for a collective rejection of colonial violence. The nascent industry of opinion polling detected no groundswell in that direction, either. A 1953 Gallup poll found that 41 percent of respondents approved of the government's handling of the Mau Mau uprising, while 23 percent disapproved and 36 percent did not know.[10] Even those figures almost certainly understate the popularity of colonial war because some who expressed disapproval favored more harshness rather than less. In a 1956 poll that found 51 percent of the sample dissatisfied with government actions in Cyprus, only 20 percent judged them "too severe," while more than twice as many (44 percent) found them "not severe enough." Backing for greater severity cut across party lines, including 37.5 percent of Liberals, 40.5 percent of Labourites, and 50 percent of Conservatives.[11]

But if war for empire could draw on powerful reserves of nationalism, racism, and jingoism, other sentiments were always present too. Anxiety, guilt, shame, and confusion shadowed the waging of war in the colonies, a tumultuous "inner life of decolonization."[12] Amid broad support for colonial war, Conservative Party agents nervously registered signs of disquiet. An internal public opinion report in January 1954 described "a feeling of uneasiness over Kenya" in the London area as press reports of "alleged ill-treatment of Mau-Mau suspects by British soldiers [were] causing concern."[13] Victories over insurgents—if they could be termed victories at all—inspired ambivalence rather than triumphalism when they finally arrived. With the announcement of a conclusion to the Cyprus conflict in 1959, Tory operatives detected "relief" along with suspicion that "a settlement of this sort might have been reached earlier and the lives of many British soldiers and civilians saved."[14] The uncertainties in public opinion reflected deeper tensions. Wars against brutal terrorists were being fought with brutal methods. Wars to defend empire concluded with the dissolution of empire.

Some voices, to be sure, were outraged rather than ambivalent. "I'll tell you now what I find very painful in the Daily Papers — Our war in Cyprus," novelist John Cowper Powys exclaimed in 1955. "Why the hell don't we clear out of Cyprus as we did out of the Sudan & the Nile and India?"[15] Strains of anticolonial and antiwar politics, isolated or co-opted during the Second World War, acquired new life with the moral shocks of counterinsurgency. When an acquaintance dismissed the Hola massacre on the grounds that the victims were probably murderous insurgents, Liberal MP Violet Bonham Carter retorted that the "character of the victim" was irrelevant: "it is the degradation of those who were able to beat them to death which matters."[16] For others, brutality proved unsettling on account of geopolitical degradation more than moral degradation; it signified the loss of power through the ineffectiveness of violence.[17] Racial prejudice was perfectly compatible with objections to colonial war on these grounds. "We cannot suppress the darkies by shooting them," ex-politician Harold Nicolson wrote in his diary shortly after Hola.[18]

Through the personal experiences of family and friends, the debates waged by politicians and activists, and the stories told in newspapers, books, radio, television, and theatre, unrest in the colonies did not stay there. The challenge for the British people was to find ways of living with the violence that they could not simply ignore. This book tells how, for the most part, they succeeded.

* * *

What does it mean to live in a society at war? It was a particular kind of war that occupied Britain for two decades after V-E Day: not "total wars" that transformed civilian life but "small wars" of the kind that had long raged on the frontiers of empire.[19] Although that Victorian-era term had given way by the 1950s to talk of "counterinsurgencies," "emergencies," and "low-intensity conflicts," the principle remained unchanged. It was guerilla fighters or insurgents who challenged British rule, not professional armies trained on European lines and equipped with the latest technology. The wars of decolonization therefore molded a very different kind of home front than the Second World War had. Anticolonial insurgents posed virtually no threat to the lives of civilians in Britain. In the colonies, they avoided big battles, relying instead on targeted raids and assassinations. As a result, the British troops deployed to combat insurgencies numbered in the tens of thousands, far fewer than the 2.9 million who served in uniform between 1939 and 1945. It was not people living in Britain but colonial subjects overseas who bore the heaviest burdens in these conflicts.[20]

Faced with the relatively small scale of colonial wars—small, that is, from the British perspective—historians have minimized the extent to which people in Britain even noticed them. Conflict in the colonies, one writes, was "far removed from the daily lives of the average inhabitant of the metropole."[21] Another argues that the wars of decolonization "left scarcely a trace in Britain's public memory."[22] With the exception of Suez, it is said, no British colonial war after 1945 caused any significant controversy.[23] These claims echo a longstanding assumption about the ease, even the peacefulness, of British decolonization in contrast to the traumatic experience of other European powers. As the story goes, no governments fell, no monarchies toppled, as the British Empire dissolved; it was indifference or approval, rather than anguish or loss, that possessed the public imagination at home.[24] While historians have challenged this view in recent years by tracing the impact of decolonization in everything from the welfare state and the financial system to national identity and popular culture, the violence committed in Britain's name overseas has not featured prominently in the reassessment.[25]

The self-flattering narrative of a peaceful end to empire—a deliberative "transfer of power" rather than a bloody, grudging struggle—has its parallel in the story long told about colonial warfare itself. A persistent myth among military strategists celebrated British counterinsurgencies for their restrained use of force: isolating insurgents from the rest of the population, winning the "hearts and minds" of civilians rather than alienating them, and so suppressing popular support for rebellion with a minimum of violence. While France in Algeria and the United States in Vietnam devolved into indiscriminate brutality, the "British way" seemed to promise something cleaner, cleverer, and more effective.[26] When General David Petraeus famously revised the US Army Counterinsurgency Manual during the invasion of Iraq in 2004, he pointed to the post-1945 British campaigns in Malaya and Cyprus as models.[27]

Thanks to a pioneering wave of scholarship, however, the British tradition of counterinsurgency now looks far more violent—and far less
exceptional—than conventional wisdom once held.[28] Curfews, checkpoints,
collective fines, house-to-house searches, and indiscriminate round-ups harassed civilians as well as insurgents. Hundreds of thousands of people were
forcibly uprooted and moved into militarized settlements; tens of thousands
more were held without trial, for years at a time, in detention camps. Judicial
safeguards disappeared and the pace of executions quickened. Soldiers on patrol destroyed homes, wrecked food supplies, and fired their weapons with
questionable justification. Police interrogators and camp guards tortured captive suspects. If the most repugnant tactics were not universal, they were not
aberrations, either. Intense, widespread, often brutal violence marked the end
of the British Empire.[29]

Could such things really happen without attracting notice or concern at
home? It has become a cliché that Britain experienced nothing like the debates
over the Algerian war that gripped France at the same time.[30] Although controversy was not totally absent on the northern side of the Channel, it appeared
sporadic and ephemeral by comparison; momentary outbursts arose from a
few well-publicized incidents, such as the Hola massacre.[31] Why the systemic
violence affecting thousands more colonial subjects, for years at a time, caused
little apparent disquiet, has been explained in various ways. Some insist that
Britain's wars really were smaller, quieter, and less brutal than those of other
colonial powers.[32] Others suggest that imagery in press coverage and popular
culture, showing English-style domestic life under siege from bloodthirsty
insurgents, made Malayan planters and Kenyan settlers more sympathetic figures than their equivalents, the *pied noirs*, in Algeria.[33]

But the most common explanation for complacency about colonial violence is also the most straightforward: the British public did not really know
was happening. Critic Paul Gilroy memorably argued that the "violent, dirty,
and immoral business" of empire was "repressed and buried," generating a
"hidden, shameful store of imperial horrors."[34] "It is only today becoming
clear," one historian writes, "how much information about the seamy side of
empire was kept from people at the time."[35] Others argue that the abuses of
decolonization were "hidden from view" or, at best, "dimly understood."[36] The
revelation in 2011 that officials had removed thousands of sensitive files from
colonies across the world when imperial rule ended, then concealed them for
decades at an intelligence facility in the English countryside, seemed to prove
the point. Unearthed documents about the counterinsurgency in Kenya
turned out to contain evidence of atrocities that the British government had

long denied, leading to an unprecedented settlement of £19.9 million for the benefit of survivors. New details likewise emerged about the scale of document destruction; while officials retreating from empire absconded with some files, they shredded and burned many more.[37] With a ruling elite so committed to keeping secrets, it is tempting to conclude that ordinary people never knew the extent of the violence carried out in their name.

But the state's grip on the flow of information was never absolute. In fact, knowledge of colonial violence rippled through British society. Networks defined by ideology, by profession, by faith, and by family and friendship all played a part in disseminating it. These communities or "circles of knowing" each processed information about British wrongdoing in their own ways.[38] They also contributed to the erosion of ignorance on a wider scale. Left-wing activists collected testimony from victims, printed pamphlets, held meetings and marches, and pressured politicians to take action. Some soldiers pasted photographs into albums; others penned letters to their parents; still others published memoirs of their experiences. Journalists recorded evidence in their notebooks, swapped stories with colleagues, and hinted at the truth in print and on the airwaves. Missionaries and aid workers witnessed atrocity, then drew colleagues back home into debates about the moral trade-offs of counterinsurgency. Playwrights, novelists, and screenwriters took audiences inside fictionalized versions of detention camps and interrogation rooms. Sometimes quietly and sometimes not, violence reached far beyond the conflict zones of empire.

Central to this history are the ambiguities of secrecy. Details about colonial violence were often treated as secrets. Officials worked energetically, and in many cases successfully, to keep them out of the press. When politicians, humanitarian leaders, and other influential figures learned about abuses through private channels, they tended to confer with government ministers behind closed doors rather than go public. But secrecy is never simply a matter of suppressing information; it also draws attention to that information, weaves networks of complicity around it, and confers a "charged status" on it.[39] One reason for this is that the disturbing accounts that did emerge into public view were all the more shocking because others were kept quiet. Another is that the never-ending work of managing secrecy, policing the boundaries of what could or should be disclosed to the public, was never itself a secret. Bureaucrats, reporters, missionaries, soldiers, settlers, and other intermediaries found themselves in the position of having to decide whether they should publicize what they knew or stay silent. This is the paradox of secrecy in a liberal society. As historian Tom Crook puts it, "citizens know what they cannot know." Even if information deemed secret by the state is "never disclosed in its fullness," liberal subjects can nonetheless "glimpse something of its existence."[40]

Suppressing information about violence proved difficult for another reason as well. While officials sought to conceal the dark side of colonial war, they could not renounce publicity altogether, because they wanted to build popular support for the conflicts. Secrecy and propaganda feed each other: one creates the informational vacuum filled by the half-truths and manipulations of the other.[41] The relationship between them assumed a particularly complex form in post-1950s Britain because the coercive dimensions of counterinsurgency were so entangled with the camera-friendly work of appealing to "hearts and minds." Detention camps were simultaneously sites of punishment and rehabilitation. Intrusive searches, mass round-ups, and forced relocations turned communities upside down in the name of protecting them.

These contradictions meant that British civilians—aid workers, nurses, missionaries—worked hand-in-glove with security forces and witnessed many of their worst abuses. They also reflected the fact that officials understood colonial war, in part, as a spectacle. The civilizing mission was a performance of stern yet benevolent paternalism. Certain kinds of violence had to be visible so that they could be folded into this narrative, justified, and even celebrated. Allowing spectators at home to participate vicariously in the "tough" choices of colonial war, at least to an extent, was a strategy for manufacturing consent. The mystique fostered by a deliberately porous secrecy, which invited spectators to peek behind the curtain of military operations, further magnified scenes of violence.[42]

The abundance of information about colonial violence was no guarantee that people would accept it, recognize it, or act on it. Phrases like "strategic ignorance" and "plausible deniability" hint at the willful cultivation of the middle ground between knowing and not-knowing.[43] Troublesome pieces of information are often converted into "inert facts," pried out of context, and filed away so that they cannot be assembled into damning conclusions.[44] All communities—institutions, social classes, national cultures—steer individuals away from certain kinds of information, through taboos, codes of etiquette, specialized functions, and ideas about what is or is not worthy of attention.[45]

By these means, the same networks that made violence knowable in metropolitan Britain also made that knowledge susceptible to controversy, complacency, and doubt. Evidence collected by left-wing campaigners was accepted or rejected along ideological battle lines. Admissions by soldiers were armed with racially tinged defenses. Missionaries and aid workers, identifying with the authorities on whom they depended for access and funding, explained away malfeasance as a necessary evil. While journalists publicized some damning details, they withheld many more, constrained by professional codes that imposed an exacting standard for verifying facts. Fiction writers, who enjoyed perhaps the greatest latitude to communicate uncomfortable truths, learned that dramatization and aestheticization could serve more easily as cathartic releases than as calls to action.

It is now a commonplace that representations of violence induce passivity, apathy, voyeurism, and desensitization instead of raising political consciousness.[46] But the ethical frailty of the spectator, or information consumer, cannot be understood in isolation from constraints on information producers. Because of their location in the imperial power structure, those who had the clearest view of brutality also felt the strongest pressures to downplay or justify it. The "circumscribed morality" of institutions and professions—the military, the civil service, the press, the churches, the aid organizations—was always shaping knowledge about violence.[47] Abstract questions of right and wrong slipped quickly into murkier dilemmas about burdens of proof and standards of evidence; about where responsibility should be assigned and who should do the assigning; about the trade-offs between working within the system and criticizing it from outside.

In some ways, this history follows an influential claim about the relationship between violence and modernity. Since the Holocaust, many thinkers have observed that modernity itself makes atrocities possible: by fragmenting responsibility across specialized roles and compartmentalized institutions; by insulating perpetrators from the flesh-and-blood consequences of their actions; by transforming unsettling face-to-face encounters into remote, impersonal, and anonymous acts.[48] Technology, bureaucracy, and other hallmarks of modernity did furnish resources for the normalization of colonial violence. But they also made violence a problem to be reckoned with in the first place. While some technologies (like aerial bombardment) put war at a distance, others (like the postal service and the television) drew it closer. Even as institutions filed evidence of violence away, they also transmitted it across time and space. Far from evading a sense of involvement in colonial violence, people in Britain were repeatedly confronted by it, as the networks of imperial modernity brought them into vivid contact with the front lines. Rather than avoiding the question of complicity altogether, they had to constantly struggle with it, to justify their response or the absence of one.

Several tactics of accommodation made this task easier. Some contemporaries cast doubt on facts about violence. Others distinguished between knowledge of violence and the duty to act on it, dwelling on the undesirable or unanticipated consequences of intervening against authority. Still others celebrated visions of racial struggle or aestheticized the grim fatalism of dirty wars. The sheer variety of these approaches makes clear that the state was not the only, and perhaps not even the most important, force in constructing knowledge about violence. Concepts such as secrecy, censorship, and propaganda—the keywords of a state-centered information economy—obscure a vast terrain of more complex attitudes. Cultivated by individuals and institutions of all kinds, the grey areas of uncertainty, ambivalence, and rationalization structured responses to colonial war.

Resistance to uncomfortable knowledge is often glossed as "denial." In the most expansive definitions, denial can be individual or social; conscious or unconscious; cognitive, affective, or behavioral; or factual ("it never happened"), interpretive ("it's not like that"), or implicatory ("so what if it was like that?"). In this way, almost any kind of willful ignorance or motivated reasoning can be glossed as denial.[49] One reason that this book invokes "denial" sparingly is to avoid this sort of conceptual inflation. No master concept can capture the variety of tactics used to contain knowledge about violence. If any idea comes close, it is disavowal, which can imply the rejection of meanings rather than the erasure of perceptions.[50] In colloquial speech, denial carries a sense of detachment from reality, as in the insult that someone is "in denial." Learning to live with violence was, by contrast, a conscious process: a confrontation with uncomfortable truths that could be minimized in various ways but never fully suppressed.

* * *

The forms of violence employed by the British Empire in the 1950s were hardly new. Torture was common practice among colonial authorities in India from the eighteenth century.[51] The indefinite confinement of suspect populations in detention camps had a long history, too, most notoriously during the Anglo-Boer War in South Africa at the start of the twentieth century.[52] Dropping bombs to render wide areas uninhabitable was standard procedure in Iraq, Sudan, and Waziristan between the world wars.[53] The counterinsurgency playbook for ground forces traveled from the late Victorian North-West Frontier to interwar Palestine and beyond. Underlying all these practices was a willingness to resort to exemplary, extrajudicial, and spectacular violence that did not clearly distinguish between combatants and civilians. Sometimes cited as an explanation for infamous events like the Amritsar massacre of 1919, this mentality was in fact normal rather than exceptional for the modern British Empire.[54]

The particular ferocity of conflict in the 1950s arose from the entanglement of imperial ambitions projected from London with local struggles for power and resources. This book concentrates on three colonial wars—in Malaya, Kenya, and Cyprus—because their brutality attracted the most sustained attention in Britain and because the use of the same counterinsurgency playbook in each case produced a common vocabulary of criticisms and defenses. While these insurgencies differed in their origins and aims, all represented dire threats to imperial rule and were drawn into the same global story of violent repression. As British personnel, tactics, and technologies circulated from one colony to another, they imposed a measure of uniformity on the fight against diverse forms of resistance.[55]

On the Malay Peninsula, stretching north from the island of Singapore to the border with Thailand, attempts to reassert British authority after the devastating Japanese occupation of the Second World War were troubled from the start. The Communists who had waged a guerilla campaign against the Imperial Japanese Army in collaboration with the British soon pivoted to rallying discontent against their erstwhile allies. The constitutional framework adopted by the British in 1948 enshrined a privileged status for ethnic Malays and their traditional figureheads, the sultans, while making citizenship and land ownership all but unattainable for the ethnic Chinese and Indian communities that comprised half of the colony's population. Chinese and Indian subjects also made up the bulk of the proletarian workforce in the engine rooms of the colonial economy, the tin mines and the rubber plantations, where European owners enforced arduous conditions with iron-fisted discipline. Faced with gathering threats to the colonial order—strikes by miners and rubber workers, violent attacks on European planters, growing enclaves of Chinese squatters on European-owned land—the British cracked down. They outlawed trade unions, pushed squatters off the land by tearing up their crops and burning down their huts, and carried out mass arrests of suspected radicals. Alienated workers, displaced peasants, and fearful activists reacted by fleeing into the jungle in 1948, forming the basis of an ethnic Chinese-dominated guerrilla army that the Malayan Communist Party would lead in attacks on British targets for more than a decade.[56]

With Communism already on the march in China and Burma, Cold War geopolitics dictated an aggressive response to the insurgency in Malaya. So did the material reality of British dependence on the Malayan economy. By early 1950s, rising demand for rubber and tin on the world market meant that Malaya alone accounted for 10 percent of Britain's overseas trade and more than a third of Britain's balance of payments in US dollars. The state of emergency from 1948 to 1960 unleashed sprawling powers of repression in an attempt to maintain Britain's place in the Atlantic alliance and keep goods and currencies flowing. Under the Emergency Regulations, which allowed for the detention of suspects without trial, nearly 10,000 were held in camps at the highest point in 1951.[57] These regulations also empowered authorities to impose curfews and limits on food supplies over wide areas. Magistrates could level collective punishments, such as monetary fines and shop closures, on villages suspected of cooperating with insurgents. The military evicted squatters and torched their homes. By the mid-1950s, virtually the entire rural Chinese population of the colony was resettled at gunpoint; more than half a million were moved into custom-built "New Villages" ringed by barbed wire, while another half a million were moved to existing towns and estates. Security forces shot people who merely seemed out of place in villages, on the sides of roads, and elsewhere. In what some soldiers later described as a cold-blooded massacre, a platoon of Scots Guards shot twenty-six unarmed rubber tappers in Batang Kali, in Selangor, in 1948. By the time the war finally ended in 1960, colonial forces had killed more than 6,000 people officially classified as "Communist terrorists." On the other side, 1,442 servicemen lost their lives, making the Emergency the single deadliest conflict for the British armed forces in the post-1945 era.

Across the Indian Ocean basin, in Kenya, tensions between European planters and dispossessed peasants likewise turned explosive. The Kikuyu were the ethnic group most affected by the expropriation of land under colonial law to benefit white settlers. Many worked as laborers on European-owned tea, coffee, and sisal plantations for part of the year in exchange for informal leave to settle and farm a portion of the land. But an influx of capital and a wave of mechanization following the Second World War empowered white settlers to force large numbers of squatters off the land, creating a landless class that swelled the increasingly crowded capital of Nairobi. There, and in the equally impoverished rural "reserves" set aside for the Kikuyu on infertile land, squatter grievances mingled with other sources of discontent. Kikuyu veterans who fought for Britain during the Second World War, and expected a reward for their sacrifices, were bitterly disappointed. The colonial state exercised its powers of forced labor to put Kikuyu women to work, for little or no compensation, on agricultural infrastructure projects. A tradition of Kikuyu resistance to colonialism, which emerged between the wars as a

FIGURE I.I Colonial secretary Oliver Lyttelton (left) rides a tank through a resettlement area in Johore, Malaya, 1951. PA Images.

backlash to missionary proselytizing, was revived under the leadership of militant politicians with links to the trade unions and the criminal underworld in Nairobi. They sought to mobilize the Kikuyu masses, in the city and the country, by asking them to swear oaths of loyalty to a revolutionary movement that became known as Mau Mau. In 1952, as the colonial state awoke to the dangers of a brewing revolt, militants began killing Kikuyu who refused to take the oath, informed to the police, or collaborated with the British in other ways.[58]

The extraordinary brutality of the Kenya Emergency, which lasted from 1952 until 1960, was driven from the outset by roughly 30,000 white settlers determined to maintain their dominance over 5 million Africans. Although Mau Mau violence overwhelmingly targeted Kikuyu loyal to the British, a relatively small number of deadly attacks on settler families unleashed a spirit of vengeance. While pressuring officials to send in reinforcements and loosen constraints on the use of force, settlers also wielded violence directly: as soldiers in the Kenya Regiment and as volunteers for the Kenya Police Reserve, which operated at times like a vigilante force. Soldiers deployed to Kenya from Britain engaged in many of the same practices—beatings, torture, summary executions—as settlers did. As in Malaya, Emergency Regulations in Kenya allowed for curfews, food restrictions, collective punishments, and detention without trial. A hastily constructed police state swept much of the Kikuyu population into a byzantine network of detention camps where physical abuse, forced labor, and disease were endemic; as many as 70,000 people were detained at any one time, and some stayed behind the barbed wire for years. Over 1 million Kenyans were forcibly resettled in militarized villages on the Malayan model.[59] While casualty figures are highly uncertain, colonial forces killed at least 10,000, and perhaps more than 20,000, people classified as insurgents. At least 25,000 additional civilians died, including many children suffering from malnutrition caused by the dislocations of detention and resettlement. Just over 1,000 members of the colonial security forces were killed.[60]

FIGURE 1.2 A night raid by security forces in Kenya, 1952. This photograph by Bert Hardy, one of the foremost British chroniclers of counterinsurgency, was first published in *Picture Post*. Getty Images.

If the British war in Malaya was propelled by economic interests and in Kenya by settler interests, the war in Cyprus was a product of strategic calculations. Faced with a rising tide of nationalism in Egypt, the British military in 1954 shifted its Middle East headquarters to the eastern Mediterranean island hopefully described by officials as a "Commonwealth fortress." Yet Cyprus had its own nationalist movement: the campaign for *Enosis*, or union with Greece, an aspiration of the ethnic Greek majority on the island dating back to the era of late Ottoman rule in the nineteenth century. It was an ideal rooted not just in linguistic affinity but in the culture of the Cypriot Orthodox Church, a cradle of irredentist politics. A fierce rivalry between the Greek community's Orthodox, conservative right wing and its secular, Communist left wing—a mirror of Second World War–era divisions in Greece—drove the radicalization of nationalist claims at precisely the moment that the British were digging in. A guerrilla movement aligned with the church and led by veteran anti-Communist fighter George Grivas, EOKA (the Greek acronym for the Organization of Greek-Cypriot Fighters), launched a violent uprising against British rule in 1955 by planting bombs in government buildings. The state of emergency declared soon afterward would last for four years.[61]

The Cyprus conflict was not a typical anticolonial struggle. This was a right-wing insurgency, on the periphery of Europe, which sought annexation by another European country rather than independence. Partly as a result of these particularities, British counterinsurgency was much less deadly there than in Malaya or Kenya: official figures showed a total of 90 insurgents, 823 civilians, and 944 soldiers or police officers killed.[62] Even so, the war acquired a reputation for brutality. This owed something to energetic propaganda efforts by Greek Cypriots and their allies as well as the island's relative proximity to Britain and the Christian identity of the insurgents. It also reflected the reality of violence that was limited in some ways—especially by the efforts of a Greek Cypriot legal community capable of pressing claims in court—but far from immune to the indiscriminate and vengeful abuses of any counterinsurgency.[63] Curfews, cordons, shop closures, and collective fines upended everyday life. House-to-house searches and mass round-ups involved casual violence by soldiers flaunting their dominance. Detention camps held roughly 2,000 prisoners at their peak in 1958. Suspects in custody were tortured, and several died under suspicious circumstances. After EOKA assassinated a British soldier's wife in Famagusta in 1958, troops went on a rampage, resulting in smashed-up shops and homes, roughly 250 injuries, and at least two deaths.[64]

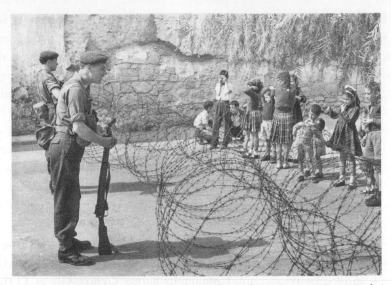

FIGURE 1.3 British soldiers police a cordon in Cyprus, 1956. Bert Hardy/ *Picture Post*/Getty Images.

What, in the end, did Britain gain by the violence of counterinsurgency? In purely military terms, the Malayan National Liberation Army and the Mau Mau were defeated, while "battlefield" success against EOKA was more equivocal. But the postcolonial states that emerged from all three wars remained within the Anglo-American sphere of influence for decades afterward. In Malaya—which became an independent state in 1957, joined Singapore and several other territories to form the state of Malaysia in 1963, and split with Singapore two years after that—the post-independence regime was stoutly anti-Communist and business-friendly. In Kenya, which achieved independence in 1963, political leaders worked to bury the controversial Mau Mau legacy and exclude its veterans from power. The independent Kenyan state bought land at market rate from the white settlers who chose to leave and transferred much of it to former colonial loyalists. In Cyprus, the claims of the Turkish Cypriot minority—and, indirectly, the Turkish state—backstopped Britain's steadfast refusal on *Enosis*. Greek Cypriot nationalists had to settle for a state independent from Greece as well as Britain, established in 1960, with power-sharing privileges for the ethnic Turkish population and swaths of territory carved out as sovereign British bases. While British expatriate minorities lost their lock on political power in all three cases—perhaps the chief achievement of decolonization—officials could congratulate themselves on forestalling more fundamental revolutions.

What might be reckoned a strategic victory by the British elite, however, was not experienced as a cause for celebration in Britain. Thousands of soldiers had been killed, and millions of pounds spent, in the name of an empire that no longer existed. Jomo Kenyatta and Archbishop Makarios, seen not long before as insurrectionist villains, were installed as heads of state in Kenya and Cyprus, respectively. Most of all, for those who lived through them, the wars themselves proved divisive and unsettling. While there was nothing new about brutality in the colonies, its reverberations were felt more deeply in Britain after 1945, for several reasons.

First was the legacy of the Second World War itself. To be sure, the war imparted no clear-cut lessons about state violence as far as contemporaries were concerned. The international organizations and treaties that emerged from the war were designed to perpetuate empires, and their capacity to use force, with minimal constraints.[65] But the widespread belief that Britain had fought a good war, in moral terms, against Germany, did complicate responses to counterinsurgency. Critics of colonial war decried the "Gestapo tactics" and "totalitarian methods" perpetrated by British authorities, unnerving parallels that rang true for many observers and even, in private, for some stalwart imperialists. Defenses of colonial war, meanwhile, did not deny excessive or extralegal violence so much as they insisted on euphemisms like "rough handling" instead of torture, language meant to evoke garden-variety callousness rather than the ideologically motivated violence of Nazism.

Second, the colonial wars of the 1950s were fought in significant measure by conscripts rather than career soldiers. Setting aside the exceptional circumstances of the two world wars, this kind of mass conscription was unprecedented in modern British history. Between 1948 and 1963, every British man between the ages of seventeen and twenty-one was liable to be called up for military service, and while exact figures are impossible to calculate, perhaps 100,000 of them actually served in colonial conflicts. Because the pool of potential colonial warriors—to say nothing of their parents, siblings, friends, and lovers—was so large, colonial war represented a looming, inescapable presence in everyday life. With conscripts circulating in and out of conflict zones, letters, photographs, and other forms of evidence reached far beyond the world of professional fighting men. Some demobilized soldiers, radicalized by the brutality of the fighting, penned gruesome memoirs and novels to justify the violence in which they participated. Others, appalled by the tactics they observed, turned to left-wing activism when they returned home. Though only a small proportion of men called up for service ultimately registered as conscientious objectors, their protests revealed creeping unease with the morality of keeping an empire by force. While critics saw conscription as an engine of militarization—propelling families across the country to identify more closely with the armed forces and react defensively to accusations of brutality—the reality was more ambiguous. Conscription widened the circle of involvement in colonial war, generating a sense of complicity along with feelings of solidarity.

Third, the age of colonial emergency was a golden age of communications. Old-fashioned information channels between Britain and its colonies, always dense, transmitted huge volumes of information about colonial war: letters from soldiers and settlers, reports from missionaries and aid workers, stories from journalists and travelers. Fueled by the expansion of air freight, the volume of British mail overseas climbed dramatically in the 1950s, peaking at 524 million letters in 1957.[66] But the vividness and immediacy that ushered colonial war into British homes was also a product of media: newspapers, which were never more widely read than in the 1950s; illustrated weeklies like *Picture Post*; radio, which remained a BBC monopoly; and, not least, the new medium of television. In print and on the airwaves, coverage of colonial war was less than uniformly jingoistic, as troubling questions about the use of force lingered in word and in image. On television, news programs like *Panorama* turned a skeptical lens on colonial war, as did a new, edgy generation of on-screen dramas about cracked-up interrogators and morally compromised soldiers.

Fourth, waves of migration from the colonies after 1948 recast debates about colonial war as struggles over British identity. Migrants from Malaya, Kenya, and Cyprus obviously had the most direct stake in these conflicts; while Greek Cypriots were the most numerous, the much smaller Malayan and Kenyan communities dominated by university students were intensely politicized. At the same time, the wider universe of black Britons—encompassing West African activists, West Indian workers, and others—constituted a new social base for anticolonial politics. For the most vocal supporters of colonial war, conversely, immigration at home and insurgency in the colonies represented two sides of the same coin: both were threats to an essentially racial conception of the British nation. While a tenuous multiracial coalition portrayed violence in defense of empire as morally bankrupt, right-wing nationalists saw it as an essential bulwark against the waning prestige and crumbling authority of an imperial race.

For all of these reasons, the colonial wars of the 1950s fueled new kinds of emotive, antagonistic, often sensationalistic politics. On the left, an array of groups—from the venerable Communist Party of Great Britain to the newly formed Movement for Colonial Freedom—focused their energies on circulating graphic evidence of atrocities and discrediting the moral status of empire. Against the global backdrop of decolonization, the profusion of reports from far-flung conflict zones refashioned a familiar pattern of isolated scandals about violence into an existential debate about whether British rule deserved to continue in any form. Leading thinkers of the New Left, including Stuart Hall and E. P. Thompson, saw the wars in Cyprus and Kenya as well as Egypt as signs of a deeper reactionary turn in British society. A home-grown fascist movement was in fact resurgent, stoking enthusiasm for racial conflict overseas and exploiting resentment about supposedly ignominious retreats from empire. The groups that led directly to the formation of the anti-immigrant National Front in the late 1960s, including the League of Empire Loyalists and the National Labour Party, drew maximum attention to their cause by staging provocative rallies, provoking brawls with anticolonial campaigners, and running candidates for public office who blended racist xenophobia with revanchist militarism.

The Suez Crisis of 1956, which hovers in the background of this story and occasionally intrudes on it, offers a revealing counterpoint to the politics of counterinsurgency. Suez was the kind of full-blown domestic emergency that other colonial wars threatened to become but never did. Parliamentary opposition was united against the government; press coverage was heavily, if not uniformly, critical; and protests filled the streets. Why Suez triggered a more powerful response than counterinsurgencies in Malaya, Kenya, and Cyprus is no mystery. An invasion of the sovereign state of Egypt, with its own seat at the United Nations, on a flimsy pretext, represented a flagrant violation of international law. As a result, the invasion exposed Britain to international pressure as conflicts that remained within the formal boundaries of empire never could. The conspicuous refusal of American support, the resolution of condemnation passed by the United Nations General Assembly, and the subsequent forced withdrawal of British troops all dealt uniquely humiliating blows to Britain's global prestige. The interruption of global trade through the Suez Canal, leading to fuel shortages and rationing, added a material dimension to the crisis which had no equivalent in the other colonial conflicts of the time.

For British attitudes to empire, however, Suez was less a turning point than a crystallization of anxieties that bubbled throughout the endless warfare of the 1950s. Here again, young conscripts were asked to risk their lives in a dubious cause. Here again, the possibility of spectacular defeat at the hands of ostensibly inferior enemies mingled with uneasiness about the methods of warfare and uncertainty about the purpose of maintaining an empire at all. A striking feature of the Suez controversy in Britain, the profusion of moralistic language, becomes more comprehensible in relation to the ongoing wars in Malaya, Kenya, and Cyprus. Critics cast the invasion of Egypt not just as a blunder but as a "shameful" act, an affront to the "conscience," a destruction of "moral authority," and a symptom of "moral decay" because debates about war in the name of empire were already morally charged.[67] The invasion of Egypt posed stark questions about the use of force as a collective, political act; counterinsurgency dramatized individual acts of bodily violence. But the distinction between these levels was never clear-cut. For this reason, the response to Suez drew on existing languages of imperial conscience while also sharpening them and giving them new currency.

It might be tempting to imagine the grey, austere, war-scarred 1950s as a time very different from our own. But what makes this history so unsettling is precisely that it does not belong to a distant past. Then, as now, states proved adept at circumventing and co-opting protections for human rights even as they paid lip service to them. Then, as now, communication links and media coverage closed the informational gap between conflict zones and home fronts without closing the empathy gap between them. Then, as now, calls for restraint on the use of force had to compete with vocal support for brutal, vengeful, and indiscriminate violence. Then, as now, the ambiguity of "emergencies" and "exceptions" that furnished the legal basis for war allowed its consequences to unfold in a twilight state of limited accountability. The patterns etched in Britain's terminal wars for empire persisted long afterward.

Besides weakening the rule of law to make way for violence, the language of "emergency" served another aim: delimiting a crisis zone in the colonies to preserve a sense of normalcy at home. Emergency was not just a temporal but a spatial concept, aimed at absorbing the echoes of violence and holding them at a distance.[68] In some ways, the mythology of far-off emergencies accomplished what it was supposed to, allowing the political elite in Britain to carry on in an atmosphere of relative stability. But even if the myth "worked" in this sense, that does not mean it should be taken at face value. Nor should its ultimate, if partial, success be seen in retrospect as inevitable. Throughout this period, the states of emergency that officials declared to fend off insurgencies in the colonies threatened to become moral emergencies in Britain. What violence looked, heard, and felt like as an empire ended; how distant atrocities became domestic problems; and what it took to keep a deeper crisis at bay is the story of Britain's age of emergency.

PART I

Knowing about Violence

I

Out of Apathy

THE POET CHRISTOPHER LOGUE was a man of political passions. Deployed to Palestine with the British Army in 1946, he was imprisoned and discharged after a clumsy effort to pass identity documents to the Zionist insurgents fighting imperial rule.[1] Back in London, he marched against the Suez invasion in 1956, the year he turned thirty years old, and then against nuclear weapons in 1958. When mobs attacked the black residents of West London for five consecutive nights that year, in what became known as the Notting Hill riots, Logue saw confirmation of his belief that "we are a racist, prejudiced nation."[2] But more than anything else in the late 1950s, he was appalled by the violence inflicted in the name of empire. "In Cyprus we are busy murdering," he observed in 1956.[3] The following year, he was horrified by the "annihilation of the Mau-Mau."[4] Logue attributed this brutality to the traditions of a state that has "thieved, raped, killed by fire, torture, and any means to hand in India, Malaya, Guiana, Nigeria, Rhodesia, and Ireland for almost 200 years."[5]

Along with playwright John Arden, director Lindsay Anderson, novelist Doris Lessing, theater critic Kenneth Tynan, and others, Logue moved in a bohemian New Left circle in London. Distaste for empire as an unholy alliance of capitalism and militarism was one of its lodestars. Inspired by a 1956 *Daily Express* story about a National Serviceman shot to death in Cyprus, Logue wrote a poem, "The Song of the Dead Soldier," that he hoped would make "a potent attack on those who want to continue the murder and anxiety."[6] The poem juxtaposes the boilerplate rhetoric of imperial-military officialdom ("Must be kept calm, must be patrolled, / For outposts are the heart and soul / Of empire, love, and lawful rule") with the fatal navieté of the conscript ("I did not know to serve meant kill, / And I did not see the captain fall, / As my life went out through a bullet hole, / Mother, I cried, your womb is done"). Logue printed and circulated 2,000 broadside copies of the poem with a polemical subtitle ("One Killed in the Interests of Certain Tory Senators in Cyprus") and a ripped-from-the-headlines epigraph from an army commander ("I am only interested in dead terrorists").[7] Reclaiming the conscript's death from the jingoism of the right-wing press, Logue portrayed it as the latest senseless episode in a cycle of violence driven by the British elite.

Most of what British people heard about brutality in colonial war did not come from impartial fact-finders but from radicals with agendas. Literary intellectuals like Logue and his friends represented just one subset of the wide and varied ranks of campaigners against colonial war, a universe that also encompassed African and Asian envoys, Christian pacifists, Communist apparatchiks, black and Cypriot migrants, university students, socialist internationalists, and trade-union organizers. Like Logue, some of these activists operated as publicists, experimenting with rhetoric and media to amplify opposition to war. Others acted as information brokers, collecting testimony and other forms of evidence from conflict zones. Together, they built a counter-narrative to the justifications for colonial war that were routinely trumpeted in Westminster, Fleet Street, and Broadcasting House. When condemnations of violence reached the same power centers—and they did, repeatedly, in the 1950s—the script most often originated with dissenters on the margins.

If this achievement has not always been recognized, one reason is that activists themselves judged their efforts harshly. As one Labour organizer complained at the height of the unrest in Cyprus in 1957, "We run meetings all right, but nobody turns up. Have you ever tried protesting to an empty hall?"[8] New Left activist and sociologist Peter Worsley complained that anticolonial campaigns struggled to convene "public meetings of hundreds while people gaze at [the ITV game show] Criss Cross Quiz in the millions." Worsley concluded that the spectacular inhumanity of the Holocaust and Hiroshima had desensitized observers and left them "inured" to the quotidian abuses of empire. That, Worsley thought, is why the murder of eleven Africans by guards at a detention camp in Kenya—the infamous Hola Massacre of 1959—failed to provoke greater outrage. "To a generation reared on paperback horrors of the concentration camp," he wrote, "another eleven make little impact."[9] The general election of 1959, which returned the Conservative government responsible for Hola, Cyprus, and Suez with a comfortable majority, seemed to offer little hope for a reckoning with the brutality of empire.

Another New Left intellectual, E. P. Thompson, drew a similarly bleak conclusion about domestic resistance to colonial war. Looking back in 1963, seven years after his break with the Communist Party of Great Britain, Thompson observed that the Cold War froze left-wing activism just as the wars in Malaya, Kenya, and Cyprus were heating up. Propaganda and paranoia divided the socialist movement; those who decried empire most vocally were tainted "by their complicity with Stalinism." In Thompson's view, Communists themselves made matters worse by following Moscow in the prioritization of anti-Americanism over decolonization. The anticolonial tradition became "formal and ritualistic," indulging in symbolic gestures that masked the "enfeebled" state of popular engagement. According to Thompson, it was only after 1956 that the global conscience of rank-and-file leftists reawakened, and even then, nuclear weapons and apartheid took precedence over the violence committed against British colonial subjects.[10]

The apathy of the masses was a perennial concern for the left. Activists' hope in the 1950s, that exposing the brutality of colonial war would inspire a collective repudiation of it, was not vindicated by events. Even so, campaigners accomplished more than they realized. They showed it was possible to dissent from the violence of empire. They created spaces—physically and metaphorically, in print and in speech, in private and in public—where events in the colonies were treated as moral emergencies that demanded a response. In meeting halls and city squares, in letters to newspapers and politicians, in student unions and conscientious objector tribunals, some said: not in our name. Amid all that has been written about the undeniable fractures, the contradictions, and the paternalism that afflicted resistance to empire, it is significant that this alternative path existed at all. Acquiescence in colonial violence was neither universal nor inevitable. It was a choice.

The Ecology of Dissent

The story of British resistance to empire is, unavoidably, centered in London. For pressure groups, proximity to the political power and press coverage concentrated in the capital was always indispensable. For activists seeking to build global movements, London offered a natural meeting place, a point of convergence for steamship lines and airplane routes where British subjects from anywhere in the world could legally disembark under the immigration regime that lasted until 1962.[11] While some came to study at universities and others to find employment, individuals from both groups were drawn into protests against empire, transforming the capital into a "junction box" for the transmission of radical ideas.[12] As the migrant population increased dramatically after the Second World War, the social base of anticolonial politics expanded, too.

When overseas subjects raised on a romantic mythology of the mother country arrived in Britain at last, the discrimination, harassment, and violence they encountered could have a radicalizing effect. Migrants-turned-activists came to see racism at home and colonialism overseas as interlocking problems.[13] In the colonies, officials' ability to criminalize activities deemed "subversive," always robust, grew virtually unlimited once a state of emergency was declared.[14] But in metropolitan Britain, dissenters remained free to mobilize. For British authorities, the price of upholding liberal pretensions to free speech—and confining legal signifiers of "emergency" to the colonies as far as possible—was a proliferating web of resistance at the heart of the empire.

One of the émigrés who catalyzed British resistance to the war in Kenya was Mbiyu Koinange. The son of a prominent Kikuyu chief, he first came to London as a student in the 1930s, finding a place in the radical Pan-Africanist circle around C. L. R. James and George Padmore. At the start of the Emergency in 1952, Koinange was again in London as the Kenyan African Union's delegate to the British government, when he was confronted with the news that authorities in Kenya had sent his father and four of his brothers into detention camps. Facing certain arrest if he returned home, Koinange emerged as the leading Kikuyu critic of the war on British soil, where he would remain until 1959.[15] He became a fixture on the left-wing metropolitan speaking circuit, addressing local Labour Party branches, Workers' Educational Associations, Co-Operative guilds, student groups, and peace groups. He compiled reports of British brutality from letters sent by contacts in Kenya and put them into the literature circulated by activist organizations. In the summer of 1953, Koinange helped to found one of those organizations: the Kenya Provisional Committee, later renamed the Kenya Committee for Democratic Rights for Africans or simply the Kenya Committee, which was dominated by members of the Communist Party of Great Britain (CPGB).[16]

Koinange himself was not a Communist. As intelligence officials concluded, he was "an ardent nationalist who is prepared to 'fellow travel' with any organization from which he hopes to obtain sympathy or assistance."[17] Like many émigrés, Koinange faced the humbling reality of dependence on British patrons to get his message out. Struggling to get by, he relied on cash gifts from left-wing patrons while teaching extramural classes at the University of London and even hauling milk bottles for the Watford Co-Op. By 1955, Koinange had fallen out with the Communists at the Kenya Committee at least partly because he maintained ties with Labour Party politicians like

Fenner Brockway and the pressure group he led, the Movement for Colonial Freedom (MCF). But Koinange's alliance with the Labour left came under strain too. Already disillusioned by the failure of the post-1945 Labour government to roll back settler control in Kenya, Koinange was wary of internal party struggles and saw Brockway as an "intriguer" "anxious to maintain the dominance of the White People."[18] Labour politicians, for their part, held Koinange at arm's length because of rumors that he was active in the Mau Mau movement.[19]

Another Kenyan émigré had more success, for a time, in forging ties with the Labour left. Joseph Murumbi had the advantages of an ethnic identity (half-Masai, half-Goan) and a religious faith (Roman Catholicism) that seemed to distance him from the insurgency, although the *Times* still tried to tar him as a Mau Mau agent.[20] Taking over the leadership of the Kenyan African Union after Jomo Kenyatta and other top figures were arrested, Murumbi traveled to New Delhi and Cairo before landing in London in September 1953. Unlike Koinange, Murumbi remained aloof from the Communists while tilting toward Brockway, who installed him as an MCF official with a modest salary.[21] But Murumbi had the same qualms about white British domination of the anticolonial cause as Koinange did, eventually resigning from MCF after what he saw as a limp response to the Suez crisis.[22] Despite an intermittently tense relationship, Murumbi and Koinange agreed on the brutality of British repression and moved in the same small community of Kenyan African students in London, which grew from just six in 1952 to more than ninety in 1959.[23]

As they came to the capital in increasing numbers, young Kenyans entered a wider world of black student activism rooted in the Pan-African tradition. A vanguard of anticolonial protest from its beginnings in the 1920s, the West African Students Union (WASU) demanded an end to "attacks" on Africans almost as soon as the Emergency in Kenya began. Later, WASU organized a boycott of Colonial Office functions for students from the colonies and joined Kenya Committee protests outside Parliament.[24] The struggle against empire "dominated all conversations" at the WASU headquarters in Bayswater, as Wole Soyinka, then a literature student, later recalled. With West African colonies already in the process of achieving negotiated independence by the mid-1950s, students from Soyinka's Nigeria and the rest of the region turned to Kenya as a cause célèbre.[25] Over time, a new generation of advocacy groups sprang up on the WASU model. One of them was the Kenyan Students Association, which in 1957 likened settler rule to "apartheid" and called for the immediate "demolition of all detention camps and the release of all prisoners held without trial."[26]

Emigrés and students also comprised the nucleus of dissent from the war in Malaya. John Eber was a mixed-race Singapore lawyer, educated at Harrow and Cambridge, who returned to Britain as a "voluntary exile" in 1953 after spending two years in a detention camp on charges of collusion with the Malayan Communist Party. Once settled in a flat in Finchley, Eber started an antiwar organization, the Britain-Malaya Committee, and recruited a succession of British leftists to join.[27] Another Cambridge-educated political exile, Lim Hong Bee, voiced more explicit support for Communist insurgents and forged closer ties with the Communist Party of Great Britain. From flats in Notting Hill and Camden Town, Lim produced a cheap mimeographed newsletter, the *Malayan Monitor*, over the protests of colonial authorities who wanted it banned in Britain as it was in Malaya.[28] Both Eber and Lim worked to build support among the fast-growing population of Malayan students in Britain, which jumped from 60 in 1947 to 1,200 in 1953, transforming the Malayan Students' Hostel in Marylebone into a hotbed of émigré politics.[29] While those students were ideologically and ethnically divided, even the staunch anti-Communists among them were troubled enough by British repression to track cases of detainees held without trial and protest to the colonial secretary.[30]

The campaign against the war in Cyprus could draw on the deepest wells of ethnic identification in the metropolis. Roughly 75,000 migrants left Cyprus for Britain in the decade and a half after 1945, most of them Greek-speaking and most settling in the capital in search of work.[31] Clustering in a swath of north-central London, Greek Cypriots left their marks on the cityscape: the Cypriot Brotherhood headquarters in Fitzroy Square, the Union of Greek Parents clubhouse in Camden Square, the Greek Orthodox Church in Camden Town. After the start of the Emergency in 1955, community leaders founded a pressure group called the National Cypriot Committee; an Orthodox priest served as the director and participants in protest marches to Downing Street wore traditional costumes.[32] Not coincidentally, one of the most assertive anticolonial voices in the House of Commons, Lena Jeger, represented much of this community in the constituency of Holborn and St. Pancras South.

The increasingly substantial, visible, and assertive presence of colonial subjects in Britain was vital to the politicization of colonial violence. These groups were hardly monoliths and did not always align with each other; to name the most obvious fault line, struggles against labor exploitation in

Malaya and land expropriation in Kenya had far more in common with each other than with a Christian nationalist uprising in Cyprus. But the collective impact of activists from the colonies made itself felt in the pressure they exerted on home-grown dissent. The left-wing internationalist tradition, with rival branches in the Communist and Labour Parties, had a history of blending lofty anticolonial rhetoric with paternalistic, parochial, and often racist reluctance to act on it.[33] This hypocrisy, though persistent, became harder to sustain over the course of the 1950s. As new forms of multiracial activism interacted with an old infrastructure of dissent, and sometimes moved beyond it altogether, the landscape of opposition to colonial war was transformed.

Ideological divisions fueled a competition among communist, socialist, and liberal leftists to champion the claims of oppressed colonial subjects.[34] The far-left wing of opposition to colonial war, defined by its willingness to defend insurgencies as heroic liberation struggles, was centered in the CPGB and offshoots like the Kenya Committee. The Labour left represented by MCF condemned colonial wars, pushed for rapid self-determination, and celebrated nationalist aspirations but stopped short of embracing violent uprisings. The pacifist left of the Peace Pledge Union and the Union of Democratic Control followed this line closely. More moderate still was the liberal-humanitarian left, which encompassed a "legalistic" wing focused on the language of rights (in the National Council for Civil Liberties and the Amnesty International forerunner Justice) and a "moralistic" wing with missionary roots (in the Anti-Slavery Society).[35] Positioning themselves as bulwarks against militant alternatives, these groups mainly aimed to shape elite British opinion from within the establishment. They also hewed more closely to a reformist, case-by-case logic of curbing empire's most conspicuous abuses. Some groups, including the "moralistic" rivals Africa Bureau and Christian Action, shifted over time from liberal humanitarianism to explicitly anticolonial politics.[36]

As E. P. Thompson observed, resistance to colonial war in the late 1940s and early 1950s was dominated by the Communists. Labour, after all, was the party of government until 1952 and launched the war in Malaya on its watch. While CPGB membership rolls hovered around the modest figure of 35,000 in the early 1950s, the party's reach extended well beyond the cadres. Boasting a circulation of 120,000 at its postwar peak, the *Daily Worker* was a platform for atrocity stories that sometimes forced the mainstream press and government officials to respond.[37] Communists recognized that wars fought in defense of rubber plantations in Malayan and coffee farms in Kenya played to their ideological strengths. As then–party recruiter Raphael Samuel recalled, it was "the Empire rather than Britain itself which served as the paradigm of 'two camp' politics, of the division between haves and have-nots, of the oppression of the many by the few."[38]

CPGB strategy called for party members and fellow travelers to carry opposition to colonial war into organizations with more political muscle: above all, the trade unions. This approach succeeded in capturing some branches while foundering on the conservatism of the wider movement and union bosses in particular.[39] When the delegate from a steel construction union proposed a resolution condemning the "reign of terror and repression in Kenya" at the 1953 Trades Union Congress, his impassioned indictment—hundreds of thousands of Africans sent into detention camps, hundreds shot without trial, bombs dropped on "defenceless people," whole villages "destroyed"—failed to carry a majority. The motion was voted down after a skeptic from the National Union of Seamen asked, rhetorically, if the

FIGURE 1.1 London Communists march to "Stop the War in Malaya" and "End the Terror in Kenya," May Day, 1953. Henry Grant/Museum of London.

authorities should "allow the atrocities of Mau-Mau to continue" by failing to enforce "law and order."[40]

This episode, and others like it, exposed a major reason for CPGB ambivalence about decolonization: fear of alienating patriotic working-class sentiment. The party had a good war after the 1941 collapse of the Hitler-Stalin pact because it could ride antifascist and nationalist waves simultaneously. In the early 1950s, CPGB leaders were still waving the Union Jack, denying that they longed for the destruction of the British Empire, and envisioning a prosperous future underwritten by the economic dependence of tropical territories. American, rather than British, imperialism loomed as the chief enemy.[41] The problem with this strategy was that West Indians, Asians, and Africans in Britain, long targeted by party recruiters, were demanding a stronger line against the empire governed from London. When the party held a first protest meeting against the Kenya Emergency at Holborn Hall in December 1952, roughly a third of the 150 people who attended were black.[42] Party member Desmond Buckle—the son of an elite Accra family who had lived in England since age ten and participated in black radical politics since the 1930s—pressed his comrades on the Executive Committee to take more forceful action against "the terror in Kenya."[43]

Black leftists had long argued that spectacular violence could unsettle British complacency about empire. As Trinidadian-born George Padmore put it in 1939: "It is only when there is some riot in Jamaica, or shooting in Palestine, or unrest on the North-West Frontier, that the average Briton is made even remotely conscious of his responsibility toward the hundreds of millions of coloured people over whom the British ruling class speciously claim to be exercising a benevolent trusteeship."[44] While Padmore doubted that epiphanies inspired by atrocity would ever be more than temporary, the spectacular violence of counterinsurgency in the 1950s prompted some Communists to question their soft line on British imperialism. William Gallacher, famed for holding a Glasgow parliamentary seat for the party until 1950, observed in 1953 that "the use of Lincoln Bombers, with all their destructive power, in Kenya," signaled the advent of a new era. Imperialists "can no longer rule as of old, with 'the iron hand coated with a velvet glove,'" he concluded. "Now it is often blatant, brutal force." Even if "ruthless Yankee imperialism" represented the future, Gallacher observed that "the twilight of British imperialism" involved the same "barbarous methods."[45] But the criticism he received from party comrades, who accused him of elevating colonial workers over British workers as victims of capitalism, underscored the limits of Communist anticolonialism.[46]

As time went on, and especially after the Hungary crisis of 1956, Brockway's Movement for Colonial Freedom seized the initiative from the Communist Party.[47] Founded in 1954, the MCF brought together émigré activists including Murumbi and Eber, a smattering of Communists and Liberals, and a wide swath of the Labour Party's left wing. The key demands in its platform were straightforward: an end to wars and emergencies followed by speedy independence for colonies across the world.[48] Within a year of its founding, eight national trade unions, seventy trade union branches, and 244 local Labour organizations voted to affiliate with the MCF, and chapters were established in eight cities besides London.[49] Along with Tony Benn and Barbara Castle, Brockway formed a nucleus of MCF campaigners in the parliamentary Labour Party whose ranks grew steadily over the course of the decade. By 1960, nearly one-fifth of the entire House of Commons had joined the organization.[50]

While the figures seem impressive, the Movement for Colonial Freedom had limited grass-roots appeal, with no more than 1,000 active members nationally at its height.[51] While a few chapters clustered in the Home Counties were still going at the end of the 1950s, the organization's presence in cities like Birmingham, Liverpool, and Sheffield had withered into nonexistence.[52] Regular meetings at the national level, held "in a big room in the nether regions of the House of Commons," drew about twenty people at a time.[53] Some activists never really moved beyond the narrower causes that drew them into MCF in the first place.[54] Doris Lessing, who observed that those meetings in the Palace of Westminster amounted to a roll call of British colonies "in various stages of unrest," drifted away because she felt that her home country of Southern Rhodesia was not getting enough attention. Disagreements erupted, too, about how to respond to racial discrimination at home and whether to link colonial issues to the living standards of British workers.[55] Lack of funds were a chronic handicap.[56] Despite the nominal affiliation of hundreds of thousands of trade unionists, MCF was never able to tap into the institutional muscle of the labor movement or the Labour Party, whose leaders kept their distance from what they perceived as a radical cause.[57]

The impact of MCF came less in orchestrating opposition to empire than in making it visible. As Brockway and Castle cemented their status as spokespeople for the anticolonial cause, journalists learned to come to them for quotes and dissidents with information. The rallying of a multiracial coalition against empire, meanwhile, fueled a potent symbolic politics. Between 1955 and 1958 alone, MCF marches occupied the imperial space at London's heart, Trafalgar Square, on ten occasions, as Cypriot folk songs and African drums mingled with the sounds of speeches and cheers.[58] Other MCF events took place in civic buildings where politicians, intellectuals, and clerics held forth on topics like "human rights in the colonies" and "civil rights in Kenya."[59] Both kinds of gatherings attracted hundreds of people, many of them black, as observers invariably noted.[60] Audiences were likely drawn to the novelty of a figure like Murumbi, a colonial subject and racial outsider, crossing the country to speak on behalf of the people British soldiers were then fighting overseas. From platforms in London and elsewhere, Murumbi wove the elements of the organization's name into a plea for liberation from violence: "I am a colonial; I come from the colonies; I am a human being. As you cherish freedom, so we cherish freedom. It is in the nature of things."[61]

One reason that the act of white Britons, black Britons, and colonial subjects joining in protest gained the visibility it did was that the empire's defenders were so enraged by it. When MCF meetings made newspaper headlines, it was usually because provocateurs from a far-right militant group with fascist origins, the League of Empire Loyalists, tried to break them up by force. Five Empire Loyalists burst into a 1958 MCF meeting on

FIGURE 1.2 Occupying the heart of imperial London: a Movement for Colonial Freedom demonstration against the war in Cyprus, Trafalgar Square, 1956. Henry Grant/Museum of London.

Cyprus shouting "Keep Britain White" and scattering pamphlets that asked, "Cypriot murderers: how soft can we get?" Twenty men yelling "Keep Britain White" disrupted another MCF meeting the following year. Brockway's Highgate flat was vandalized by extremists who painted the same slogan and swastikas all over the doorstep.[62] Besides boosting the MCF's profile, these aggressive stunts by apologists for colonial violence also confirmed one of its arguments: that war in the colonies was as much a battle for British identity as for territory or power overseas.

Organizations like the Movement for Colonial Freedom faced a generational cleavage as well as racial and ideological fissures. The leading British forces in the anticolonial cause were overwhelmingly products of Edwardian and interwar radicalism. Brockway cut his teeth in the pacifist causes of the First World War era: crusading for disarmament, fighting conscription, and defending the right of conscientious objection. Several institutional bulwarks of opposition to colonial war—the Union for Democratic Control, the National Peace Council, the pacifist weekly *Peace News*—were forged in the same moment. The National Council of Civil Liberties was founded in the anti-fascist fervor of the 1930s. The women who sat on the Kenya Committee were veterans of decades-old campaigns for suffrage and birth control.[63] While the Communist Party of Great Britain may have been most conspicuously shaped by nostalgia for yesterday's struggles, the anticolonial left as a whole remained dependent on aging traditions of activism.

The youthful current in anticolonial dissent emerged above all from the universities. While students from the colonies represented an important vanguard—their numbers climbing from around 5,000 in the early 1950s to almost 30,000 by the end of the decade—unease with colonial war was not limited to them.[64] What would soon be known as the New Left was already taking shape at Oxford in 1955–1956, with the formation of a socialist club to promote left-wing discussion freed from party dogmatisms.[65] One of its founders, a Rhodes Scholar from Jamaica named Stuart Hall, went on to argue against the Suez invasion at the Oxford Union, backing a resolution of disapproval which passed by a vote of 352 to 206.[66] As early as 1954, another young activist, Raphael Samuel, a Communist from a London Jewish family, observed in the student journal *Oxford Left* that war in Malaya and Kenya represented an intensification and normalization of empire's brutality. "Before 1945," Samuel wrote, "imperialist atrocity was occasional, incidental. Today it is an everyday occurrence."[67] Reacting against Oxford's distinctly imperial brand of conservatism, the students of the socialist club—a band of outsiders in terms of race, class, religion, and nationality—insisted on a deromanticized vision of empire.

The other wing of the early New Left emerged from a different corner of the academy, generationally and geographically. E. P. Thompson (thirty-two years old in 1956) and John Saville (forty years old) were older than Hall and Samuel, established members of the Communist Party Historians Group, and based at northern universities. They too believed that colonial war in the 1950s had become "uglier and more cynical" than its predecessors, as Thompson wrote in response to the Suez crisis.[68] As New Leftists north and south attempted a rapprochement after 1956, the resulting outpouring of manifestos was shot through with unease about "the revived aggression of British imperialism," as Hall later put it.[69] This theme ran through the journals *Universities and Left Review* and *New Reasoner*, which merged to form the *New Left Review* in 1960, and the essay collections *Declaration* (1957), *Conviction* (1958), and *Out of Apathy* (1960).

Yet tensions remained. When the radical working-class revival envisioned by older activists failed to materialize, opposition to colonial war tilted further toward university graduates in the metropolis. In London, the Partisan Coffee House in Soho, run by Samuel and Hall between 1958 and 1962, emerged as a gathering place for educated young radicals. Though best remembered as an unofficial early headquarters of the Campaign for Nuclear Disarmament, the Partisan's sleek minimalist storefront also hosted Lessing's talks on Africa and Logue's poetry readings. Broadsides of "The Song of the Dead Soldier" sold for five shillings apiece at the counter and a copy hung on the wall, an emblem of the print culture that sustained antiwar and anticolonial communities. Claiming spaces and building institutions for dissent always ran parallel to another effort: finding ways to communicate the horrors of colonial violence. War for empire came home as a war of words and images.

The Rhetoric of Dissent

Activists focused so intently on the language of counterinsurgency because pro-war arguments drew on a carefully crafted vocabulary. In describing insurgents to the public, officials employed terms suggestive of criminality—"bandit," "gangster," sometimes "terrorist"—rather than politically weighty, potentially romantic words like "rebel."[70] Authorities also downplayed the gravity of these conflicts by declaring or "police actions" and "emergencies." This designation was not just a device for managing public opinion. It also

FIGURE 1.3 Partisan Coffee House, Soho, 1958. A broadside print of Christopher Logue's protest poem about the war in Cyprus, "The Song of the Dead Soldier," is visible on the wall at left. Roger Mayne/Mary Evans Picture Library.

underpinned Britain's position that the laws of war, including the Geneva Conventions, did not apply to insurgencies within empires.[71]

Campaigners against colonial war took aim at this sanitized lexicon. Lim Hong Bee's *Malayan Monitor*, for instance, opposed the delicate phrases used at press conferences with the grim realities they concealed:

security measures	large-scale round-up and indiscriminate arrest
screening	third-degree interrogation
shot while running away	shooting at sight of suspects . . .
punitive measures	sacking and burning of towns and villages[72]

Kenya Committee activists made similar points about the spurious bloodlessness of the words used to characterize counterinsurgency. "When Kikuyus mutilate European farmers' cattle," they noted, "it is described as 'barbaric.' When the RAF drops bombs on tribesmen who have taken refuge in the forest, it is described as 'a satisfactory mopping-up operation.'"[73] Communist barrister Ralph Millner protested that "the process so politely referred to as 'repatriation'" in Kenya—the mass removal of

Africans to overcrowded reserves—masked a brutal regime of expropriation and starvation.[74]

In his famous essay on "Politics and the English Language" (1946), George Orwell observed that the word "pacification" signified actions that were far from peaceful. "Defenseless villages are bombarded from the air, the inhabitants driven out into the countryside, the cattle machine gunned, the huts set on fire with incendiary bullets." Orwell argued that euphemism was a necessary condition for "things like the continuance of British rule in India," which could be justified "only by arguments which are too brutal for most people to face."[75] Other activists carried Orwell's message into the 1950s. Alex Comfort, a pacifist, physician, and fixture of BBC panel shows, saw Orwell's "double think" as a fitting label for the euphemisms applied to colonial conflicts. "We don't torture people—we display firmness in putting down terrorists. We don't burn children alive—we only obtain results against military objectives." Although the British public "doesn't like war," Comfort argued, talk of "police actions" helped to blunt that opposition because "'police' suggests the London bobby helping children across the road, not napalm and area bombing." Comfort, like Lim, composed a glossary to illustrate the double standard of the imperial lexicon:

Our Side	Their Side
necessity	atrocity
Resistance movement	bandits, terrorists . . .
re-education area	concentration camp . . .
interrogation	torture
firmness	repression
screening	iron curtain, purge

For leftist campaigners, remaking the semantic world of press coverage and political rhetoric was a prerequisite for getting people to care about violence.[76]

Anticolonial campaigning aimed at training the public to perceive the hidden meanings of phrases dulled by overfamiliarity. "We often hear the word 'Curfew,' now familiar in BBC news from Kenya, Malaya, and Cyprus, but do we realize what it means?" one activist asked, referring to round-the-clock restrictions that could restrict access to food and water.[77] Some leftists saw media not merely as a passive conduit for government propaganda but as an active collaborator in the suppression of the truth. "Writers, political leaders, the press, and the BBC have for years combined to hide from the

British people the knowledge of how these basic rights are denied to British subjects in the colonies," Millner charged. The priority activists placed on documenting facts and compiling evidence stemmed from their mistrust of established information sources.

It also represented a response to the engrained skepticism of "atrocity stories" in Britain. A lasting legacy of the accusations leveled against the German Army at the start of the First World War—the tales of Belgian babies bayoneted and Belgian nuns raped by rapacious Huns—was the belief that the Beaverbrook press had precipitated Britain's entry into the war by whipping up public hysteria.[78] As Orwell observed in 1942, reports of brutality functioned more as political bludgeons than moral revelations, with each side believing the worst about its ideological enemies and denying the charges leveled against its allies.[79] Throughout the Second World War, and even as photographic and testimonial evidence of the Holocaust began to circulate, Britons responded skeptically to reports of atrocity on the assumption that propagandists were seeking to manipulate them.[80] This legacy presented activists in the 1950s with a dilemma: how to seize public attention with allegations of extreme brutality without sacrificing credibility in the process.

One strategy they employed was to interweave atrocity imagery with the empirical detail of names, dates, and places, anchoring emotional impact in down-to-earth factuality. In 1953, the Kenya Committee published a letter from an African correspondent who wrote: "I cannot tell you the names of all the people who have been killed, but I can mention of a few like Njoroge wa Kago (Simeoni) and Stefano, the father of Thiani: those are from Waidake school and were taken from their houses by the Kenya Police Reserve." The names of more than a dozen murdered people followed, each one attributed to a specific place and sometimes to a particular day.[81] A few years later, Cypriot nationalists circulated a list of 317 names, each one corresponding to a signed statement alleging brutality in a certain village, police station, interrogation center, or detention camp.[82] Lim Hong Bee published a roll call of Malayan villages destroyed under collective punishment in the space of just a few months.[83] Anticolonial campaigners attempted to construct not just an alternative vocabulary but an alternative geography in which coordinates on the map represented sites of suffering.

Numbers represented another front in the propaganda war. Sometimes, activists compiled their own sets of numbers to undercut official claims of carefully targeted violence. Critics of the war in Kenya tracked figures on detainees held in camps, deaths in custody, and livestock confiscations, relying on sympathetic MPs to elicit information by questioning government ministers in the Commons.[84] At other times, activists did not challenge the accuracy of official metrics of military "progress" but instead reinterpreted them as evidence of overwhelming force. Measured by numbers of soldiers deployed and tons of bombs dropped, a Communist pamphleteer argued, the counterinsurgency in Malaya had to be far more intensive than the rhetoric of "police action" against "a handful of bandits" implied.[85]

Like later human-rights activists, campaigners in the 1950s had to navigate tensions between different forms of knowledge. Did quantitative data document systemic injustices or muffle the voices of individual victims?[86] Did testimony honor the subjective experience of suffering or overwhelm causes and structures with the immediacy and partiality of emotion?[87] One genre of anticolonial literature, the first-person torture narrative, tipped decisively in the direction of shock value. English-language pamphlets for the Cypriot cause were perhaps the most aggressive in fixing readers' attention on the bodily experience of pain, plunging readers into a disorienting world of brutality removed from political contexts. Underlining the assumption that sensory details of suffering could speak for themselves, one pamphlet listed fifty-six varieties of torture allegedly practiced by the British with burning cigarettes, ice water, bright lights, and other instruments. The same pamphlet featured an array of evidentiary flourishes to combat skepticism, including samples of manuscript testimony written by victims in Greek and photographs of bruised and battered suspects.[88]

For many Britons, of course, no amount of corroboration could ever make the stories told by colonial enemies credible. Beyond a reflexive mistrust of political horror stories, insurgents had to contend with widely publicized atrocities of their own, including attacks on British soldiers and settlers. This complicated any effort to pose as sympathetic victims. In the case of Cyprus, especially, the effort to employ torture narratives as antiwar propaganda was perhaps too conspicuously coordinated to be persuasive for many Britons. Despite the prevalence of real abuses on the island, some Greek Cypriot "testimonials" were exaggerated and others fabricated.[89] While neither Malayan nor Kenyan insurgents embellished to the same extent, they faced the same problem of communicating visceral horrors without seeming to concoct macabre tales.

To strike that balance, one of the most powerful weapons activists had at their disposal was the testimony of whistleblowers: the disillusioned agents of empire who decided to go public. Their whiteness and Britishness, and the presumption of objectivity those traits carried, conferred a unique standing among critics of colonial war. As members, however marginally, of the imperial elite, they could accuse administrators, soldiers, and police officers of failing to uphold the values they shared, rather than attacking those values frontally.[90] Most whistleblowers presented themselves as loyal servants of empire who saw their idealism unexpectedly shattered by grim realities, their narratives unfolding as reluctant journeys toward painful truths.

The ferocity of the violence in Kenya prompted a succession of whistleblowers to come forward. The first to emerge as a cause célèbre was Eileen Fletcher, a social worker and devout Quaker who went to work in the detention camps in December 1954 and resigned in disgust seven months later. Her story, billed as an "eye witness account," ran as a three-part series in the pacifist weekly *Peace News* and then in a pamphlet published by MCF in 1956. The cover featured a drawing of two wide-eyed African children peering through a barbed-wire fence alongside the words "Concentration Camps... White Supremacy... Children Starved... Tortured to Death." As if to fend off charges of sensationalism, the text inside began simply: "This is a true account of things I have seen and heard myself and of things told me by responsible officials."[91]

When she decided to go to Kenya, Fletcher stressed, she was troubled by reports of atrocities on both sides of the conflict. But her work with European refugees during the Second World War led her to believe that even hostile prisoners could benefit from the sympathetic attention of a trained counselor. She quickly realized, though, that the detention system ostensibly devoted to "rehabilitation" was permeated by violence and racism, hampered by grim living conditions, and driven by vengeance rather than understanding. Fletcher's exposé guided readers through the Dantean circles of the detention process: the herding of suspects into "pens" as guards struck stragglers with rifle butts; the extraction of confessions through torture; and the long, indefinite confinement to camps with forced labor, scarce food, and sadistic guards. "I have seen cattle markets in England," Fletcher wrote, "where the treatment was better than that accorded human beings in this camp." Chillingly, she quoted other camp officials whose attitudes toward Africans ranged from malign indifference to genocidal hatred. A contractor who advocated a mass shooting of detainees shrugged and said, "Oh well . . . blackwater fever and malaria will do the trick just as well."[92]

More horrors in Kenya were detailed by another low-level functionary in the detention system. Ernest Law was an ex-army captain who found work as the storekeeper of Nairobi's main prison in 1955. After complaining about the mistreatment of detainees and the lax discipline among security forces, Law was fired and held as a virtual prisoner at Kamiti camp, where he worked without pay for five months before returning to Britain. Law eventually found his way to Labour MP John Stonehouse, a leading MCF figure, who arranged for left-wing publisher John Calder to print Law's affidavit in a slim paperback edition. The volume also contained a collection of documents on the 1959 massacre at Hola Camp and the testimony of five Algerians tortured by French security forces, which had been recently published in France under the title *Gangrène*.[93] Calder used the English equivalent of the same word to title his book in a visceral statement of corruption, decay, and rot. "For the British reader," the cover of *Gangrene* promised, "the most vital and shocking part of this book will be found in Captain Law's descriptions of the brutalities that he witnessed . . . a clear and frightening picture of police sadism, administrative collusion, and ministerial irresponsibility."[94]

Within a fortnight of joining the Nairobi prison staff, Law saw around a dozen African convicts "lying stark naked on a murram patch, being beaten and kicked with truncheons, sticks and boots, unmercifully," by a group of British guards. At Kamiti, he witnessed Africans confined in narrow, solitary cells for weeks at a time; fed meager, rancid food; exposed to extreme heat; forced to labor without pay; and repeatedly beaten beyond the point of unconsciousness. "Not a day went passed without someone being beaten up." Law was released from the camp only after writing a letter to the colonial secretary, which was smuggled into the mail by a friendly African warder and threatened to go public with stories of brutality and lawlessness.[95]

As the counterinsurgency in Kenya dragged on, other disillusioned bureaucrats came forward. One of them was Philip Maldon, who served in the Kenya Police Reserve and then as a welfare worker in the detention camps. Maldon, like Fletcher, began as a true believer in the promise of "rehabilitation" behind barbed wire. He served as the commandant of a displaced persons camp in the British sector of Berlin from 1945 to 1947, then traveled in Malaya, where he admired the New Villages. In Kenya, though, Maldon clashed with higher-ups uninterested in the hearts and minds of Kikuyu detainees. In a 1957 *Peace News* exposé published shortly after his resignation, Maldon chronicled "a 'concentration camp' atmosphere." Camp officers carried whips and fired guns indiscriminately through the barbed wire. Those accused of brutality were simply shuffled from one district to another. The denials issued by the colonial government were "pure whitewash."[96] Like other whistleblowers, Maldon wrote as an idealist whose pleas for a more humane policy went tragically unanswered.

In a few cases, critics of counterinsurgency turned confessional, revealing their own complicity as they exposed violence to public view. Peter Marris, who served as a district officer in Kenya before working as a sociologist in East London, was one of them. In the New Left essay collection *Conviction*, Marris described an incident from the early days of the counterinsurgency that made him, by his own admission, "an accessory after the fact of murder." On New Year's Day, 1954, Marris was resting on the side of a mountain road at the end of a fruitless manhunt for a Mau Mau suspect. Suddenly a police officer appeared; he was grabbing an African man by the hair and prodding him with a gun barrel as he screamed in terror. Then another African—a teenager, "unarmed, and dressed as a schoolboy, with a Boy Scout belt and a mackintosh coat"—scrambled out of the bush. A series of shots rang out while Marris's back was turned. A second police officer, a trusted subaltern, had shot the young man dead.[97]

Marris might easily have glossed this fragmented narrative as a cautionary tale about the "fog of war," the impossibility of upholding clear standards amid chaos and uncertainty. Instead, he dwelled on the moral failures that infected his every move. He "rummaged the dead boy's pockets, in search of some evidence on which a court would have sentenced him to hang." A package of ammunition materialized, "but whether it was really found on the corpse, no one seemed to know." His friendship with the police officer deterred him from pressing charges or even raising his voice. Marris was, in any case, "too astonished to be angry." With other cares and responsibilities looming, the easiest course of action was to declare the operation a success and move on. That is just what Marris did, leaving him to marvel years later that "one could commit a crime so simply—between breakfast and lunch, as it were, with his mind on . . . the files waiting in an office tray."[98] Even the moral rupture of an extrajudicial killing could recede into the background of quotidian bureaucratic routine.

Given the intensity of pressures toward loyalty, discipline, and cohesion, police officers and soldiers made the most reluctant of whistleblowers. Men in uniform were complicit if they followed orders to commit abuses and exposed to punishment for insubordination if they did not. A few nonetheless decided to break the code of silence. A pair of ex-lieutenants honorably discharged after serving in Cyprus joined Brockway at an MCF-sponsored press conference in 1957. They released a joint statement that detailed the routine beatings of detainees at Kokkinotrimithia camp and disclaimed "any political motive whatsoever." As one of them told the press: "We felt it our duty to speak. We feel that people in this country, and government officials here, have no knowledge of the harsh treatment meted out."[99]

David Larder was a twenty-year-old National Service conscript in Kenya court-martialed and cashiered in 1953 for refusing to carry out orders. Facing a conscientious objector tribunal after his dismissal, Larder reported that he had been forced to shoot unarmed Africans and chop off their hands for identification purposes. One such shooting, carried out at close range, provoked him to quit. "I had machine-gunned men and women before, but this was so close that his brains landed on my chest." Repelled by the methods of colonial war, Larder also felt sympathy for the Kikuyu cause. "It seemed to me that the Africans had everything in common with the ordinary people in England," he said, "and were struggling for the same things that British people had themselves struggled for in the past." Granted a conditional exemption by the tribunal, he crisscrossed Britain as a Communist Party speaker campaigning for Kenyan independence.[100]

What made graphic imagery of violence effective, in activists' eyes, was not only shock as an end in itself but also the echoes of fascist warfare it conjured. If some campaigners, like Peter Worsley, worried that the horrors of massacre and genocide in the Second World War set an impossibly high standard for moral outrage, many more found the analogy irresistible. Anticolonial literature invoked the iconography of an all-powerful police state running rampant. Faced with "troops, police, dogs, planes, and armored cars," the Kenya Committee reported, "thousands of terrorized families fled from their homes to roam the country."[101] An MCF pamphlet on Cyprus asked: "Can you imagine the terror of the children as they watched these, to them, foreign soldiers with bayonets and rifles, rough-handling their fathers and brothers in the dark, early hours"?[102] By focusing on threats to privacy and the family, activists turned Second World War propaganda against totalitarianism on its head. The sanctity of domestic life, once celebrated as a quintessentially British value, was under attack from the British themselves.[103]

Nothing illustrated this moral role-reversal more vividly than the image of the camp. The unique horror of extermination camps like Auschwitz was not yet widely appreciated in the 1950s because the concentration camps liberated by British troops to the west, especially Belsen, dominated the public imagination.[104] This lingering ambiguity made analogies between Nazi war and colonial war more plausible at the time than they might seem in retrospect. At a May Day rally in London in 1954, Murumbi likened the detention camps in Kenya to "Belsen and the other German atrocity camps of WWII."[105] In a letter smuggled out of the Lokitaung detention camp and published by the *Observer* in 1958, five Kenyan prisoners compared the "brutal and inhuman treatment" they experienced at British hands to "that of a Nazi concentration camp."[106] A former police officer in Kenya wrote to the press in 1958 describing camps "on the lines of Mordhausen or Mauthausen."[107] An imagistic shorthand of barbed wire, guard towers, and search lights evoked the punitive excesses of Nazism even before activists described what was happening inside.

The fascist comparisons were never merely aesthetic nor wholly focused on tactics of violence. The racial and ideological structures that made brutality possible also drew activists' attention. Fenner Brockway argued that the British public had been rightly outraged by "collective punishment against the Jewish race" and that "the principle is exactly the same" when British forces burned down huts, slaughtered cattle, and imposed curfews to deter Kikuyu from aiding the Mau Mau.[108] Some activists, including Koinange and Murumbi, accused Britain of waging a genocidal campaign against the Kikuyu.[109] Others saw the Nazi precedent above all as a cautionary tale about the dangers of willful ignorance and deference to authority. Trade unionists pointedly observed that "the German people claimed ignorance of the existence of Belsen—let us not blind ourselves to what is happening now in Malaya." New Leftists John Saville and E. P. Thompson drew a parallel between atrocity denial in Germany and the British public's acceptance of "smooth official denials" about the counterinsurgency in Cyprus.[110]

Suggesting that Britain might have its own problem of collective responsibility offered a way to unsettle complacent assumptions about the relative benevolence of its empire. Comparisons with the French counterinsurgency in Algeria advanced the same aim. Writing to the *Manchester Guardian* in 1954, historian Eric Hobsbawm linked Algeria and Kenya as sites where "there has been killing on a scale which nineteenth century observers would have described as massacre."[111] But it was the English translation of Henri Alleg's *The Question*, published in spring 1958, that made the Algerian war synonymous with torture for British audiences. Newspapers ran extracts on their front pages and 25,000 copies sold within a few weeks.[112] While many predictably read Alleg as evidence of a peculiarly French depravity, activists advanced a less flattering interpretation. Future Amnesty International co-founder Peter Benenson insisted on treating Algeria and Kenya as "particular examples of a general case." In both cases, he argued, interrogators of "unstable mind, stunted development, and weak fiber" were releasing their "primeval instincts" through sadistic violence. "Lest British readers should think they can escape responsibility by shrugging off the problem as particularly French," Benenson urged, "it must be admitted that the cap fits the British soldier almost as well."[113]

New Left intellectuals also rejected the smug moral superiority of "'our boys' don't do such things,'" the popular refrain noted by Peter Worsley.[114] Stuart Hall and Raphael Samuel cast Algeria as a warning because "the jingoism of declining imperial power" posed a threat of incipient fascism in France and Britain alike. While the scale of destruction in, say, Cyprus could not compare with Algeria, Thompson and Saville argued that enforcing an alien authority over hostile populations always corrupted soldiers the same way. Even the warped "sexual sadism" chronicled in torture narratives from the two colonies was eerily similar.[115] For Worsley, the contrasts between French and British counterinsurgency represented superficial variations within a common project of modernizing violence by transforming it into a routine, technical operation. The French electrified their torture chambers; the British perfected a whole apparatus of repression including "the hooded informer, the concentration camp village, the bomber, and the destruction of crops."[116]

A classic liberal anxiety, the infection of metropolitan society by rotten colonial mores, also galvanized New Left activists. With mounting urgency after the Notting Hill riots of 1958, they warned that soldiers who served in the colonies could be transformed into agents of racist brutality at home. Worsley identified both a macropolitics and a micropolitics of violence: the British state's reliance on warfare legitimized aggression while individual Britons learned habits of dehumanization in battle with colonial foes. As Worsley put it, "When we get Suez lunacies at the top, we get Notting Hill riots at the bottom."[117] Thompson and Saville agreed that might-makes-right amorality could not be confined to the colonies. Leaders bred cynicism by flouting the rule of law while paying lip service to it. More disturbing still, the "inhuman" occupiers of today would be the voters of tomorrow.[118] Peace activists made a comparable point about the incompatibility of rigid military training and responsible citizenship. When white supremacist mobs took to the streets, it was a sign that democracy itself had been conscripted into thoughtless violence against imagined enemies.[119]

Occasional spasms of censorship seemed to confirm the illiberalism unleashed by colonial war. Although political communication was not subject to anything like the censorship that targeted obscenity in the 1950s, the state employed a variety of informal powers that made it harder for campaigners to get their message out.[120] Many public libraries banned *Peace News* and the *Daily Worker*, the publications most consistently critical of colonial war.[121] The police in St Leonards-on-Sea, Sussex, seized copies of

FIGURE 1.4 "The New Safari": black humor and stark imagery of a summary execution in the "Kenya Report," a 1953 pamphlet from the Communist-dominated Kenya Committee. Author's collection.

Gangrene from a local bookseller and held them for several months, although no charges were ever filed. In London, the British Transport Commission forbade Calder from posting Tube advertisements for *Gangrene* that promised "the truth about the Kenya prison camps," allowing only the title and price to appear.[122]

Beyond a few scattered pockets of state-enforced silence, however, the world of radical print remained vibrant. British prosecutors resisted legally questionable entreaties from conservatives to deploy sedition and incitement statutes against activists.[123] Left-wing bookshops like Communist-run Collets in Charing Cross Road, pacifist-run Housmans in Kings Cross, and the Hammersmith Bookshop kept their shelves stocked with the latest literature. *Gangrene* sold about 20,000 copies nationwide.[124] *Peace News* maintained a weekly circulation of about 9,000; the *Daily Worker,* starting from a postwar readership of around 115,000, hovered near 50,000 after 1956. Most significant of all, perhaps, left-leaning but mainstream publications drew on the same stock of words and images as radical titles did. A drawing of gun-toting imperialists hovering over a crumpled African body appeared in a 1953 Kenya Committee pamphlet that was condemned in Parliament for "inflaming racial animosity." Less than two years later, a David Low cartoon in the *Manchester Guardian* showed a strikingly similar scene, with a few more soldiers and pith helmets added for good measure.[125]

"GOT TO STOP SOMETIME - SOONER THE BETTER"

FIGURE 1.5 Cartoonist David Low takes up the motif of khaki-clad, gun-wielding imperialists looming over an African victim in Kenya. The Manchester *Guardian*, 1955. Associated Newspapers Ltd.

The *Daily Worker* long set the standard for unflinching atrocity coverage. The paper gave space to a Cypriot journalist who said that police shoved bits of broken glass under his fingernails and a Kenyan mother who described torture, food deprivation, and random beatings.[126] Even more damaging than the first-personal testimonials were the photographs from Malaya published in the spring of 1952. Under a headline screaming "Stop This Horror," the front page on April 28 featured a photograph of a Royal Marine dangling the severed head of a Chinese insurgent before the camera. The paper ran more photographs in the days that followed; all showed British soldiers posing with corpses, or parts of mutilated corpses, as trophies. "We cannot plead ignorance," CPGB leader Harry Pollitt declared in a follow-up article that appealed to "restore Britain's honor" by bringing the war to an end. Although no other newspapers reproduced the photos, several ran stories describing them, and the colonial secretary was forced to concede in Parliament that they were genuine.[127]

While the Labour-aligned press was less consistent in criticizing colonial violence, its exposés and attacks reached much bigger audiences. The *Daily Herald*, under the editorial control of the Trade Unions Council until 1957, had a circulation of more than 2 million at the start of the decade and 1.4 million at the end, while its nominally independent cousin, the *Tribune*, added another 40,000.[128] Both papers regularly turned over their columns to party figures who led the charge on colonial issues from the left and, less regularly, to radical voices outside Parliament. The early years of the Malaya war represented a conspicuous blind spot for Labourite criticism: a typical *Daily Herald* editorial in 1950 warned that "Communist banditry" threatened "Britain's progressive mission in the Malayan peninsula."[129] Once back in opposition, however, the Labour papers vied to match the Communists in the ferocity of their attacks on other colonial wars. Journalist and historian Basil Davidson, effectively blacklisted at the *New Statesman* for his Communist sympathies, found a new home at the *Daily Herald*, where his columns on Kenya condemned "a very dirty war . . . getting dirtier every day it lasts."[130] Promising to expose "oppression wherever it occurs," the *Tribune* in 1957 devoted a sixteen-page special issue to reports of torture in Cyprus.[131] Where the Labour papers once fanned outrage about the brutality of Malayan insurgents, they pivoted to declaring that "freedom will win in Cyprus and Kenya against torturers . . . and all those in London who would prefer to hush up their misdeeds."[132]

Even in the left-leaning press, journalistic standards imposed a lawyerly caution on some atrocity coverage. The Cyprus special in the *Tribune*, drawn largely on sworn testimony by court witnesses, called for further investigations rather than resignations. When the *Tribune* later ran parts of a letter from a camp detainee in Kenya, the editors stressed that they withheld any passages based on "hearsay" rather than firsthand observation.[133] Yet sensational descriptions of suffering bodies threatened to overwhelm the caveats. A *Tribune* front page in 1957 featured an article by Labour MP Jennie Lee, who reported seeing the disfigured back of a Cypriot prisoner held at Wormwood Scrubs in London. The headline read: THESE SCARS GIVE THE LIE TO [colonial governor John] HARDING.[134] Other imagery appealed even more openly to emotion. Rising-star photojournalist Terry Fincher took a picture of a forlorn-looking Greek Cypriot boy framed by loops of barbed wire that ran in the *Daily Herald* under the headline THE BARBED-WIRE ISLAND.[135]

By the late 1950s, the traditionally staid papers of the left were playing catch-up with the *Daily Mirror*, the daily newspaper with the biggest circulation in the world in the 1950s. The tabloid owed its success to a populist voice that flattered working-class readers as "the people" while entertaining them with colorful human-interest stories. This formula did not always translate into opposition to empire; the *Mirror* initially cheered on the war against "jungle Reds" in Malaya and influential columnist William Neil Connor reliably defended British soldiers. But the paper's coverage of the Kenya and Cyprus wars, reaching 4.5 million readers every day, was overwhelmingly critical and overwhelmingly focused on brutality. In many ways, colonial violence played to the *Mirror*'s strengths. Gory details of bodily harm fit the mold of the sensational crime stories that were a standby of the paper. Patrician Cabinet secretaries, broad-acred settlers, and Blimpish army officers made for ideal villains; after 1951, colonial wars could be branded simply as Tory wars, the morally bankrupt project of a corrupt elite. The dark drama of interrogation rooms lent itself to a perennial script of British scandal that was gaining currency again in the 1950s: glimpsing the twisted behavior of the powerful behind closed doors.[136]

The *Mirror* turned against the counterinsurgency in Kenya within a few weeks of the Emergency declaration in October 1952. Faulting the government for employing "tough" measures rather than trying to win over moderate Kikuyus, the paper predicted that repression would only create more terrorists. As one headline put it, "Britain cannot shoot her way out of this."[137] According to the paper's leader writers, the "sterile policy of brute force and barbed wire" was not only tactically counterproductive but a stain on Britain's global reputation.[138] Saturation coverage of atrocity scandals in subsequent years generated headlines like these:

THE PRISONER WAS SHOUTING DON'T BURN ME
I WAS HELD OVER FIRE BY POLICE

SOLDIER SAYS: I WAS TOLD TO "CUT OFF HIS EAR"

Two Wounded Africans Were in Agony...A Dog Ripped Open Another African's Throat . . . AND THE WHITE MEN "GRINNED"[139]

On Cyprus, the *Mirror* conceded that EOKA was trying to win the war in part by smearing British soldiers. But even this did not deter the paper from sounding the alarm. When Greek Cypriot leader Archbishop Makarios held a press conference alleging abuses by British forces in June 1957, the *Mirror* labeled the performance a "vicious propaganda campaign" while splashing the gory details across the front page and insisting that "only an impartial inquiry" could "clear the air."[140]

That same month, writer Keith Waterhouse published a *Mirror* dispatch under a provocative headline: "ARE THE BRITISH CRUEL IN CYPRUS?" Waterhouse's first-person narrative left no doubt about the answer: "I have sat in the barbed wire surrounded stone courthouse in Nicosia where allegations of slaps and kicks and punches at interrogation centers are becoming more frequent every week. I have seen dozens of hair-raising statements by Cypriots alleging that British Security Forces beat and tortured them. I have talked to responsible men who hold that confessions of terrorists are obtained with threats and whippings, and who say they have seen the evidence of this ill-treatment."[141] A few weeks later, in a front-page story headlined "STOP THIS BLOODSHED NOW," Waterhouse described soldiers menacing schoolchildren with truncheons, seizing suspects from their homes in the dead of night, and staging mock executions complete with the sounds of gunfire.[142]

While the *Mirror*'s splashy tabloidism looked a world removed from activist groups' mimeographed pamphlets, the differences were more superficial than substantive. Both interwove words and images to maximize emotional impact. Both invoked the trustworthiness of photographic evidence and first-person testimony—especially from British witnesses—to substantiate claims of violence. Above all, both dwelled on body violations as a metonym for the political violations of empire. Just as the *Mirror* showed it was possible to integrate colonial war into a populist worldview, leftists learned to shed their reservations about gruesome atrocity stories.

Long a redoubt of cross-party consensus, debates about governing empire became acrimonious and divisive in the 1950s.[143] The rising prominence of atrocity stories played a decisive role in this. So did the intensifying mobilization of colonial subjects in Britain. It is true that, as the home-grown left escalated its confrontation with empire's violence, the voices of Malayans, Kenyans, and Cypriots grew less distinct. One reason for this is the racial double standard that extended the presumption of objectivity to white Britons while casting others as inherently biased. Another is that imagery of silently suffering and passive victims offered a more capacious vessel for British sympathies than the potentially menacing figure of the resistance fighter. But the conversion of overseas liberation struggles into introspective moral dilemmas also made it harder for people at home to maintain distance from violence. Paying attention to the brutality committed in Britain's name inevitably posed the question of what, if anything, Britons were prepared to do about it.

Acts of Dissent

One feature of British militarism in the 1950s brought war home like nothing else: the state's reliance on conscription. It forced ordinary Britons to grapple with questions, about the legitimacy of colonial war and their willingness to participate it, which they might have preferred to ignore. Introduced by the Labour government in 1949, mass conscription in what was officially termed "peacetime" rested on a shifting foundation of public support. Labourites in opposition after 1951 backed away from the policy, calling for a reduction in the two-year period of service, and the ruling Conservatives hinted that they were open to changes. While opinion polls in 1949 showed wide support for conscription, the situation was reversed by September 1956, with 44 percent ready to end National Service and 38 percent in favor of keeping it.[144] Conservative politicians, including Anthony Eden and Enoch Powell, were inundated with letters complaining about the burdens conscription imposed on young men and their families.[145]

Some young men tried to evade conscription by moving out of the country, often to the Republic of Ireland, or by feigning infirmity during the medical exam, which had a failure rate of around 16 percent.[146] To confront the system more openly, by declaring a conscientious objection, was a grave act. Although the infamously punitive treatment of objectors in 1914–1918 was not repeated in the Second World War or afterward, the possible consequences of refusing to fight remained daunting. Conscripts seeking an exemption had to face a tribunal made up of magistrates, sheriffs, retired military officers, and other notables. Their questions were designed not just to expose logical inconsistencies in claims of pacifism but to shame and stigmatize the applicant before the public: "Why do you prefer the life of the enemy to the life of your fellow-countrymen?" "Do you regard soldiers as murderers?" "Do you realize that other people work while you rant?"[147]

Although more than 70 percent of those who declared an objection in the 1950s were ultimately allowed to perform civilian work or non-combat work in the military, roughly a quarter received no exemption. Those who continued to resist were fined, sent to youth detention centers, or imprisoned (usually for a term of several months). Servicemen who declared an objection after enlisting faced court-martial and imprisonment by the military.[148] Even COs whose applications succeeded ran the risk of ostracism and joblessness for years afterward. Stories about local objectors, often quoting censorious remarks from tribunal officials, appeared regularly in the newspapers. At least some local councils maintained employment bans on anyone who had ever registered as a CO.[149]

Despite the risks, a total of 8,284 men appeared before CO tribunals between 1948 and 1960, roughly one in two hundred of those called up.[150] Reversing the pattern seen in the Second World War, the proportion of conscripts claiming an objection climbed steadily over the course of the 1950s.[151] The most common grounds for asserting CO status, and those most readily accepted by the tribunals, were religious objections to war in any form. Asserting political or humanitarian objections to *particular* wars, by contrast, invited almost certain denial. Although the statute books offered no guidance on what constituted a "conscientious" objection, tribunals reliably scoffed at COs who presumed to distinguish between just and unjust conflicts by their own lights.[152]

In the face of that reality, making any statement against colonial war amounted to a remarkable act of dissent. Just how many COs chose this path is impossible to say. Few records from the tribunals survive and the state apparently kept no systematic figures on the justifications provided by COs. But officials did note the kinds of language that recurred in CO applications. Some COs argued that the "answer to the problem is world government as opposed to oppressing armies in the Colonies." Others expressed unease with "the prejudices and intolerance directed against people of different race, 'class,' or colour." Still others objected to fighting for "a social system in which most of the wealth is owned by a few rich men."[153]

Many who refused to fight on these grounds had a history of activism. Practiced in disputation, they insisted on the illegitimacy of war fought for empire. A London schoolteacher who belonged to the League of Coloured Peoples cited Kenya, Malaya, and British Guiana at a November 1954 tribunal "as examples of militaristic imperialism which he could not support . . . especially since he knew that British forces were committing brutalities which he could only describe as Nazi-like."[154] The next month, a pacifist youth group leader mentioned the same conflicts at his tribunal in the capital. "I am told I am defending freedom," he declared. "But I believe that in Kenya, Malaya, and British Guiana freedom is not being defended by British troops."[155]

For Richard Pankhurst, called up in 1952 at the age of twenty-five, activism was a family affair. His mother Sylvia was a prominent suffragist, pacifist, and antifascist who shared with her son a passion for the cause of Ethiopian independence. Like other left-wing COs, Richard Pankhurst stated that he would have gladly fought fascism in the Second World War but refused to participate in wars he considered aggressive, chauvinistic, or exploitative. Appealing the tribunal's negative decision, Pankhurst reiterated that he would not "wage a war on behalf of the sectional interests of the settlers against the Mau Mau rebellion which is itself the inevitable outcome of the patently unjust Kenya Government's land policy." Denied CO status again five months later, he repeated his protest against the "criminal policies . . . which deny 5,000,000

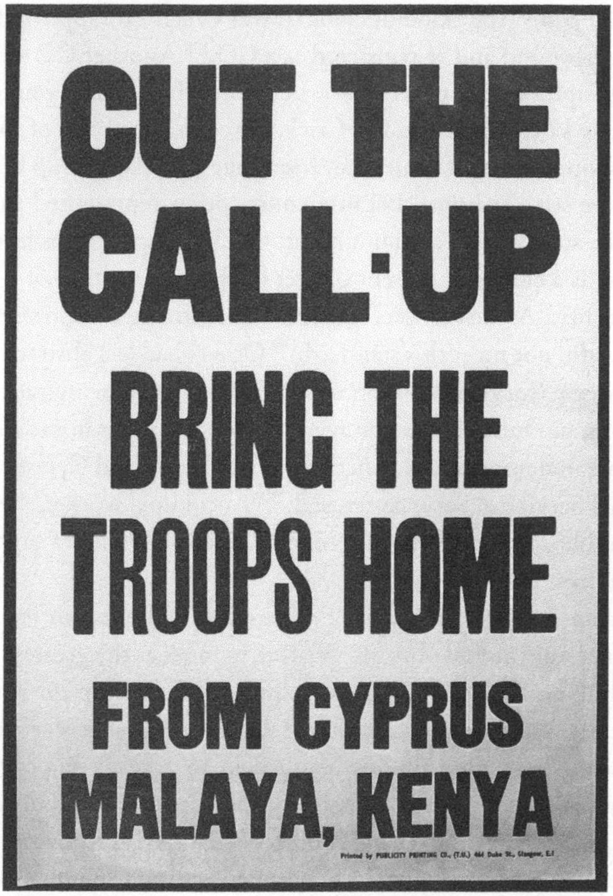

CUT THE CALL·UP
BRING THE TROOPS HOME
FROM CYPRUS MALAYA, KENYA

Printed by PUBLICITY PRINTING Co. (T.U.) 464 Duke St., Glasgow, E.1

FIGURE 1.6 A Communist Party poster against conscription for colonial wars. People's History Museum.

Africans a single elected representative in the Kenya Legislative Council and use British armed forces to arrest innocent men, women and children and to confiscate their cattle." Pankhurst was summoned to court three times, threatened with imprisonment, and fined a total of £63 (approximately £1,300 today) before finally securing a place on the CO register.[156] Even then, he did not relent in his criticism, publishing a book in 1954 that blamed "vicious police atrocities" on a "quasi-fascist phalanx of unrepentant settlers."[157]

Conscientious objectors were not always steeped in activism. By his own admission, eighteen-year-old painter David Hockney registered for National Service in 1955 without thinking much about it. It was only after the Suez invasion ("the first thing that made me politically aware") and the flare-up of violence in Cyprus (the "kind of colonial war which I disapproved of") that he changed his mind and re-registered as a CO.[158] Another CO who worked out his principles in the process of articulating them was a young political theorist named Bernard Crick. For Crick, the central problem of colonial war was not the oppression of subjects overseas but the relationship between citizens and the state at home. Because conscription represented the coercive power of the state at its maximum point, Crick thought it was justified only "when there is a clear and present danger to the very survival of a free political community." As "lesser wars of national advantage and prestige," Malaya and Cyprus did not meet this standard.[159] Others had less abstract, and more personal, reasons for registering an objection. A Guyanese migrant and warehouse laborer in Dulwich was outraged by the coup in his home country and saw the same undemocratic violence at work in Kenya and Cyprus. Called up for National Service in 1959, he refused. "As a colonial worker," he wrote, "it is incompatible with my conscience to serve or assist Britain in suppression of people like myself."[160]

For Britons beyond the reach of conscription, the forum for dissenting from colonial war was less obvious. Writing in 1960, as the greatest ambitions of the early New Left seemed to be fading, E. P. Thompson worried that British society was losing its capacity to nurture resistance. Institutions like corporations, parties, and unions had grown to a vastly impersonal scale; mechanisms of democratic accountability had devolved into bulwarks of the status quo. Anyone seeking change confronted a sense of powerlessness and hopelessness.[161] For some opposed to colonial war, collective action through the Communist Party or the Movement for Colonial Freedom offered an antidote to apathy. But for others, the act of declaring an objection to war in the colonies was meaningful in itself. Even without the formal procedures of a National Service call-up, they found ways to proclaim opposition to the violence committed in their name.

Speaking out was not necessarily a substitute for joining, organizing, or voting. Nor did it always represent an individualistic rejection of collective action. As an eminent Oxford philosopher argued at this time, words are entwined with action and with social life; they respond to other people, try to influence behavior, assert authority, and define communities.[162] Dissent from colonial war could be aimed at changing minds or simply breaking through the façade of pro-war consensus, signaling to ideological allies that they were not alone. In 1947–1948, as Parliament was approving the National Service Act and the government began to enforce it, authorities in London were unnerved by a wave of graffiti challenging conscription and war. In Bayswater, the message was: "CONSCRIPT WEALTH NOT WORKING-CLASS YOUTH" and "FREE THE COLONIES." In Shoreditch a year later: "END THE WAR IN MALAYA" and "WITHDRAW THE TROOPS."[163]

Unlike the graffiti, most protest against colonial war was not anonymous. Especially outside the big cities, where opportunities to stage mass demonstrations were limited, the most common mode of dissent was writing letters to politicians and newspapers. At a moment of growing faith in the value of the "ordinary"—a shift signified, among other things, by social scientists collecting opinions from the people they studied rather than observing them from a distance—Britons entered into national debates with confidence.[164] Already in 1948, a Gallup poll found that roughly one in ten adults had written to their Member of Parliament and one in seven had written to a newspaper.[165] Even backbench MPs, who preferred impressionistic measures of opinion to professional polling, received two or three letters a day on average.[166] One civil servant observed in 1956 that "the British citizen is now more ready to write his Member of Parliament about his grievances than he was before the war" as press, radio, and television coverage heightened the visibility of once-obscure politicians.[167] Newspapers received more letters still, hundreds each day at the national papers, and published a generous selection of them to assure readers that their voices mattered.[168] Populist papers like the *Daily Mirror*, where editor Hugh Cudlipp revered reader mail as "the people's pulse-beat," led the way in elevating the views of the masses.[169]

Perhaps more than most sources, these letters present a distorted picture. At a time when the majority of people did not write to strangers about controversial issues, those who did were disproportionately activists, university graduates, and men. Politicians habitually weed critical and trivial messages from their papers while retaining flattering and momentous ones; editors curate mailbags to match their visions of an ideal readership. Despite these limitations, the letters that survive from the 1950s have lessons to impart. One is that the British left wing could reach beyond the ranks of true believers through the letter pages of the newspapers, a surprising number of which upheld their promise of showcasing diverse opinions. Another is that the "ordinary" people who wrote letters against colonial war were influenced by activist campaigns but not beholden to them. While comparisons with fascism resonated widely, individual protests also drew on an idiosyncratic mix of guns-versus-butter materialism, national pride, imperial prestige, and evangelical judgment. They encompassed provincial concerns as well as cosmopolitan ideals, the practical as well as the philosophical, the conservative as well as the iconoclastic.

Unlike the literature produced by parties and movements, dissenting letters appealed as much to interests as to altruism. Several writers saw a trade-off between warfare overseas and welfare at home. A self-described socialist wrote to the *Luton News* warning that "imperialist actions in Korea, Kenya, Malaya and British Guiana must have repercussions on the home front . . . The country cannot have schools, houses, and hospitals and also build huge bombing planes, warships, and A and H bombs."[170] A West Yorkshire man registered a similar objection in the *Shipley News and Express* about the cost of armaments in "Kenya, Malaya, Egypt, Korea, Indonesia, etc.," draining funds away from "social services."[171] Others expressed concern about the effects of conscription on economic productivity. If soldiers were "brought home and put to useful employment as civilians," a Hartlepool Communist suggested to his local paper, "Britain's economic ills" could be cured.[172]

Letter writers often made pragmatic arguments about the futility of violence. No colony could be ruled indefinitely through coercion, they argued, because this alienated the uncommitted without ever fully defeating resistance. A *Daily Telegraph* reader in Essex recalled the failure of repression in Ireland and concluded that "the methods we are using just won't work in Cyprus." Another *Telegraph* reader, writing from Gloucestershire, made the same point more succinctly: " 'Love me or I shoot you dead' is no substitute for a sane foreign policy."[173] A paternalistic twist on this argument held that empires forfeited their moral authority, and thus their capacity for uplift, when they resorted to force. Writing to the Colonial Office, a Birmingham woman objected to brutality in Kenya on the grounds that it undermined the civilizing mission. "The downtrodden African negro," she complained, "will never learn a better way of life unless he is taught it." She urged officials to "show tribesmen who know nothing more than the law of nature, the law of tooth & claw, a better way to settle their difficulties." Humanitarianism was far from incompatible with racist condescension.[174]

Nor was it incompatible with nationalism. For some letter writers, overwhelming violence against relatively defenseless enemies offended British pride. They saw it as unchivalrous and dishonorable, a notion that gained currency during the Second World War, when the ideal soldier was imagined as a restrained, humane, and gentle warrior to contrast with bloodthirsty Nazi killers.[175] One veteran of that conflict wrote the Colonial Office to complain that tactics in Kenya violated the noble traditions of the British Army. "To turn dogs and armed men loose on entire unarmed villages," he wrote, "is like a robust man striking a pregnant woman" and "a blot on the good name of the English." A woman writing to MP Philip Noel-Baker likewise bemoaned attacks on unarmed women in Cyprus which "left a stain on the honor of our land [and] seared with shame those of us to whom that honor was dear." Like the civilizing mission, the chivalrous soldier was an imperialist standby that could be turned, occasionally, against the violence of empire.[176]

One theme of activist campaigns, the threat of racial brutality coming home from the colonies, coursed through grass-roots sentiment as well. When Labour MP Barbara Castle made headlines in the fall of 1958 for her allegations about brutality in Cyprus, several correspondents connected what happened in Famagusta to what happened in Notting Hill a few weeks earlier. As one social worker told Castle, "we cannot expect to arm young servicemen up to the teeth; teach them to kill with their hands (as they are being taught) and then hope that they will come back into the civilian community as law-abiding citizens." A Second World War veteran recalled "the disgusting attitude to and treatment of the 'wogs,' as they were arrogantly called, by some of our fellows" in India and worried that military service in the colonies was breeding a hardened generation of white supremacists. Another veteran cited the same epithet as evidence of the same pathology: "Unfortunately the hatred and suspicion of 'wogs' and all sallow foreigners inculcated by the army survives into civilian life."[177] Longstanding anxieties about the brutality of "demobbed" men, resurgent after the Second World War, assumed a new form with the backlash against black migrants.[178]

Many letter writers echoed activist claims that the moral authority accrued in the war against Germany was slipping away in the colonies. Of course, this myth of a "good war" depended on selectively forgetting Britain's bombing of German civilians and its reluctant, hastily concluded prosecution of German war criminals.[179] Yet the myth also created an opportunity for judging the brutal conflicts of the present against a precedent seen as righteous and restrained. *Manchester Guardian* readers excoriated General Gerald Templer's use of collective punishments in Malaya as a "totalitarian" homage to the "grossly repugnant" methods of Britain's "late enemies."[180] One woman told Barbara Castle that the use of indiscriminate searches, casual beatings, and indefinite detentions in Cyprus "puts us on level with Hitler and his concentration camps." Another woman writing to Castle doubted that "we are any better than the Nazis" and worried that people will "loathe us all over the world as they did the Germans." She added: "I'm ashamed that Britain has sunk so low."[181]

Complicating the Nazi comparison in the 1950s was a growing reluctance to dwell on German guilt. A Christian discourse of forgiveness, a hazy understanding of the Holocaust, a narrowly legalistic approach to Nazi prosecutions, and Cold War alliance-making all militated against efforts to hold the entire German population accountable for wartime atrocities.[182] It is all the more striking, then, that critics of colonial war seized on the principle of collective responsibility for Britain's crimes. Complicity in brutality went far beyond the individuals who struck the blows, they argued, and beyond the colonies. It stained the nation as a whole. The 1955 trial of two Kenya police officers who tortured a suspect to death prompted a *Times* reader to ask "whether we are so calloused that we can permit these atrocities to be performed on British subjects in our name. So long as we acquiesce in these brutalities we are, every one of us, vicariously responsible."[183] A few years later, the *Manchester Guardian's* coverage of a brutal round-up in Cyprus drove one reader to insist that "we cannot escape our responsibility by remaining silent. History will judge not only the attitude of the British Government but also that taken by the British public." Another *Guardian* reader, a refugee from Nazi Germany, argued that the average Briton was actually more responsible for atrocities than the average German in the Third Reich because British citizens were free to vote, protest, and otherwise pressure their leaders.[184]

Despite its vaguely juridical air, collective responsibility served above all as a secularized language of sin and repentance. Warnings of history's judgment substituted for divine judgment as a call to confession and change. Sometimes, the moral critique of colonial war was explicitly religious. A Coventry man writing to Barbara Castle worried about the initiation of conscripts into sin: "These boys are taken from their homes, forced into a life alien to Christian belief & the command 'Thou shalt not kill.'" Another man was so troubled by colonial war that he interpreted everyday misfortunes, like traffic accidents, as a sign of divine punishment for the sins committed overseas. "It will go on," he warned, "until we change our foul methods and recognize that all peoples are God's people and must be respected as such." An antiwar letter to the Colonial Office simply quoted 1 Peter 22:17 and took its meaning as self-evident: "Honor all men."[185] Old-fashioned currents of Christian pacifism and evangelical universalism fueled discontent with the violence of empire.

While rooted in knowledge of pain and suffering, vernacular arguments against colonial war were far more concerned with what violence meant for perpetrators and bystanders than for victims. Britain's prosperity and stability, its reputation, honor, and virtue, loomed as the most urgent preoccupations. Full-throated solidarity with insurgent movements was rare by comparison.

Even so, a few writers did seek to justify rebellion against unjust ruling orders. Why should Kenyans not revolt against "land hunger?" a Bedfordshire man asked his local newspaper. A Blackpool man defended Mau Mau in a letter to the Colonial Office by arguing that no human being could be expected "to endure starvation forever." A *Guardian* reader in Surrey offered what was, for the time, an unusually explicit account of the racial double standard at work in the colonies: "What is acknowledged to be unjust at home when white people are involved does not always appear to be an injustice when the victims are black and the scene is thousands of miles distant."[186]

These letters reveal the many routes available to contemporaries who wanted to reject colonial violence. The brutality inflicted by British forces was richly documented, vividly represented, and publicly debated. For some, this knowledge created an opening for arguments based on materialism and realpolitik. For others, dissent was less a calculated act than a product of emotional responses—pity, worry, anger, disgust—generated in the confrontation with atrocity. These kinds of protests ran along the boundary between guilt and shame: between the possibility of change and redemption, on the one hand, and a fatalistic sense of complicity, on the other.[187] People spoke out to stop colonial war without being at all certain that their voices would make any difference.

For this reason, the pessimistic diagnoses of activists like Worsley and Thompson are ultimately misleading. Discomfort with violence was not lacking in 1950s Britain. Neither was the willingness to take action against it. Even the political handicap imposed by organizational and ideological fissures can be overstated. Vivid representations of violence accomplished what was arguably their leading tactical aim: to energize a left wing that could not agree on thornier questions about timetables to independence, constitutional arrangements, or the balance of power among indigenous groups. The apparent shortcomings of protest against colonial violence were less decisive in the end than the extraordinary effectiveness of the ideas and institutions arrayed on the other side.

How the moral uneasiness that activists worked so hard to cultivate was contained and counteracted by opposing forces is the story of the following chapters. Uneasy consciences could be managed with an ethics of violence, which developed reasons for looking away from brutality, or an epistemology of violence, which cast doubt on whether it was happening at all. They could also be relieved through the cathartic dramatizations of fiction, theater, film, and television. Perhaps the most disturbing response of all sought to reshape conscience directly through the encounter with violence. In some ways, this tactic made a virtue of necessity because the brutal realities of colonial war became so widely known. But apologists for brutality also understood that the prisms through which many Britons saw violence—from nationalist pride and masculine adventure to racial solidarity and racial anxiety—made it anything but a source of anguish.

2

War Stories

LURKING BEHIND HIS suave manners, James Bond of Her Majesty's Secret Service was notorious for a touch of cruelty. This sadistic streak, which critics have plausibly attributed to creator Ian Fleming's private predilections, was explained by Fleming himself as a legacy of Bond fighting insurgents in the colonies. "Something a bit cold and dangerous in the face . . . . May have been attached to Templer in Malaya. Or Nairobi. Mau Mau work. Tough-looking customer." Contrasting Bond's rough-hewn masculinity with "the sort" usually seen in a London gentleman's club, Fleming in *Moonraker* (1955) evoked an underworld of take-no-prisoners ruthlessness.[1] This brief, almost cryptic allusion to colonial war seemed to assume that the dark deeds committed by British fighters, far from genteel society, were already becoming common knowledge.

The stories soldiers tell about war often omit graphic details of violence. They do so for many reasons: reluctance to appear callous, fear of turning civilians against the military, language breaking down in the face of world-shattering extremity.[2] But wars do not always inspire silence. Nor do they necessarily depend upon it. As the conflicts of decolonization were being fought, participants and observers recounted acts of brutality in explicit fashion. Relayed in conversations, letters, memoirs, and novels, these disclosures faced few obstacles on their journey from conflict zones to domestic audiences. Far from colliding with taboos, straining the limits of representation, or slipping into the censor's grasp, the violence of counterinsurgency was discussed more or less freely by contemporaries.

There was a tradition of talking and writing about experiences of this kind. From the Indian Rebellion of 1857, to late Victorian clashes on the North West Frontier, through the South African War, the Anglo-Irish War, and the Arab Revolt in Palestine, Britons described torturous reprisals, indiscriminate shootings, and collective punishments.[3] Sometimes, they did so to flaunt their toughness and justify pitiless methods against racial enemies. Sometimes, they chronicled violence to express doubt, anger, or shame about it. Often, paradoxically, they did both of these things at once. Ambivalence was a longstanding feature of narratives about colonial violence, which conveyed the thrills of domination along with feelings of remorse.[4]

These entangled sentiments threatened to break apart in the war stories of decolonization. As unalloyed disgust with brutality became more common, so did unapologetic celebrations of maximum force. While dissenters saw graphic violence as evidence of depravity, their opponents invoked the same imagery for very different ends: to savor the pleasures of vengeance and initiate civilians into the harsh realities of battle. Even writers critical of violence hinted at its inevitability or flattered their readers with dramas of troubled conscience. Spreading the word about brutality was an imperfect strategy for restraining warfare because it was also a means of building support for it.

Messages from the Front

If knowledge about violence was more or less open in different "circles of knowing," the military was home to the tightest circles of all: communities that forged solidarities through casual and sportive attitudes toward violence.[5] Some regiments ran competitions between units to see which could rack up kills the fastest. On the wall of the Devonshire Regiment's headquarters in Kenya, a brightly color-coded "scoreboard" tracked each company's progress, one body at a time. At least one commanding officer offered a cash prize for the first kill on a tour of duty.[6] In Malaya, the practice of decapitating insurgent corpses—ostensibly for identification purposes—devolved into macabre souvenir-hunting and trophy-collecting.[7] Images of mutilated bodies were pasted into photo albums alongside festive snaps of campfires and parties.[8] An insider's language of slurs and jokes traced the dehumanization of enemies, the erosion of restraints, and the creep of impunity. Soldiers in Cyprus enthused about "showing the wogs who is boss" and laughed about reports on the use of force "going to Strasbourg," the seat of the European Commission of Human Rights.[9]

It is difficult to draw conclusions about the representativeness of these practices because incentives to keep them quiet were strong. Repeated statements from the top of the military hierarchy condemned misbehavior and warned of consequences. While courts-martial and criminal trials were relatively uncommon, the risk of prosecution could not be ignored, either.[10]

Soldiers were also highly conscious of their image at home. Following press coverage and political debate from a distance, they bristled at the left-wing criticism described by one soldier in Cyprus as "filthy mud-slinging."[11] Their defensiveness was rooted in experience. Some of the fiercest controversies to engulf the military in this period happened when military folkways—the athletic-style rivalries, the inside jokes, the ludic preoccupation with enemy bodies—were suddenly exposed to public view.

But knowledge held within the unit always had a way of rippling outward. Conscripts awaiting deployment from barracks in Britain traded stories and pondered their readiness for dirty war. "I dare say it would be better to be in Kenya, as you say in the thick of it," one National Serviceman wrote his parents in Basingstoke from a base in Northern Ireland, "though there's no glory in shooting tribesmen."[12] In the field, freshly assigned officers were sometimes shocked to learn what passed for standard procedure in their new postings.[13] Military doctors noticed suspicious injuries on the bodies of the prisoners they were called to examine. A National Service medic serving with the Royal Army Medical Corps in Cyprus was regularly asked to determine whether battered and frightened suspects at a police station were "fit for 'further questioning."[14] The bureaucratic demand for quantitative data sent other evidence of excessive force up the chain of command. When discrepancies opened up between numbers of insurgents killed and numbers of weapons collected, officials had to work hard to deflect the obvious conclusion that soldiers were shooting innocent civilians.[15]

Acts of brutality could become public knowledge by many different paths, including activism, whistleblowing, and journalism. For the most part, however, personal experiences of violence did not pass directly into front-page news. They were shared first among family and friends. Intimate relationships allowed for frank conversation of a kind otherwise uncommon outside the military. Whether these disclosures amounted to boasts or confessions, they could be excruciatingly vivid. One young National Serviceman who spent two tours of duty in Cyprus described to his father the details of "the rough stuff that the military teaches them"; for instance, "fingers or thumbs inserted inside the mouth and a quick pull splits the sides of the flesh of the cheek."[16] A veteran of the Kenya Emergency showed his brother a trophy photograph of "an African having his arms sawn off."[17] A Londoner with "friends and acquaintances who did their National Service in Kenya" heard "some horrible stories of happenings there" and was likewise struck by the casual sadism of a relative who returned from service in Cyprus. "It is no use using rifle butts against Greeks," one joke went, "they are so greasy that only bayonets will do the trick."[18] Techniques and idioms of brutality, hair-raising stories and macabre souvenirs, anguished admissions and offhand remarks—all brought the cruel realities of colonial war into civilian life.

So did another form of communication. In some ways, it is remarkable that soldiers' letters communicated as much about violence as they did. Wartime correspondence often followed informal propaganda scripts that played down dangers in favor of domestic banter.[19] Many soldiers saw epistolary life as an escape from conflict, a means of staying in touch with the civilian world and reassuring loved ones rather than chronicling grisly experiences.[20] Almost inevitably, however, letters that went beyond the briefest updates in the 1950s touched on the dark side of counterinsurgency. While some soldiers may have suppressed details that risked upsetting their families, others dispatched meticulous, daily or near-daily chronicles of events to sustain relationships at a distance. Violence was not necessarily worth concealing from relatives because so much of it was dully routinized in the form of patrols, searches, and round-ups. Conversely, exceptional moments of life-and-death violence could be worth recording precisely because they were exceptional: a dramatic rupture with the mundane and, sometimes, with the soldier's own moral code.

When soldiers did choose to write about brutality against colonial subjects, they could do so with a surprisingly free hand. As in earlier conflicts, the state subsidized mail traffic between overseas troops and the home front as a morale-boosting measure, at a cost of more than £1 million annually by 1954.[21] Military letters were carried either by the civilian post at a reduced rate, as happened in Malaya for the entire Emergency, or by the forces-only field post offices that proliferated during troop build-ups; Kenya had six FPOs and Cyprus seven in the 1950s.[22] While officers at the unit level had the authority to open letters sent by their men, they exercised it sparingly. Military authorities recognized that invading privacy in this way bred resentment among rank-and-file soldiers, annoyed officers with additional work, and strained unit cohesion. More to the point, it made little sense to crack down on disclosures by soldiers without imposing military-style discipline on civilian mail and press coverage at the same time.[23] Centralized censorship bureaucracies for both military and civilian mail were wound up quickly after 1945 and, with them, the blackout marks and censor's stamps that visibly marked postal surveillance.

Imperial scrutiny always focused most intently on the mail of non-white soldiers and their potential to spread subversion.[24] Political anxieties about white British soldiers and their families at home, muted by comparison, focused more on the blowback from heavy-handed censorship than on the

FIGURE 2.1 Officials sort mail for soldiers at an Army depot in west London, 1958. PA Images.

dangers of unsettling revelations. Delays or interruptions in the mail service for overseas troops reliably provoked outrage in Parliament.[25] Political pressure to keep letters moving quickly helps to explain why even during the Second World War, only a fraction of soldiers' mail (perhaps 7 or 8 percent) was actually reviewed by censors.[26] Another lesson learned in that war was that loosening strictures on the transmission of information made letters more revealing and thus more useful for surreptitious surveillance.[27] Perhaps most significant, officials after 1945 understood that implementing a formal censorship regime for letters sent to Britain would undermine their contention that colonial wars were not really wars at all. The atmosphere of "emergency" could hardly be confined to the colonies if a conspicuously intrusive bureaucracy monitored correspondence between conscripts and their families.[28]

If every letter contains elements of distance and connection, some soldiers wrote because they wanted to register just how far they had traveled from the moral universe they knew at home.[29] The sense of disorientation, as old restraints fell by the wayside and familiar values were inverted, shaped many letters. "I must get some more of the yellow bastards before I return," a conscript nearing the end of his tour in Malaya in 1952 wrote to an old school friend. Then he reflected: "Surprising how one feels like that, but one looks impassively on bullet holes and dead bodies now, except on one's own chaps . . . Lust for blood! In a year's time, I suppose, all this will seem as far away as England does now."[30] A National Serviceman writing home from Cyprus likewise admitted that "we have all become very bloodthirsty." He saw counterinsurgency as "a most unsavory job" because "you have orders to shoot at any one you see who might be going to throw a bomb, and you cannot tell if it's a bomb or a stone."[31] Another conscript writing to his parents compared Cyprus to "a penal servitude camp" and "a complete-rough house" where career officers were "only too delighted to see the 'Wogs' bump each other off."[32] In all of these cases, soldiers used letters to express the tension they perceived between imperial-military values and metropolitan-civilian values. Correspondents at home, though physically distant from conflict zones, were often the first to hear objections to colonial war precisely because they helped to anchor soldiers in the world they knew before.

The impulse to manage disorientation by chronicling it, maintaining distance from the "inside" by staying in touch with the "outside," may have been especially pronounced among National Servicemen who had never served in uniform before. But it was not unique to them. Letter-writing always offered a refuge for unhappy soldiers, a zone of relative privacy for venting frustrations with brothers-in-arms who were otherwise inescapable.[33] A Royal Highlander in Kenya writing to his father in Scotland unburdened himself in the wake of Operation Anvil, which forcibly removed tens of thousands of Kikuyu from Nairobi in 1954. At the Mackinnon Road detention camp, he reported, detainees "were made to run the gauntlet" with "a few rifle butts in action." "I saw all this from the roof of a carriage," he added, "and I was rather disgusted with the whole episode; quite unnecessary violence to people who may or may not be found guilty."[34] A South London police officer recruited to serve in Kenya wrote to his former workmates in Streatham with tales of suspects beaten until they "confess something," prisoners dying in their cells overnight, and police shooting at unarmed men in the bush. "Compared with coppering in London, this really shakes you," he wrote. "I am sure all this Gestapo stuff never got anyone anywhere."[35] An army officer in Kenya employed the same analogy in a letter of his own, writing that the "Gestapo tactics" of herding men, women, and children into stockades—leaving them exposed to the elements with no food and little water—"makes me feel ashamed to say that I am British."[36] Disillusionment, the feeling of lofty standards disappointed and proud traditions tarnished, motivated some counterinsurgency fighters to pick up their pens.

Soldiers troubled by British abuses often felt that they belonged to the minority. One of them was a National Service conscript and classical scholar named Ian Martin, who served as a Greek interpreter in Cyprus in 1957–1958. His letters home portrayed the regular soldiers in the Royal Ulster Rifles as casually brutal and spoiling for a fight. They staged provocative marches in the hope of triggering riots which they could then put down by force. "Showing the flag, they call it, or 'showing the wogs who is boss.'" As his fellow soldiers smashed up shops, went on a looting spree, and beat civilians with batons, Martin heard one of them enthuse that "he hadn't enjoyed himself so much in years." During a search operation in one village, Martin watched as an old man kept for hours in a cage in the boiling sun was beaten when he signaled for help. "And we fondly imagine that we are superior and more civilized than the Germans, Japanese, etc.," Martin wrote bitterly.[37]

It was not only the brutality of his fellow soldiers that disgusted Martin but the deceit of the men at the top. "To keep up the farcical pretense of no ill-treatment," he wrote, "everyone in authority has perjured themselves again and again." When British officials received allegations, their investigations consisted of asking accused soldiers to respond and then accepting their self-serving statements without question. Dishonesty, in the form of plausible deniability, became routinized. It even determined the kinds of blows soldiers used to strike their victims. "You can of course get away with anything in this country," Martin wrote, "as long as you don't leave any bruises, but just 'poke people around a bit.'"[38] Other soldiers also complained about the corruption of language. "'Interrogations' is one word" for the questioning of suspects by Special Branch officers, conscript Martin Bell reported from Cyprus. "The most used, most noncommittal, and most misleading."[39]

Most soldiers and police officers were not dissenters, even to the modest extent of communicating disquiet to family and friends. The details they shared came not in conscience-stricken confessions but in casual references, flashes of braggadocio, and vengeful outbursts. A colonial adventurer named Geoffrey Hedger-Wallace played up the sportive quality of his service for the Kenya police in a letter to a friend. "It's forest work, so you shoot first and ask questions later," he wrote. "I bagged another two Mau Mau yesterday morning . . . Why don't you come out here to see for yourself? I can take you out on a couple of patrols if you like."[40] National Serviceman Crispin Worthington was so open about the desire for revenge after insurgents killed a comrade in Malaya that even the cold-blooded murder of a prisoner was grist for a letter to a friend. "I hate the Chinese' guts," he wrote. "They stink . . . One of our Dyaks cut the throat of a wounded one. I felt no pity. It squared us for Grady."[41] In a letter to his MP, a Fife man serving with the RAF in Cyprus wrote that he feared "being shot in the back in the typical greasy Greek manner." One day, he predicted, British soldiers looking to retaliate would "take a walk with their Sten guns and blast a few Greeks."[42]

Major Richard Unett of the Yorkshire Light Infantry wrote almost daily letters to his Staffordshire family as he served successively in Malaya, Kenya, Aden, and Cyprus between 1948 and 1957. His war stories took the form of routine duties punctuated by occasional, thrilling bursts of violence. For Unett, it seemed, anything other than the use of force represented a tedious diversion from the real work of soldiering. "My patrol today was quite uneventful," one letter from Malaya reported. "We nearly shot an old man, who got scared & thought about running, but otherwise 'nix.' "[43] Several weeks later, Unett described the destruction of a squatters' settlement in Penang as a welcome release from the monotony of patrol. "We arrested all the male inhabitants— 45 in all. All empty houses were burnt down and some only inhabited by a single man. The troops loved it ... To be actually encouraged to burn (certain) houses was the next thing to paradise." Underlining the game-like pleasures of counterinsurgency, another letter spelled out "the analogy of the jungle as a warren & the bandits as rabbits." Far from concealing the destructiveness of war, Unett detailed it a mixture of indifference and playfulness.[44]

When Unett struck a more somber tone, it was to justify brutality as the unfortunate yet unavoidable byproduct of military imperatives. A Chinese Malayan man kept "squatting" and "manacled" in British custody was so old that he "could hardly totter," but he had been found in possession of a gun, so "that was that." A Cypriot man shot to death by British troops after throwing stones during an operation turned out to be "the village idiot & meant no harm, but the soldiers weren't to know that."[45] Even those faint stirrings of regret were undercut by the enthusiasm Unett displayed whenever restraints on the use of force fell by the wayside. He described guard duty at a Nicosia prison one night as "a real picnic" because his platoon had the task of suppressing a riot. "The [commander] took in five toughs & dealt with each cell in turn; result—complete quiet."[46] Unett expressed hesitation about serving in Cyprus only once, when he feared missing out on what promised to be a more eventful campaign in Aden. The authorities there "will tell the insurgents to pay up a fine of money & rifles," he told his parents, "or else we will raze their villages & crops. It might be quite fun ... Everyone expects some resistance & the Assault Pioneer Platoon is dying to blow down houses!"[47]

Letters from civilians in conflict zones rarely displayed such delight in warfare. But here, too, flashes of uneasiness were overwhelmed by other

sentiments. The vicarious thrills of military spectacle, the feeling of vulnerability among pervasive threats, and assumptions about the necessity of harsh
measures all kept civilian observers from registering alarm about counterinsurgency measures even as they described their brutality. Writing to his sister
in London, a coffee farmer in Kiambu, Kenya, noted that a security sweep
that passed through his estate and killed seven "terrorists" bore "a rather
dreadful similarity to a rat hunt." But he also described it as "quite exciting"
while downplaying the dangers with a morbid joke: "It is quite a job to see
that the over-enthusiastic military do not massacre one's own people working
in the coffee."[48]

For non-soldiers, violence made a natural subject for letters home because
its intrusions into everyday life were unusual and unpredictable. After arriving
in Nairobi from Lusaka in 1954, a career colonial bureaucrat named Henry
Barlow quickly realized that his neighborhood doubled as a battlefield. "It is
a strange life in many ways," Henry Barlow wrote to his brother and sister-in-
law in Shropshire. Barlow described hearing a radio report about the shooting
of suspected insurgents by security forces, only to learn later that the incident
happened a mile from his home. Another night, he listened to the distant
crackle of machine-gun fire echoing across his garden.[49] Less often, Barlow
described the upheavals in African communities. Touring Kikuyu territory
outside the city, he found an eerily depopulated landscape that was the result of forced resettlement. "The countryside is completely empty," he wrote.
"Not a soul anywhere." Around the perimeter of the hastily constructed New
Villages, meanwhile, authorities had ordered the "entire" resettled population to dig twelve-foot-deep trenches as a security buffer. Barlow described
these scenes as "rather depressing" and "rather sad." But he also saw inevitability rather than injustice at work around him, attributing the "tragedy of
the Emergency" to a rebellious tribe "which had completely destroyed its *own*
property and put *itself* back scores of years." His use of the passive voice elsewhere—"pressure is being put on the population"—betrayed a reluctance to
portray the British as agents of the hardships he witnessed.[50]

Barlow was not a hardened ideologue of white supremacy. His impatience
with settler dominance prompted him to leave the colonial service in 1958 for
a job with the Anglican Church in Northern Rhodesia. There he worked for a
fiercely anti-apartheid prelate and remained in what became the independent
state of Zambia until his retirement in 1972. Yet the indiscriminate repression of the Emergency in Kenya never seemed to offend Barlow's liberalism.
Though his letters often referred to the conspicuous absences of Africans who
disappeared into the security machine, his tone was always matter-of-fact

rather than anguished or outraged. Sometimes, it was even bemused. "This morning the police were taking up a lot of Africans from our area," the post-script to one letter read. "Several people have had their servants removed. I only hope I shan't find the house empty when I return!" The phlegmatic wartime pose that treated violence as a strange spectacle, a necessary evil, or a punch line blunted the urgency of revelation.[51]

Other civilians were outraged, though, and they too chronicled their experience in letters. Like military mail, civil mail was no longer subject to systematic and visible censorship after the end of the Second World War. This does not mean that postal communication was shielded from the prying eyes of the state. By the early 1960s, domestic security service MI5 was secretly opening 135,000 letters in Britain every year, a large proportion of them from overseas since delivery delays were less likely to arouse suspicion.[52] Anticolonial activists living in London, including Mbiyu Koinange and George Padmore, were among those targeted by surveillance on dubious legal grounds.[53] Here too, however, surreptitious monitoring served the interests of the state more effectively than blacking out or preventing the delivery of letters. The security services' desire to track "subversives" without detection took priority over stopping the flow of embarrassing information. Only a sharp-eyed intelligence veteran like Graham Greene, receiving a letter from Kenya, could easily spot an envelope that had been tampered with.[54]

Politicians and activists in Britain came to depend on a steady stream of detailed letters from informants in the colonies. For Britons living overseas, a well-documented letter that reached the right hands offered a rare chance to influence debates at home. A rubber planter wrote ex-MP Stephen King-Hall in 1949 to complain about British soldiers in Malaya ransacking homes, stealing money and jewelry, and condemning suspects on slim evidence. The planter's view that such "methods and behavior bring more recruits to the Communists than they capture or shoot" reached thousands of subscribers through King-Hall's newsletter.[55] At the Fabian Colonial Bureau, left-wing activist Hilda Selwyn-Clarke learned much of what she knew about the Cyprus conflict from a friend who moved there in 1956. He wrote to her about cases of innocent men languishing in jail and the sight of "whole families wait[ing] to be moved from their homes with their men folk in cages."[56] Nothing appalled him more than the orgy of reprisals by British soldiers in Famagusta in October 1958: "One chap was suffocated in an overcrowded lorry. Six might have been suffocated in a cell last night . . . In each case we are told that it serves them right."[57]

For the tight-knit subculture of settlers in Kenya, letter-writing offered a way to air misgivings about colonial war in private without "letting the side down" in public. Even as Elspeth Huxley staked out a position as a vocal defender of settler interests, she and her relatives were trading anxious letters about the callousness of security forces. Writing to her husband in London from the family farm in the White Highlands, Huxley reported that "the police arrest these people on the word of informers, and goodness knows how many are guilty and how many are not . . . No one knows, or can know, what goes on in the way of bribes and intimidation."[58] When Huxley returned to Britain, her mother, Nellie, kept her updated on the menacing atmosphere back in Kenya. One letter described a police reservist who laughed while saying that he would seize two Mau Mau suspects working on the farm and that Nellie would "never see them again."[59] Other settlers remained reticent about violence, even in letters to confidants, because they feared lending credence to criticisms by activists. Writing to her mother in Britain, an army wife who volunteered for the Kenya Police Reserve while her husband was stationed in the colony bristled at the image of "trigger-happy, whip-cracking tyrants who would kill an innocent Kikuyu as soon as look at him."[60]

Only a fraction of what contemporaries knew and communicated about colonial violence is accessible to historians today. Many letters were never sent, never saved, and never deposited or published. Whether correspondents feared repercussions for themselves, wanted to avoid casting aspersions, or simply perceived disturbing subjects as sensitive subjects, exchanges about violence were often premised on discretion. And yet, it would be wrong to assume that knowledge about brutality was always kept in confidence. The same mix of motivations that brought descriptions of violence into private letters could propel them into more visible spaces as well. While some soldiers and settlers feared scrutiny from the metropolitan public, others invited it, by publishing vivid accounts based on their experiences.

The Pleasures of Pulp

A cottage industry of counterinsurgency books sprang up in the 1950s. Some were marketed as memoirs, others as novels. In practice, many occupied an ambiguous space between genres, with thinly fictionalized real-life experiences overlaid on conventional plots and sometimes eclipsing them altogether. Along with the motives that attracted generations of readers to colonial war stories—fascination with exotic settings, enjoyment of vicarious adventure, identification with masculine heroes—publishers looked to the new market of conscripts and their families. Army officer Arthur Campbell's manuscript about Malaya captured the attention of an editor at Allen & Unwin because it described "the life which these National Servicemen, scarcely out of childhood, are leading while they pursue an unseen enemy in dense jungle, in swamps, and over mountains."[61] The growing sense that events in Malaya, Kenya, and Cyprus belonged to a historic wave of empire-toppling revolt drove literary production as well. By 1956, the *Illustrated London News* noticed, publishers were unleashing "a stream of [novels] about British rule under the stress of Asian or African revolution."[62]

Like the letter-writers who confined their observations to family and friends, many authors felt that the story of colonial war could not be told without explicit violence. If these details entered letters as a function of inner pressures and personal relationships, their inclusion in novels and memoirs always represented a performance intended for public consumption. These performances could serve literary ends: to impress readers with gritty realism, to certify the experiential bona fides of the author, to raise the stakes of the moral dilemmas or psychological crises experienced by the characters. It could serve a variety of ideological projects, too, from horrified indictments of British misconduct to appeals for solidarity with British soldiers and settlers. What is clear is that brutality was neither a taboo subject nor the preoccupation of antiwar and anticolonial writers alone.

In fact, most popular writing about counterinsurgency blended reactionary politics with aspirations to mass appeal. These books owed stylistic debts to pulp and genre fiction—including crime, mystery, juvenile adventure, and romance—which favored sensationalism and sharply drawn lines between heroes and villains. Some were written by actual veterans of the conflicts. Others were penned by children of empire with close ties to the settler world: figures like Charles Thurley Stoneham, who was born in India and served in Kenya during the First World War; Mary Margaret Kaye, the Simla-born daughter of an Indian Army officer with family roots in the Raj; and Lavender Lloyd, the daughter of a British Army officer who grew up in Kenya. Still others were written to order in Britain by seasoned genre hands. Gordon Landsborough, the author of an especially exploitive Cyprus novel called *The Violent People* (1960), was a paperback publisher and prolific writer who penned more than seventy titles, including war thrillers, Westerns, and science fiction, many of them dashed off in just a few days.[63]

There was nothing inherently authoritarian about pulp or genre writing.[64] But the authors of colonial war stories could draw on precedents for the aestheticization of violence. In the detective stories and comic books of the 1920s and 1930s, characters like Bulldog Drummond and the Black Sapper operated outside the law to dispense rough justice.[65] The Cold War vogue for hardboiled fatalism and the lurid racial fantasies in American "macho" magazines offered more up-to-date models of stylized brutality.[66] Counterinsurgency writing also reflected the influence of a new explicitness in visual culture, exemplified by the "horror" comics filled with surreal imagery of death and dismemberment.[67] In Britain, the resulting moral panic about grotesque pictures in the hands of children extended from clergymen, magistrates, and conservative parents to the Communist Party, culminating in a 1955 Act of Parliament that attempted to ban "horror" comics altogether.[68]

Controversies like this stemmed from uneasiness about American cultural influence as much as graphic violence itself. Ironically, however, modes and styles borrowed from American popular culture proved well suited to justifying British imperialism. Mass-market war stories brought a blunt ideological sensibility to the page-turner form, coupling vivid portrayals of brutality with a flaunting disregard for liberal pieties. Whether elaborate scenes of suffering should be read as documentary or fantasy remained unclear, but either way, they initiated readers into the rites of violence. Presented as a bracing antidote to metropolitan naïveté, this was violence without apology: untroubled by qualms, calculated to terrorize, and reveling in the suffering of racial others. If these books could be said to share a philosophical outlook, it was "combat gnosticism," the belief that only front-line fighters and settlers possessed the experience necessary to appreciate the uses of violence.[69] To justify the actions of British forces—to air grievances, settle scores, and press the case for tough tactics—reactionary war stories gloried in gruesomeness.

One thinly fictionalized memoir, *Spearhead in Malaya* (1959), was written by a colonial police veteran named J. W. G. Moran. It came with General Templer's ringing endorsement; he called it "a first-class book" and praised Moran for having been "on such close terms with his men." This is a more telling remark than Templer probably intended. The tension between the European officer protagonist, Moran, and his Malay and Chinese subalterns is a major theme of the book. Moran wins their respect, ultimately, by meting out violence. When he arrives in an unfamiliar village to take up a new assignment, a Malay headman asks how he would deal with a suspect who refuses to give information. The newcomer responds:

> "Circumstances would have to be taken into account. I might even think of shooting the person," I replied slowly with a greater show of calmness than I thought I possessed . . .

"You believe in brutal methods? The law of the jungle, tuan?"

"Where circumstances demand it, yes. I do not believe in half measures, inche."

"An eye for an eye. A tooth for a tooth."

"Definitely."

Moran soon gets the chance to put his precepts into practice. His men detain a self-described rubber tapper with immaculate papers but suspiciously pristine hands. When the suspect protests that he has the right to go on his way, Moran is enraged by the challenge to his authority. He also sees an opportunity to show up the humanitarian squishes at home:

> A slightly educated type, I mused . . . . There is only one way to deal with these situations. If the press critics think they can do it better, then let them come out and try.
>
> I slapped him across the mouth with the back of my hand. He reeled a pace or two. I slapped him again, harder. A thin line of blood trickled down his chin. He spat out a loosened tooth. He sank to his knees, moaning.

When the suspect makes a lunge at his captor, Morgan strikes him again, harder this time, "right in the guts . . . This time he stayed down, hissing like a punctured tyre." Moran's success in rendering him unconscious has two immediate consequences: Moran's subalterns begin to look at him with admiration for the first time, and the suspect, when he wakes up, has abandoned his belligerent attitude. Only a little more physical terror is required to elicit the location of an insurgent camp in the jungle: "I shook him like a rat. His eyes shot up and down like ping-pong balls. I did not release my grip on him . . . . At last he became calm and spoke." With comic-book-style simplicity, *Spearhead in Malaya* proposed violence as a solution to the problems of the Emergency. Whether by intimidating insolent subordinates or humbling treacherous rebels, beating suspects offered a reliable way of putting "natives" in their place. By breaking conspicuously free from the constraints of law and morality, brutality proclaimed the unanswerable nature of British authority. Finally, and almost incidentally, it succeeded in shaking loose the tactical information needed to win the war.[70]

Moran was hardly the only author to revel in the pain inflicted on enemy bodies. In describing the satisfaction of killing long-elusive foes, memoirs and novels reflected the influence of another venerable genre, the "guts and gore" hunting adventure story.[71] Insurgents ran "like rabbits out of a burrow" or "writhing snakes." Seen up close, they resembled "harried, hunted animals" or "emaciated monkeys."[72] Struck by gunfire, they collapsed "as ducks drop in a shooting gallery."[73] These stories fixated on the bodies of their slain enemies because they signified the hard-won success that might happen only once, or not at all, on a months-long tour of duty. In other words, corpses were trophies.[74]

Writers who served in the security forces did not usually admit to mutilating enemy corpses themselves. More often, they explained postmortem injuries as the accidental byproduct of fierce combat, the unavoidable effects of the climate, or the overzealousness of indigenous collaborators serving with British troops (such as the Kikuyu Home Guard in Kenya or Dayak "headhunters" in Malaya). But if writers deflected responsibility for the destruction of bodies, they also did not conceal their pleasure at seeing it. Some narratives devolved into sado-pornography with fantastic—and perhaps fantasied—images of spectacularly tortuous deaths for enemy fighters.[75] This is how James Macdonald's Malaya memoir *My Two Jungles* (1957) described the cathartic thrill, if not the sexual release, of killing a long-sought foe: "The Combat Section joyfully opened up, ridding themselves of the hours of idle frustration in the ceaseless pressure of their fingers on the triggers.... When I had pumped those bullets into Chong Choy, I had also released in myself my hatred for the terrorists. I felt too empty to hate anyone."[76]

The graphic violence in counterinsurgency stories seized readers' attention. Occasionally, it provoked unease, as when the *Times Literary Supplement* complained that Moran "saves his strongest writing for the mangled death that he and his men inflicted."[77] Far more often, though, reviewers celebrated gore as evidence of authenticity. This was particularly true of books written by soldiers. The rapturous reception of Arthur Campbell's 1953 memoir *Jungle Green*—reviewed in more than a dozen national and provincial publications, serialized in the *Liverpool Echo*, adapted as a BBC radio play, and selling more than 20,000 copies in just three months—provides a case in point.[78] Although Campbell made clear that elements of the story were fictionalized, the fact that he had served as an officer with the Suffolk Regiment in Malaya was cited in almost every review and lent weight to the depiction of violence. Announcing that the book contained "one of the most ghastly hand-to-hand fights-to-the-death which I have ever come across," the reviewer for *Illustrated*

London News concluded that "truth can be nastier than fiction, but it should be faced." Writing for the *Observer*, Harold Nicolson called it a "bloodthirsty story" but "completely authentic."[79] Reviews repeatedly praised Campbell for conveying the strange intimacy and harsh brutality of counterinsurgency. "The ultimate work of killing has reverted, as often as not, to its most primitive instruments: the knife to cut, the bare hands to throttle," the *Yorkshire Post* related. The *Manchester Guardian* enthused that "the grim beastliness of the limited but hideous war is made to hit one hard in the face as no documentary film is every likely to do," citing an especially nasty detail about the treatment of insurgent corpses.[80]

Even writers who avoided gory extremes found ways to describe the pleasure of inflicting pain. Their books promised the vicarious thrill of seeing enemies mocked and punished at time when British power looked ever more precarious. Clearly assigned roles of dominance and submission became more enticing in fantasy as they receded in reality, "offering a sense of mastery over what were otherwise terrifying ambiguities."[81] The paraphernalia of fetishism made a brief appearance in W. R. Loader's *Not Yours the Island* (1956) when a constable taunted by flag-waving Cypriot schoolgirls "longed for the freedom to drag these spitfires by the hair into a quiet corner in the company of a leather strap."[82] Other stories drew on an idiom of schoolboy pranks and prefectural discipline that reduced enemies to naughty children. In Oswald Wynd's *The Gentle Pirate* (1951), the British hero humbles a Chinese insurgent-turned-gun-runner by grabbing him "by the seat of his wide flannel trousers," hoisting him over his shoulder, and tossing him into the water "screaming and kicking" while a crowd of onlookers laughs.[83] Without causing serious injury, Wynd's protagonist still managed to achieve the humiliation that readers of colonial war stories came to expect.

The anxiety that British imperialists might be humiliated themselves, by subjects mocking their authority, produced elaborate fantasies of punishment. In Diana Buttenshaw's *Violence in Paradise* (1957), set in Cyprus, characters complain that the floggings meted out to rioting schoolboys are insufficiently painful; one comments that the boys at English public schools are caned more harshly for "dodging cold baths." Frustrated by this restraint, the heroine of the novel, an army officer's daughter named Ginny, concocts a scheme to deliver the maximum of pain and embarrassment to a group of young demonstrators without actually killing them. She commandeers a water hose, connects it to a hydrant, and mows down them down with glee, at which point the story veers abruptly from Wodehousian comedy to graphic violence. Bodies lie in the streets "writhing and fighting for the breath that had been knocked clean out of them"; Ginny's confederates pepper their victims with pellet guns as they try to stagger away. Buttenshaw suggests that mischievous children must sometimes be beaten at their own game. If only the British stopped holding themselves to a higher standard than their enemies, they could quickly set things right.[84]

Counterinsurgency writing was shot through with frustration at the constraints under which British forces supposedly labored: the shackles of law, tradition, and morality. A favored set-piece was the debate between a squeamish naïf, often visiting a colony for the first time, and a battle-hardened realist who invariably gets the better of the argument. In M. M. Kaye's *Later Than You Think* (1958), a young English woman is disgusted by the notches cut into the verandah railing on a plantation, each one representing an insurgent killed in the jungle. In reproaching his guest for misplaced sentimentality, the planter vents his frustration with a legion of critics passing judgment from their armchairs at home: "So you think I'm appalling and barbaric because I allow the boys to cut a tally of their kills on my verandah rail, do you? You are not the only one. There are uncounted thousands of soft-hearted and fluffy-minded—and abysmally ignorant—people who would agree with you . . . I get a little bored by people who broadcast views on something that is, to them, only a problem on paper." He goes on to argue that only settlers in the colony could understand just how "filthy and abominable" the Mau Mau were. Proximity, conferring knowledge, also conferred the right to judge what sort of violence was appropriate to the situation. "You cannot conduct a campaign against a bestial horror like the Mau Mau with gloves on," the planter declares.[85]

Sometimes, entire novels were structured around a protagonist's gradually dawning appreciation for the virtues of brutality. In Gordon Landsborough's Cyprus novel, *The Violent People* (1960), traveler Roy Holder is initially alienated by the bloodlust of the other Britons he encounters on the island, civilians as well as soldiers. But an encounter with a reasonable-sounding captain in the Royal Engineers, who startles Holder at first by admitting that troops sometimes "behave brutally," begins to inculcate a more sympathetic view. "You can't expect men in danger to continue to behave like gentlemen," the captain explains. "There's too much danger for them to go on leaning over backwards to be gentle to the naughty Cypriot. The men have had enough of it, and quite humanly are hitting back in retaliation."[86] The portrayal of soldiers as stressed and imperfect, rather than blandly heroic, may have served to disarm readers suspicious of agitprop. But when the focus shifts from British troops to Cypriot insurgents, Landsborough abandons the subtle shades for a lurid palette. Dispelling the ambiguity that hovers over the early pages, EOKA rebels are revealed as "the violent people" of the title; they are sadistic thugs who torture Turks to death for sport and serially rape the captive English woman Holder has come to rescue. In the end, a daring escape from near-certain death confirms Holder's contempt for the "fools who found perverse pleasure in running down his country." It is the British who are most vulnerable in the age of decolonization, he realizes, the British who should be seen as victims rather than oppressors. Holder finds himself in the same perilous position as those ordinary men in uniform, targeted simply

FIGURE 2.2 Counterinsurgency pulp: popular fiction like Gordon Landsborough's *The Violent People* (1960) offered fantasies of vengeance, justifications for violence, and sentiments of victimization in lurid tones. Orion Books.

"because they had been born in a territory marked England, and the British were no longer wanted."[87]

Again and again, counterinsurgency novelists expressed bitter contempt for metropolitan liberals, condemning them as clueless do-gooders who failed to appreciate the sacrifices of soldiers and settlers on the front lines. Characters in Buttenshaw's *Violence in Paradise* complain that the mistreatment of Cypriot suspects causes far more consternation at home than the deadly attacks on British men in uniform. "They can murder as many of us as they like and call it their struggle for Freedom," a corporal fumes, "but if we hit back every now and then, we're the brutal oppressors." The heroine, Ginny, shares his disgust that "some horrid little Socialist" is always speaking out in the Commons on behalf of "the Sops." John Appleby's *The Bad Summer* (1958), also set in Cyprus, excoriated the "professional liberals, often roving newsmen, who blackguarded" the British government with unfair accusations. In C. T. Stoneham's *Kenya Mystery* (1954), the hero channels settler discontent with the "Whitehall wallahs," complaining that their "cumbersome legal procedure" allows Mau Mau suspects "to get off nine time out of ten." A character in another Kenya novel, Lavender Lloyd's *The Verandah Room* (1955), claimed that the British public sympathized more with African insurgents than white settlers: "Old ladies will knit them socks and comforters no doubt . . . just because they are black and seem from so far away to be pathetic and downtrodden."[88]

From this perspective of aggrieved victimhood, the frank description of violence was a virtue in itself. If the public could be taught to see matters with the same grim clarity as front-line fighters, perhaps they would come to appreciate the emptiness of liberal niceties. In a weird mirror image of anticolonial writing, apologists for colonial violence often made a point of rejecting euphemism. Instead, they flaunted their brutality and racism as proof of tough-mindedness. This was a moral universe in which slogans like "shoot first and ask questions afterwards" were intended not as condemnations but as badges of honor.[89] References to "Gestapo methods, hanging the culprits and all those who give them asylum," were framed not as indictments but as roadmaps to victory.[90] The racial slurs that peppered these writings signaled the same defiant rejection of constraints. With so much of popular culture reveling in brutality, how could antiwar novelists hope to stir the conscience of the public?

Liberal Fiction and Its Discontents

Even novelists who took a critical view of colonial war usually did so as disillusioned imperialists rather than champions of insurgency. Despite slowly gathering intimations of change, white metropolitan voices continued to dominate the British literary world in the 1950s. After the surprise success of Amos Tutuola's *The Palm-Wine Drinkard* (1952), London-based editors scrambled to cultivate non-white and non-British-born authors.[91] But the resulting boomlet of literature—which, like migration flows from the colonies to Britain at the time, was predominantly Caribbean and West African—had little to say about the ongoing horrors of colonial war. The rare Mau Mau novel to feature a Kikuyu forest fighter as the protagonist, *The Leopard* (1958), was written by black Jamaican writer Victor Stafford Reid. While *The Leopard* briefly referenced the castration of prisoners by British authorities, it lavished far more detail on the bloodlust of the insurgents: their pleasure in "splendid," "beautiful" revenge against white bodies; their erotic fascination with guns and pangas; the elaborate, flesh-rending tortures visited on captured policemen. Even Reid, who saw inspirational parallels between Kenyan and Jamaican liberation struggles, found it difficult to resist the primitivist tropes of imperial propaganda.[92] Approaching the violence of decolonization obliquely, through history, offered another possibility in the 1950s. Chinua Achebe's *Things Fall Apart* (1958) narrated a version of the 1905 British massacre at Ahiara, Nigeria, and concluded with a bitterly ironic comment on the "pacification" campaign that destroyed Igbo society. But for the most part, it was only in retrospect—after the wars of decolonization ended—that those who sided with anticolonial uprisings gained access to the means of literary production.

Before this shift, British writers who questioned counterinsurgency typically identified as troubled observers rather than rebel sympathizers. Instead of giving voice to resistance, novels such as Michael Cornish's *An Introduction to Violence* (1960) and George W. Target's *The Missionaries* (1961) meditated on the guilt of the imperialist conscience. While appalled by brutal violence, they set its spectacular violations in a wider and murkier world of moral uncertainty. Target later reflected on the questions that fascinated him: "Are we responsible for the violence done in our name by the government?" "Is it rational to wage anything but total war?" "Is it possible to be rational about anything so utterly irrational as war?"[93] Their preoccupation with the dilemmas of the individual in a complex world is reason to call them liberal novels.[94] Amid the wave of reactionary thrillers, they attempted to strike a delicate balance: making sense of colonial war's depravity without glamorizing or excusing it. But in the moody introspection they brought to scenes of brutality, liberal fictions came perilously close to putting a high-toned gloss on jingoism.

What Target called "the wicked and cruel things done to chained and defenseless men" in Kenya was the subject of *The Missionaries*. One of the novel's protagonists, a burnt-out doctor, recounts a litany of grotesque abuses he witnessed at a detention camp. They climax in a vaguely Hola-like massacre: an escape attempt that provokes a mass shooting and then a frenzied attack on the survivors.[95] In many ways, *The Missionaries* reads like a simple inversion of apologias for brutality. Here, it is the left-wing activists who get the better of polarized arguments: "When colonial people fight for their freedom we call it nasty names, except when they happen to be fighting the Russians."[96] The treacherous fifth columnists of reactionary fiction, meanwhile, have become impotent gadflies: "There were protest meetings, letters in the *Guardian*, *Spectator*, *New Statesman* . . . and nothing happened, not a blind thing." As the novel's setting shifts from the site of the massacre to a colorless southeast London, the characters struggle to understand the horrors of Kenya in retrospect. Underlining the threat of wars coming home, one speculates about the presence of a "murderer among us ... [who] has probably settled down in a place very like this, salesman, likes his half-pint at The Bird-in-Hand, pillar of society."[97]

In liberal war stories, violence against colonial subjects did not resolve tensions, remove uncertainties, or bring adventures to a close. It lingers in ways that haunt characters and disturb relationships. The dust jacket for Cornish's *An Introduction to Violence* promised an unsentimental look at the counter-insurgency fighters "who have found a way of living with their job of killing"; they revel in "drunken parties and shows of bravado, which they need to help them forget." The story centers on a conscience-stricken National Serviceman who watches British forces murder a wounded insurgent in the forest and is gripped by disturbing memories afterward. When he subsequently recounts the episode to a love interest, he agonizes over which details to share and which to withhold, confessing that he will never forgive himself for failing to save the man's life.[98]

But if the violence in liberal fictions was explicit in some ways, it was shrouded in haziness at the same time. Like other literary treatments of brutality—stretching back to Joseph Conrad's *Heart of Darkness* (1901), which exercised an almost inescapable influence—liberal novels favored a style of "hallucinatory filminess," with trance-like flashbacks and other surreal touches wrapping the narrative in an aesthetic of mystification.[99] Then too, liberal novels were marketed with many of the same sensationalistic touches as their reactionary counterparts, their dust jackets adorned with spear-wielding warriors and shadowy mobs gathering outside farmhouses. These affinities were not confined to the packaging. In an exchange that could have been lifted from the pages of counterinsurgency pulp, the seasoned army officer in *An Introduction to Violence* reproaches the weak-kneed conscript for his sentimentality: "What's the point of taking [the prisoner] in so that the doctors can patch him up and hang him afterwards? Besides, that's only giving the devil a chance to recover and get back to do some more mischief. We'll shoot him now . . . What clause from the Geneva Convention d'you think he had in mind when he shoved that elephant-gun bullet up the breech of his gun?"[100] In their insistence on moral ambiguity, liberal writers gave some of the best lines to apologists for brutality.

Little wonder that the same audiences which applauded militarist novels for bracing authenticity found liberal fictions unsatisfying. Siding with the battle-hardened veterans over the traumatized newcomers, reviewers found the protagonists too "quixotic" and "sensitive" to be realistic.[101] These were, after all, uncomfortably hybrid narratives, steeped in the consciousness of empire's abuses yet clinging to old-fashioned themes of moral extremity in the tropics. In these stories, as in generations of colonial adventure tales before them, distant frontiers served as testing grounds for the virture of lonely heroes. While the boundaries between good and evil were no longer so clearly defined as they once were, the concern with British character remained.

Characteristic of liberal novels was a tendency to question the means of colonial war but not the ends, holding out the possibility of morally acceptable counterinsurgencies. In *An Introduction to Violence*, the conscript disgusted by the killing of a prisoner nonetheless maintains that Mau Mau "has got to be smashed by every means available" because overwhelming force "is the only treatment that these people understand or expect."[102] *The Touch of Pitch*, a 1956 Mau Mau novel by British Army colonel W. B. Thomas, fused elements of the liberal conscience novel and the reactionary thriller to demonstrate that the dirty wars of empire could be cleaned up. The hero is an army captain who cracks down on the brutality he finds everywhere in Kenya, upbraiding a settler policeman for asking questions with his fists, reprimanding a subaltern for using slurs, and rejecting the folk wisdom that "the only good Kuke is a dead Kuke." The villain of the piece is an unreconstructedly racist settler, deep in debt, who sets the story in motion by stealing an older man's money and murdering him with a panga to stage the crime like a Mau Mau assault.[103] Absolving the army from the stain of atrocity by scapegoating boorish locals, Thomas cast colonial war as a test of national honor, with a prospect of redemption once by-the-book metropolitan regiments take charge.

One of the most celebrated writers of the day brought a different sort of ambivalence to the portrayal of violence. Anthony Burgess launched his career as a novelist with *Time for a Tiger* (1956), the first installment of a trilogy set in Malaya, where he worked for years as a schoolteacher. Like many younger male writers in the 1950s, Burgess turned a withering satirical gaze on established institutions in general and the British Empire in particular. His Malaya novels are stocked with blimpish colonels and reactionary settlers who signal their villainy with sadistic racism. An "ex-Army type of planter" in *Time for a Tiger* bursts into a rage when an unexplained noise intrudes on his cocktail hour: "Bloody Club servants. I'll tan his black hide. I'll put a bullet through him. I'll castrate him. I'll put out his toe-nails with pincers."[104] For Burgess, though, a world-weary sense of irony blunted any sense of political urgency. Even in his most pointed critiques of colonial war, fatalism triumphed over outrage. "Some think the war will never end," he wrote. "There are no decisive engagements, nor real victories. It goes on and on, the sniping, the gutting, the garroting, the thin streams of jungle-green troops, the colossal waste." This was a prose-poem of imperial entropy, not a polemic, motivated as much by frustration with the decay of the colonial state as disgust with its violence.[105] The blend of satire and apathy in Burgess's Malaya novels is inseparable from the indignity of what he later recalled as "the white man [being] thrown out of this final corner of the British Empire."[106]

More radical literary treatments were possible. An ex-National Serviceman who served in Malaya, Alan Sillitoe, painted a sympathetic portrait of a left-wing conscript who refuses to shoot at insurgents in *The Key in the Door* (1962). Unlike Burgess, Sillitoe saw Communist rebellion as a legitimate response to oppression. Yet the novel, in thrall to the coming-of-age template of many National Service fictions, depicts little violence and presents the army as more shambolic than destructive.[107]

The same cannot be said of Han Suyin's *And the Rain My Drink* (1956), a novel that anatomized colonial violence by discarding literary conventions and leaping across genres. Han, the *nom de plume* of Rosalie Matila Kuanghu Chou, likewise defies easy categorization. Most likely born in Henan province to a Chinese railway engineer father and a Belgian mother, she attended Catholic missionary schools in Beijing, then trained as a doctor in Brussels and London. After a passionate affair that inspired the best-selling autobiographical novel *A Many-Splendoured Thing* (1952), Han married Leon Comber, a British Special Branch officer stationed in Malaya.[108] It was there, caring for patients at Johore Bahru General Hospital and hosting a steady stream of intelligence and military officials at home, that Han was plunged into colonial war. "The Emergency," she remembered later. "We lived and breathed it; it penetrated our pores, we chewed it with every mouthful of food."[109]

Already in *A Many-Splendoured Thing*, Han signaled her sympathy with Chinese Communism and her distaste for the unreal world of British expatriates. These sentiments deepened on contact with Malaya's age of emergency. Leveraging her connections as a Special Branch wife, Han gained access to the dark recesses of the security apparatus and paid weekly medical visits to a New Village near Johore Bahru. While her husband's colleagues maintained that the British presence was "necessary to protect the good people against the bad ones," she ferreted out some dissenting voices.[110] "I have had many talks with army officers, who over a beer, in the quiet evenings, deplored the acts they were forced to commit, like rounding up whole villages," Han wrote in an unpublished manuscript from 1954.[111] A dispatch she published in an American newsmagazine that year painted an equally grim picture of "a country in a stage of siege." Crushing curfews, confiscations of food, and ubiquitous armed patrols created an "atmosphere of resentment and hostility." Rather than winning hearts and minds, the British "exhibited a fatal tendency to emphasize and to evaluate success in terms of 'kills.'" As shooting competitions between regiments "became a kind of sport," violence was unmoored from any political objective.[112] "Once you give small men who have no understanding of Asia, authority, they all turn into small sadists," she told her American publisher. "I am upset and sick with horror nearly everyday."[113]

Like Han's earlier writings, *And the Rain My Drink* is transparently rooted in personal experience. But while the narrator is identified as Dr. Han Suyin, a Chinese-speaking doctor recently arrived in Malaya, the novel can hardly be described as a first-person narrative.[114] Han drops out of the story for long stretches, sometimes yielding to a third-person omniscient narration, sometimes introducing faux-documentary sources, such as an insurgent's diary, a police report, and a questionnaire distributed by propaganda officers. Han also shifts the setting repeatedly, from the bureaucratic warren of the interrogation centers where captured fighters are questioned, to the insurgent hideouts in the jungle, to the detention camps where suspects are held without trial, to the New Villages where Chinese civilians are resettled, to the government ships that carry deported subjects to China. As critics noted at the time, most characters surface for a few pages and then disappear, thronging a punctuated series of episodes with hardly any continuous narrative at all.[115] *And the Rain My Drink* often reads less like a fiction than a reporter's notebook, a loosely stitched assemblage of quotes and color.

FIGURE 2.3 "I am upset and sick with horror nearly everyday": Han Suyin circa 1960. Ernst Haas/Getty Images.

While this fragmented style was criticized as a literary failing, it succeeded in portraying a vast, impersonal system at work. In the novel, individuals and their moral sensibilities do not count for much as the war machine grinds on. The characters who thrive are those who internalize its values, most conspicuously an ex–Indian Army officer and Palestine veteran named Tommy Uxbridge, who takes command of a New Village. "His notion of the world, like Mont Blanc, consisted of a white top and a submissive yellow-brown-black base," Han writes.[116] The "war-not-war" prosecuted by men like Uxbridge flattens lives and landscapes with Olympian indifference. Armored cars topped with machine guns rumble down streets; barbed wire converts productive land into sterile surveillance zones. The resettlement process encapsulates this bleak inhumanity: "In six hours the whole population had been carted away, the pigs slaughtered, the crops smashed, the whole area destroyed by fire."[117]

And the Rain My Drink is the rare antiwar novel of the period that left liberalism behind. The title was taken from a Chinese Communist anthem celebrating the jungle as a utopian refuge from British oppression: "I will go to the forest for justice / . . . The wind for my garment and the rain my drink, / We build a new heaven and earth."[118] Unsurprisingly, Comber lost his Special Branch post and Han her hospital job when the book was released. One ex-official critical of the war had half-jokingly warned Han about the backlash: "The only ones who will dislike it will be the Tommy Uxbridges and admirers of General Templer!"[119] But in Britain, as opposed to Malaya, the book was hardly treated as the stuff of sedition.

Even the harshest criticism of colonial war, it turned out, could be enjoyed as an object of ethical consumption. A leading arbiter of middlebrow literary taste, the Book Society, ensured the commercial success of Han's novel by naming it a monthly selection, mailed automatically to thousands of members.[120] The *Tatler* praised it for showing a "terrible situation" "without prejudice." The *Birmingham Daily Post* suggested that Han's background made her more objective than "an English novelist" and able to "see beyond the headlines." The *Illustrated London News* wallowed almost masochistically in Han's flaying of "half-hearted liberalism and grotesque, inevitable injustice" in the prosecution of the war as well as the "Führer complex" that possessed characters like Uxbridge.[121] In confronting the dilemmas thrown up by empire, Han's readers could imagine themselves as protagonists in the drama of conscience more sympathetically portrayed by other writers.[122]

Campaigns against torture are often described with the language of secrecy and disclosure: the breaking of silences, the shattering of taboos, the shining of light into dark corners. But the outpouring of writing about colonial violence, in private and in public, demonstrates that transparency had no intrinsic politics. Graphic revelations served the aims of those who wanted "tougher" wars and "cleaner" wars as well as those who wanted no war or no empire at all. Even the crimes described in Han Suyin's exposé could be savored by readers who had no intention of trying to change them. If some contemporaries found satisfaction in vicarious violence, others found it in the contemplation of moral failure. Feeling uneasy about brutality proved that, even if British rule was devoid of humanity, at least some British individuals were not.

These kinds of self-flattering rituals would be taken up by other well-meaning observers of colonial war, including missionaries, aid workers, and journalists. But less subtle tactics of accommodation also emerged from the confrontation with counterinsurgency. The defiant refusal to apologize for brutality was not confined to pulp fictions and khaki memoirs. Arguments for violence without limits found support from elements of the political, military, and media elite; a resurgent far-right movement; and some ordinary Britons.

PART II

Justifying Violence

3

Violence without Limits

THE OFFICIALS RUNNING colonial wars worked to keep unsettling details about violence out of sight.[1] When total concealment was not possible, they sanded down the rough edges of the truth by targeting selected details for refutation. But the suppression of information operated in tandem with another tactic: the candid acknowledgment of brutality. While seeming to contradict denials about excessive force, these admissions actually complemented them. Doubt could be cast on the most explosive allegations while the point of investigating further was called into question. Portrayed by some as quotidian routine and by others as grim necessity, violence proved more difficult to attack when it was already in the open.

Colonial violence is usually thought to have left few traces in the language of British politics.[2] A quiet tradition of "liberal militarism"—preferring high-tech weapons to mass mobilizations and full-scale occupations—may be the closest thing to an official ideology for the use of force, in the colonies and elsewhere.[3] But the intricacies of liberalism (while endlessly fascinating to historians) distract from what the wars of decolonization reveal most dramatically: the appeal of illiberal militarism in Britain. This was not an elite policy doctrine but a popular language of resentment. Its tenets were the rejection of legal and moral restraints on soldiers in the field, intolerance of debate and dissent at home, and the embrace of national greatness and racial prestige as paramount values. When officials shrugged off brutality against Britain's enemies as unimportant or unavoidable, they created a space for more radical apologetics.

Justifications for untrammeled violence reached back to the suppression of revolt in the mid-Victorian empire and the controversy that followed the Amritsar Massacre of 1919.[4] The prospect of imperial collapse revived them in a new, existential key. Would Britain remain a great power capable of working its will on far-flung adversaries? Or would it suffer the humiliation of internal enemies and overseas insurgents degrading its authority? While violence without limits attracted the most fervent support from a resurgent fascist movement, the same ideal struck chords of identification beyond the fringe. Backbench politicians, right-wing publications, and their supporters gave wide currency to the language of illiberal militarism. For them, the most brutal features of colonial war were neither embarrassing secrets nor necessary evils. They signaled commitment to an order worth fighting for.

In Defense of Brutality

Like their counterparts in other times and places, British authorities at the end of empire almost invariably denied that torture happened on their watch. In the absence of an "unambiguous threshold" distinguishing callousness from torture, officials semantically downgraded the seriousness of the abuses they oversaw.[5] They portrayed violence as casual rather than sadistic, individual rather than systematic, and undisciplined rather than planned. Yet employing this strategy meant conceding that violence was real, pervasive, and not easily controlled.

"Roughness" and its variants—vague, colloquial language reminiscent of the schoolyard—were favorite euphemisms for the conduct officials were willing to admit. In Cyprus, colonial governor Hugh Foot conceded that "roughness can and does take place" in the pursuit of suspects, while Army Chief of Staff Victor Fitzgeorge-Balfour told the press that "we are not plaster saints and a bit of roughness is sometimes unavoidable."[6] During a visit to Kenya, Scottish Unionist MP Walter Elliot declared: "This is a rough world. In an emergency like this there is a great deal of roughness used at times, but there is a sharp distinction between roughness and brutality."[7] On a BBC radio show in 1963, a parade of military men denied that British troops engaged in "torture" but copped to an array of lesser offenses. Host Alun Gwynne Jones, who commanded a company in Malaya, admitted that "we have not always been as scrupulous in practice as we are in theory . . . . It may be inevitable that soldiers get a little rough with people captured in the field." A veteran officer of the Malaya and Cyprus conflicts agreed that "acts of brutality have been carried out by individuals and added that "a bit of sharpness is bound to produce the right result." General Templer himself offered BBC listeners an equivocal attitude toward violence. "On the spot I dare say there's a bit of rough stuff, with fists so to speak . . . But torture in the proper sense of the word can never be justified."[8] While deflecting the torture label undercut a sense of urgency, authorities conceded almost everything else in the process.

Expanding the boundaries of excusable violence was also a standard tactic in the right-wing press. At the height of the scoreboard scandal in Kenya, Lord Beaverbrook's *Daily Express* defended competitive killing as evidence of an admirable "offensive spirit."[9] More common were the sliding scales of culpability that distinguished the ostensibly trivial infractions committed by British troops from other, grander iniquities. Without going so far as to celebrate shooting people for sport, the *Spectator* insisted that abuses in Cyprus did not rise to the level of moral emergency: "Soldiers sometimes grew impatient, sometimes bloody-minded, sometimes violent; but there was never systematic defiance of international law."[10] On the same slippery grounds, one journalist writing about Cyprus argued that "there had been some rough handling . . . But there was no evidence . . . of a cold and bestial British terrorism."[11] These were the vanishingly fine lines and continually lowered bars that made it easier to acknowledge violence.

Some observers relied on contrasts with other nations—real, exaggerated, or imagined—to lessen the burden of British guilt. A doctor in Cyprus took comfort from his belief that neither the "German method" of collective punishment nor the "French method" of interrogation with electrodes played a part in the counterinsurgency there. Whatever the British did was not "torture," he felt, while struggling to articulate the distinction: "Justice often becomes rough . . . There were unofficial beatings-up, inevitable, not advocated."[12] "Torture" became an otherwise empty signifier for unjustifiable violence, a designation British counterinsurgency escaped on the basis of benevolent intentions and haphazard execution. It was always something that other people did.

Efforts to cast British violence in a less sinister light laid the foundation for brasher defenses of brutality. Tactical and moral justifications fed on each other: dirty wars could not be won with clean hands and underhanded enemies did not deserve to benefit from the rules of armed conflict. The *Daily Telegraph* asked why soldiers should "observe a gentleman's agreement in jungles which contain very few gentlemen."[13] "In a war of this nature," the *Western Mail* of Glamorgan, Wales, agreed, "it would have been a miracle if there were not" "acts of brutality."[14] The *Dundee Courier* agreed: "The Mau Mau are fighting this war without regard to rules. It would not be surprising if they provoke unorthodox retaliation."[15] According to a retired RAF officer, the duplicity of Mau Mau fighters made it unavoidable to shoot first and ask questions later.[16]

Dwelling on the ugliness of colonial war, apologists for violence flirted with a maximalist position that portrayed the very idea of restraints on violence as hopelessly genteel and absurdly detached from reality. "Isn't it a bit naïve to suppose . . . that troops who had their own comrades murdered when hunting terrorists can observe all the niceties of Marquess of Queensbury rules?" a BBC host asked on the *Tonight* program in 1958.[17] A young corporal in Cyprus posed a similar question to a newspaper reporter: "What do you expect us to do with them? Sit them down and give them all cups of tea?"[18] An ex-serviceman who served in Palestine came forward to defend his counterparts in Cyprus by arguing they have "a filthy job to do . . . I would not hesitate to shoot the lot."[19] Decorated army officer Frank Kitson freely confessed that the soldier in Kenya would take sometimes "the law into his own hands and strike a blow where one seemed necessary, because the existing legal methods of dealing with the situation were not good enough."[20]

While euphemistic evasions played a part in the defense of violence, then, so did explicit calls for ruthless force. Far from falling into disrepute after the Second World War, the language of exterminatory warfare surfaced repeatedly in colonial counterinsurgency. General John Harding compared Malayan insurgents to mosquitos who could never be eliminated by swatting them one at a time because "the real answer lies in destroying their feeding and breeding grounds."[21] "Nothing short of a war of extermination is likely to clean up" the Malayan peninsula, the *Coventry Evening Telegraph* warned in a 1951 story on the Communist sympathies of the ethnic Chinese population.[22] One white Kenyan settler told a Rotary Club meeting in Worcestershire that the "Mau Mau thugs should be exterminated," while another published a book proposing that they "be kept in the forests and there exterminated one by one."[23]

Playing up the barbarism of one's enemies to relax strictures on the use of force was a time-honored tactic. Long applied to colonial warfare, arguments for explicitly retaliatory attacks on civilians surfaced again during the Second World War, in debates about RAF attacks on German cities.[24] But while critics of civilian bombing in the 1940s were dismissed as fringe gadflies, critics of brutality in the 1950s were attacked as insidious threats to security, a sign of hardening illiberalism.[25] With the perpetuation of empire hanging in the balance, right-wing commentators hammered away at the idea that the mere act of questioning British tactics amounted to dangerous subversion. As a Tyneside newspaper put it, "the menace [of insurgency] cannot be fought with votes of censure or by the exaggerated misgivings of armchair observers at home."[26] Seeking to elevate the armed forces above the tussle of democratic politics, this view cast parliamentary oversight as a dangerous burden on British fighting men. "It would be deplorable if anything said in Parliament gave our forces, especially those from Britain, the idea that everything they do would be minutely examined for faults," the *Dundee Courier* opined.[27] Measured against the physical courage of soldiers in the field, what sort of authority could politicians claim? "I think it is high time some of you showed more interest in those who are fighting so that you can sit in comfort on your well-upholstered backsides in the House of Commons," read a typical letter to MP Tom Driberg.[28] Another Labour MP, Richard Crossman, felt that the pro-Boers had an easier time in their day than critics of colonial violence in the 1950s. Protesters had never been villainized so intensely, he thought, and "the belief in 'our soldiers, right or wrong,'" had never been stronger.[29]

The bitterness directed at critics of violence flowed through several channels. The Cold War politics that framed leftism as inherently traitorous was one. Given the prominence of Communists and fellow travelers in the anticolonial cause—a perpetual annoyance for Labour Party leaders—the specter of disloyalty was probably inevitable. Imperialist right-wingers seized the opportunity to equate criticism of counterinsurgency with subversion. As one Tory militant thundered at a 1953 party meeting: "Every form of sedition in the British Empire finds congenial supporters on the Opposition benches in the House of Commons. That is something new; it is something serious and it could be something disastrous."[30] For their part, left-wing activists recognized that the stigma of Communism undercut their credibility and constrained their ability to reach a wider audience. "Anyone who has dared raise suggestions of violence against the Security Forces," Peter Benenson observed, "has been branded as a 'red.'"[31] Noting the "marked increase in repression" by colonial powers in 1954, historian Eric Hobsbawm complained that British opinion "too often has remained muted for fear of encouraging 'communism.'"[32]

The nebulous concept of morale, which flourished as never before during the Second World War, also heightened the intensity of attacks on critics of colonial war.[33] Language that cheered Britain's enemies or disheartened its defenders could have life-and-death consequences. The editors of the *Manchester Guardian* hesitated to condemn British abuses because they worried about "endangering lives (by encouraging intransigence of EOKA)" and "lowering morale (especially of the troops)."[34] Because only decisive force could bring rebellions to an end, a variation on this argument held, anything that planted hesitation in soldiers' minds imperiled civilians. "The arm chair critic may easily do more harm than good," a retired colonial policeman warned Graham Greene, after the novelist voiced concerns about brutality in Kenya. "More innocent people have suffered in the long run from the man on the spot fearing to be 'rough' than from official 'atrocities.'"[35]

Another force contributing to the demonization of antiwar and anticolonial campaigners was mass conscription. "How few families there must be who have not had some member who has served in Africa or the East!" activist Peter Worsley exclaimed.[36] The British Army had become a "people's army," its once-unsavory reputation burnished by the Second World War and its claim to universality entrenched by National Service. The growing inter-penetration of military and civilian cultures made it difficult to attack brutal tactics without appearing to attack ordinary Britons. As Crossman noted, "the suggestion that National Servicemen may be fighting an unjust war outrages every father and mother in the land."[37] Benenson likewise concluded that allegations brought a "surge of emotional support for the Government, for everybody has some relative or friend who is a soldier or a policeman, and feels bound to defend him, saying 'Our Jim could never do a thing like that.'"[38] As Mary Towler, the Yorkshire woman who had no trouble believing rumors about brutality in Cyprus, noted in her Mass-Observation diary: "Let anyone criticize 'our lads' & suggest they aren't angels of mercy, then the fat is in the fire." By violating this taboo, Towler observed, left-leaning Labour MP Barbara Castle had "put her foot in it" politically.[39]

No politician condemned brutality more forcefully than Castle or re-ceived more attacks as a result. Her measured comment, after a visit to Cyprus in the fall of 1958, that soldiers were encouraged "to be very tough in searching villages," triggered a hysterical response. A blaring headline in the right-wing tabloid Daily Sketch charged her with "a stab in the back for our troops."[40] The left-wing Daily Mirror rapped her for "blackguard[ing]" soldiers with a "gross and all-too-easy slur" that was "absolute rubbish."[41] A hostile BBC interviewer accused Castle of lending credence to the Athens Radio propa-ganda that branded British troops as "felons and filthy cannibals." Didn't her criticism add "fuel to the flames" of the terrorist campaign? Wasn't it "harmful and unhelpful" to attack soldiers who were risking their lives every day?[42] Castle's own party leader, Hugh Gaitskell, issued a statement repudiating her comments and pledging Labour's categorical support for the troops.[43] While Castle stressed that her criticism was aimed at the architects of colonial policy rather than ordinary soldiers, she was heckled throughout the election season of 1959.[44] Two years later, her intervention on Cyprus was still generating hate mail. "Leave our soldiers alone," demanded an elderly woman who noted that her father had fought in the Crimean War and her husband in the South

African War. Another correspondent told Castle to "shut her big mouth and listen to people who have brains." Some letters contained violent threats. An anonymous message from a self-styled "Patriot" declared Castle a "bloody traitor" and called for "the treatment she would have had in Russia. Shoot the bastard."[45]

Misogyny fueled the backlash. Fantasies of renewing manhood on rugged frontiers always lurked behind the glorification of colonial violence.[46] After 1945, however, a new emphasis on ideals of welfare and community in the Colonial Office seemed to threaten the "feminization" of empire.[47] A sense

FIGURE 3.1 Labour MP Barbara Castle, one of the most prominent critics of colonial violence, in London after her return from Cyprus, 1958. PA Images.

of masculinity under siege was underscored by the prominence of women in protests against brutality, including Labour MPs Castle, Lena Jeger, Edith Summerskill, and Eirene White; Liberal MP Violet Bonham Carter; and Kenya whistleblower Eileen Fletcher. Castle's BBC grilling on Cyprus opened with the question: "are you looking at this as a woman or as a politician?"[48] At the height of the Cyprus controversy, several newspapers expressed distaste for the anger displayed by left-leaning women. "The note they strike is not gentle and tender," *Daily Mirror* columnist William Connor complained. "It is muscular, harsh, vibrant — and usually wrong."[49] The *Daily Express* branded Castle and company as "unfeminine, unhumorous, unrelenting . . . . It seems to be the mistake of women in politics that they shout for too loud and too long."[50]

Resentment about the seemingly inexorable retreat of empire inspired longing for the no-holds-barred prosecution of colonial war. This sentiment was bolstered by a selectively recalled past of violence without limits, signified above all by the massacre ordered by General Reginald Dyer in Amritsar, India, in 1919. Long a heroic figure for British fascists, Dyer was lauded again in the 1950s as a model for imposing order through decisive force.[51] A retired Raj official in Sussex celebrated the Amritsar precedent in a 1958 letter to the *Daily Telegraph* that claimed "the whole [uprising] was over in a week" after the shooting.[52] Another Anglo-Indian pensioner made the same point to the *Wiltshire Times*, stressing the parallels between India in 1919 and Cyprus in 1956 while praising Dyer for averting a full-blown rebellion.[53] A *Yorkshire Post* reader likewise speculated that "firm action at once, with a man of General Dyer's type in command, could have saved the troubles in Malaya, Kenya, and Cyprus."[54]

Despite mounting evidence of brutality, it became an article of faith on the British right that the conduct of colonial war in the 1950s was crippled by humanitarian softness. The red-meat rhetoric tossed out at Conservative Association dinners indicted the "sloppy" sentiment that led the government to be "weak where it should be firm, and kind where it should be harsh," as Tory MP Ralph Rayner, a retired brigadier, told a Coventry audience in 1954. "As far as our Empire is concerned," he declared, "our conscience has become overdeveloped."[55] Nothing alarmed right-wing critics so much as controversies about atrocity, which they interpreted as evidence that soldiers' hands were being tied behind their backs. "ARE WE TOO 'KID GLOVE' WITH MAU MAU?" asked a 1954 headline in the *Lancashire Evening Post*.[56] Whenever authorities modulated violence for strategic ends—offering amnesty in surrender drives, holding trials for suspected insurgents, negotiating over the terms of withdrawal—conservatives howled that the "velvet glove method should end and be replaced by repressive tactics."[57] Another retired brigadier felt sure that the memory of Amritsar's aftermath, with Dyer "ignominiously sacked" at the behest of "liberals and labourites," deterred authorities from taking stronger action against insurgents.[58]

The drive to unshackle military force from legal and bureaucratic restrictions acquired the status of a right-wing *cause célèbre*. One *Daily Mail* reader voiced frustration with "talk of conference and compromise" in Cyprus "when drastic action is the one thing required." Another letter to the *Mail* claimed that "two or three men given authority to do so could clean up Cyprus in a month."[59] Removing limitations on the use of force was some-times interpreted as a quasi-biological imperative rooted in the Darwinian logic of self-preservation. When the Oxford Union nearly carried a resolution that "rules of war are obsolete and illogical" in a 1952 debate, its proponents argued that "a nation's first duty is to survive."[60] One Conservative politician, an ex-army officer who attributed his leadership qualities to lessons learned "in the hills of Palestine," argued that "we must have the moral fiber to main-tain law and order in our possessions, without which we face extinction by younger nations."[61]

Whether or not decolonization threatened the destruction of Britain, it unquestionably represented its humiliation. Above all else, the simmering resentments of frustrated nationalism drove popular support for colonial war. Conducting interviews in Stevenage after the general election of 1959, left-wing researcher Raphael Samuel found voters preoccupied with the promise of "keeping Britain great," as he put it. One lower-middle-class housewife longed "to put England back where it used to be," to restore an era when "England was looked up to in the world." A machine operator fumed about the trajectory of decline he traced from India to Egypt to Cyprus: "These little countries, they seem to just throw us out when they feel like it, whereas one time they wouldn't have dared do that . . . . I don't think we should let other people trample on us the way they do."[62] A 1958 survey of working-class Conservative voters across the country unearthed the same anger and disbelief about a world in which Britain could no longer dictate terms. "I think we kowtow to too many people," a shop owner in Acton grumbled. A Lancashire woman, more explicit about the racial indignities of decline, complained that "the Black countries . . . are telling us what to do now."[63]

Anxiety about decolonization did not necessarily translate into enthu-siasm for war. As a Stevenage woman asked: "Why should all those boys be killed if [colonized peoples] get their independence anyway? Let them rule themselves and make a mess of it if they want to."[64] But for others, military force represented an obvious antidote to the indignities of decline. Working-class voters in the 1958 study made the point repeatedly: "We need to defend ourselves." "We've got to keep our strength up." "We want to be strong so that no one can try to push us about."[65] When Labour politicians branded their Conservative rivals as "war-mongers," the accusation fell flat. Critics of military action consistently paid a greater political price than apologists did: driven out of parliamentary seats, demonized by the press, buffeted by hostile questions.[66]

Belligerent nationalism, stoked by war in the colonies, made it easier for governments to weather controversies over conscription, nuclear weapons, and Suez. It also threatened to overwhelm whatever uneasiness existed about the treatment of colonial subjects. At a time when majorities of the public still supported floggings and executions for criminals at home, many struggled to see anything illegitimate in the harsh suppression of rebellions against British authority.[67] A twenty-year-old East London man told researchers that he found nothing objectionable in the deaths of eleven African detainees at Hola

FIGURE 3.2 Soldiers of the Brigade of Guards, some accompanied by wives and girlfriends, march from Wellington Barracks to Waterloo Station en route to Malaya, 1948. PA Images.

and found the criticism "grossly overdone." "When you think of what the Mau Mau's done," he said, "I couldn't really find much sympathy for them."[68]

Underlying this indifference to the fate of racial others was racial solidarity with white Britons overseas. One Conservative MP privately reported that "if you shot a thousand black men I wouldn't lose a vote. But if 50 Europeans in Kenya were scuppered shortly before a General Election we could lose several, because ... most people know someone in Kenya and would be concerned for them."[69] For the same reason, rightists saw support for harsh tactics as a litmus test of national loyalty. Responding to an immigrant from Cyprus who criticized the counterinsurgency in his homeland, a Tyneside man snapped, "I'm British and proud of it and what your countrymen have received from our men they will no doubt have thoroughly deserved."[70] For defending rebels against empire, the left appeared to its enemies not merely as subversives but as race traitors—willing to defend "anyone except their own kith and kin," as a Norfolk man wrote to the *Daily Mail*.[71]

The desire to uphold British authority through overwhelming force was sometimes crudely racist. At a dinner for ex-servicemen in 1957, a retired brigadier blasted politicians who "don't know Orientals like we do, they don't know that the only way to deal with them is to kick their backsides."[72] A teenager in the East End, who slurred Cypriots as "greasy" and "slimy," enthused about sending the army "to put a couple of rounds into them, that'll quiet them down, won't it." A Stevenage woman told an interviewer after the Suez crisis that she wanted "an H-bomb dropped on the whole of Egypt. It's a stinking place anyway. They're a fat lot of wogs."[73] In comparatively genteel tones, press commentators warned that the decisive suppression of uprisings was a prerequisite for maintaining racial prestige. Restraining the use of force, conversely, risked racial humiliation. "To shout before you shoot," the illustrated weekly *The Sphere* opined, "quite certainly breeds contempt for you among rebels and thugs of every race and colour."[74] The *Dundee Courier* advocated "ruthless action" against Mau Mau on the grounds that "weakness would present Africa with the spectacle of a white government, offshoot of a great empire . . . set at naught by native thugs and gangsters."[75]

Explanations for the brutality of colonial war usually work from the ground up. Settler culture, the frustrations of guerrilla conflict, and the logistical pressures of mass detention all point to violence as the product of tensions within the colony. But public opinion in Britain also enabled brutality. Though far from universal, a reservoir of unshakeable support for the most extreme forms of repression acted as a buffer against humanitarian outrage. Officials contending with accusations of softness as well as cruelty could escape accountability in the stalemate between polarized camps. Even as radicalization went further in rhetoric than in practice, fantasies of unlimited violence and absolute destruction created a context for the abuses that did take place. They made them easier to imagine and to defend.

The Fascist Romance of Colonial War

Admiration of brute force, hostility to dissent and parliamentarism, commitment to racial community: the values of the far right were not confined to the fringe in the age of colonial war. This does not mean that zeal for violence against colonial subjects was necessarily "fascist." The term suggests a degree of ideological coherence not found in most apologias for brutality. Classic elements of fascist ideology—the politicization of private life, the mobilization of the masses, the utopian reimagination of the future—played no part in British debates about colonial war. In the metropole, authoritarian violence generated excitement in large part because its effects were felt elsewhere; it was a rhetorical ideal that could be expressed within the existing system rather than a form of action aimed at toppling it. There was no conspiracy of settlers and officers working to overturn the government in London, no well-drilled cadres in the streets demanding the installation of a military-imperialist regime. Brutality against colonial subjects required no radical break with the established order in Britain. The danger of the fascist label is that it exoticizes and marginalizes the home-grown illiberalism of an empire long rooted in racial violence.

Even so, contemporaries found it difficult to overlook the resemblances between fascist war and colonial war. Left-wing activists were not alone in seeing the parallels. Writer Lawrence Durrell, who served as press officer for the colonial government in Cyprus, privately worried about the impulses he saw unleashed there. "If you could . . . see the behavior of the Cyprus Police, Malaya, Palestine police," he told a friend in 1958, "you would be scared at the strong vein of brutish fascism the British have in their unconscious. The minute Habeas Corpus goes out, and the hundred juridical safeguards which we have built up, it is astonishing how jackbooted and truculent we become."[76] Appalled by an upsurge of jingoism during the Suez crisis, Oxford don Hugh Trevor-Roper observed that "that there is in England, as in other countries, a fascist world: the world of lower-middle-class conservatives who have no intelligence but a deep belief in violence as a sign of self-importance; who hate foreigners, especially if they come from 'inferior' races; and who, gratified with the spectacle of such violence against such people, even if it fails in its object, are prepared to shout, in unison, 'il Duce ha sempre ragione' ['the Leader is always right']."[77] More than a rhetorical device employed by left-wing campaigners, the fascist analogy represented an attempt to explain the breadth and depth of enthusiasm for authoritarian violence in the colonies.

That enthusiasm was most fully developed on the extreme right wing of British politics. This was terrain occupied in the 1950s by a motley array of groups, most with connections to Oswald Mosley's interwar Blackshirt movement, although their leaders were reluctant to claim the fascist label they once embraced. Even without achieving notable success by the measure of membership rolls or electoral results, the League of Empire Loyalists, the National Labour Party, and the White Defence League demonstrated the porosity of the boundary between the margins and the mainstream. In their speeches and pamphlets, far-right activists outlined the same sorts of apologias for colonial war as less ideologically committed Britons did in letters to editors and politicians, in social surveys, and elsewhere. The extreme right both reflected and amplified the concerns of larger constituencies.[78]

This was a two-way traffic. Extremists looking for a path to mass appeal exploited popular anxieties about imperial retreat. At the same time, provocateurs broadcasting sentiments once considered unsayable or taboo shifted the boundaries of rhetorical possibility. Decades of far-right attacks on the flabbiness of the liberal elite—its reluctance to take forceful action, its crippling deference to laws and norms, its failure to defend the racial nation—forged a language ready-made for the discontents of decolonization. Several leading figures in the Conservative governments of the 1950s, including Colonial Secretary Alan Lennox-Boyd, had a history of involvement with Mosleyite fascism.[79] What is more, the same constituencies that rallied to the Blackshirt movement in the 1930s had an outsized presence among the most bellicose voices captured by newspapers and surveys in the 1950s: the Home Counties redoubts of military and imperial pensioners; the declining industrial zones of Lancashire and Yorkshire, where ancestral Tory loyalties often trumped class solidarity; and London's East End, with its long tradition of xenophobic violence.[80]

It was the Palestine Emergency of 1946–1948 that first mobilized the far-right movement on behalf of colonial war. With British soldiers fighting Zionist insurgents, the conflict presented a conspicuous opportunity to harness anti-Semitism—the lodestar of far-right ideology—to the resentments of decolonization.[81] While Britons were already prone to discounting the specificity of Jewish suffering in the Second World War, Zionist guerilla attacks on British forces in Palestine accelerated the transformation of the war's quintessential victims into alien and threatening others.[82] A series of attacks by the Irgun—including the King David Hotel bombing in July 1946, the flogging of three soldiers in December 1946, and the Officers' Goldsmith Club bombing in March 1947—unleashed a wave of revulsion in Britain. This anti-Semitic backlash climaxed after the killing of two British Army sergeants by insurgents near Netanya in July 1947.

Under the headline "Hanged Britons: Picture That Will Shock the World," the *Daily Express* ran a large front-page photograph of the slain officers dangling from a tree with their hands tied behind their backs. An orgy of violence across Britain followed. Mobs gathered in Liverpool, Manchester, and London; more than three hundred Jewish properties, including shops and synagogues, were destroyed.[83] A Lancashire newspaper editor published an editorial declaring Jews "a plague on the country" and proposing a pogrom as "the only way to bring them to the sense of their responsibility to the country in which they live." He was acquitted of seditious libel after a trial in which the *Daily Express* photo figured prominently.[84] Throughout the conflict in Palestine, graffiti with messages like "Hitler Was Right," "The Jews Are At War with Britain," and "Germans Were Hung For Killing Jews, When Will Jews Hang For Killing Britons?" appeared on city streets, sometimes accompanied by the telltale lightning bolt symbol of Mosley's followers.[85]

This surge of anti-Semitism did not translate into a recruiting boom or an electoral boost for the extreme right. But the battle cry of British greatness threatened by treacherous racial enemies continued to echo after the retreat from Palestine. The far-right group most intently focused on imperial decline, the League of Empire Loyalists, purveyed a conspiratorial anti-Semitism that saw Wall Street, the United Nations, and other American-led global institutions as stalking horses for Jewish interests. While the Soviet "Red Empire" represented an obvious rival to British power, a more insidious threat came from the "Dollar Empire," which one League pamphlet described as the "anti-British, anti-White, and anti-Christian conspiracy which has its headquarters in New York."[86] The organization's director and chief propagandist, Mosley disciple Arthur Chesterton, identified the hidden hand of Jewish plotting in uprisings across the empire and in the supposedly vacillating response of the British government. For Chesterton, the dissipation of so much power and territory could only be explained by an "orgy of betrayal."[87]

Steeped in the vulgar Darwinism of the far right, Chesterton celebrated violence as an expression of racial vitality. The clearest sign that "the people of England" might be "a decadent and doomed race," he warned around 1960,

FIGURE 3.3 League of Empire Loyalists waving the Union Jack, London, late 1950s. Marx Memorial Library/Mary Evans Picture Library.

was the mounting failure to maintain empire by force. "Is it for this that our men have hanged from trees in Palestine, died in the jungles of Malaya, been stabbed in the back in Cyprus? Did they do that for us to shrug our shoulders when the very heritage they fought to defend is handed over to the terrorists who slew them?"[88] Portraying the British dead as martyrs asserted a claim to the ground on which their blood was spilled. It also underlined the idea of colonial war as a source of order: "a citadel of strength and a guarantor of peace," holding the line against a sea of "potential anarchy."[89] Above all, Chesterton saw empire as a field of racial competition, built through centuries of "struggle, exertion, achievement" and now ripe for the reconquest that would allow Britain to "restore her greatness."[90]

The League of Empire Loyalists had a short life, from 1954 to 1967, and its membership rolls peaked at around 3,000 in the late 1950s, with heavy representation from military-imperial veterans and settler colonists.[91] Although a younger generation of fascists bristled at the LEL's seeming elitism, they shared many of the group's beliefs: empire as a proving ground of racial prestige; attacks on empire as a betrayal of racial identity; violence as an energizing, purifying, and unifying force. The new breed of fascist groups that spun off from the LEL, led by the National Labour Party and the White Defence League, added anti-immigrant and anti-black rhetoric to the traditional mix of far-right concerns. But these sentiments, too, derived some of their venomous intensity from the wars of decolonization.

For right-wing extremists at the end of the 1950s, colonial wars were traumatic above all because they signified the breakdown of racial order. A 1959 story in *Combat*, the National Labour Party newspaper, opened with the enraging sound of tom-tom drums in Trafalgar Square for an African Freedom Day celebration. This "sad spectacle in the heart of a great nation" marked the triumph of groups like the Movement for Colonial Freedom, which defended "the 'rights' of any race or nation other than their own."[92] The NLP continually fulminated about breaches in the defenses of Britishness. Critics of the Cyprus war showed "more concern for the welfare of EOKA terrorists than their own British constituents"; the Colonial Office treated the white settlers of Kenya, "our own flesh and blood," as "expendable"; left-wing outrage at the Hola massacre made "martyrs out of monsters."[93] Like Chesterton, who argued that "racial discrimination" was "throughout Nature . . . a clean and wholesome thing," NLP publicists sought to legitimize an explicitly racial form of British nationalism.[94] As Colin Jordan of the White Defence League cried at a 1959 Trafalgar Square rally, under a banner reading "Keep Britain White": "This square has seen meetings for African nationalism, Cypriot nationalism, Greek nationalism. Just for a change, we are having a meeting for British nationalism!"[95]

The demonization of anticolonial fighters throughout the 1950s furnished a script for fear-mongering about immigration. Sensationalistic *Combat* headlines about crimes committed by West Indian immigrants ("BLACKS GO BERSERK: WHITE MAN MURDERED") could have been lifted verbatim from news stories about Mau Mau. In another echo of colonial war, Cypriot immigrants were folded into the narrative of "black" criminality and subject to the same accusations of hoarding public resources such as council flats.[96] Boundaries between colonial battlefields and British streets likewise blurred in the fascist romanticization of racial violence. The same far-right groups that incited attacks on black Londoners, with deadly consequences at Notting Hill in 1958, reveled in fantasies about the murder of colonial subjects. A 1959 *Combat* story described Mau Mau as "lice" and invited readers to "to strain the tendons of the fingers in mute yearning for the spade-grips of the machine-gun!"[97] Even as anti-Semitism remained a fixture in *Combat* and like-minded publications, a new set of racial enemies joined the Jewish world conspiracy in far-right demonology.[98]

The plausibility of representing colonial wars, in retrospect, as humiliating failures buoyed the far right into the 1960s. Seen through the lens of racial surrender, the memory of these wars refused to fade into a self-soothing narrative of magnanimously relinquished power. The embittered rhetoric of hard-right imperialists makes it difficult to accept one historian's verdict that Britain in the age of decolonization avoided a "patriotic revolt against the treachery or incompetence of national leaders" because it "escaped military defeat."[99] Rightists held the weak-kneed liberalism of both major parties responsible for what they saw as the abandonment of white settlers in Kenya. Standing for Parliament at Petersfield in 1964, an LEL candidate asked: "How is it possible to vote for supporters of an administration which handed over a beautiful country like Kenya, pioneered by British courage and made prosperous by British brains, to the obscene Mau Mau cult? . . . Why has it become fashionable for Party politicians . . . to prefer foreign interests to British interests, to back the Black man against the White man, to force civilized governments over vast tracts of the earth's surface to make way for government by savages?"[100] Another LEL figure, a retired Indian Army officer named Richard Hilton, insisted in 1968 that British soldiers fighting colonial wars had been stabbed in the back by treacherous politicians. "Ruthlessness will always stop guerrilla war . . . . It was the British Government, *not* the fighting men, who gave up the struggle."[101] When a seemingly endless series of wars failed to secure British dominance, jingoism curdled into disillusionment with the governing elite and fear of racial degradation.

While reaching back to the 1930s in some ways, then, the far-right response to decolonization also anticipated the "authoritarian populism" of the 1970s and 1980s. Stuart Hall coined the term in 1979 to describe a form of politics, pioneered by the National Front and co-opted by Margaret Thatcher's Conservative Party, which weakened democratic culture while retaining most "formal representative institutions." Appealing to racial grievance and especially to resentment of non-white immigrants, it asserted the need for "law and order" against disorder, decay, and conspiracy.[102] In the Thatcher years, it was still possible to see the 1950s as a wilderness period for the radical

FIGURE 3.4 "White Africa Betrayed": the racial resentments of decolonization energized the radical right. A fascist demonstration in Trafalgar Square,
1961. PA Images.

right, with extremists kept on the sideline by consensus-style Conservatism
and immigrant-bashing not yet widely exploited as a political weapon.[103] But
colonial war had a more formative and lasting impact on right-wing politics
than this narrative suggests. Panic about the softness and treachery of the
ruling class, enthusiasm for leaders breaking rules in defense of the nation,
and fear of insidious racial enemies all deepened in response to the frustrated
violence of decolonization.

From the Cambridge spies to the Profumo affair, a series of scandals in
this period signified the entwinement of sexual and political corruption
at the heart of "the Establishment."[104] Apologetics for colonial violence
exploited the contrast between effeminate gentility and muscular patriotism.
Condemning the "soft men" of metropolitan Britain while lauding the "true
men" among settlers in Africa, as LEL pamphlets did, transformed a long tradition of frontier romance into a self-flagellating narrative of decolonization.[105]
Ultra-imperialist peer Lord Salisbury, commiserating with white Rhodesian
leader Roy Welensky in 1962, complained that the British people had been
"emasculated by the welfare state."[106] The prominence of women in criticisms
of colonial violence—along with a few men, including MP Tom Driberg and

journalist Michael Davidson, notorious for their homosexuality—bolstered the idea that the strength on which empires depended was rotting from within.

An alternative, masculine, and frankly authoritarian style of leadership was modeled by the counterinsurgency commanders who made their names in the 1950s. Lingering admiration for General Dyer created an opening for two charismatic figures, Gerald Templer and Frank Kitson, who built reputations as master strategists while flaunting disregard for constraints on the use of force. An adulatory portrait of Templer, published in 1955, appeared in a volume revealingly titled *A Law Unto Themselves*.[107] By the 1970s, the retired Templer was still touting collective punishment in Malaya as "harsh, maybe, but most effective," while Kitson, then commanding troops in Northern Ireland, hinted that the army stood ready to restore order against "political extremists" in mainland Britain.[108] The monarchy's embrace of both men wreathed their strongman inclinations in patriotic symbolism. Templer, who briefly left Malaya in 1952 to attend Queen Elizabeth II's coronation, was awarded a knighthood in the Queen's Birthday Honours of 1955 and later served as a colonel in the Household Cavalry. Kitson received a long string of royal honors before his 1982 appointment as Commander-in-Chief, Land Forces, of the British Army. Incorporating counterinsurgency icons into ceremonial tradition hallowed colonial war as the defense of the nation.[109]

The popular hunger for leaders willing to take strong measures and articulate unpleasant truths was most powerfully revealed in the backlash against immigration.[110] While animosity for anticolonial insurgents did not cause hostility to non-white migrants in Britain, it did provide a template for expressing it. Historian Bill Schwarz has argued that the racial mythology of settler society—the sense of besieged, victimized whiteness honed in places like Kenya—gave shape to the "populist language of politics" at home.[111] Black Britons with no connection to East Africa found themselves harassed as potential enemies in casual encounters from London to Liverpool: "Are you a Mau Mau lady?" "Go back to Mau Mau land."[112] The language of insufficient toughness and crippling liberalism suffused the reaction against immigrants. Nativist listeners writing to the BBC after a 1958 broadcast on race relations argued that reluctance to fight "the invasion of the blacks" revealed a pathological "sickly-sentimentality."[113] One correspondent claimed to speak for those who "love their country and hate to see it degraded and made to look foolish by over-tolerance."[114] Greek Cypriots likewise attracted hostile attention from the self-styled defenders of racial hierarchy. One researcher recorded the explosive reaction of a Teddy Boy after a café owner smacked one

FIGURE 3.5 Field Marshal Sir Gerald Templer (right), with Lord Mountbatten, in a Household Cavalry ceremony, Windsor, 1965. PA Images.

of his friends for sitting on a table. As he put it, "I just don't like to see a white man hit, I mean a Greek hit a chap of my own nationality."[115] The tense racial atmosphere of counterinsurgency—lurking threats, endless reprisals, endangered prestige—had a long afterlife.

These pressures left a lasting mark on the Conservative Party in particular. A familiar pattern of intraparty politics, with militants vigilant for betrayal by ideologically suspect leaders, was fueled by recriminations over the retreat from empire. The top of the party splintered when Lord Salisbury, the grandson of the Conservative prime minister, resigned from the Cabinet in 1957 over Prime Minister Harold Macmillan's Cyprus policy. Disturbed above all by what he saw as the abandonment of "our friends and kinfolk" in Africa, Salisbury worried that Macmillan and his ministers had failed to recognize the stakes of "a white versus black racial world conflict." Decolonization, he wrote later, empowered "the blacks who have no sympathy with Britain and all that Britain stands for."[116]

Grass-roots Tories likewise attributed national decline and imperial withdrawal to the misguided liberalism of political leaders. While this vituperation focused most intensely on Labour politicians, the continued dismantling of empire under Conservative governments after 1951 turned some of that anger inside the party. Local Conservative associations passed resolutions upbraiding party leaders for insufficient commitment to empire.[117] Confiding to a group of mostly Tory peers at a London club in 1958, Lord Halifax observed that "the difficulty of the Government is that they are tied by their local Conservatives, who do not yet realize that we are no longer a Great Power, and that the days are past when we could assert our authority with a Maxim gun."[118] Though not yet perceptible in electoral terms, mistrust was growing among rank-and-file Conservative voters susceptible to the fascist rhetoric of imperial greatness and racial solidarity. A Warrington man and lifelong Conservative voter wrote to the party's Central Office in 1957 to complain about "a so-called Conservative Government which is perpetually letting the country down." His grievances echoed those of the extreme right: "The Liquidation of the Empire under the supervision and influence of the USA," the "appalling influx of Coloured people into the country," and the failure to defend "the White British way of Life."[119]

The most significant vehicle for radicalizing the Conservative Party from within was the Monday Club, founded in 1961 by local Tory activists with backing from Salisbury and other right-wing peers. Organized in protest against Macmillan's "Wind of Change" speech, which conceded the inevitability of decolonization, the Monday Club began by issuing communiqués against the desertion of white settlers in Kenya and grew more extreme over time. In 1965, the group expressed solidarity with the white-supremacist regime of Rhodesia rebelling against the British government, and in 1968, it backed Enoch Powell's anti-immigrant "Rivers of Blood" speech. The group went on to defend apartheid South Africa as well as Rhodesia and to campaign for the voluntary "repatriation" of non-white migrants from Britain.[120] While National Front extremists belonged to the Monday Club, so did dozens of Conservative MPs, and its positions enjoyed widespread popularity among the party faithful.[121] Like the National Front, the Monday Club began to fade only in the mid-1970s as Thatcherite Conservatism co-opted its grievances.

Zones of British settlement preoccupied the right wing on the grounds that decisive battles for national character were taking place there. Defenders of colonial war longed for the hardening of sensibilities because it was not the brutality of counterinsurgency, but the reluctance of so many to accept it, that they viewed as a symptom of moral decline.[122] A *Yorkshire Post* reader spoke for many on the right with the lament that "we are reaping today in Cyprus, as we have in other parts of the Empire we once had, the harvest of our own folly, weakness, and liberalism."[123] Artist Wyndham Lewis, notorious for his fascist sympathies in the 1930s, likewise blamed "the 'Liberalism' in this unhappy land" for encouraging insurgencies. Referring to the left-wing barrister who defended Jomo Kenyatta against accusations of sedition, Lewis wrote, "I would have [Denis] Pritt and all his friends shot."[124] Anxieties about waning toughness reverberated between imperial and domestic politics, most conspicuously in the backlash against policies to liberalize criminal justice, from the abolition of penal flogging in 1948 to the limitation of capital punishment in 1957. Right-wing voices predicted that softening the treatment of lawbreakers in Britain would set a poor example for colonies "just emerging from the Stone Age," as one Tory peer put it in 1955.[125] In Bournemouth, Conservative activists were as outraged by their MP's support for the abolition of hanging as for his opposition to the Suez invasion. The party faithful allegedly complained that he "didn't want the blood of either Englishmen or Arabs. What's a Tory MP for?"[126] Viewing liberal sentimentality as the root of the problem, defenders of colonial warfare chose to attack it frontally, by reveling in brutality.

But if this strategy proved effective at stirring jingoistic passions, it also carried risks. Unease about colonial war was diffuse and inconsistent yet unpredictable and sometimes powerful. While transparency about violence did not guarantee moral outrage, neither did it ensure a permanent state of indifference. Conscious of the potential for backlash against brutality, officials cultivated relationships with journalists, missionaries, and aid workers because they feared that the wrong kind of detail slipping into public view could still undermine support for counterinsurgency. Because so much was already known about violence, the problem for those in charge of colonial war was not how to maintain an ironclad grip of secrecy, but how to avoid the tipping-point revelation that turned apathy into resistance.

4

The Claims of Conscience

EMPIRES ARE SPACES of moral confusion. The capacity to help others is bound up with the desire to dominate and the power to harm. These contradictions grew sharper in the age of decolonization. Colonial subjects were simultaneously victims to be rescued and enemies to be crushed; promises of welfare and development worked hand in glove with brute force.[1] Little wonder that contemporaries endlessly questioned the ethical imperatives of counterinsurgency. What responsibilities flowed from living at the heart of a violent empire? Did the British people share a "universe of obligation" with overseas communities composed of insurgents as well as citizens?[2] Could conscience be expressed in opposition to other values—faith in institutions, respect for authority, loyalty to queen and country—or only in concert with them?

Two traditions spoke directly to the principles at stake in colonial war: Christianity and humanitarianism. From parish churches to street-corner chapels, British Christians experienced counterinsurgency as a problem of faith. Disentangling the rights and wrongs of these conflicts took the form of an ongoing debate that unfolded in sermons, prayer services, and missionary projects. Nominally secular humanitarian groups shied away from explicit judgments as they prioritized the relief of suffering over the salvation of souls. But they too confronted the task of honoring universal creeds and moral commitments in the maelstrom of violence.

Some Christians and humanitarians raised their voices against colonial war. For the most part, however, neither tradition proved incompatible with the brutal repression of colonial subjects. Many churches and aid organizations had long since made their peace with the inevitability of war. Few were immune to the pressures of patriotic solidarity.[3] Even so, the conviction summoned to rationalize and justify the dirty of the 1950s was striking. As missionaries and aid workers absorbed mounting evidence of unchecked violence, they found a multitude of reasons to keep quiet and keep working with the state. The logic of casuistry—applying ostensibly universal principles to murky real-world cases, spinning out the myriad consequences of alternative choices, and accepting the necessity of accommodation with an imperfect world—offered an ethically respectable alibi for inaction. As they engaged in elaborate moral calculations, weighing the virtues of compromise against the vices of complicity, the reckoning most often came out on the side of empire.

Praying for Peace

Although religious influence weakened dramatically in late twentieth-century Britain, the early years after the war witnessed an Indian summer of Christian piety.[4] Whether measured by church memberships, Sunday-school enrollments, or participation in the rites of confirmation and communion, Protestantism expanded at a pace not seen since Victorian times.[5] While these institutional gains happened unevenly, religiosity was flourishing beyond the walls of church and chapel as well.[6] Politicians and pundits interpreted the victory over fascism as a providential act of God, identifying Britain as a "Christian nation" in an oft-repeated rhetorical formula. The first-ever mass television event in Britain, the coronation of Elizabeth II in 1953, projected a resplendent vision of national community that was deeply sacral and distinctly Anglican.[7] American preacher Billy Graham packed crowds into Wembley Stadium and White City on a series of evangelizing tours, while religious broadcasting reached millions of radio listeners and television viewers each day.[8] Even the New Towns, classrooms, and hospital wards of Labour's welfare state left a prominent place for the Church of England.[9]

While the postwar resurgence of Christian Britain had a decidedly conservative bent, some spiritual leaders used their platform to question the morality of colonial war. Drawing on a long tradition of Christian socialism, these were charismatic yet controversial figures whose criticisms of counterinsurgency overlapped with campaigns against apartheid, nuclear weapons, and Cold War militarization. Several of them—including Methodist leader Donald Soper, a prominent left-Labourite, and his co-religionist Leslie Weatherhead, the minister of City Temple in Holborn—entered radical politics through the pacifist movement of the 1930s.[10] Others—including the infamous "red dean" of Canterbury, Hewlett Johnson, and the "red vicar" of Hackney, Stanley Evans—were enchanted by the promise of the Soviet Union and maintained their Marxist commitments through the early years of the Cold War.[11] For Anglican clerics John Collins, Trevor Huddleston, and Michael Scott, the struggle against the apartheid regime in South Africa shaped their vision of decolonization as a moral process and their impatience with racial hierarchies maintained by force.[12]

Christian leftists protested colonial violence for many different reasons. But they shared a sense that antiwar and anticolonial politics extended from their spiritual convictions. Preaching in London in the late 1950s after a stormy departure from South Africa, Huddleston warned against the hypocrisy of shutting one's eyes to suffering in the colonies while clinging to pieties. "To proclaim the Christian gospel in Africa . . . is a mockery of God if, whilst proclaiming it, you allow men to be treated as beasts." Collins, the canon of St. Paul's Cathedral, reached the same conclusion. "Religion and politics are interdependent," he argued, not "distinct, fenced-off areas of human activity, each with its own appropriate code of behavior." Respectable churchgoers put off by topical sermons were clinging to an illusory belief that "there might be one morality for private and another for public life."[13]

With Collins in the pulpit, churchgoers at St. Paul's grew accustomed to the violent end of empire intruding on Sunday worship. In a sermon after the Suez invasion, Collins insisted that deploying force in a bid to retain geopolitical influence was both deluded and immoral. "Bereft of much of our worldly power and prosperity," he declared, "we go on believing that Britain's greatness is in her material and military might." The hunger for prestige ensnared the nation in sin; accepting a diminished role in the world, by contrast, promised spiritual renewal. "The old ways with their reliance on the sword have been tried and found wanting," Collins urged his parishioners. "Let us as a nation move out of the shadow of death."[14]

Collins, a pacifist, had preached against military action before.[15] But his warnings about the corrupting effects of warfare grew more insistent over time. Like other leftists, he traced the outbreak of racial violence at Notting Hill in 1958 to a "lust for blood and violence" bred by militaristic policies. He castigated the wars in Cyprus and Kenya for embodying an un-Christian instrumentalism that treated human beings as means to the end of national self-interest. "To hang and punish young men and young women . . . to impose collective punishments . . . these and all such oppressive acts are, in my opinion, sin. That such sin is conducted in our name is a disgrace." Privileging imperial power over the sanctity of life led inevitably to atrocity, Collins warned.[16]

In their effort to redefine the empire's enemies as the empire's victims, radical clergymen painted vivid images of suffering. Preaching at Canterbury

Cathedral in 1957, Stanley Evans described Cypriots "living their lives at the end of a gun, watched, supervised, cajoled, forced." While Methodist clergyman Leslie Weatherhead acknowledged the "terrible deeds" perpetrated by Mau Mau to worshipers at City Temple, he stressed that both sides had blood on their hands. "Are we quite happy about Lincoln bombers dropping thousand-pound bombs on comparatively unarmed African people, including women, with apparently no concern for the wounded and mutilated?" Identification with besieged settlers should not translate into moral detachment where others were concerned, Weatherhead argued, adding that "no Christian can sit back complacently, shutting his mind away from what is going on in Africa." One commentator in 1954 estimated, only half-jokingly, that "cases of maltreatment of the African are denounced from half the pulpits of Britain."[17]

Religious radicals argued that a false sense of moral superiority was justifying violence. Holding an empire by force, they insisted, was no righteous cause. Evoking the seemingly endless cycle of killings and reprisals in Cyprus, Evans cited an ominous warning from Matthew 26:52: "He that takes the sword will perish by the sword." Congregational minister John Marsh observed that Britain had long pledged fealty to the principle of self-determination and had no right to deny it to "a resentful population just because we have the brute force to do so . . . We may well be found fighting against the Divine Order." After the rampage by British troops in Famagusta in 1958, the Cardiganshire Congregational Union passed a resolution that condemned British troops for cruelty and declared them no better than the Soviet soldiers who marched into Hungary in 1956.[18] Religious criticism of the war in Kenya revolved around the indefensibility of fighting to preserve settler privileges. An Anglican clergyman near Berwick-on-Tweed in 1958 denounced a war fought for "greedy men that would take everything from the native and leave him starving." Soper called for the expropriation of all white settlers in Kenya, arguing that the defense of their wealth had led to "reprehensible, brutal, and obscene" behavior by "some of the soldiers out there."[19]

Some lay believers were also outraged by the violence committed in Britain's name. As a Lancashire man upset by the war in Malaya told the Archbishop of York in 1952, "no one with a spark of Christianity in them could possibly agree with what is going on in the East, where the natives are demanding their freedom from the rule and exploitation of so-called Christians and being met with the extensive use of the strong arm."[20] A Birmingham woman in 1952 urged Colonial Secretary Oliver Lyttelton to sue for peace in Kenya by reminding him that "we call ourselves a Christian people and are celebrating our Queen's coronation with all religious rites."[21] Quaker Philip Radley, who ran a hostel for international students in Gower Street, upbraided the archbishop of Canterbury for his reluctance to condemn atrocities in Kenya. "I have wished," Radley wrote despairingly, "that you would voice the Christian feeling in this country that, whatever the tragic events in Kenya, each African is a human being, an individual precious in the sight of God."[22]

Radley was not the only believer driven to action by the 1953 court-martial of British Army Captain G. W. B. Griffiths, who was charged with mutilating Kenyan suspects. The Anglican rector of St. George's in London's East End held "a service of reparation" for what he called "the evil and cruelty which hold sway in Kenya today." A statement adopted by the worshipers in attendance condemned the "terrible revelations of the recent trials" as well as the use of area bombing, which showed "contempt for human life—provided only that it was black." Declaring a spiritual mobilization against sin, the Anglicans of St. George's asked God's forgiveness for their "acquiescence in this terrible state of affairs."[23]

While left-leaning Christians dominated the field of antiwar protest, the cause of insurgents in Cyprus inspired sympathy among religious conservatives because they saw the conflict as a tragic rift between Orthodox and Protestant Christians. The evangelical revival movement known as Moral Rearmament argued the case for reconciliation on the grounds that pious Western nations had to unite against the threat of Soviet atheism. As Moral Rearmament spokesman Peter Howard explained in 1959, "It cannot go on, two of the sister nations of Europe destroying each other with the world so near the abyss." Howard urged his fellow Britons to acknowledge the wrongs they were committing against Cypriots and seek forgiveness for them. "I hate the hypocrisy of us British," he declared. "We get furious when Khruschev kills people who fight for freedom in Hungary—but when the people of Cyprus ask us for their freedom, we say no." Citing details of sadistic torture reported by the Greek-language press, Howard attributed British "cruelty" to the degrading effects of "homosexuality and immoral living in Britain."[24] A Liverpool man writing to Conservative Party politician R. A. B. Butler in 1956 likewise cast the counterinsurgency in Cyprus as an unholy war. He complained that the Tories were repressing "a kindly Christian people" and warned that they would "have to answer to God for their sins."[25] For some believers, warfare against European Christians inspired objections even when other conflicts did not.

Fear of ceding moral authority to other movements drove leaders of the established church to take their own stand on colonial violence.[26] Criticizing

British attacks on the Greek Orthodox Church, Archbishop of Canterbury Geoffrey Fisher and other members of the Anglican hierarchy urged the government to negotiate with rebels in Cyprus and posed tough questions in the House of Lords about detentions and executions.[27] In the first year of the Kenya Emergency, the executive committee of the Anglican Church Missionary Society (CMS) issued a statement urging "maximum restraint" by security forces, while the Anglican newspaper *Church Times* treated atrocity allegations as front-page news. By 1954, Fisher was publicly, if grudgingly, acknowledging "abuses of power among those enforcing law and order" in the war against the Mau Mau.[28]

The most forceful Anglican protest against the Kenya counterinsurgency came with the Church Missionary Society's 1955 pamphlet, "Kenya—Time for Action!" The "abuses of power" it described—indiscriminate round-ups, violence during interrogation, and indefinite detention—echoed familiar criticisms by left-wing activists. Besides carrying the imprimatur of the established church, what made the CMS pamphlet so striking was that it insisted on viewing abuses in Kenya as a spiritual rot infecting Britain along with its colony. "Confess before God *your* failure to be sufficiently concerned," the pamphlet urged. "Acknowledge that where there has been failure by Christian men and women on the spot . . . you share in that failure." The path to atonement proposed by CMS led from introspection to activism: the pamphlet concluded by urging readers to write their Members of Parliament requesting an independent inquiry.[29]

Detailing the human consequences of political choices, stretching webs of obligation across the world, and co-opting the imperialist language of duty, Christian moralism furnished a powerful language for reckoning with colonial violence. It was a language that stung consciences and, in a few instances, prompted hidebound institutions to act. But the anguish voiced by faith-based critics of empire also hints at a less triumphant view of their role. Their fervor stemmed in part from the recognition that they were swimming against the tide of Christian sentiment. Most believers had no trouble reconciling faith with colonial warfare. For all their eloquence, religious activists had every reason to see themselves as voices in the wilderness.

God On Their Side

The British Empire long nurtured a reputation as a godly enterprise. Allegedly un-Christian practices in other cultures—slavery, polygamy, child marriage— offered a perennial justification for conquest, bolstering British pretensions to represent something greater than materialistic greed and lust for power. Christianity and militarism grew closer in the second half of the nineteenth century as hagiographies of fighting men poured off the presses, the moral reputation of the soldiery improved, and religious organizations adopted army-style discipline in turn. The new ideal of "muscular Christianity" challenged the evangelical emphasis on domesticity by celebrating heroic, manly independence as the foundation of conscience. War in the colonies, seen as uniquely suitable for chivalric tests of moral fiber, began to assume the complexion of holy war: heathen enemies demonized, fallen fighters hallowed as martyrs, the chords of "Onward, Christian Soldiers" echoing across the battlefield.[30]

What renewed this tradition in the 1950s was the conviction that new enemies threatened the moral order of empire. The leading lights of British Christianity condemned the authoritarian state "which rounds up in concentration camps those it suspects, makes its prisoners slaves, and subjects its opponents to torture," as Leslie Hunter, the bishop of Sheffield, put it in 1953. But rather than targeting the abuses of colonial war, this criticism was aimed at the "totalitarian" governments of the Communist bloc.[31] For Christian authorities, Cold War polemics denouncing godless dictatorships took precedence over imperial self-criticism. As Bishop of Coventry Cuthbert Bardsley warned in an ominous address to the city's business leaders, "a rising tide of nationalism and racialism bids fair to swamp the Western world with its age-old Christian and democratic heritage."[32]

Figures at the commanding heights of religious hierarchies threw their weight behind colonial warfare. Eminences dropping into conflict zones received lavish welcomes from the military and delivered spiritual seals of approval for counterinsurgency in return.[33] Visiting Malaya in 1951, the fervently anti-Communist Archbishop of York, Cyril Garbett, delivered morale-boosting sermons on "the British way of life" and toured Templer's armed settlements with gusto. Where critics saw grimly punitive camps ringed with guard towers, flood lights, and barbed wire, Garbett returned home with rosy visions of a grand "social experiment." According to the archbishop, agriculture and pasturage were flourishing, shops and cinemas were proliferating, and "educational, medical, and welfare opportunities" abounded. Unless thwarted in Malaya, Garbett warned, the Red menace would spread across Asia through a campaign of "murder and blackmail."[34]

Archbishop of Canterbury Geoffrey Fisher offered no hint of discomfort with counterinsurgency tactics during a tour of Kenya in May 1955. Instead, he celebrated African Christians for their "faith onto death," hallowing the war against Mau Mau with the rhetoric of martyrology. After leading an Anglican service at the Limuru girls' school where his niece worked as headmistress, Fisher heard the testimony of an African clergyman who had nearly been stabbed to death by insurgents. Bleeding from knife wounds, the man reportedly told his attackers: "I have drunk the blood of Christ and that is enough for me." A photograph distributed by the propaganda arm of the colonial government showed Fisher draping a benevolent hand over the man's shoulder above the caption: "He Meets Man Tortured by Mau Mau." Another photograph showed Fisher walking between rows of neatly arrayed African soldiers as a large gold crucifix hung from his neck.[35] Counterinsurgency leaders, for their part, embraced the identity of Christian warriors. General Templer's top aide in Malaya poured messianic anti-Communism into his diary: "It is a light of Christianity against a fanatical evil, and such a struggle has never been easy or decent."[36] In Kenya, the anti-missionary origins of the Mau Mau movement cemented a Manichean sensibility that saw insurgents as demons, their Christian victims as martyrs, and the authorities who stood between them as heroes. Colonial secretary Oliver Lyttelton recalled that, as he penned memoranda about Mau Mau, "I would suddenly see a shadow fall across the page—the horned shadow of the Devil himself."[37]

Faith stiffened the resolve of soldiers in the field as well. One company commander in Malaya experienced an impromptu prayer service in the jungle as an oasis of Christian virtue. As he remembered it, "the church walls were the rubber trees rising straight upwards. Behind the walls . . . lurked the legions of Anti-Christ."[38] The military chaplains serving alongside men in uniform doled out spiritual comfort while skirting awkward questions of conscience. A study of active-duty RAF chaplains found that nearly four in ten of those interviewed in the 1960s would raise no objection if the airmen in their unit used torture. "If one can get the truth that way and save lives, I would not protest," one commented. Several chaplains defended "far from pleasant" methods, such as "slapping someone around," so long as they stopped short of sadistic extremes. A Nonconformist chaplain excused moral slippage of this kind as a "problem of applying Christian standards in a non-Christian world."[39]

The humanitarian crises provoked by counterinsurgency opened another route to religious involvement. Hundreds of thousands of people in Malaya and Kenya alike were uprooted by the forced move into militarized settlements; in Kenya, hundreds of thousands more were detained in the camps where officials promised to "rehabilitate" ex-Mau Mau adherents. Many Christians concluded that this massive dislocation provided an opportunity

FIGURE 4.1 Archbishop of Canterbury Geoffrey Fisher, seen here visiting Kenya in 1955, urged the public to trust colonial authorities even as reports of wrongdoing mounted. Kenya Department of Information/Herskovits Library, Northwestern University.

for service—offering medical care and counseling, leading English lessons and welfare classes, building schools and clinics—and also for winning converts. As far as missionaries were concerned, the populations branded as suspect by imperial officials could be seen either as wayward sinners crying out for spiritual guidance or as refugees uprooted by senseless conflicts. That missionaries effectively took sides in those conflicts by carrying out the imperial program of winning "hearts and minds" was overlooked. As long as officials allowed them to deliver welfare and education with a pious bent, missionaries could see work in the resettlement zones and detention camps as God's work.

Mobilizing on an impressive scale, Christians from many denominations helped to keep the machinery of resettlement and incarceration running smoothly. More than four hundred missionaries—some recently expelled from Communist China, others directly recruited from Britain—operated in the New Villages of Malaya.[40] In Kenya, at least fifteen missionaries plied their trade in the detention camps, half a dozen more lived in the new settlements, and another two dozen were spread across community centers in greater Nairobi and mobile welfare units in the countryside. One detention camp, Athi River, was conceived as a full-bore experiment in the power of Christian conversion; several camp administrators belonged to the Moral Rearmament movement and eventually migrated to camps throughout the system.[41] In both colonies, the confessional sensibility of "hearts and minds" campaigns—encouraging civilians to publicly admit and renounce their support for insurgency—aligned with the work of saving souls. So did a Cold War–tinged sense of purpose that saw uprooted communities as uniquely vulnerable to atheistic Communism.[42]

The involvement of British religious institutions meant that many people at home perceived counterinsurgency through the lens of spiritual mission. For every Anglican, Presbyterian, Methodist, or Quaker who went to the colonies, thousands of co-religionists at home were reading stories about their exploits, raising funds to support them, and hearing appeals to join them. Anglican services featured prayers for the missionaries working on the front lines. Picture books for Sunday schools showed Christian workers helping families settle into the Malayan New Villages with hymns and homilies about "the love of the Lord Jesus."[43] Church newspapers drummed up a sense of urgency among potential volunteers and donors. "You now have a chance to help your fellow-Christians in Kenya do the most vital job of all, among the bewildered, distressed, questioning youth of the Kikuyu," read a typical appeal. Getting insurgents to renounce their violent ways was heralded as a demonstration that "the power of the Holy Spirit . . . can still overcome the forces of evil in black or white."[44]

Faith-based campaigns involved heart-rending humanitarian appeals. One pamphlet for Christian Aid featured a photograph of bone-thin Kenyan children in tattered clothes alongside images of huddled masses from Europe and Asia. The BBC spotlighted the group's 1955 Kenya Appeal as a "Week's Good Cause," helping to raise nearly £50,000 from ordinary people as well as corporations like Barclays, Lloyds, and ICI.[45] The missionary response to counterinsurgency blended the centuries-old rhetoric of conversion with the modern preoccupation of rescuing civilians displaced by conflict. The fact that the British government bore much of the responsibility for displacing its own subjects was elided along the way. In this way, the language of "emergency" transformed the uncomfortable reality of ongoing state violence into something like a natural disaster.[46]

In the face of British Christianity's overwhelming public support for colonial war, flashes of dissent like the "Time for Action" pamphlet proved short-lived, drawing counter-criticism from within the church and ultimately receding amid the deluge of pro-government propaganda. No matter how distinguished the pulpits they occupied, clerical radicals always faced resistance in their own backyards. Parishioners organized pilgrimages to telegraph their displeasure with left-leaning sermons, and Members of Parliament called for the dismissal of the most outspoken preachers.[47] In the Anglican case, pressure also came from the heights of the ecclesiastical hierarchy. With Canon Collins, Fisher wrote that he did "everything I can to restrain" him, subjecting the junior cleric to reprimands that turned "very hot and argumentative and fierce."[48]

While a handful of high-profile dissidents grabbed headlines, most Christians discomfited by colonial violence voiced their qualms discreetly. But very few of those with troubled consciences perceived their involvement with violence as an unambiguous wrong. Rather, they saw a clash of competing values, an ethical balancing act most often navigated through private hand-wringing and public reticence.

For some Christians, entanglement with any kind of state authority risked compromising their principles. If missionaries appeared too close to colonial officials, they worried, prospective converts might question their motives and end up resisting the gospel.[49] Others pointed out that material and medical forms of aid were easily decoupled from the spiritual mission they hoped to advance. Was the kind of work done by Christian Aid "really giving the cup of water in Christ's name," one missionary wondered, or merely "sponsoring secular activity under Christian auspices?"[50] For religious pacifists like the Quakers, aid work in wartime was not necessarily out of bounds, but the danger of crossing the line into complicity with violence was ever present. "Those taking up this service," one Quaker leader stressed, "must not feel too prickly about 'security' and the presence of the barbed wire." Another acknowledged that, "to some Friends here at home, their very presence in such a setting implies an unwarrantable compromise."[51]

The heaviest burden on Christian consciences came from flesh-and-blood details about the abuses committed by British authorities. With their ecclesiastical hierarchies and missionary networks stretching across the world, their privileged access to camps and settlements, and their close ties to government officials, religious institutions amassed an impressively complete picture of colonial violence. Reports traveled from ministers and aid workers in the field to higher-ups in London, Oxford, and Edinburgh; missionaries circulated newsletters to their contacts at home; visiting dignitaries caught glimpses and heard rumors of the worst. All of this information gave ample cause for concern.

In Malaya, missionaries who welcomed the opportunity to ply their trade in the New Villages suffered no illusions about how the "villagers" had gotten there. The East Asia secretary of the CMS described the process of forced resettlement in a book published in 1954:

> The first thing a squatter family knew about it was the arrival of a police official with a few Indian or Malay constables, all heavily armed. The family were told in language they could scarcely understand to pull down their home and load the materials on to a waiting truck. If they started to argue they were warned that refusal to obey would mean the burning down of their home. When the demolition was completed the family, with such of their home and their belongings as were transportable, were taken to a clearing within a perimeter fence of barbed wire, shown a piece of bare ground, and told to rebuild their house. This was to be their new home.[52]

In Cyprus, emissaries of the Moral Rearmament Movement heard from the governor himself that British forces had done "terrible things."[53]

The alarms sounded most insistently in Kenya. Christian idealists who set out to "rehabilitate" troubled African souls were soon disillusioned by the realities of the colonial police state. "Some of the camp commandants, and other officials, pour ridicule upon all efforts to change the outlook of the African," a CMS aid worker wrote to a colleague in London in 1955. "They believe in one thing only, and that is force and a firm hand."[54] An Anglican missionary writing to family at home chronicled the horror stories of Kikuyu men who were loyal to the government but nonetheless found themselves trapped behind the barbed wire of detention camps for years.[55] Others noted that the punitive impulse of British policy fed a lawless atmosphere of racial vengeance. "In many areas," another Anglican missionary wrote to his friends and family in 1954, "an average Kikuyu hardly knows which to fear the more—Mau Mau or the Forces of Law and Order. By either he may be robbed or beaten or carried off or killed at any time and there is little chance of redress." He added that "Africans, and especially Kikuyu, are so often messed about, disregarded, treated as though they were of no account, not human beings at all." There was no hint of Christian mercy in counterinsurgency as these missionaries saw it.[56]

As knowledge of violence rippled outward, institutions found themselves confronting difficult choices. For the Church of England, a moment of reckoning arrived as early as January 1953, when the CMS dispatched its Africa secretary, Canon T. F. C. Bewes, to investigate conditions in Kenya.[57] What Bewes saw and heard there was intensely disturbing. Innocent men lay in the hospital with broken bones after beatings inflicted by security forces. One European policeman told Bewes that he extracted information from suspects by "putting an up-turned bucket on a man's head and then beating it up with a metal instrument for up to half an hour," a procedure that left some victims deaf. Other officers admitted using a metal clamp to chop off fingertips and even to castrate. The reign of terror was necessary, they told Bewes, because once ordinary people "were more afraid of us [than the Mau Mau] we shall get the information we want."[58]

Weighing his outrage against a sense of institutional loyalty, Bewes decided to work through the established channels of church and state, setting bureaucratic wheels in motion behind the scenes instead of exposing them to public scrutiny. He first wrote a letter to Kenya's colonial governor, Sir Evelyn Baring, describing the abuses he witnessed. Although Bewes demanded answers, he also deferred to Baring's lofty position and promised to shield him from embarrassment as long as the situation improved. "I am very anxious that information of this kind should not go into the Press," Bewes wrote, "for I am sure that we must do all that we can to prevent inflammation of passions on either side." He even volunteered to "try and put the positive side of anything I have seen" in a press conference before his departure from Nairobi. By confining ugly details to elite circles, Bewes expressed a very establishment sensibility.[59]

The missionary tried to strike a bargain with Baring. In exchange for his silence in public, he expected decisive action to crack down on abuses. Once that happened, Bewes made clear, "I should feel much happier about keeping my mouth shut!"[60] Having spent twenty years as a missionary in Kenya, he also knew that the work of saving souls depended on the good will of colonial officials.[61] So while Bewes continued to press for a more humane counterinsurgency, he did so in an ambivalent way that signaled his reluctance to rupture the alliance between church and state. At a London press conference in February 1953, Bewes mentioned "third-degree methods" but was "unwilling to give many details of such violence or to put his charges into strong language," as the *Manchester Guardian* put it.[62] Addressing a group of parliamentarians in the House of Commons a few weeks later, Bewes obeyed a Tory MP who "warned him" to "keep off the subject" of police brutality "as this would embarrass the government." By first withholding details and then dropping the accusation, Bewes left many MPs with the impression that he had no evidence of wrongdoing.[63]

Bewes's ambivalence fed an atmosphere of doubt about violence in Kenya. But he believed that he had done his "duty" by delivering confidential reports to a series of establishment pillars: first Baring, then Fisher, and finally Colonial Secretary Oliver Lyttelton.[64] Bewes took his cues from Fisher, another institutionalist who preferred discreet consultations to public contretemps. The archbishop encouraged Bewes's instincts against whistleblowing even when all the signs from Kenya pointed to a cover-up. "I can conceive good reasons why the result of the inquest should be kept secret," Fisher reasoned about the case of a man who died in police custody. "It is not merely that the authorities might be embarrassed. It is possible that if they are trying to build up the morale of the Police and get rid of bad things like this, publication of a report . . . might hinder and not help."[65] When a woman in Oxfordshire sent Fisher a *Daily Worker* story detailing atrocities in Kenya, the archbishop replied with a homily about the irresponsibility of the newspaper's editor. "His right course would be himself, privately, to approach the authorities and seek to strengthen their hands in tackling any such practices, if they exist, of which they would certainly disapprove. That is a far more useful and responsible thing to do than to publish a letter of this sort in his columns."[66] For Fisher, as for Bewes, political virtue was deferential and discreet.

One of the ways that churchmen justified not going public was to impose an exacting standard of proof. Even in private, they raised endless questions about the reliability of the stories they received. They also hinted that anything short of legally admissible evidence lessened their obligation to act. In a statement drawn up after his meeting with Lyttelton, Bewes stressed, "I have no evidence that could be produced in a Court of Law, as to extreme measures taken by the police."[67] Seven months later, Bewes told Fisher that letters he received from missionaries in Kenya confirmed "a good deal" of the atrocities described in the *Daily Worker*. But, he added, "the real difficulty is to be able to give properly certified evidence and to be sure that it is also up to date."[68] The bishop of Chichester, George Bell, likewise observed that "it is extremely difficult to get at the true facts of what is happening in Kenya."[69]

The insistence on clinging to uncertainty is curious since colonial officials privately admitted to wrongdoing. As Baring told Bewes after the *Daily Worker* article appeared, "there no doubt are things done by the Security

Forces which should not be done."[70] In a conversation with Bell around the same time, Baring acknowledged abuses by career police officers, soldiers in the Kenya Regiment, and settler volunteers in the Kenya Police Reserve.[71] But Baring blunted the impact of these disclosures by playing up the threat of misinformation from anticolonial propagandists. With so many "mischief-makers willing to make false accusations," the governor warned, gleaning the truth about violence was no simple task.[72] Exploiting an atmosphere of ambiguity about facts, officials made churchmen less confident about pressing their claims in public.

Theology, too, offered justifications for proceeding cautiously and quietly in response to violence. Confronting a student who wanted him to condemn the Mau Mau campaign, Fisher preached the virtues of restraint. Venting outrage brushed against the sins of judgmentalism, egoism, and wrath. "One of the real evils of to-day," Fisher declared, "is that people jump to wrong conclusions about everything and explode their indignation on things great and small."[73] At other times, the archbishop projected an almost fatalistic acceptance of violence. Savage behavior by British forces came as no great surprise in a conflict where savagery reigned on all sides. Responding to the gory details related by Bewes, Fisher sighed: "As always when you get a sinful condition like this, all kinds of other things break out all round it and the thing becomes extremely difficult to control." A few months later, Fisher commented that the war in Kenya "is a Civil War—evil things are done."[74] Against the backdrop of brutal attacks against Kikuyu Christians and British settlers, the archbishop saw Kenya as a place where conventional morality no longer applied.

This equivocal attitude to atrocity was shared by other Anglicans. A long-time CMS missionary in Kenya, Peter Bostock, revealed his ambivalence to a London colleague in November 1953. Despite the steady pressure exerted by churchmen on government officials in private, Bostock admitted that "excesses and atrocities by members of the Security Forces" seemed to be increasing in frequency. "I believe that if the truth were known," he wrote, "Europeans have been guilty of many more cold-blooded murders of Africans in the past twelve months than Mau Mau have been guilty of murdering Europeans." And yet, he refused to expose British malfeasance in public, taking a fatalistic position on the inevitability of violence just as Fisher did: "It seems to me that we are witnessing the sorry spectacle that unredeemed human nature is utterly ugly whatever the color of the skin, and feelings run high." Bostock also justified his silence on the grounds that forces more sinister than British imperialism lurked in the world. Even as he acknowledged that British crimes matched Mau Mau crimes in their brutality, Bostock insisted, "When all is said and done, I consider that our Government is much better than most Governments in the world, and there are many enemies who wish to discredit the British before world opinion." The temptation to "raise a stink" through publicity had to be resisted because "such a course would only play into the hands of the enemies of our way of life."[75]

From this mix of motivations and rationalizations, a familiar rhetorical line took shape when Anglican authorities spoke in public. Colonial officials were heeding their calls for a more humane war, they claimed, and conditions in Kenya were improving as a result. In a book published in 1953, Bewes wrote that "talk of third degree methods is happily dying down."[76] Fisher assured an ecclesiastical gathering in February 1954 that the church "has been using all its influence and is now satisfied that everything that can be done by the controlling power is being done."[77] In fact, Anglican prelates had simply decided that communicating their concerns to the Colonial Office and Government House marked the end of their intervention. Behind closed doors, Fisher pledged his influence "to see that any further discussion is damped down." He maintained this attitude even as a Church of Scotland minister in the colony warned that the security forces had yet to change their ways, as CMS officials released the "Time for Action" pamphlet, and as the bishop of Mombasa privately admitted to "the continued occurrence of incidents of an untoward nature." Whistleblowers within the Anglican world were discouraged and isolated by a culture that emanated from the uppermost levels of the hierarchy. Faced with a choice between humanitarian activism and genteel collusion, the established church overwhelmingly behaved as an arm of the establishment.[78]

So, to a surprising degree, did a prominent bastion of Christian Dissent. The most celebrated of all whistleblowers in the Kenya conflict, social worker Eileen Fletcher, was a Quaker. But when she went public with her account of the detention camps in 1956, the Society of Friends raced to distance itself from her testimony and even discredit it. The man coordinating Quaker efforts in the colony blasted Fletcher in the press, telling a Reuters correspondent in Nairobi that she had given a "totally unfair picture" riddled with "striking inconsistencies." Back in London, the chair of the Friends Service Council's Kenya Committee told the *Times* that Fletcher suffered from an "unbalance" that recognized "little else but injustice and oppression." He also stressed that she had gone out to Kenya as a government employee rather than a missionary under Quaker auspices.[79]

The reputation of British Quakers for rigidly principled pacifism was always an oversimplification. In the era of the Second World War, some Friends celebrated the "martial virtues" instilled by service in uniform and by youth organizations such as the Boy Scouts.[80] Even so, the vehemence of the reaction against Fletcher was striking. The expression of individual conscience, hallowed as "witnessing" or "testimony," long occupied a place at the heart of Quaker tradition. Yet instead of respecting Fletcher's statement as a moral act, Quaker administrators denigrated her as emotionally unstable. She "must suffer from inhibitions & repressions of long standing," one commented. She has "proved something of a problem child all round," another observed. Yet another deemed her revelations "at best, one-sided, and at worst, the work of someone who is embittered." They implied that, while other Quakers in Kenya were doing difficult work to improve conditions, Fletcher was simply lashing out.[81]

Even if things were as bad as Fletcher said, her coreligionists reasoned that the tactic of exposé was counterproductive. A Quaker working in Kenya predicted that Fletcher would set back the humanitarian cause because settlers there were so resistant to criticism from "newcomers or outsiders."[82] Others complained that Fletcher had launched a partisan crusade that could only alienate the government in power. She brought her story to the left-wing newspaper *Peace News*, after all, and the MCF crowd took up the issue in Parliament.[83] Fatalism offered further justification for silence. Given the brutality of the insurgency, one missionary observed, there was "reason to be thankful that the situation did not bring out greater cruelty and repression than it has done." Amid such horrors, what gave Fletcher the right to insist on clear-cut standards of right and wrong? Kenya in the age of insurgency was no place for moral clarity. Rather, it was a place where, in the words of one Quaker administrator, "good and evil are inextricably and frighteningly interwoven."[84]

An array of relativistic evasions muted the Quaker response to violence. One administrator claimed that the treatment of Mau Mau detainees "does not compare too unfavorably" with the "maltreatment and even beatings" meted out to British convicts in prisons at home. Another acknowledged that extracting confessions in detention camps bore the hallmarks of a totalitarian "police state," but insisted on the benevolence of the British version compared to its Iron Curtain counterparts. This was Christian social work, not political indoctrination, as evidenced by the fact that confessions had "a tremendous spiritual effect on those concerned." Pitting an empire of faith against an empire of atheism excused many sins.[85]

Even as they tried to undercut Fletcher's allegations, the administrators at Friends House in London quietly wondered whether they had become complicit in violence. "For some time," one admitted, "I have been feeling that our 'eyes and ears' on the spot have not been sufficiently active or observant as to some of the injustices going on at the present time." The head of the Kenya Committee questioned "whether we have done enough in the past to make clear our intense dislike of such actions."[86] Quaker leaders recognized that aid work in counterinsurgency involved a precarious balancing act. As missionaries busied themselves with the workaday demands of schools and clinics, they had to weigh the value of "long-term solutions" against the danger of "acquiescence in wrongdoing." Their zeal for reconciliation, a key concept in Quaker thought, risked achieving peace at the price of allowing injustice to flourish.[87]

When Quaker leaders spoke out against violence in Kenya at last, they did so only because ordinary believers across the country expressed outrage at the statements made in their name. As Fletcher undertook a speaking tour of meeting houses from Cornwall to Hull, her supporters flooded Friends House with petitions demanding a forceful denunciation of British atrocities. "Are we so compromised by our work in Kenya," one dissident asked, "that we must not speak as a Society against flagrant injustice?" Another complained that the ideal of reconciliation had been warped "to give more support to any evil system . . . than anyone who opposes evil with vigor." After a month of such protests, the national Quaker body, the Meeting of Sufferings, finally sent a letter to the Colonial Office condemning abuses in the detention system. Even this statement failed to defend Fletcher and accepted government claims that "much has already been done to remedy" abuses by security forces. Mirroring divisions within the Church of England, voices of protest in the Quaker community had to contend with an institutionalist elite bent on defusing controversy and dampening conflict. For Anglican and Quaker leaders alike, deference and discretion overrode the claims of conscience.[88]

Casuistry and Complicity

Genteel distaste for confrontation was a powerful counterweight to humanitarian concern. Like any other institution, churches were subject to pressures from the outside world and shaped by the social aspirations of its leaders. But Christian quietude in the face of colonial violence was not only expressed in secular terms. Believers often justified their position theologically, balancing the virtues and vices of whistleblowing against the virtues and vices of participation in counterinsurgency. Constraining dissent involved a moral calculus.

For all the sanctity that Protestant tradition accorded to individual conscience, theologians long grappled with the difficulties raised by treating the inner voice as a guide to behavior. If conscience was a kind of common sense, accessible to everyone on their own terms, what did that mean for values such as authority, stability, and community?[89] How could intuitive pangs of conscience be tested against other, and possibly more rational, sources of moral knowledge? Questions like these were the lifeblood of casuistry: the application of moral principles to particular cases to determine the proper course of conduct.[90] Beginning in the seventeenth century, the practice of divine casuists issuing guidance to laypeople evolved into a variety of literary and legal texts aimed at training individuals to forecast the consequences of their actions. Advice columns, epistolary novels, and statute books came to reflect post-Lockean skepticism about the existence of any innate moral sense. They sought to discipline vague moral impulses with finely graded distinctions and case-by-case exceptions.[91]

The secularization of casuistry mirrored its decline in theological practice.[92] But in the first half of the twentieth century, anxieties about the radical individualism of conscience staged a revival in British religious thought. One reason for the resurgence of what was now called "Christian ethics" or "moral philosophy" is that the new sciences of mind drew attention to the dark and irrational forces lurking behind ostensibly moral reasoning. Another is that the emergence of a new social category in the First World War, the conscientious objector, dramatized the anarchic dangers of letting conscience run free against states and armies. It was in this atmosphere of instability that Protestant thinkers once again urged believers to question, parse, and analyze their moral sensibilities before acting on them. As one Anglican theologian of this generation put it, the conscience was not an "infallible guide" but a "delicate instrument."[93]

A recurring assertion in theological texts of the 1930s, 1940s, and 1950s was that attacking established institutions represented a grave and potentially sinful step. The claims of conscience "cannot be fulfilled in isolation," one treatise warned, and any Christian who tried to do so ran the "danger of becoming a crank and an eccentric." Another cautioned that "free and vigorous criticism . . . all too easily degenerates into cheap and facile disparagement."[94] The most visible proponent of subordinating moral impulses to social stability was Kenneth Kirk, the Regius Professor of Moral and Pastoral Theology at Oxford from 1933 to 1938 and Anglican bishop of Oxford from 1937 to

1954, whose books were standard texts for "any Anglican priest ordained before 1950."[95] In Kirk's view, the laws of the state had a prior claim on Christian
obedience so long as they were constitutionally legitimate and reasonably
just. Even when those conditions failed, Kirk argued, "it may be part of the
Christian's duty to obey [anyway] in order to avoid scandal or disturbance."
Subjective judgments of right and wrong had to yield to the higher values of
respect for authority and the cohesion of the social order.[96]

   This mistrust of moral dissension, so well-suited to the needs of a wartime state, was partly the product of wartime imperatives. The theology of
deference that Kirk perfected in the 1920s bore the traces of his horrified response to a polarized home front in the First World War, when he served as
a chaplain with the British Army. Kirk's later sermons recalling this period
bemoan the pervasive cynicism that undermined trust in the ruling elite. "We
lost confidence in everyone, we lost confidence in our leaders, and all sorts of
evil rumors grew up about them . . . . Every hint, every slip, every discrepancy
of conduct was magnified by infidel minds to tarnish the reputation of a general, or a Minister of the Crown." Suspicion of the nation's leaders revealed
a lack of faith and a refusal to recognize the goodness in a divinely ordained
world. "A faithful soul would believe that with all our faults and follies—
and we all have them—everyone of us, from the Cabinet downwards, was
trying to do his best." So Kirk urged his flock to go forth "and try and spread
again that faith in our leaders," casting the maintenance of morale as a sacred
duty.[97] The elevation of confidence over conscience also reflected what Kirk
termed his "repugnance to Bolshevism." For Kirk, communism transgressed
by incarnating the worst vices of individualism: self-righteousness, suspicious-
ness, mistrust of others. Trapped in the disenchanted world of dialectical materialism, the communist "imputes evil where there is none" and cannot help
glimpsing "ulterior motives and hidden malevolence." Dissenters of all kinds
risked slipping into the same misanthropic, corrosive sensibility.[98]

   Imprinted by decades-old traumas of mobilization and dissent, the moral
guidance offered to Anglicans in the 1950s sacralized deference to authority.
Breaking the social contract for reasons of personal conviction required overwhelming certainty. Giving the example of a servant who doubts the morality
of an order, Kirk instructed that "its legality may be presumed" as long as
"the master is habitually law-abiding and there is no clear evidence that the
command is illegal."[99] This was, in effect, a theology of the status quo. The
deference granted to authority, the value placed on maintaining community,
and the demanding standard of proof required to challenge either one offered
manifold justifications for inaction in the face of injustice. As "red vicar"

Stanley Evans observed, the casuist tradition had been warped into a prop of unquestioning civil obedience, preventing British Christians from grappling with moral problems while denying the right of rebellion to oppressed peoples in Malaya and Kenya.[100]

The Church of England played an outsized role in shaping Britain's theology of conscience. This reflected, among other things, the Anglican effort to craft an accessible, undogmatic, interdenominational brand of Protestantism that might plausibly speak for British society as a whole.[101] But skepticism of moral individualism was broadcast by other traditions as well. Quaker literature dwelled on the inevitability of compromising ethical ideals, at least to some extent, as long as one lived in the world. Impassioned denunciations of wrongdoing shut down the possibility of influence over future decisions; they also, sometimes, camouflaged self-regarding sentiments with the sheen of righteousness. "It is all too easy to condemn the actions of others without charity and without proper weighing of the issues," one Friends pamphlet cautioned. "One's motives on such occasions can be very mixed and not unconnected with pride."[102] Another Quaker publication pointedly noted that criticizing others ("the attitude of protest") tended to conflict with Christian virtues of empathy and forgiveness ("the attitude of reconciliation").[103]

While liberal Protestants dwelled on the frailty of moral subjectivity, their evangelical and conservative counterparts defended hierarchies of authority more forcefully. In his celebrated BBC lectures, broadcast in 1943 and reprinted many times afterward, C. S. Lewis observed that the Christian society envisioned by the New Testament is "always insisting on obedience," beginning with "obedience (and outward marks of respect) from all of us to properly appointed magistrates."[104] The divinely ordained state, presumptively worthy of pious obedience, was a fixture of evangelical ethics. One theologian proclaimed that "any proper authority" must be "willingly accepted" and "obeyed." A Presbyterian divine observed that the evangelists of the New Testament enjoined loyalty even to the pagan Roman Empire, in a sign of the value they placed on compliance with the state.[105]

Although the language of casuistry was less explicit than in Anglicanism, the same habits of fine-grained moral reasoning found a foothold in other traditions too. A Nonconformist missionary who witnessed what he described as "unofficial cruelty" in Kenya's detention camps provides a case in point. Why did he continue to profess "sincere admiration for Government's methods"? First, he insisted that formal policies prohibited violence and that camp administrators enforced them as best they could. Second, he suggested that even well-meaning camp workers were imperfect sinners like anyone else: "the human element always comes into every situation." Finally, and most importantly, he insisted that the good done by saving souls outweighed the suffering inflicted along the way. Even detainees deprived of their possessions and cut off from their families for years could find happiness by embracing the gospel. "Their faces were often aglow, their spirits radiant," he claimed. Transcending the hellish reality of the camps, faith offered a fore-taste of heaven, where "the wood and barbed wire compound gates [will] be "exchanged for the pearly gates."[106] The conversion narrative was a microcosm of the larger effort to transfigure inhumane wars into spiritual undertakings.

Aiding Counterinsurgency: The British Red Cross

Relief for victims of counterinsurgency did not come exclusively through reli-gious channels. Though founded by devout Christians, the international Red Cross movement adopted secular principles of neutrality, impartiality, and independence from its beginnings in the 1860s. Its leaders pledged to refrain from moral judgments to maintain their apolitical status and secure cooper-ation from warring states. While religious bodies might praise some conflicts as righteous or condemn others as unjust, the Red Cross has traditionally avoided the question of why wars happen and whether they are justified. This trade-off lies at the heart of "classical" humanitarianism: making war civilized by giving up on the dream of preventing it or ending it.[107]

And yet, even without passing judgment or seeking converts, humani-tarian groups like the Red Cross have often occupied the same space as re-ligious aid organizations. Both kinds of institutions appeal to the claims of conscience, to feelings of compassion and empathy, and to transcendental values that sanctify the relief of suffering.[108] Spiritual and secular aid workers alike have confronted the world beyond the West with a paternalistic sense of mission. In Britain's empire after 1945, missionary and humanitarian groups both cared for colonial subjects uprooted by counterinsurgency. Both also risked compromising their values on the front lines of colonial war.

What constrained the Red Cross movement from speaking truth to power was, above all, its entanglement with the nation-state. By the end of the nineteenth century, Red Cross societies at the national level controlled the lion's share of relief funds and carried out the bulk of aid work for the benefit of their own citizens. Meanwhile, the Geneva-based international committee—which itself often followed the call of Swiss national interests—saw little to gain from criticizing other governments or seeking to act without their permission. The Holocaust, in which the German Red Cross actually participated and the international committee proved reluctant to intervene, remains the most notorious case of humanitarian aid compromised by national power.[109] The response to colonial violence after 1945 exposed the same marked deference to state authority. When the international committee sent Red Cross observers to Kenya and Cyprus in the late 1950s, their remit was carefully circumscribed, their findings kept secret, and their biases strikingly pro-colonial. The result was an implicit stamp of approval, in the public eye, for the British way of counterinsurgency.[110]

The British Red Cross Society (BRCS) based in London carried out the day-to-day operations of counterinsurgency relief. More than fifty nurses and welfare officers from the British chapter were stationed in the New Villages of Malaya.[111] Another seventeen British aid workers went to Kenya, some in the detention camps and others in the Kikuyu reserves.[112] In Cyprus, where the absence of a massive resettlement project lessened the need for manpower, the national chapter sent four nurses along with an administrator and a Greek-speaking liaison.[113] Like their missionary counterparts, BRCS workers projected a benevolent image of British power that contrasted with the iron fist of counterinsurgency. They distributed food and clothing, cared for the sick and wounded, gave lessons in childcare and hygiene, and fought the spread of disease.

Aid workers were also the bearers of lofty ideals. In accord with the humanitarian principle of neutrality, BRCS nurses treated the occasional wounded insurgent as well as British soldiers and refused to disclose enemy locations to the authorities.[114] A nurse who worked in Malaya and Cyprus summarized the organization's philosophy: "You shouldn't take sides . . . . If you had a guerrilla in one bed and a British soldier in another bed, you would treat them both the same way." Neutrality went to the heart of the organization's identity, the foundation of its claim to "bridge the gulf between nations, linking them by mutual acts of kindness," as a 1956 fundraising appeal put it. Britons were encouraged to take pride in their national chapter precisely on the grounds that it transcended national ties. As a laudatory BBC report proclaimed in 1951, the BRCS was "dedicated to the suffering humanity of the world without reference to color, creed, or caste."[115]

These doctrinal pronouncements appeared to leave little room for ambiguity. But what did neutrality mean in practice for an organization so closely tied to the British state? The chairman of the BRCS, Lord Woolton, was a Tory politician and businessman tapped by Winston Churchill to run the Conservative Party organization from 1945 to 1951. The vice chair, Lady Limerick, was born into a distinguished military family that traced its lineage back to the first duke of Wellington. The pedigree of BRCS administrators in the colonies was just as distinguished: the Malayan branch was headed by the chief justice of the colony, the Kenya branch by a former mayor of Nairobi, and the Cyprus branch by the deputy governor. Links between the ruling elite and the BRCS went so deep because the organization was seen as a valuable propaganda vehicle. If one wanted to boost "British prestige," Woolton told a fundraising audience in 1957, "I don't know anything that's doing so much to help it, all over the world, as the work of the British Red Cross." Imagining medical care as a kind of soft power exemplified the wider attempt after 1945 to repackage British influence through humanitarian service.[116]

If officials saw missionaries as useful allies in their effort to win hearts and minds, they welcomed the help of BRCS workers even more warmly. In Malaya, Kenya, and Cyprus, the colonial government invited aid workers to the front and paid their salaries. One of Templer's men praised them lavishly for "establishing confidence between the Government and the people."[117] A district officer in Kenya opined that "one Red Cross worker was of more value than a battalion of soldiers in combating Mau Mau influence, and she is less costly than that in any case."[118] In Cyprus, where the military base at Episkopi doubled as headquarters for BRCS programs across the Middle East, the militarization of humanitarianism was even more pronounced. Despite the national chapter's objections, Red Cross jeeps with a nurse in the driver's seat often had a Tommy with a machine gun in the passenger seat.[119] The colonial governor enthused that BRCS relief would "strengthen his position" against EOKA by providing a "balance" to "strong arm tactics" and showcasing the "benevolent attitude of the British people."[120] It is no surprise that officials saw the BRCS fitting so comfortably into the war effort. While cultivating an unthreatening public image, the Red Cross—like many humanitarian organizations after the Second World War—operated according to military logics of logistics, supply, and discipline.[121]

Besides financial support, state backing gave the BRCS an entrée into conflict zones where civilians otherwise had little access. This privileged position cemented the organization's claim to preeminence in the humanitarian industry—and to donations from the general public—over rivals like the St. John Ambulance Association. But occupying a front-row seat to counterinsurgency brought complications as well.

The dilemma was felt most acutely in Kenya, where evidence of neglect and cruelty overwhelmed the BRCS from the earliest days of the Emergency. Touring the detention camps in 1954, the organization's director of overseas operations, Joan Whittington, recorded a succession of horrors in her diary. At Kajiado, where more than 1,200 were detained, she noted "very bad conditions, no disinfectant, swarms of flies, buckets for [latrines] . . . All sleeping on concrete floor with no mats, babies looked ill." At Nyeri, there was a "great shortage of water." At Rumuruti, where the prison walls crawled with bugs and latrine buckets overflowed, authorities imprisoned children because their parents refused to reveal information.[122] Another Red Cross worker described the "quite horrifying" transit camp at Nakuru, where detainees slept without bedding on rain-soaked floors, as "unfit to house animals." Yet another aid worker warned that crowding in the isolated, arid reserves—where authorities were transferring Kikuyu agricultural workers and their families en masse—threatened to cause a famine.[123]

As they testified to an emerging humanitarian crisis, BRCS observers noted that deliberate violence posed as great a danger as bureaucratic neglect. The "extreme view" among settlers, one noted in 1953, was "that the Kikuyu tribe should be wiped out."[124] The brutality meted out by security forces drew the notice of some aid workers. Whittington referred to the "bad reputation and lack of adequate discipline" among soldiers and police officers. Another BRCS worker, stationed in Maua in 1958, told Limerick that Africans in custody "have quite a tough time . . . the interminable herding, interrogating, beatings, & so on." While expressing hope that the colonial administration would adopt a "more humane" policy than it had in the early years of the conflict, she did not seem optimistic.[125]

While disturbing information flowed into BRCS headquarters from the field, activists at home urged the organization to take action before it was too late. The member of a BRCS branch in Bexhill worried that Africans shipped to the reserves "and unable to get sufficient food there are faced with mass starvation. That some officials advocate starvation as collective punishment to some Mau Mau crimes seems grimly unjust and unworthy of anybody claiming to be a member of civilization."[126] Activist cleric Michael Scott wrote the Red Cross, too, citing "very distressing reports about near famine conditions" and asking if any relief operations had yet been organized.[127]

Some of the most damning and detailed accounts of British violence came from the Geneva-based International Committee of the Red Cross (ICRC). Undertaking fact-finding missions in response to allegations of torture, delegates from Geneva visited detention camps in Kenya between 1957 and 1959. Because ICRC officials believed that openly challenging state authority would run afoul of their commitment to neutrality, they did not publicize the findings, delivering confidential accounts of their concerns to the British government instead. In their first report on Kenya, in 1957, ICRC officials demanded an immediate end to the use of whipping as punishment, although conditions in the camps were deemed adequate otherwise. In a second report, delivered at the height of the Hola Camp controversy in 1959, they issued a far more sweeping criticism against "the abuses committed in applying corporal punishment and subjecting certain detained persons to brutal treatment during questioning." This observation did not go unnoticed by the BRCS; someone in the organization's London headquarters flagged the passage with heavy markings in pencil.[128]

The BRCS received repeated warnings that counterinsurgency in Kenya was unleashing a humanitarian catastrophe. How did the organization respond? Its efforts to combat hunger and disease likely succeeded in easing the worst effects of both. By the middle of 1956, aid workers in hard-hit areas were distributing hundreds of penicillin doses and thousands of bowls of soup every month.[129] Despite their enviable access to government officials, however, BRCS officials never pressed them on the root causes of suffering: the policies that displaced whole populations, separated detainees from their families, and restricted those left behind to overcrowded zones of confinement. On the contrary, the BRCS championed these policies, participated enthusiastically in executing them, and brushed back criticism with gusto. Even as the organization relieved some suffering, it helped to keep a cruel and broken system running smoothly, not least by throwing its reputation behind the claim that the counterinsurgency met humanitarian standards.

In public, BRCS administrators gave their seal of approval to forced labor in the detention camps, promising that "hard agricultural or construction work" would "purge those detained of the Mau Mau poison." In private, they advocated keeping Kikuyu men behind the barbed wire indefinitely, so that women left at home could be exposed to the benign influence of Western aid workers for "as much time as possible."[130] BRCS officials also insisted, in language streaked with racist condescension, that food, clothes, and housing in the camps represented a vast improvement over the usual standards of Kikuyu life. The detention camps were "so comfortable," one administrator improbably claimed, that they amounted to a reward for rebellion. "It obviously paid to be a bad boy."[131]

Above all, the BRCS worked to shield the colonial government from scrutiny. When the ICRC proposed visiting Kenyan camps and prisons, their British counterparts insisted that they had the situation under control and that "essential humanitarian rules were being observed."[132] BRCS officials also maintained that the torture ban in the 1949 Geneva Convention did not apply to Kenya. The Emergency was no civil war, they argued, but mere "banditry"

FIGURE 4.2 Performing humanitarianism: a British Red Cross worker in a detention camp, Kenya, 1957. ICRC Archives.

or a "tribal outbreak" to be dealt with, like any other criminal offense, under the jurisdiction of the sovereign authorities. This was the very same argument used by colonial officials to thwart independent investigations. Not coincidentally, BRCS administrators coordinated their response to Geneva with the Colonial Office.[133] "Endeavoring to interfere in what a nation might well consider its domestic province," Lady Limerick argued, would compromise the ICRC's "unique privileged position" of neutrality.[134]

In the end, British government officials—facing the glare of negative publicity at home and overseas—decided to admit international observers to the detention camps in Kenya after all.[135] Yet, even as these visits took place, the BRCS continued to run interference for the empire. To avoid setting a precedent, the organization's leaders emphasized that the British government had voluntarily invited the ICRC to Kenya, to provide "help and advice" in an informal way, rather than acceding to an "official" inspection mandated by the Geneva Convention.[136] The British chapter also insisted that the visitors from Geneva confine themselves to the narrowly defined issue of living conditions for detainees. How detainees ended up behind barbed wire in the first place, how their families managed to survive for years without a breadwinner, and whether individuals actually convicted of Mau Mau-related offenses received fair trials were all deemed out of bounds.[137] Finally, in concert with the British government, the BRCS demanded that the reports written by ICRC observers remain secret. Long after those observers went home, the British organization sternly warned the ICRC against publicizing its findings or even sharing them with other humanitarian groups.[138]

The BRCS had good reason to react defensively to scrutiny of the camp system. From the earliest days of the Emergency, the organization was deeply entangled with it. BRCS workers observed most screening operations, during which security forces interrogated suspects, and assumed a degree of responsibility for the care of detainees behind the barbed wire. Some camps received daily visits from BRCS workers carrying out medical inspections. At least one nurse comforted children with blankets and milk while interrogators assaulted their parents.[139]

Even when they witnessed inhumane conditions, BRCS workers rationalized and defended the actions of the colonial state, which they saw as a bulwark against the pernicious threat of African terrorism. At every level, the organization replicated the attitude of the authorities, treating all Kikuyu as presumptively suspect and excusing British transgressions as well-intentioned efforts to combat savagery. Whittington, who railed against the "Mau Mau scourge," complained that international observers paid far more attention to detainees than to the disfigured victims of Mau Mau attacks. She felt alienated and disgusted by those she was supposed to care for: "very wild looking people," she wrote in her diary. Whittington believed that, if children went hungry when British authorities detained their parents, the detainees were to blame because "the African does not put the child first."[140] The aid worker in Maua who witnessed security forces beating suspects likewise saw little cause to blame the authorities. Violence against Africans, she thought, was "unpleasant to think about but, I suppose, inevitable under the circumstances." The leaders of Mau Mau were "black Hitlers." Operating as an extension of the colonial state at war, the BRCS absorbed its logics and prejudices.[141]

These attitudes flowed from the highest echelons of the organization. For Lady Limerick, mounting knowledge of British abuses never translated into a sense of obligation, much less a sense of urgency. When she visited a detention camp in 1958, Limerick noted that newly arrived detainees "sleep on the ground with a couple of rugs, 50 to a hut"; visiting another camp a few days later, Limerick watched female detainees forced to squat before a seated panel of interrogators. What stirred her outrage was not the behavior of British officials—she thought they did their best with an "extremely difficult job"—but rather the "scurrilous and unjustifiable attacks" they had to endure from journalists and MPs at home.[142] Back in London, when apprised of the beatings that accompanied interrogations in Maua, Limerick expressed neither surprise nor outrage. Instead, she worried that the security situation might result in "added work" for the Red Cross nurse on site. She also waxed rhapsodic about the local flora: "I can imagine how beautiful the country will be beginning to look with those lovely blue delphiniums out on the hills."[143]

In Cyprus, too, the BRCS resisted acting on evidence of neglect and abuse. Here again, some of the most damning observations were gathered by observers with the International Committee of the Red Cross. On a 1957 visit to Pyla camp, a delegate from Geneva registered "numerous complaints" of "harsh treatment suffered during questioning by the police" and noted "actual traces of such treatment" himself. While he confined these observations to a private report in accordance with Red Cross policy, he publicly complained that British authorities had barred him from the police stations where interrogations—and, reputedly, the worst violence—took place. On a second visit to Pyla the following year, the same observer found further evidence of beatings by British troops along with leaky roofs, dirty lavatories, and stagnant wastewater.[144]

Far from expressing concern, the BRCS again rushed to protect the counterinsurgency from interference. One aid worker stationed on the island, a veteran of the Special Branch in Malaya, dismissed Cypriot "tales of brutality" as "silly lies" and "wild charges."[145] When the ICRC first proposed visiting the sites where insurgent suspects were held, British Red Cross administrators insisted that the colonial government would set the conditions and that only British aid workers would carry out any relief efforts afterward. BRCS officials protested, vehemently, when word of the international inspections made it into the press. They expressed outrage when their counterparts in Geneva proposed sending supplies to make life more comfortable for the detainees. They even tried to undercut sympathy for EOKA suspects by urging support for the "victims of Greek aggression" as well.[146]

The BRCS followed the government line, too, in casting doubt on the relevance of humanitarian norms in anticolonial uprisings. This went beyond parsing the language of the Geneva Conventions to questioning even the hallowed principle of neutrality. As the group's chairman, Lord Woolton, saw it, "EOKA is a rebel organization in a British position and is, therefore, engaged in a civil war . . . . These people are rebels who come under an entirely different classification from the neutrality that the Red Cross is charged to show in time of war." Although other BRCS leaders did not put the case in precisely those terms, the sentiment lurking behind Woolton's opinion was widely shared. Stateless insurgents, attacking the empire from within, did not merit the same consideration as more traditional enemies.[147]

In short, the British Red Cross amassed detailed reports about abuses by British authorities, kept them from the public, and did nothing to rein them in behind the scenes. On the contrary, BRCS higher-ups worked energetically to airbrush the image of counterinsurgency, thwart investigations by non-British "outsiders," and chip away at the protections which existed for the benefit of detainees. Little wonder that one ICRC official was struck by parallels with the darkest chapter of Red Cross history. "I do not see a difference," he remarked in 1955, "in the position of the British Red Cross and the position, 20 years ago, of the German Red Cross concerning the Concentration Camps in Germany."[148]

It is conventional to describe humanitarian work in terms of painful, inescapable trade-offs, through the language of "moral dilemmas" and "hard choices."[149] The Red Cross movement has long taken a distinctive line on one dilemma in particular: whether to speak out or remain silent in the face of atrocity. Already in 1948, as criticism of its response to the Holocaust was mounting, the ICRC cast doubt on the value of naming and shaming: "For the Committee to protest publicly would have been not only to outstep its functions, but also to lose thereby all chance of pursuing them, by creating an immediate breach with the government concerned."[150] As rival aid organizations in later years advocated a more vocal response to wrongdoing, Red Cross leaders continued to insist on the priority of gaining access to people in need. Public condemnation, they argued, was counterproductive. It might vent emotion but was unlikely to change the behavior of rogue states (except, perhaps, to turn them against humanitarian assistance). For many Red Cross administrators, in other words, this particular sort of choice did not appear very hard at all.[151]

The value placed on discretion in Red Cross culture helps to explain why the British chapter responded as it did to counterinsurgency. Working with governments to deliver aid has long been the default position of Red Cross organizations everywhere—a far cry from issuing pronouncements on the moral quandaries of warfare. But this is not only, or even mainly, a story about making necessary compromises to achieve higher goals. What kept BRCS officials quiet in the face of counterinsurgency's horrors was not neutrality but partisanship. They hardly felt confined by discretion when publicity might advance British interests, which is why cheery, white-uniformed BRCS workers regularly appeared in newspaper reports and propaganda films. Unlike their counterparts in religious aid organizations, BRCS administrators did not even pretend to wrestle with ethical dilemmas or weigh competing values. Their faith in the justice of the British cause went unquestioned.

Moral language was ubiquitous in the age of counterinsurgency. Christians described ongoing struggles between good and evil while humanitarians spoke of the urgent obligation to help human beings in need. Although both kinds of language promised moral clarity, they actually led to endless moral compromise. Christian warriors found justification for violence in the Manichaean stakes of a crusade against atheism and terrorism. Conscience-stricken Christians saw so much sin on all sides, and in their own potential role as dissenters, that they chose incrementalism and fatalism over speaking out. Aid workers conceded the barest definition of humanity to the empire's enemies, then denied their political legitimacy and their claim to be treated justly.[152] Appealing to morality proved far more effective at rationalizing behavior than changing it. Invoking lofty values—even if only to reason them away—shrouded complicity in the trappings of reluctance, benevolence, and care. By entertaining the claims of conscience, those who enabled colonial violence could at least say that they did so with the best of intentions.

PART III

Living with Violence

5

Covering Colonial War

AN AFRICAN MAN speaks into a microphone on the streets of Nairobi. The device is held in front of him by Edward Ward, a star BBC correspondent, as Ward's wife Marjorie, a BBC producer, looks on. The scene, captured in an indistinct *Radio Times* photograph, heralded a rare occurrence.[1] From the heart of a conflict zone, a colonial subject was discussing colonial war for a mass British audience. This was not just empty symbolism: the Wards' 1955 broadcasts on radio and television lent a conspicuously sympathetic ear to black Kenyans and attracted controversy as a result. The rocky reception of their reporting reveals a larger truth: news about counterinsurgency was less a steady stream of propaganda than a fractured field of ideologies and pressures. Caught in the middle, the colonial subjects who wanted to make their voices heard first had to contend with the mediating force of journalism.

Reporters on the front lines have long been shadowed by suspicions of partisanship. Swayed by the thrill of combat, the lure of colorful copy, and old-fashioned patriotism, they have sometimes acted more as cheerleaders than observers.[2] Yet the narrative of professional detachment corrupted by militarism simplifies as much as it illuminates.[3] Reporting on Britain's wars at the end of empire was striking less for its jingoistic uniformity than for its tensions. Journalists did glamorize the use of force, sensationalize the plight of British victims, and elevate imperialist voices over those of dissidents.[4] But they also offered disquieting glimpses of violence: violence that failed to distinguish between civilians and fighters; violence that affected women, children, and the elderly; violence with no clear rationale and no end in sight.

These crosswinds arose from a paradox and an irony. The paradox was that, in order to justify the brutality of counterinsurgency, it was sometimes necessary to draw attention to it. The irony was that codes and standards designed to enforce neutrality in journalism actually favored war and empire. Humanitarian exposé had to compete not only with flag-waving partisanship, but with reportorial modes designed to insulate reporters from controversy: forensic skepticism, judicial evenhandedness, and press-conference stenography. When journalists decided against making violence the story, it was not because those professional strictures fell apart on the front lines, but precisely because they remained in force. Facing an uncertain journey from reporters' notebooks to front pages and airwaves, colonial violence became one story among many, rather than headline news.[5]

Journalists have always encoded attitudes to authority in the standards and practices of their profession. Some sources carry more weight than others; some kinds of information are deemed more reliable than others. Without explicitly taking sides, these "hierarchies of credibility" tilted the scales against critical coverage of colonial violence.[6] It was a dynamic that applied to other colonial wars, too, as Frantz Fanon noted in Algeria. "Even the most liberal of the French reporters never ceased to use ambiguous terms in describing our struggle," Fanon wrote. "When we reproached them for this, they replied in all good faith that they were being objective. For the native, objectivity is always directed against him."[7] Colonial violence was far from invisible in the British press. But it was seen through a glass darkly.

Sights and Sounds of Violence

Most Britons experienced colonial warfare as a media event.[8] Like the bulk of war coverage, then and now, reporting on counterinsurgency in the colonies was far from immune to the lure of national solidarity. Soldiers and policemen in the news usually appeared as sympathetic figures: ordinary young men doing their best in a dangerous situation, courageous heroes protecting vulnerable civilians, skilled professionals restoring order with tactical sophistication. Insurgents, by contrast, were portrayed as bloodthirsty fanatics, who lurked dishonorably in forests and jungles, targeted women and children without scruple, and tore into their victims with savage enthusiasm. Favoring events over structures, media reports depicted rebellions as eruptions of violence within an imagined universe of stability rather than the latest moves in an ongoing struggle for power.[9]

It might be tempting to view the soldier's-eye perspective of most news coverage as a failure of professionalism. In fact, battlefield dispatches belonged to a distinct genre of reportage that long followed its own set of rules. The war correspondent's institutional authority, commercial audience, and sense of purpose all depended on conveying the vicarious experience of combat with vivid, thrilling details. Although this did not necessarily translate into partisan one-sidedness, it did privilege spectacle over exposé, fueling an appetite for dramatic set-pieces that officials proved adept at exploiting. The value placed on immediacy in war reporting left a deep imprint on British perceptions of counterinsurgency.

In the first half of the twentieth century, the vast scale and surreal extremity of total war frustrated reporters' efforts to craft neatly etched dramas.[10] The searches, round-ups, and other discrete outings of counterinsurgency represented a kind of return to the "little wars" of the Victorian era, which could be narrated as adventure stories with identifiable characters and comprehensible stakes. The novelty of war coverage in the 1950s was the depiction of these small-scale conflicts in vivid sensory media. More than ever before, imagery and sound rivaled text as the currency of news, a shift accelerated by the rise of television but not confined to it. The share of newspaper column-inches devoted to pictures rose dramatically over the course of the decade: by 29 percent in the *Daily Mail*, 50 percent in the *Daily Express* and the *Daily Mirror*, 160 percent in the *Daily Herald*, and 300 percent in the *Daily Telegraph*.[11] The increasing use of smaller-format cameras, easily interchangeable lenses, and fast film stock heightened the spontaneity and intimacy of photographs that appeared in newspapers and in illustrated weeklies like *Picture Post*.[12] Although the weeklies and the cinema newsreels were both losing their audiences to television in the 1950s, they continued to reach millions of people each week. The visual record of counterinsurgency was profoundly shaped by journalists working for "old" media: from celebrated photographers Bert Hardy and George Rodger in *Picture Post* and Terry Fincher in the *Daily Herald* to the mostly anonymous cameramen who supplied moving images for newsreel services Movietone News and Pathé News.

Lively, personalized storytelling in broadcast news developed over the course the 1950s. On radio and television alike, the classic BBC format—studio-bound announcers reading scripts in a carefully modulated, deliberately impassive style—long remained a fixture of news programs.[13] But the success of the wartime radio program *Radio Newsreel* prompted BBC producers to experiment with less scripted, less stately, and timelier formats that featured sound recorded outside the studio.[14] Dramatic tape of an American TV correspondent reporting on riots in Cyprus in May 1956 inspired the inaugural news editor of Independent Television News (ITN) to begin using sound recorded on location in tandem with camera footage.[15] By the end of the decade, a new generation of television programs, like *Roving Report* on ITN and *Panorama* on BBC, were showcasing the firsthand accounts and subjective impressions of correspondents in the field.

The explicit political orientation of news outlets varied widely. The newsreels, the Beaverbrook papers, and the *Illustrated London News* were the most stridently patriotic; ITN, *Picture Post*, and the *Daily Mirror* had a populist edge that flirted with radicalism in varying degrees; the BBC, awkwardly, was both a creature of the Establishment and a self-styled neutral arbiter. Yet all were shaped by a moment of fierce competition for mass audiences. Across media, genres, and titles, the quest for compelling sounds and images of colonial war imposed a measure of unity.

In elevating dramatic scenes and sympathetic protagonists, counterinsurgency coverage mirrored popular culture. Like the *Eagle*, *Wizard*, and *Battle*, all widely read comics in the 1950s, the illustrated weeklies pitted hardy but isolated heroes against unforgiving conditions.[16] The *Illustrated London News* favored wide-angle shots that dramatized the vulnerability of British forces and the immensity of the task they faced: a thin column of soldiers surrounded and overshadowed by jungle; a pair of soldiers on a mountain ledge, looking out at a thick blanket of forest below; a long procession of detained suspects winding across a field.[17] Images in *Picture Post*, likewise centered on the stresses of counterinsurgency, were typically framed with a tighter lens. The smaller scale foregrounded tense encounters between security forces and civilians: an impromptu interrogation conducted through a crack in the

FIGURE 5.1   On location: ITN correspondent Reginald Bosanquet in Nicosia, Cyprus, for *Roving Report* in 1958. ITN/Getty Images.

door; a pat-down search of a suspect standing with arms outstretched; a revolver held inches from another suspect's face.[18]

The physical demands of fighting insurgency inspired awestruck treatment. Newsreels showed troops wading through neck-deep swamps and hacking through undergrowth in Malaya while inviting viewers to imagine "the steamy heat, about ninety degrees, the mosquitos, the leeches, and all the rest of it." As soldiers clambered over a stony hillside in Cyprus, Movietone's announcer observed that "patrols are tackling the job thoroughly" even though "the countryside presents many difficulties."[19] Air strikes on rebel camps furnished a thrillingly perilous backdrop for some stories, with soldiers crawling toward enemy locations amid flying bullets and thunderous explosions.[20] Even the relative tedium of house-to-house searches could assume the heroic dimensions of an endurance test. Frequent cuts and fast-paced orchestral soundtracks left the impression that soldiers were constantly in motion, and in danger, as they scrambled over rooftops, burst into doorways, and squeezed into confined spaces.[21]

While the same motifs resonated in broadcast news, narrative differences amplified the dramatic impact of soldiers fighting insurgents. Beyond the hourly news bulletins—which employed the same quick, telegraphic style as newsreels did—radio and television allowed stories to unfold vividly in time. When broadcast correspondents accompanied British troops into conflict zones, the distinction between observer and participant all but collapsed, as the moment-by-moment travails of the unit were relayed to audiences at home. With relatively infrequent cuts and breathless first-person narration, journalists placed their listeners and viewers in the position of soldiers beset by danger.

Few broadcasts matched the theatrical flair of BBC correspondent Stewart Wavell's radio dispatch from Malaya in March 1953. The scene was set with the voice of a regimental commander preparing his men to stage an ambush in the jungle. Thanks to an unusually good piece of intelligence, he announced, the kind of opportunity the soldiers had been awaiting for years was finally at hand. "Your hearts will be going like sledgehammers," he told them, "because you'll be lying there," hidden on the side of the road, waiting for a group of enemy fighters to emerge from the jungle. "Keep breathing slowly and carefully," the colonel advised. "I know it from my old days of big game hunting . . . If you do that, you will shoot straight . . . Good luck to you."[22]

The next voice listeners heard was Wavell's own. As he lay alongside a group of soldiers behind a clump of brush, Wavell dropped his voice to a near-whisper. "Now we're all sitting here waiting very tensely. We're all sapped to the skin from perspiring and we're feeling dreadfully tired. But the great moment we've been waiting for is going to come." To avoid detection by enemy sentries, Wavell related, he and the other men were pressed against the ground from head to toe. A front line of gunners inched forward, very slowly, on their bellies. "This last 30 yards have been a sharp agony of suspense," Wavell intoned.[23]

Suddenly, gunfire broke out. Amid the shots and the shouting, Wavell raised his voice but only communicated the confusion of the scene: "Spraying the whole of the road ... Flying in all directions ... They're going away ... I can't see anything." Then, between long breaths, Wavell managed to describe what he had seen. "What happened was ... four bandits came forward ... dressed in khaki ... and then the firing began." As the frequency of gunshots in the background gradually tapered off, Wavell described seeing one insurgent crumple under fire and another tumble out of a tree. The tally, he reported a few moments later, was one insurgent killed and one wounded.[24]

Along with a sense of nerve-racking perils, war reporting projected confidence that British authorities were equal to the challenge. A portrait of overwhelming force emerged from images of helicopters and bombers streaking across the sky, convoys rolling through city streets, and rows of neatly aligned soldiers picking up weapons in unison. Military code names like Operation Anvil and Operation Black Mac, favorite bits of reportorial color, reinforced the image of clockwork efficiency. Even without the benefit of sound or motion, print outlets found ways to portray the forward momentum of British forces on the page. A 1955 *Illustrated London News* feature on Cyprus condensed the life cycle of an urban operation into a sequence of snapshots: the troops outfitted with gas masks, helmets, and riot shields; a crowd scattering as clouds of tear gas waft; a few young men standing still, hands raised in the air, as soldiers close in.[25] Images of civilians passing through checkpoints, submitting to pat-downs, and standing behind barbed wire were staples of counterinsurgency coverage across media, establishing an orderly visual counterpoint to the chaos of insurrection. Even if the outcome of the wider war remained uncertain, signs of progress—suspects questioned and detained, hideouts raided, weapons confiscated—accrued with each operation related by reporters.

Beyond the front lines, many journalists offered a similarly optimistic vision of colonial war. Their stories on the detention of captured fighters and suspects conformed to a government-approved narrative that downplayed brute force in favor of tactics of persuasion, the so-called battle for "hearts and minds." A *Picture Post* feature on Malaya included before-and-after photos of detained insurgents, contrasting the drab uniforms, grim expressions, and rigid postures of Communist ideologues with the relaxed, sunny, and thoroughly Westernized appearance of the fortunate ones "who changed their minds." A story on the camp system in Kenya, headlined WASHING THE SOUL OF MAU MAU, likewise offered up the spectacle of "converted" detainees in bright white uniforms dancing harmlessly or sitting docilely on the grass.[26] A 1955 BBC television report on Kenya, featuring pictures from the detention camps of Tebere and Mwea, rhapsodized about life behind the barbed wire as an uplifting and joyous experience. "Propaganda talks lead to confessions, the start of a new way of thinking and living. Men jump to their feet and admit their sins, perhaps with a sincerity of a simple people." All-day mandatory labor was described as an innocuous way of keeping detainees "occupied."[27]

War reporters favored the British side, too, in the personalities they chose to feature. Generals, governors, and other top officials had the opportunity to express their views in frequent, deferential interviews, while rebel leaders remained underground. The figures who attracted the most sympathetic treatment were British civilians menaced by insurgent attacks. Journalists lavished detail on the disrupted patterns of everyday routine: the claustrophobia of curfews and confinement, the creeping mistrust of servants and workers, the revolvers and shotguns kept always at hand. When a settler's son or a soldier's wife was killed, newsreel cameras captured the funerals, complete with the sight of pallbearers carrying the coffin and grief-stricken relatives following close behind.[28] Images of backyard gardens and cozy farmhouses transformed into conflict zones offered instant points of identification for audiences at home.[29]

Stories about British civilians balanced a sense of the peril with morale-boosting tales of sturdiness under fire. Reporters stressed that, in the context of counterinsurgency, "it's not only troops who are in the fight but everyone who lives in the country." Far from helpless victims, British women were portrayed as battle-hardened combatants who could be as ruthless as circumstances required. After showcasing the hibiscuses in her garden, a planter's wife in Malaya coolly told a BBC correspondent about the time she noticed an insurgent aiming a gun at her: "I'm good with a shotgun and I quickly pulled down my shotgun and luckily I got him in the head." In a singsong voice, she added: "I was quite envious of my husband when he shot one the other day . . . . They don't deserve any mercy."[30] A few months later, the story of two middle-aged women in Kenya who shot down Mau Mau attackers in their living room rated a breathless play-by-play on the BBC and a cover photograph in the *Illustrated London News*.[31] Initially unsure of how to portray the "atmosphere" of counterinsurgency on film, Universal News cameraman Ronnie Noble decided to foreground the weapons settler women held at their side. The juxtaposition of danger and domesticity became a staple of newsreel iconography.[32]

War reporting always risked straying into propaganda by privileging vivid scenes over causes and contexts. But there were times when the sensory richness of media instead undermined seamless visions of heroic counterinsurgency. The endless demand for images of what were, after all, brutal conflicts fought at close range inevitably captured some unsettling moments in the frame. The need to portray British soldiers and civilians as effective combatants meant that the violence they perpetrated could be romanticized or rationalized but never entirely obscured. As Claire Mauss-Coupeaux observed of the French war in Algeria, "images of victory are also images of violence."[33] Even when they hastened to provide explanations for morally ambiguous situations, reporters could not help drawing attention to them, and to the fact that appearances alone left a damning impression.

Cracks in the façade of counterinsurgency coverage appeared when the text and the subtext of an image were at odds. Newsreel announcers implored viewers not to rush to conclusions at the sight of suffering colonial subjects. When British soldiers in Cyprus frisked a bewildered old man guiding a rickety cart down the street, the voiceover pointed out that "the most inoffensive-looking peasant might be concealing an arsenal of weapons or a head full of anti-British intentions."[34] Far from denying that broad-brush security measures swept up blameless civilians, many newsreel stories explicitly admitted it. But by describing such tactics as a tragic necessity, narrators tried to steer viewers from conscience-stricken outrage to resigned acceptance. One Pathé announcer warned grimly that "until the Mau Mau are destroyed, the innocent too must suffer," as the camera showed a sea of Kenyan children sitting on the ground under armed guard. In seeking to harden the hearts of the British public, stories like these offered a glimpse of war's inhumanity.[35]

Newsreels sometimes defended violence that was plainly vengeful rather than tactical. After Cypriot insurgents murdered the wife of a British soldier in 1958, troops in Famagusta broke into homes, smashed windows, and arrested and assaulted scores of men. What was so remarkable about the coverage of these reprisals was not the attempt to justify them but the absence of any real attempt to conceal them. "It would be surprising indeed if the troops naturally enraged by this cold-blooded act of EOKA thugs had carried out their search and made their arrests with kid-glove methods," the Movietone announcer conceded. As the camera showed a line of cars with shattered windows, he admitted that "tempers were strained." As a dozen Cypriot men wandered down the street with bandaged heads, he noted that "protests were made later about rough treatment during the round-up of suspects." Euphemisms about tempers and roughness attempted to minimize the gravity of the violence. But in choosing not to suppress the footage of fractured skulls, newsreel producers appeared confident that outrage at the fate of the soldier's wife would outweigh outrage at military brutality.[36]

In print, captions took the place of narrators in reinterpreting potentially troubling scenes. Journalists at publications like *Picture Post*, where images were meant to tell the story, found themselves in the awkward position of urging readers to mistrust their eyes. In 1952, the weekly ran a Bert Hardy photograph of a teenaged Kenyan girl ringed by half a dozen armed askaris and a trench-coated, fedora-wearing official with his back turned to the camera. It is night; the blanket in an askari's hand suggests that the girl has been rousted from bed. There is fear in her face. Yet the caption assures that her treatment is deserved. "She looks innocent—but she had helped to beat up a boy younger than herself."[37] Another *Picture Post* story, sixteen months later, featured a George Rodger photograph from Nairobi. A long line of young African men, arms tucked behind their heads, await a pat-down from a police officer with a

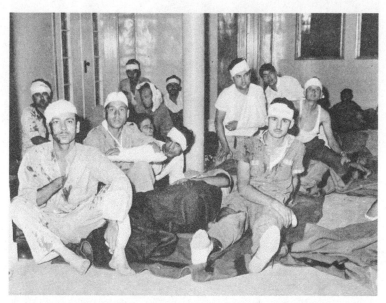

FIGURE 5.2 Images of the bandaged heads and bloodied clothes of Greek Cypriot men injured by British troops in Famagusta in 1958 circulated widely in newsreels and print. Mary Evans Picture Library.

rifle slung over his shoulder. One of the men grins puckishly at the lens as the caption poses an ominous question: "Is the absence of incriminating arms— or a smile—a guarantee of innocence?"[38] The counterinsurgent truism that appearances deceive became a refrain, ironically, in publications devoted to photojournalism.

The urge to herald tactical shifts as turning points brought glimpses of the pulverizing force directed against colonial subjects. A 1953 BBC radio feature on Malaya broadcast a government spokesperson's claim that what happened at Permatong Tinggi "really began to win the war," prompting the correspondent to explain: the inhabitants of the Penang village refused to offer information about food smuggled to insurgents, so soldiers "bulldozed it flat" and sent them to a detention camp for a year.[39] Even the spare, telegraphic prose of the BBC's radio news bulletins detailed the deployment of new weapons and vehicles, the advent of fresh crackdowns and campaigns, and the

FIGURE 5.3 A security operation in Kenya, 1952. Press coverage of counterinsurgency offered reasons not to worry about seemingly disturbing images. Bert Hardy/*Picture Post*/Getty Images.

destruction they inflicted on insurgents and civilians alike. A report in April 1952 described plans to drop plant-killing chemicals on Malayan jungles so that "as the terrorists have less access to food, they will be forced out of their lairs by hunger." One June evening in 1953, the lead story of the 6 p.m. bulletin announced a new "scorched earth policy" in Kenya: cutting off food to fighters "already suffering from hunger" and demolishing huts "to give security forces a better field of vision." Other reports noted that "collective punishment" policies in Kenya, including the confiscation of cattle, were aimed at Kikuyu merely suspected of aiding insurgents or withholding information.[40]

The authority granted to war correspondents' subjective impressions was a propaganda boon as long as they identified with the soldiers surrounding them. But the vividness and immediacy of their reporting sometimes communicated unease instead. A *Panorama* reporter commented in 1958 that Mau Mau detainees were "being set free after a brain washing which seems to make some of them as lifeless as zombies." The same year, a *Panorama* piece on Cyprus opened with another reporter standing outside Pyla detention camp, where he noted that more than five hundred people were being detained without trial and called the barbed wire "a grim sign of the emergency under which the people of Cyprus are still living."[41] At other times, journalists left the ambiguities of striking images to speak for themselves. The same close-up shot of a captured insurgent in Malaya, his face caked with blood, appeared in newsreels and on television. So did footage of British troops setting fire to straw huts as a woman and her child toddled past.[42]

Journalists striving for cinematic effects in print also narrated unsettling scenes of violence. Reporting from Malaya in 1948, *Observer* newspaper correspondent Patrick O'Donovan described the visit of colonial police officers to a squatters' village. Because the inhabitants were unable or unwilling to provide any information about the recent murders of two British estate managers, the police set to work burning the village to the ground. O'Donovan watched as the squatters rushed to salvage a few belongings—torn blankets, pots and pans, a sun hat—before a detective flicked his lighter at the thatch. "The hut burst into a slow explosion of flame and the family stood and watched, ankle-deep in all they had. That happened five times. Once a child started to scream. Others just stood, their faces marble-cold." Like the newsreel announcers and caption writers, O'Donovan signaled that he was not leveling a criticism of the punitive British policy, which he described as "necessary." But he also pointed out that the squatters were now "as frightened of the police as of the Communists" and expressed hope for "a more constructive solution." By 1950, in a book recounting the same episode, O'Donovan confessed that he felt a twinge of excitement witnessing the operation at the time and was sickened by it in retrospect. "God forgive me," he wrote.[43]

The personal voice of war reporting could register alienation, anger, even disgust with the British side. On the BBC, the journalists who voiced qualms most clearly were the husband-and-wife team of Edward and Marjorie Ward. Their special report on Kenya aired on the Home Service on the evening of Tuesday, April 19, 1955. It opened with a recording made in a village near Embu where security forces were carrying out a hut-to-hut search for Mau Mau insurgents. "Several shots have been fired," Edward Ward said, "and now you can hear . . . this terrible eerie sound of the women wailing." After describing the body of a seventeen-year-old boy murdered by Mau Mau, he pointed out that far more Africans than Europeans had died on both sides of the conflict. "How many Mau Mau have been shot, hanged, killed with poisoned arrows, bombed?" he asked. "There are no true figures — one knows only that 40,000 are in detention camps and prisons." Several voice actors then reconstructed a cocktail party attended by the Wards in Embu, during which settlers casually referred to Africans as "primitive savages" and expressed a desire to see them hanging from trees. When one settler complained that people back home did not appreciate the hardships of pioneer life on the East African frontier, Edward Ward replied with withering skepticism: "Oh, come off it. You came out here to escape the English social revolution."[44]

Such impassioned outbursts were rare in stories about colonial war. Along with the ambiguous images and defensive rationalizations, however, they attest to the unease that ran through counterinsurgency coverage. After all, the firsthand testimony of war correspondents had to share columns and airtime with a steady stream of stories about alleged abuses emanating from courtrooms, Westminster, and Whitehall. These were mostly terse accounts of official proceedings: courts-martial of British soldiers accused of misconduct, trials of accused insurgents where the use of torture to secure confessions was raised as a defense, parliamentary debates, and commissions of inquiry. Of course, right-leaning tabloids tended to ignore or distort these stories, just as left-leaning tabloids amplified and sensationalized them. But the sober establishment outlets that saw themselves as keepers of a definitive factual record—the *Times*, the *Manchester Guardian*, and the BBC—covered the procedural dimensions of colonial violence with regularity.

Though lacking the drama of front-line war reporting, and rarely treated as front-page or top-of-the-hour news, these stories constituted a long-running drumbeat of disclosures.[45] Procedural revelations were slow to come out of Malaya, although a 1951 *Manchester Guardian* story described witnesses in a court case alleging police brutality that "ranged from threats with revolver shots, kickings, punchings, and severe beatings with a rattan cane to the insertion of a needle under the finger nails."[46] The pace quickened in Cyprus, where a Greek-backed propaganda campaign and activist legal community forced allegations into public view, and in Kenya, where reports of excessive force were pervasive from the earliest days of the counterinsurgency. One of the most notorious and widely covered cases of the decade was the court-martial case of Captain Griffiths in Kenya. It occasioned unusually graphic language by broadsheet standards. The *Times* and the *Guardian* both headlined testimony about the severing of a prisoner's ear; a *Times* editorial even condemned soldiers for approaching their duties in the spirit of "an afternoon's shoot or a pig-sticking match."[47] Another reliably conservative broadsheet, the *Yorkshire Post*, editorialized against "methods of so-called interrogation which were in fact torture."[48]

While the quality papers reached relatively narrow audiences, the same cannot be said for BBC radio, which chronicled official responses to violence even more meticulously. A government statement read over the airwaves in April 1953 acknowledged cases of "indiscipline," "unlawful injury," and "rough handling" in Kenya with the half-justification, half-admission that "occasional errors of judgment were inevitable."[49] A few years later, an interviewer confronted Cyprus governor John Harding with allegations of "harsh and brutal methods" against civilians.[50] The BBC also brought listeners into the courtrooms where cases of excessive force came under legal scrutiny. When an appeals court judge in Kenya found that screening teams were "softening up" suspects to "extract information" and that authorities probably "knew about it and condoned it," the BBC reported his complaint. Another news bulletin quoted a witness, in the court-martial of two British soldiers in Cyprus, who saw marks on the back of a suspect, suggesting that he had been "struck with a chain" during interrogation.[51]

BBC coverage of House of Commons debates allowed MPs aligned with the Movement for Colonial Freedom to press their case before a wide audience. Radio listeners heard Labourites blast collective punishments as "totalitarian" and "fascist," chemical sprays as "immoral and ineffective," and many other tactics as brutal and unjust. Why were officials "starving villagers" in Malaya, MPs asked, instead of winning hearts and minds?[52] Why were Kenyans who had never been tried for a crime, much less convicted, forced to labor in camps under the threat of flogging? Why was the government in Cyprus refusing to investigate dozens of "documented cases" of "brutality" by security forces?[53] Sharp questions about mysterious deaths in custody, unseemly competitions to rack up kills, and innocent people swept up in raids were all relayed by BBC newsreaders.

Scripted talks and interview shows gave parliamentary critics of colonial violence another platform. Speaking on the BBC program *At Home and Abroad* in April 1955, Liberal-turned-Labour MP Dingle Foot protested the lack of due process for detainees in the Kenyan detention camps. "Many thousands of Her Majesty's subjects" had been imprisoned, Foot declared, "not because they have been found guilty of any offence but because they are believed by the authorities to have taken some part in the activities of Mau Mau . . . . There has been no opportunity for the detainees to answer the charge or even know what is alleged against them."[54] Returning from her visit to Cyprus in 1958, Barbara Castle declared on BBC's *Tonight* that the government had misled the public about the extent of injuries inflicted by "tough behavior" among British soldiers.[55] Even some officials expressed qualms about counterinsurgency on the air. A former government spokesman in Malaya, reflecting on parallels with the conflict in Kenya in 1955, worried about the fear-soaked atmosphere generated by raids, checkpoints, and camps. "Perhaps the greatest danger of terrorist movements," he told a late-night BBC audience, "is that the process of dealing with them generates a 'Police State' mentality. And that, in the end, is as destructive of human freedom as the worst of terrorist outrages."[56]

The British media was no propaganda machine. Troubling images and subversive sentiments could and did break through to the public. And yet, crucially, they never went unchallenged. Damning images were undermined by captions and voice-overs; disturbing accusations were paired with reassuring statements from government spokesmen; disembodied accounts of wrongdoing competed with memorable, sympathetic scenes of soldiers and settlers. What forces acted against the exposé mode in reporting on colonial war? One way of answering that question is to track the facts about atrocity that were seen and heard by reporters but never communicated to a wider audience.

The Politics of Professionalism

To judge from the attitudes of the correspondents themselves, it is surprising that the coverage was not more uniformly critical. The *Times* reporter in Malaya in the early 1950s, Louis Heren, was a self-described "Cockney radical" who disliked the colonial elite for its "greed and opulence," its "pompous and status-ridden" ways, and its exploitation of "racial antipathies, resentments, and hatreds." General Templer and his aides considered him a Communist and tried, unsuccessfully, to get him fired.[57] Legendary foreign correspondent James Cameron, who spent most of the 1950s at *Picture Post*, frankly identified as "socialist and most especially anti-imperialist." While covering Cyprus, news of the Suez invasion prompted him to exclaim "I feel ashamed to be English!" at a Nicosia watering hole.[58]

Some of the most committed left-wing journalists hopped from one counterinsurgency to another, driven by a sense of obligation to expose injustice. A stringer for the *Observer* and the *News Chronicle*, Michael Davidson spent much of his time in Malaya quarreling with General Templer, who once greeted him with the words, "I think you're a shit." "Well, sir," Davidson replied, "I don't think too much of you."[59] From his perch in Singapore, Davidson quietly encouraged Templer's Labour opponents in Parliament. "Keep bashing at this frightful man Templer and his madness," he told Tom Driberg, citing the policy of collective punishment at places like Tanjong Malim.[60] By 1955, Davidson had landed in Nicosia, where he joined the staff of the newly founded *Cyprus Times* and went on to publish front-page exposés of torture. His colleagues thought that Davidson's experience in Malaya made him an especially passionate, and fearsome, foe of the government. As one colleague put it, "he knew the routine and could anticipate most of the steps on the road to repression," from curfews and identity cards to punitive fines levied on whole villages.[61] Davidson's publisher at the *Cyprus Times*, Charles Foley, printed such critical coverage of the war effort that the state adopted a raft of censorship regulations and targeted him for prosecution.[62]

In Kenya, a *Times* journalist observed in 1954, virtually the entire press corps was "anti-settler and they are very keen on ferreting out misbehavior."[63] It came as no surprise that left-leaning papers like the *Daily Mirror* trumpeted evidence of excessive force and found themselves resented by many soldiers as a result.[64] But antiwar and anticolonial responses cut across partisan lines. The Kenya correspondent for the *Daily Telegraph*, for instance, was impressed by the "ragged band of rebels" who "defied the British army" and appalled by the "mockery of British justice" in summary trials and brutal interrogations.[65] Reporting for the BBC, Edward and Marjorie Ward quickly decided that the settlers were unreconstructed racists, "so greedy and so stupid," as Edward Ward put it later.[66] The settlers, for their part, saw reporters as "bloody Bolshies" who did not understand the colonial way of life. They raised tens of thousands of pounds to launch a propaganda outfit, the Truth about Kenya Committee, aimed at combatting what they saw as "jaundiced" reports in the mainstream media.[67]

Not every reporter in the colonies assumed an adversarial stance, of course, and some grew close to the figures they covered. The *Guardian's* man in Singapore was flown home at government expense in 1956 to secretly advise the colonial secretary on peace negotiations.[68] In Cyprus, *Guardian* correspondent Nancy Crawshaw assured her government sources that she disagreed with the paper's critical editorials on the counterinsurgency, which she described as "extremist." "I have felt a deep frustration at not being able to convince them that unjust and ill-founded criticism merely makes the problem worse," she told one official.[69] Other journalists sympathized with colonial war on ideological grounds. The *Daily Mail* reporter who covered Kenya put down concerns about violence to "the lunatic fringe of the extreme Left."[70]

Ultimately, however, the biases of individual journalists mattered less to public perceptions of violence than one might expect. One reason for this is that editors back home had powerful tools at their command for policing the biases of overseas reporters. They could alter the copy they received or decide not to run it at all. They could issue story assignments in addition to approving or rejecting pitches from the field. Finally, they could ensure that no one journalist had anything like a monopoly on coverage of a story, by dispatching processions of roving correspondents to supplement the output of locally based stringers. In Kenya, London-based colonial correspondent Oliver Woods regularly dropped in to do his own reporting for the *Times*, even though at least four other correspondents filed stories from there. In Cyprus, the *Times* had no fewer than eight reporters between 1955 and 1961.[71] Even the most opinionated journalists had to work within the constraints of a system.

As a result, the heroic, individualistic style of the war correspondent was not the only, or even the dominant, mode of reporting on colonial war. The bread-and-butter stories that filled newspaper column inches and BBC airtime were largely factual, spare, and detached. They focused heavily on official events and statements—press conferences, dignitary visits, policy shifts, legal proceedings—while playing down the experiences and personalities of the reporters who relayed them. Many newspaper stories were attributed to unnamed "correspondents" in Singapore, Nairobi, and Nicosia. The *Times* did not introduce bylines until 1967.[72] The announcers for BBC radio bulletins were likewise anonymous, allowing their famously regimented tone to project what Lord Reith called a "collective personality."[73] Even on television, where the possibilities of vivid first-person testimony were greatest, nightly newscasts long featured desk-bound announcers reading a script and introducing filmed reports. Until the late 1950s, for technical reasons, those reports only rarely featured correspondents speaking directly into the camera and relied on studio-recorded voiceovers instead.[74]

This impersonality reflected a growing sense that information, not commentary or advocacy, was the journalistic coin of the realm. The wartime examples of Reuters and the BBC, which burnished their reputations by conveying reliable news despite close ties to the state, cast a long shadow.[75] While old-fashioned patriotism persisted in the newsreels and illustrated weeklies, the ideal of neutral fact-gathering was gaining strength. It was only in this period that many newspapers abandoned a longstanding convention by placing news, rather than editorials or advertisements, on the front page: the *Manchester Guardian* in 1952, the *Scotsman* in 1957, the *Glasgow Herald* in 1958.[76] Amid rising costs, growing dependence on advertisements, and new competition from television, newspapers faced pressure to appeal to the largest possible audience, loosening their connection both to political parties and to the ideological preferences of their proprietors.[77] The impact of television as a medium likewise elevated reportage over opinion. Crisp descriptions of scenes and events represented the new gold standard; commentary began to feel verbose, inauthentic, and extraneous by contrast.[78]

Mirroring these structural changes in the industry, British journalists after the war increasingly saw themselves as professionals defined by training and standards. In 1947, the newspapers owned by Lord Kemsley (including dailies in Manchester, Newcastle, and four other cities) started a scheme for new recruits to supplement on-the-job experience with lectures, seminars, and courses at technical colleges. Five years later, a coalition of owners, editors, and trade unions founded the National Council for the Training of Journalists, which implemented a version of the so-called Kemsley system on a national scale. Most aspiring reporters were required to meet minimum educational standards and navigate proficiency tests that assessed news judgement along with practical skills like shorthand and typewriting.[79] The journalistic career was changing shape from an ink-stained artisanship to a specialized and regimented vocation. The growing influence of trade unions in newsrooms reinforced the sense that journalists were less accountable to owners than to their own professional community.[80]

The function of the modern journalist was summarized by one contemporary handbook as "the securing and presentation of facts."[81] Reliability mattered more than originality; every piece of information which made it into print or on the air had to be confirmed and verified beyond all doubt. Journalism manuals singled out institutional sources of information—press attachés, government relations officers, libraries, and museums—as vital allies in the reporter's work. Standard reference books like the *Encylopaedia Britannica* and *Who's Who* were considered indispensable tools "every hour of the day and night"; so were press clippings from other newspapers.[82] Journalistic practice in these accounts was not a matter of investigation or interpretation so much as data collection, which one handbook envisioned as tapping "the fountains of information from which flow rivers of facts."[83] The first page of Charles Rigby's *The Staff Journalist* (1950) referred to the much-quoted wisdom of legendary *Manchester Guardian* editor C. P. Scott—"comment is free, facts are sacred"—as "something like Holy Writ."[84] In the words of a rare contemporary who questioned the reigning empiricism, "the average journalist . . . in his simple, sentimental, and unthinking way . . . still believes that most news is 'natural' news, of which he is the mere recorder."[85]

This was a code defined not just by accuracy but by objectivity. That is a notoriously amorphous term, but the imposition of constraints on individual agency—through strict rules and automated procedures, the cultivation of distance between the observer and the observed, and the accumulation of details rather than the construction of generalities—was always central.[86] The robust form of objectivity that prevailed in British journalism after 1945 enjoined a "passive," almost "stenographic," form of empiricism.[87] Reporters should confine themselves to collecting and disseminating facts beyond dispute; anything that might draw attention to the correspondent's own subjectivity or agency was considered suspect. If "advocacy" ever appeared in a news article, *Times* editor Ralph Deakin declared, "we feel that it should be indirect, as though the Correspondent, in presenting a forefront of facts, were also presenting the best arguments, not as his own opinion, but as the best, or widest, or deepest opinion available in his territory."[88] His successor, William Haley, likewise insisted that maintaining a position of detachment—reflecting reality rather than intervening in it—was essential. While obliged to report "what is happening regardless of whether it reflects credit or discredit on the Government in power," Haley declared in 1953, "the point is that a *Times* correspondent . . . has to be above the battle, not one of the contestants."[89]

One consequence of this sensibility is that the gap between what reporters knew and what they communicated to the public was sometimes vast. The colonial correspondent for the *Times*, Oliver Woods, paid annual visits to Kenya during the early years of the Mau Mau revolt. As early as December 1952, he told his colleagues in London, "I am very distressed by the cases of 'beating up' which continue to occur." Some British-born Kenya

Police Reserve officers at a station in Laikipia, he reported, were "torturing prisoners, if what is alleged is true, in a sadistic manner." At another police station where Mau Mau suspects were being held for interrogation, Woods "noticed that two out of three had bandages around their heads." A year later, in December 1953, Woods heard from a high-ranking British official—the chief native commissioner, Edward Windley—that police reserve officers were torturing Africans at a station in Thompsons Falls and that the settler-dominated Kenya Regiment was "shooting far too many Africans." A briga-dier in the King's African Rifles admitted to Woods that his own soldiers "had been rather beastly to some prisoners." A *Times* correspondent told Woods that another reporter "had seen European police beating African prisoners on the head with revolver butts."[90]

The damning details seemed to mount with every moment Woods spent in Kenya. And yet not one of them ever made it into the stories he published in the *Times*. The closest Woods came to exposing colonial violence was a single line in the second paragraph of a story, which ran on November 6, 1952, label-ling police action as "indiscriminate and rough." The headline under which this story ran—"Limited Results of Campaign against Mau Mau"—was re-vealing. British misbehavior made news in this case not because it violated moral norms but because it revealed strategic failures. As Woods observed in the story, "interrogation has alienated as many as it has deterred."[91] In this con-text, a cursory and euphemistic reference to "rough" treatment made far more sense than dwelling on the details of torture, which might risk the appearance of bias or sensationalism. Woods's impassive language insisted that violence merited public attention not as the cause of suffering or as an occasion for outrage, but as the object of a cost-benefit analysis for colonial policy.[92]

If Woods seemed to sanitize the ugly realities of empire, he did not do so from a sense of patriotic or sentimental attachment. As he confessed to his editor during a trip to central Africa in 1953, "I don't really 'like' white settlement at all, if one is looking at it in terms of likes and dislikes."[93] From Kenya, he wired to his editors every scrap of evidence about torture that came into his hands, though he stopped short of filing a condemnatory story as he wrestled endlessly with the reliability and consistency of that evidence. He expressed frustration at his inability to piece together a mosaic of reliable facts; much of the information that came to him was unpublishable because it was secondhand, off-the-record, or both. As he put it in January 1954, "it is very difficult to get the facts about brutality in Kenya. Where incidents occur, there is naturally a conspiracy of silence. This is turn produces rumors which on investigation nearly always turn out false . . . It is very difficult to get any coherent picture out of all this." Woods worried that even the firsthand evidence he possessed was not incontrovertible. While the sight of imprisoned Africans in bandages suggested that "they had been hit at some time," he pointed out that "it might have happened any other way."[94] For Woods, as for many of his fellow journalists, fear of printing an inaccurate fact outweighed the fear of concealing suggestive evidence.

For its part, the colonial state in Kenya worked to exploit professional constraints by manipulating the information available to reporters. After Operation Anvil, a military action which removed almost the entire Kikuyu population from Nairobi in the spring of 1954, journalists struggled to find sources other than white British settlers, soldiers, and administrators in the city where they were based. One correspondent noted that few Africans "dared to show their face" there, while another was reduced to surreptitiously interviewing taxi drivers.[95] Officials, meanwhile, shrewdly leveraged their position to keep reporters close. They wielded the carrot of access, from interviews at Government House to army missions in the jungle, along with the stick of vocal complaints about accuracy and fairness. A reporter who filed a critical story might find himself summoned for a dressing-down by the governor.[96] Even that passing reference to "rough" treatment, Woods noted, had got the police commissioner "after my blood."[97]

Above all, officials shaped coverage by filling reporters' notebooks with a steady stream of facts and figures. Three times each day in Nairobi—at 11 a.m., 4 p.m., and 9 p.m.—press aides issued typewritten situation reports or "sitreps" describing the latest military action and tallying the casualties on both sides.[98] They supplemented this ready-made copy with frequent, not-for-attribution conversations, encouraging a sense of complicity and shaping the perceptions of reporters and editors without having to commit themselves in print. Quietly leaked numbers made a particularly strong impression on Woods. After a government source told him in December 1953 that 150,000 arrests to that point had led to just twenty-four official complaints, Woods concluded that there may be "a lot of rough stuff but I think there is little real sadism."[99] Sources inside the state bureaucracy spoke with the authority of a comprehensive knowledge, however spurious, which insurgents in the field had no hope of matching. Officials offered facts; rebels, whistleblowers, and witnesses could reply only with anecdotes.

Times coverage of the campaign against Mau Mau was not exactly a whitewash. But the damning stories about legal cases and parliamentary accusations coexisted with reports about exculpatory investigations, government denials, and individual acquittals. The swirl of seemingly contradictory information helped to validate the official line that abuses were rare and isolated rather than pervasive and systematic. Amid the swirl of charges and counter-charges, journalists hesitated to invest their own authority in support of one side or another. Weighed against assertions, both public and private, from a pha-lanx of official sources, the reliability of Woods's own observations appeared shaky. The most disturbing of them therefore stayed, unpublished, in the "Confidential Memorandum" file at the *Times* office on Printing House Square.

A yawning gap between public knowledge and private knowledge also defined Kenya coverage in the Kemsley-owned *Sunday Times*. After nov-elist Graham Greene dropped into the colony for a few weeks in 1953— supplementing his income, as many successful writers did, with occasional journalism—he published a pair of stories that warmed the hearts of officials and settlers.[100] Greene portrayed left-wing MPs holding forth in Westminster as hopelessly out of touch with the vicious crimes committed by Mau Mau: "the group of burnt huts, the charred corpse of a woman, the body robbed of its entrails." British administrators, by contrast, were progressive types drawing up plans to combat soil erosion and lift the color bar; white landowners were salt-of-the earth farmers. Just one line buried deep in Greene's second story, predicting that "trigger-happy" security forces "would not come out of the struggle unstained," hinted at a darker story on the British side.[101]

In the letters he wrote to his cousin Catherine from Kenya, however, Greene's unease with the counterinsurgency was far from veiled. "I'm very bored—& very pro-Kikuyu," he told her shortly after arriving. "I don't know what the white settlers are making so much fuss about." Many of them, he wrote later, had devolved into "a kind of white Mau Mau."[102] Greene's concerns with the British campaign continued to mount after returning home. Revealingly, he chose to voice them not in his capacity as a bylined correspondent, but as a private citizen. In a letter to the editor of the *Times*, just two months after his *Sunday Times* articles, Greene wrote of mutilated African bodies left to rot outside a police station and of soldiers "who fire first as soon as curfew calls and look at papers afterwards." Warning against the temptation to justify such acts as a response to Mau Mau atrocities, Greene observed that the Bren gun, the British Army's weapon of choice, "can produce a result as horrible as the panga," the machete favored by Mau Mau.[103]

Even as a merely personal account, Greene's letter represented a coup for the anticolonial cause. Greene received more than a dozen letters applauding him for breaking a code of silence about British misdeeds. "At last," a London woman wrote, "they have published a letter on this horrible business saying what should be said." But after blowing the whistle on the letters page of the *Times*, Greene refused to press the issue further. He soon moved onto other causes, like the malign influence of American anti-Communism, and new literary projects, like *The Quiet American*. Greene's subsequent silence about the "white Mau Mau" did not mean that the news from Kenya improved. On the contrary, Greene continued to receive reports of atrocities from the colony for years afterward. As he told one correspondent, however, he feared looking "like a propagandist." To another, he wrote, "the only people who go on reminding us of these things are contributors to the *New Statesman* or some such paper."[104] Making colonial violence a signature issue would have spelled a loss of influence by tying Greene's authority to a partisan campaign. Though he enjoyed far more autonomy—and, perhaps, more moral authority—than most newspapermen, he was unwilling to trade his identity as a professional writer for that of an advocate or gadfly. Greene reserved his fire for the occasional stinging line tucked into novels like *A Burnt-Out Case* (1960): "Hola Camp, Sharpeville, and Algiers had justified all possible belief in European cruelty."[105]

Neither the *Times* nor the *Sunday Times* offered an especially hospitable environment for anticolonial politics. But even at proudly left-leaning publications, objectivity placed a heavier burden on allegations of atrocity than on government denials. At David Astor's *Observer*, long lionized as a progressive champion of decolonization, evidence of British wrongdoing in Kenya struggled to make it into print.[106] After a week in Nairobi in October 1954, reporter Cyril Dunn had amassed an impressively comprehensive dossier of horrors. As he wrote to Astor, "There are thousands of Kikuyu, Embu, and Meru children wandering about the terrorist areas without parents, the parents being either dead or detained. They are showing signs of an undernourishment disease which turns them grey." The New Villages had no sanitation facilities and children were dying of measles every day. The screening of suspects involved "beatings, ridicule," and other "Darkness at Noon pressures." The detention system invited comparison with the gulag: "People 'vanish.' Europeans go round trying in vain to find out what has happened to servants they've had for ten or fifteen years. Detainees in the camps have often heard nothing of their families for a year or more, and vice versa."[107]

Rather than rushing Dunn's dispatches into the paper, Astor sat on them for months, while his correspondent waited with mounting impatience in East Africa. The story that finally ran in mid-December, after Dunn protested the long delay, was a watered-down revision seemingly calculated to lull readers into apathy or boredom. The printed version favored balance and generality over vivid scenes of suffering, employing vague euphemisms about "improper acts" and "unorthodox methods of interrogation." No mention was made of orphaned children, disease-stricken settlements, or vanishing detainees. Most striking of all, the lede preemptively deflected criticism from the government, claiming that "officials deplore cases where their own high standards are disregarded."[108]

Caution prevailed over urgency at the *Observer* again in 1958, when correspondent Colin Legum agreed to hold off publishing a damning letter from Kenyan detainees in the Mariira camp. Officials worked to raise doubts in his mind with a two-pronged strategy: off-the-record rebuttals to specific allegations and on-the-record testimonials about camp conditions from medical and missionary observers. Although he was refused access to see the camp for himself, Legum ended up printing a story ("Kenya Frees 1,000 Each Month") that affirmed the rosy official narrative of a benevolent, rapidly disbanding detention regime.[109]

Other left-wing outlets also proved reluctant to credit evidence of colonial violence. At the reliably Labourite *Tribune*, editor Mervyn Jones received bundles of photographs showing the abuse of African bodies at British hands. But Jones decided that, because "no one could prove who was doing the killing and torture, or prove who it was that was suffering," the images could not be printed.[110] By the fall of 1953, reports of atrocity had been filtering out of Kenya for a year. But the editorial writers for the *Daily Herald* remained adamant that "It is hard to pass a final judgment here in Britain . . . . We need facts."[111]

The *New Statesman* trod cautiously with Kenya, too, despite its proud self-image as "one of the text books of colonial liberation."[112] Editorials did condemn settler vigilantism, repeatedly, and letters from white correspondents related stories of "indiscriminate terror" and "ruthless cruelty."[113] But when editor Kingsley Martin in 1953 received letters from Africans describing beatings, rapes, and other abuses suffered at the hands of security forces, he decided against publishing them. Although these accounts came from different witnesses, in different parts of the country, and in some cases were validated by locals he knew personally, Martin was haunted by the possibility that partisans had fabricated the lurid details to advance their own agenda. "Is this propaganda?" he wondered. While the skeptical, independent sensibility of Martin's *New Statesman* led to criticism of government claims, the same attitude silenced some anticolonial voices.[114]

In Cyprus, as in Kenya, only a fraction of what British reporters knew about violence ended up in print. When talking among themselves, members of the press corps on the island half-jokingly referred to Special Branch interrogators as "H.M.T.s": "Her Majesty's Torturers."[115] Reporters heard chilling details from interrogators who wanted to unburden their consciences without going on the record. Michael Davidson, writing for the *Observer*, "was told by a man working at the Troodos interrogation center that a colleague of his . . . was in the habit of tying a string to a prisoner's genitals and giving a tweak when his questions weren't satisfactorily answered." Another Special Branch source of Davidson's referred to torture as an open secret: "You know what goes on—we all know."[116] A *Manchester Guardian* reporter vented to his editors about the beatings that took place in Famagusta after the murder of a British soldier's wife in 1958. He called it "lynch justice without the lynching, calculated brutality of the basest kind." *Guardian* correspondent Nancy Crawshaw admitted that unpublished cases of brutality were "far worse" than the ones featured in her stories.[117]

Where did the pressure to suppress details come from? Some, no doubt, originated with government sources. Even at left-leaning papers, journalists needed to maintain relationships with officials to keep the information flowing. During his stint as press officer for the Cyprus government, Lawrence Durrell cultivated ties with potentially hostile reporters by meeting them at the airport and treating them to the lavish hospitality of his villa. "I had six hundred pressmen in six months," he bragged to a friend in 1958. "The house was a river of gin; no time to myself. But I inspired several million miles of prose in praise of a highly questionable policy."[118] For journalists, leveling harsh accusations in print risked shutting off the spigot of access. It also created serious legal exposure for libel. When the *Observer* published a letter from five Kenyan detainees in Lokitaung camp in 1958, alleging beatings, malnutrition, and other abuses, the British district officer mentioned by name promptly filed a lawsuit in London's High Court. Within six months, the *Observer* was forced to settle, and he won a substantial cash settlement along with a retraction in print.[119]

But reporters who covered colonial war did not typically see themselves as censored or silenced. Rather, they internalized incentives against provoking controversy, stressing uncertainty and weighing counterarguments as they debated how far to go in print. When *Guardian* correspondent Nancy Crawshaw broke from her usual practice to acknowledge that "rough handling takes place" in a published article on Cyprus, she hastened to add that allegations were "part of an intensive campaign to discredit the British" and "grossly exaggerated."[120] The editor of the *Cyprus Mail*, Kenneth Mackenzie, was likewise conflicted. He privately admitted that "our troops do go in for some pretty rough stuff" but complained that the torrent of accusations and counter-accusations made it "almost impossible to ascertain where exactly the truth lies." He represented this uncertainty in graphic form, with a hand-drawn sketch that showed the "Truth" hovering somewhere between the "British Version" at one extreme and the "Greek Version" at the other.[121] The fact that anticolonial Cypriots were indeed waging a well-organized campaign to dramatize and, in some cases, fabricate abuses by British forces only heightened reporters' reluctance to put their credibility behind lurid accusations.[122]

The BBC was, if anything, even more dogmatic than newspapers about enforcing the dictates of objectivity. One BBC executive, without apparent irony, cited Charles Dickens to describe the work of overseas correspondents: "Their brief has been, to quote Mr. Gradgrind, 'Facts alone are wanted in life.... You are not to see anywhere what you don't see in fact."[123] The director of foreign news, preparing for a special broadcast featuring overseas correspondents in 1955, reminded the BBC's man in Nairobi that "we don't want to get involved in any deep political questions, so you should keep your answers as factual as possible." While the causes and consequences of the Mau Mau rebellion were considered off-limits, permissible topics included whether insurgent attacks had affected the reporter personally and whether he carried a gun.[124]

This concern with events rather than causes, consequences, or meanings flowed from the top of the BBC hierarchy. New Zealander Tahu Hole, who served as news editor from 1948 to 1960, frustrated many correspondents by imposing a two-source rule and applying it in the most literal way imaginable. If Reuters ran an Associated Press story verbatim, Hole considered this confirmation for purposes of the rule.[125] By redefining reliability as replicability, this policy made it difficult, if not impossible, to report any information—the lonely whistleblower's claim, the traumatized survivor's fractured testimony—that strayed beyond the approved communiqués of official sources. Professionalization as the tightening of rules, codes, and standards marginalized voices beyond the state.

This is ironic because the usual story told about the BBC in this period centers on the broadcaster's heroic willingness to speak truth to power. In 1956, Director General Ian Jacob defended broadcasting editorials critical of the government's Suez policy in stirring terms: "If the BBC is found for the first time to be suppressing significant items of news, its reputation would rapidly vanish, and the harm to the national interest done in that event would enormously outweigh any damage caused by displaying to the world the workings of a free democracy."[126] In fact, the proud myth of editorial independence during the crisis, cherished long afterward, was overblown. BBC officials ran programming ideas past Downing Street, on-air commentators mostly parroted the government line, and opposition to the invasion across Britain and the world received scant coverage.[127] The BBC's coverage of the counterinsurgency in Kenya exhibited the same paradox: neutrality in principle coexisted with deference to government in practice.

The BBC's correspondent in Nairobi for most of the Mau Mau uprising, Ian McCulloch, had a penchant for ceremonial occasions and human-interest set pieces. He reported one story about the archbishop of Canterbury laying the foundation stone for a memorial to victims of Mau Mau and another— ideal for Empire Day, he said—about a ten-year-old settler girl who bandaged the wounds of an African farm worker after a Mau Mau attack. For Christmas 1954, he covered the lighting of the Christmas tree outside Nairobi city hall, a pageant featuring African carol singers, presents for needy children, and a speech from the colonial governor. It is little wonder that some BBC executives worried about the dangers of sanitized coverage.[128] But it turned out that skeptical and probing reportage was far more vulnerable to accusations of bias than McCulloch's dutiful stenography.

When the 1955 prime-time radio special by Edward and Marjorie Ward foregrounded African suffering and mocked white settlers, the reaction from the Conservative government was predictably furious. Colonial Secretary Alan Lennox-Boyd complained that the program "displayed a clear bias" and pressed for the cancellation of a planned rebroadcast overseas.[129] Less predictably, perhaps, few BBC journalists were moved to defend their colleagues against political attacks. One complained that "the word 'settlers' in this feature regularly introduces a point of view which is distasteful, extremist, or untenable," citing the use of actors' voices as an especially egregious offense.[130] Another faulted the Wards for taking "sides against the settlers" and added: "if it is true that in private in Kenya they made no secret of their anti-settler feelings, they were wrong to do so."[131] Bowing to internal and external pressure, BBC director-general Ian Jacob decided to cancel the rebroadcast. While "containing a good deal of quite accurate reporting," he told Lennox-Boyd, it "left out so much of what was required to make it a true representation of the highly complex situation that exists." By expressing a point of view that seemed to emanate not from attributed sources but from themselves, the Wards proved vulnerable to the charge that they had crossed the line between skeptical detachment and opinionated intervention.[132]

The BBC would never again cast a comparably unflattering light on the conflict in Kenya. As late as 1958, a visiting correspondent for the television news-magazine program *Panorama* was still pitching softball questions to the officials in charge of detention camps and failing to challenge the evasive answers he received. When asked how Mau Mau detainees were induced to confess to having taken oaths, one camp commandant prevaricated: "Well, it's very difficult to say. I, even myself, I wonder sometimes how they do confess . . . . It's really amazing how they do confess, I just don't know how it is."[133] Here, as in other stories on Mau Mau, BBC journalists covered the detention camps as a bureaucratic problem of classifying and managing populations rather than as sites of extreme violence. From this perspective, constantly updated official figures on the numbers of detainees—a handy metric of progress toward the goal of winning hearts and minds—were among the most newsworthy items to emerge from the camps.[134]

Whether on the airwaves or in print, most colonial violence made news only when the state was forced to recognize it. By journalistic standards, political debates and legal proceedings—criminal trials, court-martials, cases investigated by international bodies—were unambiguously newsworthy. This encouraged reporters to adopt a legalistic mentality, adjudicating claims with rigorous standards of evidence that left a heavy burden of proof on the accusers. The very idea of the fact, as a discrete and documented unit of knowledge, was a legacy of the Anglo-American judicial tradition with its ingrained presumption of innocence.[135] In the colonial context, taking cues from the legal system also meant absorbing the values of an institutional culture that habitually deemed "native" testimony untrustworthy and unreliable.[136]

The dominance of procedural stories imparted an adversarial structure to news about violence, underlining journalists' role as neutral arbiters rather than active agents of knowledge production. They performed that role nowhere more clearly than in coverage of parliamentary speechmaking. Commons debates had a potentially enormous impact on public awareness of colonial violence because a committed group of left-wing Labour and Liberal MPs exploited that forum to hold the government accountable.[137] But for journalists, this tactic meant that allegations about torture were subject to the same skeptical response as any other blow in a partisan tussle. It also reduced them to passively relaying claims and counter-claims. This report, from an hourly news bulletin on the BBC Home Service in May 1952, provides a case in point:

Mr. [Tom] Driberg (Labour) asked what enquiries had been made into the methods used by police officers in interrogating suspects in Malaya. Mr. [Alan] Lennox Boyd said there had been many rather wild accusations of ill-treatment and it was clearly in the Communists' interests to propagate those stories. He said any specific allegations had been investigated, and in a few cases where cause had been shown, stern action had been taken. Mr. Driberg said the Colonial Secretary should be asked to investigate this subject. Mr. Lennox Boyd replied that more time and trouble should be devoted to considering the problem of the police officers themselves in their appallingly difficult task. He said much time spent in checking ill-founded allegations could have been better employed in helping to bring the dreadful war to an end.[138]

Apologists for colonial violence, in turn, exploited distaste for partisan squabbling to deflect scrutiny.

For critics of colonial war, the journalistic hesitance to take sides created a quandary. They recognized that allegations carried the most weight when "serious and responsible" outlets reported them, as Anti-Slavery Society activist Thomas Fox-Pitt observed in 1956. But because the most influential media institutions were also the most cautious, news of wrongdoing usually ended up in the pages of "sensational and emotional" publications "with a strong party bias."[139] Colonial violence was thus marked as a cause rather than a story. The papers that covered it most consistently, like the *Daily Worker* and *Peace News*, were those that had the least credibility with the public or the establishment.

Whether politically aligned or ostensibly neutral, British news organizations presented a mixed and uncertain picture of what was happening in the colonies. Reports of atrocity appeared regularly but in ways that diminished their urgency: framed as allegation rather than fact, counterbalanced with steadfast denials, contradicted by other stories, played down by opinion writers, and buried on inside pages. In an age when sights and sounds traveled rapidly across time and space, colonial violence was no secret. But neither was it treated as a moral emergency.

6

Performing Colonial War

AS COLONIAL WARS dragged on, Hollywood sent reinforcements. Claudette Colbert came to London's Pinewood Studios to film *The Planter's Wife* (1952), a Malaya drama that opened with an on-screen dedication to the planters "daily defending their rubber trees with their lives."[1] With Mau Mau as a backdrop, Victor Mature and Janet Leigh shared top billing in *Safari* (1956), a film produced by Columbia and shot in Technicolor on location in Kenya, which played like a shoot-'em-up Western transposed to the jungle. Another Mau Mau film, the MGM production *Something of Value* (1957), had more ambivalent politics, signaled by the interracial casting of Rock Hudson and Sidney Poitier as lifelong friends divided by the insurgency.[2] But liberalism was hardly a trend in the empire films of the 1950s. Even as decolonization accelerated, Hollywood stars were still lending their talents to a run of Raj adventure pictures that barely updated the formulas of the 1930s: Tyrone Power in *King of the Khyber Rifles* (1954), Mature again in *Zarak* (1956) and *The Bandit of Zhobe* (1958), and Lauren Bacall in *North West Frontier* (1959). British cinema was not yet ready to abandon the romance of imperial authority, a thin red line holding back the tide of insurgency.[3]

The injection of glamor into old-fashioned genres marked another front in the waging of colonial wars as media wars. Even more than newsreels or novels, cinema held the promise of stirring visceral responses and forging sentimental bonds. Rubber planters, coffee farmers, and other expatriate communities with an uncertain claim on affections at home stood to gain from the reflected charisma of popular stars. When Hudson and Dana Wynter played a Kenya settler couple in *Something of Value*, and British stars Dirk Bogarde and Virginia McKenna did the same in *Simba* (1955), they softened the image of a not-much-loved overseas caste associated more with aristocratic hedonism than family values. Along with a Malaya picture starring

Peter Finch and Mary Ure, *Windom's Way* (1957), these films placed romantic couples in peril, domesticating political anxiety with the reassuringly familiar beats of melodrama.[4]

Even faint stirrings of unease on the big screen played like superficial concessions to changing times, aimed at rehabilitating empire rather than end it. The stereotypical "bad" imperialists in *Simba*, *Something of Value*, and *Windom's Way* were conspicuously outclassed by more humane British characters with bigger roles. While these pictures nodded to the legitimacy of anticolonial grievances, they undercut them by dwelling on the barbarism of opposition movements, hinting at the anarchy of a postcolonial future, and holding out the possibility of salvation from white paternalists.[5] The advent of Technicolor opened up new possibilities for reactionary film by exoticizing "color" and dramatizing its incursions across boundaries.[6] If the cinema of colonial war is largely forgotten today, that is a mark of its success in meeting the quotidian needs of the propaganda moment.

But film was not the only medium for entertainment about colonial war. By the late 1950s, a new generation of dramas about uneasy soldiers, traumatized families, and cracked-up interrogators were crowding theater stages and television screens. Literary critic Raymond Williams observed that the characters and spectators of drama in this period increasingly resembled one another: they sat in domestic spaces and responded to messages from the outside world. This uneasy connection between the familiar and the distant—between the comforting fixtures of the everyday and the unpredictable intrusions of "the knock on the door" or the letter"—provided an ideal metaphor for wars coming home.[7] Abandoning the usual propaganda pattern, these dramas showed inner life threatened by the violence of imperialism rather than insurgency. Instead of adventure and romance, they drew their tension from ethical dilemmas and guilty consciences.

Imperial administrators who succeeded in keeping a tight rein on film production, by offering subsidies, information, and access to locations, watched unhappily as gritty war stories broke through in other media.[8] After a 1961 BBC television drama on the campaign against EOKA, one official observed that "the Cyprus troubles, Mau Mau, and in a different way the Communist insurrection in Malaya" would "form the staple of many books and plays built around the theme of violence. I fear we must live with it."[9] By then, moody, deromanticized portrayals of colonial war had been taking shape for years. The oppositional edge of the London theater scene—the Communist-dominated Unity Theatre, the experimental Theatre Workshop, and the critically feted Royal Court Theatre—led the way in dramatizing colonial war with dark tones. The new television networks of the BBC and ITV, hungry for material to fill airtime and drawn to stories that seemed "serious" as well as suspenseful, developed a similar aesthetic for much bigger audiences. Even Hollywood eventually caught up to the bleak new style. The descent from grandeur to despair, famously signaled by the two-part structure of *Lawrence of Arabia* (1962), also defined Cyprus films like *Private Potter* (1962) and the Malaya picture *The 7th Dawn* (1964).

Not coincidentally, the peak moment of the dark war drama in the late 1950s and early 1960s arrived as the end of empire began to seem inevitable. Favoring the muted shades of fatalism over the bright colors of outrage, these stories condemned brutality above all for its pointlessness. For writers captivated by the theme of "decommitment," colonial wars did not generate new causes to rally for so much as they illustrated the disintegration of old faiths.[10] While some dramas inverted the values of old-fashioned imperial adventures, by casting yesterday's heroes as today's villains, many more reveled in moral ambiguity, by showing characters trapped within a tradition they did not create. Dwelling on the grim inescapability of violence was less a call to action than a form of catharsis, allowing audiences to indulge their uneasiness about futile and ugly wars.

Acting Out Atrocity: Violence on Stage

Kenneth Tynan's *Observer* review of *Look Back in Anger* in May 1956 is remembered as a landmark moment in theater history, when John Osborne's play found an eloquent defender amid a torrent of early criticism. Playing up the theme of generational rebellion, Tynan celebrated the restive anti-establishment sensibility embodied in protagonist Jimmy Porter. Less often remembered is that Tynan identified the establishment with the use of colonial violence. Summing up the character's "automatic rejection of 'official' attitudes," Tynan wrote: "One cannot imagine Jimmy Porter listening with a straight face to speeches about our inalienable right to flog Cypriot schoolboys."[11]

It was a curious choice of example—and not only because Cyprus is mentioned nowhere in the play. As critics have long recognized, Porter may have mocked the pomposity of empire, but he also mourned the passing of British power, with more than a little nostalgia for the Edwardian heyday of the Raj represented by his father-in-law. Osborne's anger targeted the indignities of decline as well as the conservatism of the traditional elite.[12] Given that Tynan had a habit of injecting anticolonial politics into his reviews—a 1958 play about the Hungarian Revolution left him longing for "a similar treatment of Suez"—there is nothing surprising about his attempt to wring a polemical message from a more ambivalent text.[13] But the attempt itself raises questions. Had socialists like Tynan come to expect attacks on colonial war from the London stage by the middle of the 1950s? Or were they merely hoping for the advent of a political theater whose promise had not yet been realized?

At a time when partisan identification was still overwhelmingly determined by social class, the theater world was no bastion of anticolonial leftism. Stage designer Oliver Messel took Violet Bonham-Carter by surprise in 1959 when he commented that he "just couldn't stand" the Hola massacre; he had always been a loyal Conservative and had no qualms about Suez.[14] Actor Kenneth Williams, conversely, was appalled by the cynicism of Suez but bristled at the sight of a "practically all negro" group protesting at Speakers' Corner a few years later. "They proceed to run down the 'colonialists,' 'imperialists,' etc.," he complained in his diary, "but seem to forget that few other countries would afford them the privilege of freedom to abuse so fearlessly."[15] Even at the Royal Court, which cultivated a reputation for thumbing its nose at authority, director Lindsay Anderson thought that the label of "socialist theater" was "largely nonsense . . . . The tone was far more humanist than intellectual." Although several Royal Court figures joined the antinuclear movement of the early 1960s, director William Gaskill remembered, "our degree of political commitment varied" and "most of us dropped out after the first day" of the Aldermaston march.[16]

The structures underlying theatrical production in London tilted the field against political activism and formal experimentation alike. With nearly one in five West End theatres destroyed by bombing during the Blitz, commercial rents doubled and a handful of wealthy real-estate companies came to dominate theater ownership. Their high overhead costs and managerial outlook fostered a risk-averse culture built around star-driven, crowd-pleasing productions.[17] State funding from the Arts Council offered a partial respite from these incentives, but not for explicitly left-wing or avant-garde theater.[18] Although the comparatively upscale Royal Court did benefit from public subsidies, the effect may have been more constraining than liberating, as the theater's management committee anxiously monitored the politics of the material performed onstage.[19]

Of course, the state maintained another, blunter, form of control over theatrical expression in the censorship powers of the Lord Chamberlain. The enforcement of cultural standards by a royal appointee seemed anachronistic by the end of the decade: attacked by critics like Tynan, circumvented by loopholes, mocked by irreverent new styles of playwriting, and questioned even within the Lord Chamberlain's Office, which feared a humiliating loss of face as authority slipped away.[20] Yet officials continued to insist on script changes and, in some cases, denied licenses and prosecuted producers when shows ran afoul of what they saw as established codes of decency. While rough language, obscenity, blasphemy, *lèse-majesté*, and homosexuality were the most strictly enforced taboos, controversial treatments of war and empire also drew the censors' ire.[21]

These pressures meant that, for most of the 1950s, the fiercest denunciations of colonial violence played in niche theaters with strong ideological identities. The most prominent of these was the Unity Theatre in King's Cross. Heir to the socialist theater tradition forged in the Popular Front of the 1930s, the Unity was run largely by Communist activists and kept afloat by membership fees and block bookings from left-wing groups. Like other institutions on the far left, the theater suffered in the early years of the Cold War as the Communist Party declined, trade unions cut ties, and financial pressures mounted. The creative program stagnated, too, leaning ever more heavily on "classic" plays of working-class life and old-fashioned music-hall acts.[22] But the Unity in the 1950s also maintained a significant advantage in the mounting of onstage protest. As a club theater, it was exempt from the Lord Chamberlain's scrutiny on the grounds that performances were open only to registered members and therefore "private." This loophole made it possible to mock authority figures and address topical issues far more explicitly than on the commercial stage.

Some Unity productions drew on the "Living Newspaper" tradition inspired by Soviet agitprop and Popular Front theater in the United States. In its classic form, the Living Newspaper interspersed verbatim excerpts from press stories and parliamentary debates, read aloud by an onstage narrator, with dramatic scenes played by actors. This technique represented an explicit attempt to link the poetic truth of the stage with the factual truth of the "real world." It also offered a critical rereading or alternative version of the news aimed at challenging dominant interpretations of documented facts.[23] Even when they strayed from the hallmarks of the Living Newspaper genre, plays critical of colonial war took up the same project of reworking the knowledge generated by journalists.

One of them was a drama of the Malaya Emergency, *Strangers in the Land*, which ran for two months at the Unity beginning in November 1952. The thirty-seven-year-old playwright, Mona Brand, was an Australian with a history of left-wing activism then living in London. Inspired by the *Daily Worker*'s sympathetic treatment of the insurgency, Brand conceived the play as a corrective to hostile coverage in the right-wing press, told from the perspective of a young woman who visits her planter-fiancé in Malaya and is abruptly initiated into the ways of colonial war. As one reviewer summarized the story, the heroine "is so shocked by the behavior of the English towards the Malayans that she decides to go home again rather than risking becoming like them."[24]

Although the violence in *Strangers in the Land* happens offstage, it keeps intruding on the bungalow living room that is the play's only scenery. The juxtaposition of domestic comfort and savage warfare is established from the opening scene, as planters return from a bandit-hunting expedition to trade war stories over cocktails. "Pour me a drink, will you, there's a good chap," the fiancé says after making his entrance. "We've fixed those swine, anyway. There are one or two that won't be fit for much now." The presence of the newcomer, Christine, prompts a round of expository chatter covering the gamut of counterinsurgency measures: the destruction of squatter settlements ("not a shack left in Bukit"), food restriction ("the ration cut should have taught them their lesson"), and forced resettlement ("we've got 500,000 natives in camps now").[25] These unsettling details are the stuff of casual banter at the start of the play and impassioned diatribes at the end, as Christine journeys haltingly toward political consciousness. After a village is leveled by British forces, she finally exclaims: "It's just a graveyard of burnt-out shacks . . . . How many villages will they have to destroy before we can feel ourselves safe from the women and little children?"[26]

Strangers in the Land turned a spotlight on acts of war that were widely known but not always condemned as atrocities. Brand seized on the collection of morbid trophies by security forces as the most shocking, and most readily dramatized, form of brutality. A 1952 BBC radio report, featuring a planter who hung the caps of slain guerillas above the bar in his bungalow, was copied almost verbatim into the script. When Christine asks about a similar display onstage, the other characters "smirk with slightly drunken mirth," as the script put it.[27] A later scene alludes to the 1952 *Daily Worker* photographs of British soldiers posing with mutilated corpses. The cocktail hour comes to an awkward end when a planter's wife staggers onstage, announces that she has discovered a pair of severed heads in a bag, sobs hysterically, and calls her husband a murderer. When the others hint that the woman is mentally disturbed and hustle her away, they seem to admit that the imperialist code requires untroubled coexistence with brutality.[28] By juxtaposing details, montage-like, from different news stories, Brand constructed a heightened version of reality that sharpened the moral dilemma for audiences.

For all the fierceness of its politics, *Strangers in the Land* was not agit-prop. Brand rejected an attempt by Unity's director to rewrite the play with "a finale of liberation fighters marching on with flags flying" and hoped that the "Somerset Maugham atmosphere" would attract a broad audience of middle-class theatergoers.[29] That was never likely for a show, mounted at a Communist-dominated theater at the height of the Cold War, which portrayed Britons as callous killers. But the Lord Chamberlain squashed any possibility of reaching a wider public. Unusually, the censors refused to consider any revisions to bring the script into compliance, warning instead that public performance of the play might lead to a "breach of the peace." Performed only in brief runs for club audiences in London, Surrey, and Liverpool, *Strangers in the Land* remained stranded in political purgatory.

The Theatre Workshop, led by Joan Littlewood and based at the Theatre Royal in Stratford from 1953, was likewise constrained by censorship but endured long enough to outflank it. While Theatre Workshop had roots in the same Workers' Theatre Movement as the Unity, it relied more heavily on formal experimentation in the tradition of Brecht. Among the techniques aimed at disrupting bourgeois theater's stuffy conventions, Theatre Workshop productions blended song, dance, and dialogue in an unpredictable fusion of styles; broke the "fourth wall" by calling out to members of the audience; and encouraged endless improvisation. Performers rewrote scripts as they rehearsed and worked topical references into their lines, practices guaranteed to antagonize the Lord Chamberlain.[30]

Littlewood's response to the Palestine Emergency prompted an early collision with the censors. In Manchester in 1947, she witnessed anti-Semitic mobs roaming the streets after the *Daily Express* published its front-page photograph of British soldiers hanging from trees in Palestine. In typical Theatre Workshop fashion, Littlewood and her collaborators seized on a text that could speak to the moment: Friedrich Wolf's *Professor Mamlock* (1933), the story of a Jewish doctor who fails to recognize the threat of Nazism until it is too late. They interpolated Wolf's script with several freshly written scenes depicting the Manchester riots.[31] But the Lord Chamberlain refused to allow them and even banned any mention of the street violence from the program. What Littlewood bitterly called a "castrated version" of the piece played to a mostly empty house for a week and sent the company into debt.[32]

Like the Unity, Theatre Workshop had troubles in the 1950s beyond the threat of censorship. After years on tour in pursuit of working-class audiences, veteran performers felt unsure about settling in London. With scant support from the state, finances were tight, while the demands of experimental and popular entertainment proved difficult to reconcile. But by the end of the decade, the avant-garde daring embodied by Theatre Workshop was suddenly fashionable. Between 1959 and 1961, five productions transferred from Stratford to the West End, a lucrative revenue stream fueled by properties like Brendan Behan's *The Hostage* and Shelagh Delaney's *A Taste of Honey*. It was not just that commercial producers, hungry for original material after 1956, were casting a wider net than ever before. It was that the brand of transgression Theatre Workshop cultivated in this period—irreverent and tragicomic, concerned with sexuality and race as much as class, celebrating "the vitality of the excluded"—marked a colorful departure from the dour drama of much socialist realism.[33] Just as the Lord Chamberlain's writ was beginning to run out, Littlewood found a marketable formula for subversive theater.

Behan's *The Hostage* (1958), a rowdy carnival that left blood on the floor, portrayed colonial violence as a toxic national tradition. The title character is a British soldier held by the IRA as he awaits execution in retaliation for the hanging of an IRA prisoner in Belfast. The setting, a Dublin boarding house of ill repute, is stocked with eccentrics who are venal and hedonistic rather than ideological; the only character of firm political commitments is a senile English Protestant who has confoundingly embraced Irish republicanism. Yet Behan treats English nationalism as equally deluded and even more dangerous. The lyrics of the old man's big musical number, "The Captains and the Kings," links the romantic imagery of Englishness with colonial conquest and racial chauvinism:

> Far away in dear old Cyprus,
> Or in Kenya's dusty land,
> Where all bear the white man's burden
> In many a strange land.
> [...] And we sigh for dear old England,
> And the Captains and the Kings. [...]
>
> Let us cease to run ourselves down
> But praise God that we are white.
> And better still we're English [...][34]

Later, at the close of Act Two, the soldier picks up the theme with an endorsement of racist violence that undercuts sympathy for his impending fate:

I love my dear old Notting Hill, wherever I may roam,
But I wish the Irish and the n******s and the wogs,
Were kicked out and sent back home.[35]

Behan sustains a tension in the audience's relation to the soldier. He has been conscripted, literally, into the service of myths inherited from older generations, a mirror image of the IRA prisoner whose fate is entwined with his own. "He's only eighteen, same age as us National Service blokes," the soldier observes of his counterpart. The man held hostage for the crimes of empire is too young to vote and "never bloody-well asked to be brought here."[36] Even without the pointed mentions of Cyprus and Kenya, audiences would have understood the symmetry between the two hostages not only as an Anglo-Irish story, but as a parable for the ideologically exhausted, self-destructive wars of decolonization.

In what becomes almost a ritual incantation, the script rehearses the global itinerary of colonial war whenever the hangman's noose is mentioned:

OFFICER: Irishmen have been hanged by Englishmen at eighteen years of age before now.
PAT: Yes, and Cypriots, Jews, and Africans.

Later, a character quotes a sign at a street protest: "England, the hangman of thousands. In Ireland, in Kenya, in Cyprus."[37] Throughout the play, the soldier—and the audience—are instructed in the repertoire of British military occupation. "The police walk the beats in tanks and armored cars," one character says of Northern Ireland. "The British turned a tank and fired shells into people's homes," another recalls of the Easter Rising. The drumbeat of atrocity offers an implicit response to the soldier's cry: "What do I know about Ireland or Cyprus, or Kenya or Jordan or any of those places?"[38] Distinctions between Ireland and other conflict zones are always slipping in *The Hostage*, deepening the sense of colonial violence as an endlessly recurring nightmare.

Originally written in the Irish language and staged in Dublin, *The Hostage* was translated and extensively reworked under Littlewood's supervision before the London premiere. The script's allusions to colonial war, which multiplied over the course of this process, helped to anchor the action firmly in the present and heighten the story's relevance for an English audience.[39] They also advanced Littlewood's goal of thumbing a defiant nose at the censors. The revision that emerged from rehearsals at Stratford was packed with references (John Foster Dulles, the Wolfenden Report, the Virgin Mary, the Royal Family) and characters (the flamboyant prostitute Rio Rita and his black lover) of a kind long deemed taboo by the Lord Chamberlain.[40] It was only because officials feared a confrontation with the increasingly well-respected and well-publicized Theatre Workshop that they accepted script alterations rather than denying a license altogether.[41]

Audiences had no trouble reading the play as an indictment of colonial war. Publicity around the opening suggested that Behan modeled the plot on the taking of British hostages in Cyprus and Egypt.[42] In an ecstatic *Sunday Times* review that helped to make the play's reputation, Harold Hobson described the sting of its anticolonial rhetoric: "It has lines alleging the brutality of the British in Kenya, in India, in Cyprus, that strike an Englishman across the face like a lash." Another review read the play as a brief for "Cypriot nationalism" even more than Irish nationalism.[43] Though true believers were discomfited by its sudden commercial success, Theatre Workshop at the end of the 1950s had found a way to blend political subversion and aesthetic innovation without losing an audience.

If Unity and Theatre Workshop occupied the radical edge of theater against empire, the Royal Court Theatre emerged as the home of the uneasy imperial conscience. A series of plays staged there in the years after *Look Back*

FIGURE 6.1 Joan Littlewood and the cast of Brendan Behan's *The Hostage* rehearsing at the Theatre Royal, Stratford East, London, 1959. J.B. Hanley/Paul Popper/Popperfoto/Getty Images.

in Anger responded to the violent end of empire with melancholy meditation instead of protest or mockery. The ghost of socialist theater lurked in the wings of the Royal Court; the first general manager and later artistic director, Oscar Lewenstein, was a former member of the Young Communist League and veteran of the Unity Theater in Glasgow. But playwrights and producers at the Royal Court made no systematic attempt to translate ideology into art. Osborne and others who described themselves as socialists were mostly expressing a nebulous anti-establishment sentiment, chastened by the disillusionment of 1956, rather than advocating a program.[44] Unlike the theaters that grew directly out of the Popular Front, the Royal Court did not valorize the working-class spectator but looked instead to the Fabian tradition of George Bernard Shaw, tweaking the hypocrisy of middle-class audiences within the confines of literary convention. With Oxbridge-educated aesthetes in key positions and elite patrons easing the flow of Arts Council subsidies, the fabled rebellion on Sloane Square had its limits.[45]

Yet Royal Court playwrights in the late 1950s kept returning to the dark side of colonial war, a theme that fit the anti-establishment mood and served other purposes too. Some were purely dramatic. The realism that dominated at the Royal Court was not synonymous with naturalism; dialogue put ideas in conflict rather than reproducing everyday speech and characters expressed social tensions rather than idiosyncratic personalities.[46] To achieve these aims without sacrificing believability, playwrights had to construct tense situations of a kind that might plausibly happen to ordinary people. Colonial war offered an abundance of them: the experience of combat, the relationships disrupted by conscription, the violence that came home as trauma or loss. What heightened the dramatic stakes even further was the representation of these conflicts as morally suspect. Wars fought by dubious means, for uncertain ends, placed characters under greater pressure than heroic crusades.

While his politics were notoriously ambiguous, Osborne went from flirting with imperial nostalgia in *Look Back in Anger* to diagnosing its malignancy in his next play, *The Entertainer*, which debuted at the Royal Court in April 1957. Laurence Olivier played the title character, Archie Rice, a seedy, middle-aged music-hall performer whose repertoire of flag-waving songs and lewd jokes is wearing thin. Where Behan and Littlewood treated the music hall as a living source of inspiration, Osborne set out to anatomize its decay and, with it, the creeping rot of jingoism. As the debacle of Suez unfolds offstage, imperiling Archie's conscripted son, Archie's act remains trapped in the fantasy world of Edwardian bluster:

Those bits of red still on the map
We won't give up without a scrap.
What we've got left back
We'll keep – and blow you, Jack!

When the curtain comes down on the show-within-a-show, the focus shifts to the dysfunctional Rice family, for whom the chauvinism rings hollow. Archie's father Billy, a music-hall veteran and living link to the Boer War era, is disoriented by the upsurge of resistance to empire: "People seem to be able to do what they like to us. Just what they like. I don't understand it. I really don't." Archie's wife drunkenly questions the justice of conscription: "I don't know why they send these boys out to do the fighting. They're just kids, that's all." And Archie's daughter, who attends the great antiwar rally in Trafalgar Square, reflects bitterly on the troubles of the half-brother who declares a conscientious objection rather than serving: "He'd have been better off in the Army—sticking a bayonet into some wog." All are devastated when, in the midst of celebrating the conscript's expected return, they learn that he has been killed in Egypt.[47]

Left unclear is whether Osborne sees war for empire as intrinsically wrong or merely pathetic because British power has already fallen so far. The contrast between Billy and Archie Rice hints at a conservative fable about the entwinement of moral and geopolitical decline. The "genteel-seeming" older man, loyal to family and country, sets a standard unmet by the younger, a serial philanderer and tax cheat who is "dead behind these eyes." And yet, the generational differences do not always work in Billy's favor.[48] While both men are racist, Billy's repeated outbursts verge on the pathological. While both men build careers on jingoism—and thus rank among the "licensed pedlar[s] of emotional dope to every audience in Britain," as Tynan commented in his *Observer* review—it is Billy who embodies this tradition's vexed moment of origin.[49] The only sample of the older man's act heard onstage is the 1899 tune "The Absent-Minded Beggar," a song used to raise funds for wounded soldiers, widows, and orphans during the Boer War. It is a reminder that, even in the supposed Edwardian golden age, patriotism was streaked with blood. The song's final line, repeated by Billy for emphasis, is "pay, pay, pay!" *The Entertainer* shows the heirs to an empire paying the price for it.

Doris Lessing's *Each His Own Wilderness*, which premiered at the Royal Court in 1958, likewise cast empire as a generational burden. The play, which juxtaposes the *engagé*, 1930s-style leftism of a mother with the exhausted, 1950s-style apathy of her son, is concerned less with the persistence of dangerous myths than with the loss of ideals that might challenge them. Lessing draws a straight line between the waning of political commitment and nihilistic forms of warfare. One of these is nuclear war—the play opens with the sound of an atomic blast—and its mocking refutation of the left-wing faith in humanity's capacity for improvement.[50] The other is colonial war, portrayed as more obviously meaningless than ever before and lacking any redemptive purpose. When the mother celebrates her son's release from National Service in the opening moments of the play, neither can treat the usual imperial-militarist pieties as anything other than a bad joke:

> MYRA: It's luck you weren't in Cyprus or Kenya or Suez—keeping order [*laughing angrily*]. Keeping everything tidy . . . You might have been killed for something you don't even believe in.
>
> TONY: You're so delightfully old-fashioned. Getting killed for something you believe in is surely a bit of a luxury these days? Something your generation enjoyed. Now one just—gets killed.[51]

Here again, conscription works as a metaphor for the difficulty of escaping complicity in empire. It also symbolizes democratic breakdown because the state's ability to squander young lives on a transparently hollow cause dramatizes the futility of political action. "If the 5,000 people killed themselves tomorrow in Trafalgar Square as a protest against—everything, the six powerful men up there wouldn't care, they wouldn't even notice," another young character despairs. While Osborne portrayed colonial war as a retreat into fantasy, Lessing dwelled on the wreckage of those illusions and the cynicism that grew out of it.[52]

If family dramas offered a sturdy vehicle for bringing colonial wars home, the violence inflicted by soldiers overseas ran up against the limits of the genre. With their characters confined to sitting rooms, Osborne and Lessing both alluded to atrocity rather than representing it. For other playwrights—including several members of the National Service generation—atrocity belonged at center stage. Willis Hall was one of them. Born in Leeds, Hall volunteered for the regular army on the eve of conscription and ended up serving in the Malayan Emergency. After returning to Britain in 1954, he spent several years churning out scripts for the BBC before authoring his first stage play, *The Long and the Short and the Tall*, which ran at the Royal Court for three profitable months in 1959 and then progressed to a national tour and West End run. Set in a tattered, claustrophobic hut in the Malayan jungle, it is the story of seven British Army soldiers—a carefully constructed cross-section of the nation, including a Welshman, a Scotsman, and a Cockney—who debate whether to kill a disarmed prisoner as enemy forces move in.

Nominally, the action takes place during the Second World War and the prisoner is a soldier in the Japanese Imperial Army. But the echoes of counterinsurgency were inescapable in 1959: the atmospherics of an isolated patrol confronting a lone enemy; the press coverage that mentioned the Malayan jungle setting without specifying the time period; the National Service pedigrees of Hall and some of his actors. Michael Caine, who performed the lead role on tour, told reporters that "he knew many National Service lads out in Malaya who could have stepped straight from the pages of this brilliant play."[53] Reviewers touted the play as a gritty exposé of contemporary warfare. Under the headline "Lid Off Life in the Jungle," the left-wing weekly *Reynolds' News* called it a must-see for "mothers who want to know what their sons are really like when they get into uniform."[54]

The portrayal of army life in *The Long and the Short and the Tall* is resolutely anti-heroic. At a time when popular culture was awash in celebratory narratives of the Second World War, Hall set the story in the moment of maximum humiliation for British imperialism in that conflict: the fall of Singapore in 1942. The soldiers charged with holding the line are bigoted, quarrelsome, undisciplined, and unsympathetic. The Cockney Private Bamforth, with his endless, obnoxious chatter and contempt for authority, bears a strong resemblance to Jimmy Porter. There is no hint of redemption as the curtain comes down on "the screams of dying men" and a lone survivor waving the white flag.[55] Themes of questionable sacrifice and abject surrender, rarely articulated in the collective memory of the Second World War, became more intelligible in relation to the ongoing loss of decolonization. Whether or not audiences grasped the intricacies of Malayan independence two years earlier, they would have recognized that 1942 did not mark the last British retreat from a territory on which British blood was still being spilled in 1959.

Glimpses of callous behavior by British soldiers onstage mirrored contemporary anxieties as well. The soldiers' conversation reveals a thriving informal trade in "souvenirs" looted from enemy corpses. When the prisoner is finally shot, a disgusted Bamforth shouts, "You've got the biggest souvenir of all .... Take that and hang it on the front room wall."[56] Even in Brand's *Strangers in the Play*, the bag with severed heads remained offstage. In *The Long and the Short and the Tall*, the victim is visible, though silent, for most of the show. Played by Japanese-born actor Kenji Takaki in the Royal Court production, he works to establish a bond with his captors by showing photos of his family and telegraphing his emotions with expressions and gestures. His death also takes place fully onstage. As the stage directions put it: "The bullets slam home into the body of the Prisoner like hammer blows. The Prisoner doubles up and falls to the floor." This graphic violence marks the climax of a long argument during which the prisoner's fate is often in doubt, even though the illegality of killing him never is. "There's such a thing as the Geneva Convention!" one soldier points out shortly after the capture.[57]

The story traces the gradual but near-inexorable transformation of conscripts into killers. Just after the prisoner is captured, only one of seven soldiers advocates executing him: "We whip him out and knock him off, that's all. We can't take prisoners. We're out to do a job."[58] By the end of the play, six out of seven have come to accept the same view. Military service in the play is inherently brutalizing, wearing down humane impulses and encouraging aggressive ones. Though the mixture of motivations—self-preservation, vengeance, racism—varies from character to character, the trend is clear. As the commanding officer comments, the capacity to kill is "inside all of us. That's the trouble. Just needs fetching out."[59] The one-two punch of the final sequence, the shooting of the prisoner followed by the decimation of the unit, does not signify a causal connection so much as a savage irony. They have killed an unarmed man in a futile cause, losing their honor along with the battle.

No wonder even admiring reviews described *The Long and the Short and the Tall* as "anti-war" or "pacifist" "propaganda."[60] Yet the play also managed to succeed as commercial entertainment, culminating in a 1961 film adaptation. Perhaps the politics of *The Long and the Short and the Tall* were just ambiguous enough to permit less-than-subversive readings. The blow-by-blow process of brutalization could be seen as justification rather than cautionary tale. One plausible interpretation is that the men never become brutal enough; their squeamishness leads them to use a noisy gun instead of a silent bayonet, alerting the enemy to their position.[61] What is more, the hyper-naturalism of the dialogue—the saltiness and the slurs, the regional accents, the repetitions and digressions—contributes to an almost documentary quality that submerges moral judgment in surface description.

The complacency-inducing tendency of naturalism represented a deepening preoccupation for the British theater world at the end of the 1950s. Debates about the politics of form were driven not just by the experiments of the Theatre Workshop but by a wider fashion for Bertolt Brecht. Tynan cited him ritually in his reviews, the front page of the *Times Literary Supplement* touted his virtues, and festivals and theatres performed his plays with increasing frequency after the Berliner Ensemble toured London in 1956.[62] The Brechtian ideal of "modernist," "interventionist," or "epic" theater, disrupting comfortable assumptions about everyday experience to expose social structures, had always been a lodestar at Stratford East. It eventually found a foothold at the Royal Court, too. The Writers' Group began meeting there in 1958 and developed into a self-styled cell of radical theater opposed to the commercial productions of playwrights like Osborne and Hall.[63]

While the dangers of passive spectatorship and vicarious pleasure always shadowed portrayals of colonial violence, the Brechtian vogue of the late 1950s renewed attention to them. Brecht had warned decades earlier about relying on graphic imagery in theatrical protests against fascism: "Some people may believe that it is enough to describe the atrocities, particularly if great literary talent and genuine anger lend the description urgency . . . . What long explanations could be needed? The reader will surely leap up and restrain the torturers. But comrades, explanations are essential."[64] The idea of "anti-naturalism," which became a slogan among British Brechtians, warned against the assumption that even vivid and seemingly unambiguous images ever spoke for themselves.[65] The British reception of Brecht stressed other elements as well. One was an uneasy atmosphere of "exaggerated lawlessness . . . an embittered and anarchic reaction against the shortcomings of orthodox mortality," as a leading critic put it in 1959.[66] Another was the motif of the failed revolution, which Raymond Williams later summarized as characters who are "defeated but you can see why they were defeated, so it is your job to go home and make your own revolution."[67]

One of the dramatists in the Writers' Group at the Royal Court, John Arden, fused these elements into the play that became *Serjeant Musgrave's Dance* (1959). Like Hall, Arden grew up in the shadow of conscription, emerging from two years of National Service at Maresfield Army base in the late 1940s with a jaundiced view of the military. "Everyone in it was either daft or crooked or pissed-off," Arden wrote later. "As an institution it served no useful purpose except to get the walls of the latrines clean for once in a while, and to keep the documents at HQ in a reasonably ordered condition . . . . The fact is, the entire Army, as a conscript organization, was an insane institution."[68] But it was the 1958 riot of British forces against civilians in Famagusta that prompted him to write a play about the madness of colonial war.

Serjeant Musgrave's Dance is the story of a group of Victorian soldiers so traumatized by the atrocities they commit that they bring the war home in a deranged attempt to remedy the injustice. The colony where they are posted, "a little country without much importance except from the point of view that

there's a Union Jack flies over it," is never named. But the echoes of contemporary conflict are clear. "Kill *him*, kill *them*, they're all bloody rebels, State
of Emergency," is how one soldier describes the orders they are given. The
violence they unleash against civilians is purely vengeful, a reprisal for the
murder of one of their own. The routine practices of counterinsurgency slip
easily into a rampage: "It's easy, they're all in bed, kick the front doors down,
knock 'em on the head, boys, chuck 'em in the wagons."[69] Arden even modeled the death toll in the play on the figures from the Famagusta incident, a
detail he described as "quite deliberate."[70]

Under the pretext of recruiting for the army, Musgrave and a ragged band
of deserters return to their hometown in the mining country of northern
England. Because their intentions are not clearly explained for most of the
play, the climactic scene plays as a shock. On a platform bedecked with Union
Jacks, the men turn a Gatling gun on the townspeople—and, pointedly, the
audience—while hoisting the skeleton of their murdered comrade high above
the stage. "We've earned our living by beating and killing folk like yourselves
in the streets of their own city," one of the soldiers says. "Well, it's drove us
mad—and so we come back here to tell you how and to show you what it's
like." With a twisted moral logic, Musgrave decrees that twenty-five townspeople should die in retaliation for the victims of colonial violence because
five of them died in retaliation for a single soldier's death. The timely arrival
of a troop of Dragoons is all that prevents him from carrying out his plan.
One rebel is killed, Musgrave and another survivor are jailed to await their
hanging, and the moral indictment they have leveled is quickly forgotten.
The townspeople drunkenly celebrate the restoration of order as one of them
sings: "End of a bad bad dream. Gush forth the foaming stream."[71]

The contradiction at the heart of Musgrave's character, which one reviewer summarized as "violent, coercive pacifism," baffled critics in 1959.
Arden responded that making Musgrave an impeccably liberal hero would
have evaded the problem that made events like Famagusta possible: the "over-
powering urge to match some particularly outrageous piece of violence with
an even greater and more outrageous retaliation."[72] Arden underlines the difficulty of any resistance to empire by showing how deftly authority figures
exploit a pervasive atmosphere of militarism. The town Parson sanctifies the
recruiting drive with the argument that Britain "is great because of the greatness of its responsibilities." At the end, even the alienated mineworkers are
content to celebrate the restoration of a threatened status quo rather than
take risks for a cause they do not see as their own.[73]

By turning a gun on the audience, Arden made an uncomfortable statement about complicity with violence. By making the rebels flawed and letting them fail, he warned against any easy escape from it. Not surprisingly,
the conspicuous denial of catharsis in *Serjeant Musgrave's Dance* left many
spectators unsatisfied. Almost universally rejected by critics, the play ran at
the Royal Court with empty seats and heavy losses, even as the theater's creative leadership championed it. Only from the mid-1960s did the play's reputation began to improve with a flurry of revivals and repertory performances,
the start of a gradual ascent into the canon. This long-term success owed
something to Stuart Hall, who championed the play in the inaugural issue
of *New Left Review* and encouraged "every Left Club, every CND group,
and . . . every provincial theater" to produce it. Noting parallels with *The
Entertainer* and *The Hostage*, Hall praised Arden for transcending them, by
confronting the irony of an inhumane campaign for humanity. How to construct an anticolonial politics that did not collapse under the weight of its
own emotional intensity was, Hall thought, the lingering challenge posed by
the play. "Musgrave's dance is *our* dance—as surely as the 'foreign war' the
soldiers have deserted is Cyprus or Kenya or Nyasaland."[74]

Coming after a string of hit plays on the same subject, the overwhelmingly hostile reception of *Serjeant Musgrave's Dance* in 1959 hardly showed
that colonial violence was taboo. On the contrary, Arden's unconventionality
expressed the anxiety that it was becoming all too familiar through tame and
routinized gestures of unease. The same worry motivated another avant-garde
experiment that emerged from the Writers' Group at the Royal Court in 1959,
a one-night, largely improvised show called *Eleven Men Dead at Hola Camp*.
Dramatists Keith Johnstone and William Gaskill assembled a group of black
performers, most of them writers rather than professional actors, to act out
scenes from the parliamentary report on the killings while a narrator recited
portions of the text. Over the course of three hours, they staged a Mau Mau
initiation ceremony; satirized the "languid, stiff-upper-lipped" response of
white settlers; showed warders learning how to wield their weapons without
leaving visible marks; portrayed the massacre itself; and led a discussion with
the audience.[75]

Eleven Men Dead at Hola Camp—which played on a Sunday night, when
the Royal Court operated as a "club" theater to avoid censorship—signaled
the resilience of the socialist theater tradition. The "Living Newspaper"
became a living parliamentary report, with performers simultaneously focusing attention on official language and eliciting a subtext from it. In the
stripped-down tradition of agitprop, the stage was bare of scenery; clubs and

shovels were the only props and masks the only costumes. With the action centered on a dialogue of words and bodies, the climactic scene played like a "surrealist tableau," as one of the performers, Nigerian writer Wole Soyinka, remembered later:

> The Narrator at a lectern under a spot; a dispassionate reading, deliberately clinical, letting the stark facts reveal the states of mind of torturers and victims . . . The beatings begin: one to the left side, then the back, the arms—right, left, front, back. Rhythmically. The cudgels swing in unison . . . In terms of images, a fluid, near balletic scene.[76]

The surreal quality of the scene was, in part, a measure of its daring. Black performers wearing white masks were reenacting a British colonial massacre on a London stage a little more than four months after it happened. The House of Commons had not yet debated the report of the official enquiry and no charges had been filed. As Gaskill recalled, the Royal Court's board of directors was "shit-scared" to stage something so "positively political"; they insisted that a lawyer clear the idea in advance and printed a disclaimer in the program that the show was "a dramatic exercise" rather than a "reconstruction." But in a lively atmosphere of fourth-wall-breaking, at least one performer cried: "If you think this was not a political statement, you're out of your mind!"[77]

In retrospect, the limitations of *Eleven Men Dead at Hola Camp* seem obvious. Freedom from censorship came at the cost of a tiny, one-night audience. The format, with white dramatists shouting suggestions at black performers, offered a painfully vivid display of patronizing liberalism. But Soyinka was most bothered by the fear that even a spare, Brechtian representation of the massacre risked aestheticizing violence. As they performed the guards' dance of death, were they restoring the humanity of eleven dead men or merely repeating the injury? Although he stayed onstage for the rest of the show, Soyinka sat out the massacre scene because he felt queasy about the politics of dramatization. As he put it almost three decades later: "When is playacting rebuked by reality? When is fictionalizing presumptuous? What happens after playacting?"[78]

By the end of the 1950s, the staging of colonial violence had come a long way from propaganda. The taboos once enforced by the state had crumbled. Just as significant, dramatizations of colonial violence flourished in a cultural space defined by aesthetics rather than ideology. The audiences that watched an IRA sympathizer singing about Kenya and Cyprus, a family collapsing under the weight of the Suez crisis, and an Army unit murdering a prisoner in Malaya were not there because their Communist Party branch or trade union booked a block of tickets. From Stratford East and Sloane Square to the West End, bleak portrayals of empire's brutality reached those looking for an entertaining night out, the latest literary fashion, and perhaps a frisson of transgression. But Soyinka's warning shadowed the widening appeal of gritty war narratives. Performances intended as a moral reckoning, he worried, could be experienced as "an exorcism, a certificate of release," or "a soporific" instead.[79]

Bringing the War Home: Violence on Screen

Nothing confirmed the transformation of anti-heroic war stories into mass entertainment more than their uptake on television. The new medium's capacity for departing from the propaganda line was the product of an unsettled yet creative founding moment. Veterans of early television drama later delighted in puncturing the myth of a "golden age" by pointing to the severity of technical constraints, the stodginess of the production bureaucracy, and the quiet threat of state surveillance.[80] Yet the small screen in this period still emerged as a home for edgy, politically conscious entertainment. For a time, conditions aligned to produce a polyphonic culture of television drama, which elevated auteurist voices with relatively little pressure from generic templates and ideological guardrails.

This was partly a function of the fact that producers in the drama departments of the new television networks had abundant airtime to fill and a desperate need for fresh material. This meant that any script that cleared bars for technical practicality and dramatic interest stood an excellent chance of being produced.[81] Prestigious anthology series such as BBC's *The Wednesday Play* and ITV's *Television Playhouse* functioned as showcases for revolving casts of writing talent; an expectation of changing perspectives from week to week was built into the form. At the same time, the cultural ambitions of television's founding generation—the desire to claim the prestige of a significant art form—rested heavily on the reputation of "serious" or "provocative" drama. This created a real, if circumscribed, space for controversial subjects and subversive politics. "In order to be serious," critic John Caughie observed, "drama occasionally has to appear to overstep limits, to show what has not been shown before."[82] Finally, television drama in its early years took cues above all from the theater. This connection was partly aspirational and partly the function of technological limitations. Performances were broadcast live from studio sets, essentially stages with cameras, until the mid-1960s.[83] Reliance on theatrical models and theatrical talent meant that the social realism which dominated the British stage after 1956 jumped quickly to the small screen.

The teleplay format lent itself to anti-heroic narratives. In contrast to cinema's emphasis on adventure and escape in wide open spaces, early television drama was set within enclosed, often claustrophobic, interiors that underscored the drama of emotional turmoil.[84] Characters elaborated their anxieties in long, verbal exchanges. With television screens so small and the flickering images they projected so indistinct, directors favored medium shots and close-ups in which actors' faces filled most of the frame. This was dubbed the "talking heads" style.[85] Stanislavsky's method, filtered through a new generation of "television theater" in the United States, was another influence pushing teleplays toward psychological studies of stressful situations and tense relationships.[86] The dramas in this tradition were structurally limited in their capacity to convey the vicarious thrills of colonial war. They were, by contrast, almost custom-designed for uneasy meditations on it.

The Kenya drama *The Flame in the Forest* signaled the teleplay form's ideological unpredictability early on. First performed at a missionary exhibition in Liverpool, it aired on BBC television in 1956, just three months after the Methodist minister who wrote it submitted his script to the network's drama department.[87] The thirty-minute play, set in a missionary's bungalow, indicted white racism as the root cause of the Mau Mau crisis. The villain of the piece is an engineer's wife who rants about "dirty black[s]" and expresses the desire that security forces would shoot more of them. By contrast, the insurgent leader responsible for the offstage deaths of several characters (played by Guyanese-born actor Dan Jackson) is portrayed as a reluctant rebel driven to radicalism by British hostility. "When I came home from your country, where they despised me for the color of my skin, I knew that I must save my people," he says near the conclusion a long deathbed soliloquy. When the insurgent's brother, a loyal subject distressed that "European soldiers and the police" are killing Africans, walks off in the final shot, he hints that his once rock-solid faith—in Christianity, in nonviolence, in the British Empire—has begun to waver.[88]

The play's justification of African resistance came with a healthy dose of paternalism. The ostentatiously forgiving attitude of a missionary's wife, who comforts the dying insurgent even though he has killed her husband, hints at an ideal of reconciliation rather than decolonization. But viewers took notice of the challenge to knee-jerk jingoism. According to the BBC's Audience

Research Department, viewers found the play "very rewarding" because it went beyond "the orthodox white view" to offer "a sympathetic interpretation of the feelings of the African rebels." One woman in the sample even came away with the impression that "terrorists are not just thugs, they are idealists too."[89] While some conservative papers managed to salvage a more palatable message, the *Daily Mail* complained that Davey gave "most of the argument" to an insurgent "preaching revolt and revenge."[90]

If fiction allowed some soldiers to explore sanguinary fantasies, the imagined situations of the teleplay created opportunities for others to acknowledge the trauma of war. In the fall of 1958—less than two months after a BBC television interviewer browbeat Barbara Castle over her criticism of soldiers in Cyprus—the network aired a drama by Willis Hall about the death of a National Serviceman and its after-effects. Rather than sentimentalizing the loss as a tragic sacrifice, *Airmail from Cyprus* attacks its senselessness and the propagandistic haze surrounding it. The serviceman's mother, a mentally frail widow named Mary Hodgson, assumes that her son Peter has died a heroic death fighting insurgents. But Mary's daughter has concealed the truth from her: he was shot during a futile attempt to escape murder charges after impregnating his Cypriot lover and stabbing her to death, killing two military escorts in the process. It is a parable about the chasm between what every soldier's mother wants to think of her boy in uniform and the tawdry, brutal reality.[91]

When another serviceman from Peter's unit unexpectedly visits the family home in a northern town, he is appalled to learn of the deception—and, even more, of the sister's expectation that he will help to perpetuate it. The serviceman bitterly mocks the "VC Boys' Book of Heroes stuff" the mother clings to and reaches for comparisons to the most outlandish adventure fantasies: "Just for the book, like, how did he save my life? . . . Was I being scaled by Indians and he rode up? . . . Who she think he was? Errol Flynn?" Like the real-life mothers who recoiled from Castle's rhetoric, Mary refuses to accept the truth about her son's military record when John finally blurts it out. "Do you think you know my son better than I did?" she cries. Delusion keeps the heroic myth intact: in her final scene, Mary talks to a framed photograph of her dead son as she huddles by the fire. Along with hints about John's disturbed state—he keeps nervously referring to himself as a "head case"— Mary's detachment from reality underlines the theme of minds shattered by war. Perhaps unsurprisingly, the unsentimental treatment of an ongoing war unsettled the BBC audience panel, which gave *Airmail from Cyprus* a

FIGURE 6.2 "Do you think you know my son better than I did?" Denial about a dirty war in the BBC teleplay *Air Mail from Cyprus*, 1958. BBC Photo Library.

below-average rating. "One expected something about how good our troops were—not their homicidal instincts," one viewer complained.[92]

Yet the trauma involved in perpetrating violence was a recurring theme of counterinsurgency stories on television. A 1961 Malaya teleplay on the BBC, *The Terrorists*, implied that the moral monsters of the title were British soldiers deranged by brutality. Set in the waning days of the Emergency, the story revolves around characters like Rutter, a sergeant who has "spent too much time in the jungle," speaks openly of his pleasure in killing, and compares shooting "little yellow men" to "killing an animal." Another soldier in *The Terrorists* awakens from a disturbed dream to confess that he murdered a female insurgent because she reminded him of his unfaithful wife. His lover, herself an unfaithful army wife, complains that she has "lived with too many military psychopaths and their crazy little stories."[93] A 1961 ITV teleplay starred Tom Courtenay as *Private Potter*, a young soldier in Cyprus who ruins an army raid by crying out during the stealthy approach to an EOKA hideout. The outburst, Potter claims, is prompted by a sudden and dazzling vision of God. But it is also a symptom of his aversion to combat. "In all my life I've never had the guts to hit anyone," he says. Played by Courtenay with a mix of sincerity and fragility, Potter represents the humanity that is driven

to breakdown by the pitiless demands of war. "The machine must be kept
in perfect running order," insists the brigadier who advocates Potter's imprisonment. "A saint in the army is a non-conformist. And there's no room for
them."[94]

Lamenting the dehumanizing effects of war in general, television drama
in the late 1950s and early 1960s also stressed the moral confusion particular to counterinsurgency. In *The Terrorists*, the intimacy of jungle combat
haunts even a seasoned officer: "Out here you kill them one by one and
you see their faces, before you kill them and after." Almost as a matter of
course, small-screen dramatizations assumed that colonial war involved systemic brutality and ever-expanding webs of complicity. The protagonist of
the 1961 ITV drama *The Night of the Apes* is a conscript who returns to his
Welsh hometown after two years in a military prison and a dishonorable dis-
charge. His offense: refusing an order to shoot an unarmed EOKA prisoner
believed responsible for the deaths of several British soldiers. The script, by
television sound technician Terence De Lacey, exploits the irony of a soldier
punished for "lack of moral fiber" while showing far more of it than everyone
else. From the chapel-going father who throws him out of the house to the
local rowdies who beat him up, zeal for retributive violence galvanizes the
community.[95]

For television writers, as for playwrights, the figure of the conscript offered
an irresistible symbol of the conflict between compulsion and conscience.
That is why the small screen was flooded with bleak stories of young National
Servicemen trapped in violent quandaries. But this device contained within it
the potential for ambiguity. Conscription-as-metaphor could portray Britons
as reluctant participants in colonial war and even as the victims of it. Stories
preoccupied with the degradation of British morality left little room for the
stories of non-British men and women (who were conspicuous by their absence in *Airmail from Cyprus*, *The Terrorists*, and *The Night of the Apes*). A fatalism that saw corruption as all but inevitable also confounded questions of
responsibility. In wars as dirty as these, could anyone be faulted for failing to
keep their hands clean?

A central figure in the cultivation of this ambiguous aesthetic was television writer Troy Kennedy Martin. Best known in later years for *Z Cars*, the
BBC drama about morally compromised cops on a northern housing estate, he launched his career writing about morally compromised soldiers in
Cyprus, where he did his National Service with the Gordon Highlanders.
Kennedy Martin's debut, the 1958 BBC teleplay *Incident at Echo Six*, told
a simple story about a chaotic situation. After soldiers receive fragmented

reports of an attack on an isolated police post, they are overwhelmed by injured survivors, fuel shortages, and communication breakdowns while a conscript slowly bleeds to death. As in *The Long and the Short and the Tall*, the dialogue in *Incident at Echo Six* is driven by soldiers feuding with each other on the path to brutalization. The script pits two types against one another: the cautious, by-the-book conscript who worries about civilian casualties versus the trigger-happy conscript who itches to break the rules. The hothead, tellingly named Savage, wants to "take it out on the villagers" and is only just talked out of firing machine guns at civilian homes. But he is also the most vividly realized character, raging against all those at home who fail to grasp the grim realities of the war and acting as a charismatic mouthpiece for combat gnosticism. Savage's conviction that the British are fighting the war at a handicap—"cabined, cribbed, confined by a set of rules designed to placate the rumblings of three countries' politicians"—seems to be vindicated in the final scene, when the ambulance arranged by his rival fails to arrive and their wounded comrade dies as a result. While Kennedy Martin signaled concern about the moral degeneration of counterinsurgency, he also hinted that a more "savage" attitude could save British lives.[96]

Some viewers of *Incident at Echo Six* were shocked at the sight of a soldier dying on screen and worried about the impact on relatives of servicemen

FIGURE 6.3 Audiences were shocked by the on-screen death of a conscript in a morally ambiguous war, in the climactic scene of Troy Kennedy Martin's BBC teleplay *Incident at Echo Six*, 1958. BBC Photo Library.

who might be watching. Others complained about the portrayal of undisciplined and quarrelsome soldiers. But an overwhelmingly positive audience response—"I found it difficult to believe we weren't watching the real thing," one viewer enthused—secured Kennedy Martin's status as a BBC star and set the stage for another grim Cyprus teleplay three years later. Kennedy Martin's *The Interrogator* was recorded at the new BBC Television Centre in White City in December 1961 and broadcast on a Friday night soon afterward. Virtually the entire story unfolds in a Special Branch office as the protagonist, Police Superintendent James Fallon, stands under suspicion of killing a suspect who disappeared during a failed operation. Facing a suspension that takes effect in twelve hours, he has one long night to discover the location of an EOKA ammunition dump by questioning the suspects in custody.[97]

Like *Incident at Echo Six*, *The Interrogator* walks an uncertain line between dramatizing moral regression and justifying it. Fallon is a veteran of colonial policing in India, Malaya, and Kenya, "perhaps a bit hard boiled, too long in the bush." He pulls a gun on one suspect and "grills the living daylights" out of another by keeping him awake for days and sending him to a detention camp when he refuses to talk. In production notes for the cast and crew, Kennedy Martin spelled out "the idea that the harder you fight terrorism, the more likely you are to catch the disease." The metaphor of counterinsurgency as contagion was, of course, a staple of the reactionary war writing, which insisted that defeating a barbaric enemy required barbaric methods.[98] Fallon not only battles insurgents but also the elite nationalists who whip up allegations against him ("that damned mob of lawyers") and the Whitehall bureaucrats who tie his hands with red tape. While he gets rough with suspects, the script insists that he never crosses the line into "torture," in an echo of imperial officials' euphemistic evasions. A Greek Cypriot character even exculpates Fallon's casual roughness by distinguishing it from the high-tech horrors of Gestapo "brain-washers with their hypos and their textbooks."

The television drama domesticated colonial violence. This was not just a matter of making brutality a familiar plot point but, increasingly, of fashioning it into a comprehensible choice for sympathetic characters. The BBC Cyprus drama *One Morning Near Troodos* (1956) concluded with a previously affable army sergeant, outraged by the death of a civilian, "viciously kick[ing]" and taunting an EOKA leader.[99] The climax of ITV's Cyprus play *Arrow in the Air* (1958) showed a soldier torturing a suspect with a burning cigarette to give up the location of a ticking bomb.[100] As Soyinka, Brecht, and others warned, moral visions grew muddled even as violence gained in vividness.

The apologetic use of torture imagery reached a high point—or nadir—in the 1961 ITV drama *Negative Evidence*. Set in the fictional Asian colony of Khurani, a composite of Malaya and other insurgent hot spots, it is the story of a brusque young army officer suspected of torturing a suspect to death. This suspicion is held even by those close to him because he does not conceal his racist contempt for the insurgents or his fondness for rough justice. He treats his friends to a slide show of war photographs, including one of a village he and his troops leveled. "Nigs Nogs used it," he says, employing a favorite slur, "so we had to shoot it up." "What happened to all the people who lived in those huts?" someone asks. "Damned if I know," he responds. But the sanguinary insouciance turns out to be misdirection. A liberal character makes a fool of himself when he tries to prove that the soldier really did commit torture. When the tough-talking military man is exonerated in the end, the distinction between justifiable ruthlessness and inexcusable sadism is again upheld. As one character comments: "You can't send a man off into the jungle to fight terrorists year after year and expect him to come back still believing in fairies."[101]

Reluctance to treat soldiers as heroes was more pronounced on television than in any other medium. But bleak war stories often provided self-flattering explanations for the violence they exposed. In flaunting the nastiness of colonial war to fend off criticism, dramas like *Negative Evidence* echoed the manipulative techniques of reactionary war fiction. What made the heroic adventure mode obsolete was not just the ubiquity of knowledge about brutality, but the increasingly unavoidable recognition that the battle for empire was lost. While this brute geopolitical reality made a degree of bleakness inevitable, it also shaded into the doomed romanticism of characters who insist on doing their duty, no matter how great the likelihood of failure or how profound the warping effects on their own personalities.

The dramaturgy of colonial war bore a close relation to the theology of colonial war. Exquisitely ambiguous fables about means and ends, suspicion and doubt, displaced concerns about actual existing conflicts in Malaya, Kenya, and Cyprus. An aestheticized brand of fatalism offered an outlet for moral disquiet. As theorist Roland Barthes observed while France fought in

Algeria, "The state of war is conjured away under the noble drapery of tragedy, as if the conflict were the essence of evil itself and not a particular evil (which could be remedied)."[102] Colonial war began as a subject of popular drama and ended up a setting, a mere backdrop for individualized showdowns and inner conflict.

Epilogue

THE AFTERLIVES OF COLONIAL VIOLENCE

BY THE END of the 1950s, colonial violence intruded so regularly on British life that the responses it called forth were almost ritualized. When a scandal broke, the various players knew their roles and the script followed a predict-able course. A novel by Labour politician Maurice Edelman, *The Minister* (1961), rehearsed the pattern with cynical ease. In a fictional British colony in Africa, soldiers kill thirty-six unarmed protesters, a moral calamity that represents political opportunity for an array of intriguers in Westminster. Set almost entirely in a narrow slice of central London, *The Minister* is a story about how colonial massacres become objects that circulate through the corridors of power. The newspapers splash the death toll on the front pages "like a cricket score." The colonial secretary and his staff debate whether the killings should be described as "tragic" or "unfortunate." The colonial gov-ernor supplies smooth explanations for the fractured skulls of arrested men ("in the dark and confusion, it's what you might expect") and opening fire at the protesters (they were "hostile and excited").[1]

In the mobilization of opinion outside Parliament, a depressingly fa-miliar stalemate takes shape. At one outpost on the ideological spectrum, a Movement for Colonial Freedom–like group, the Campaign for a Free Africa, sounds the notes of troubled conscience but is easily discredited as a Communist front whose members believe that "white is never right." At the other extreme, a politician rallies "Flog-the-Wogs" sentiment with an unapol-ogetic defense of racial violence. His speech at a party conference is peppered with racial slurs and attacks on "the knock-kneed, sob-sister, yellow-bellied fellow-travellers . . . who have raised their lilac flag of surrender as a substitute for the Union Jack."[2] Edelman casts a seasoned politician's world-weary eye on both sides, which are equally useful to Machiavellian insiders as pawns.

Although far from flattering to anticolonial activists, *The Minister* reads like a disillusioned response to the Hola massacre. While some details recall the Sharpeville massacre of 1960, there are many more knowing references to counterinsurgency in Kenya: the indefinite detention of nationalist politicians, the banning of machetes under Emergency Regulations, the existence of protocols governing where to strike blows on the bodies of recalcitrant suspects. Mirroring the Hola story, too, the controversy set off by the massacre in the novel is intense but ephemeral. The jaundiced assessment of one veteran politico character appears amply justified: "I think the British public doesn't dislike force provided that it's short, sharp, and rewarding."[3]

Like *And the Rain My Drink* five years earlier, *The Minister* was a Book Society selection, heralding another installment of colonial guilt as middlebrow entertainment. But Edelman's novel was also an epitaph for the moral paralysis of the 1950s. All the ingredients for a massive repudiation of violence are represented in *The Minister*: activists in the streets, allies in Parliament, undisputed facts, front-page photographs of crumpled bodies. Yet the forces of empathetic action are ultimately outmatched. Atrocity awakens bloodthirsty revanchism as well as horrified humanitarianism; political operators prove adept at deflecting and dampening opposition. The novel's main character, the colonial secretary, gets to wash his hands of scandal and ascend smoothly to 10 Downing Street. *The Minister* treats the flight from empire as a golden opportunity to make Britons the protagonists of their own story once again, and, above all, to break free from the moral quagmires of the decolonization era.

The end of empire did not eradicate feelings of obligation to Britain's former colonies. But post-imperial ethics soon shifted to the comfortable terrain of alleviating distress, especially from hunger and natural disasters, for which Britain bore no obvious responsibility.[4] That exit from empire offered some measure of relief from moral burdens is apparent from the near-total silence of official memory culture on the violence of decolonization. To this day, standard British history textbooks have little or nothing to say about the emergencies in Malaya, Cyprus, and Kenya. Museums stuffed with artifacts of bombing, codebreaking, and rationing during the Second World War treat the subsequent colonial conflicts as sideshows if they mention them at all. Even the deaths of British soldiers in the colonies have been relegated to the margins—literally—of memorialization, their names squeezed into the leftover space on monuments to the fallen of the two world wars.[5]

It is not difficult to see why post-imperial societies' eagerness to leave empire behind is often described with the language of "forgetting" and "amnesia." Yet these metaphors imply an involuntary and irreparable loss of memory. The afterlives of Britain's colonial wars have been shaped instead by intentional and only partly successful efforts to suppress the past. Beyond the heights of state-sanctioned memory, there was no great silence, no sudden imposition of taboos, after the wars of decolonization ended. Nor was the violent end of empire rendered invisible by displacement onto scenes of flag-lowering ceremonies and other benign "screen memories."[6] The same fierce accusations, uneasy self-reproaches, and troubling images that preoccupied contemporaries in the 1950s continued to do so in the 1960s, 1970s, and 1980s. Without apparent interruption, unease about colonial violence was managed retrospectively as it had been contemporaneously: by talking about it, writing about it, and acting it out.[7]

The booming market in postcolonial literature was among the forces ensuring a long afterlife for colonial violence. If they existed at all in the 1950s, taboos on literary production crumbled after 1960 as British publishers snapped up novels and memoirs written from the perspective of insurgents against British rule. A heroic narrative of the EOKA campaign seen through the eyes of a young guerilla sentenced to hang, *The Age of Bronze* by Greek diplomat Rodis Roufos, was published by Heinemann in 1960.[8] Three years later, Oxford University Press published *Mau Mau Detainee*, J. M. Kariuki's first-person account of the detention system in Kenya. This marked the inauguration of a new genre, the Mau Mau memoir, at least ten of which would be published by 1980.[9] The Oxford don who brokered the publication of *Mau Mau Detainee*, Margery Perham, wrote a foreword to the book that attempted to mitigate the horrors described inside by portraying an overwhelmed rather than malevolent colonial state. Even so, she admitted, the brutality detailed in the book would "have a deeply disturbing effect" on British readers.[10]

The 1964 publication of Ngũgĩ wa Thiong'o's debut, *Weep Not, Child*, marked another milestone. The first-ever novel in English by an East African author, it was set in the Kenya Emergency. Written out of disillusionment with the early years of national independence, Ngũgĩ's fictions portrayed Mau Mau in a tragic rather than a heroic register. But like other anticolonial writers, Ngũgĩ traced a trajectory from rising discontent with an unjust system to the breakdown of communities, families, bodies, and minds in the vise of the imperial war machine. In matter-of-fact language, *Weep Not, Child* and his next novel, *This Grain of Wheat* (1967), described the torture, forced labor, and summary executions suffered by Kikuyu fighters and civilians at

British hands just a few years earlier. With the inclusion of Ngũgĩ's novels in the Heinemann African Writers Series, later acquired by Penguin, the crimes of counterinsurgency in Kenya secured a place in the literary canon.

If the cultural capital of postcolonial writing helped to preserve knowledge about violence, so did older traditions of creative protest. The formal daring and subversive politics of radical theater lived on in plays like Peter Barnes's *Sclerosis*, which ran briefly in London and Edinburgh in 1965 and showed British soldiers torturing an EOKA suspect by electrocuting him and submerging his head in water. The soldiers take buns from a tea trolley and chat amiably while their victim lies unconscious, bloody, and soaking at their feet.[11] The progressive tradition in television drama likewise prevented a slow fade into oblivion for colonial wars. The premiere episode of the ITV police series *Gideon's Way* (1964) featured an authoritarian cop with a history of "special duty in Cyprus and Kenya" raging against political protesters in Britain. "These troublemaking fanatics are scum, dirty scum!" he rants. "I'd like to see the whole ruddy lot of them locked up." A band of Mosley-style blackshirts depicted in the episode come across as even more deranged. A fascist character who attacks the Movement for Colonial Freedom as "a conspiracy to hand over our people in Africa to the black murderers" turns out to be a bomb-planting terrorist.[12]

The counterinsurgency backstory became a favorite device for writers looking to telegraph the menace of their characters. Sometimes, these were passing references that functioned as an "absent presence," an invocation of unseen but powerful influences.[13] That even brief allusions could communicate sinister associations testifies to the collective memory of colonial wars as dirty wars. One of the disgraced soldiers who team up to rob a bank in Basil Dearden's film *The League of Gentlemen* (1960) is a Cyprus veteran "cashiered for shooting EOKA suspects." Scottish playwright C. P. Taylor dropped a similar detail into his 1977 drama *Bandits!* by making a Newcastle gangster an ex-National Serviceman who brings a gun and an unstable personality back from Malaya. "I bloody killed people, too," he tells the audience. "Supposed to be communists. Who the fuck knew who the hell they were or what they were doing in that jungle . . . . Don't know how many I shot."[14] Other backstories were more elaborate. In the final installment of the BBC's *House of Cards* drama, *The Final Cut* (1995), audiences learned that twisted politician Francis Urquhart had killed two unarmed men as a young soldier in Cyprus. It was a fittingly dark origin story for the character who lied and murdered his way to 10 Downing Street. The figure of the brutalized veteran, and the threat he poses to British society, remained a symbol of colonial wars coming home for a long time.

The tradition of National Service fictions maintained a more ambiguous kind of memory about colonial war. Two coming-of-age stories written by Malaya veterans, Leslie Thomas's novel *The Virgin Soldiers* (1966) and Peter Nichols's play *Privates on Parade* (1977), offered at least a hint of nostalgia for youthful misadventures. Yet both stories also sharpened the juxtaposition of the farcical and the deadly, presenting British characters as breathtakingly ignorant of their complicity in violence. In *The Virgin Soldiers*, the basis for a 1969 film, a group of callow conscripts careen from adolescent jokes and sexual exploits to jungle ambushes and urban riots. In one chaotic moment of unrest, the protagonist fires wildly into a crowd and ends up disfiguring a Chinese loyalist; in another, the Singaporean prostitute he cares for is kicked to death by rampaging soldiers. *Privates on Parade*, adapted into a 1982 film starring John Cleese, makes an even bigger punch line of military discipline by building the story around a song-and-dance troupe of flamboyantly gay soldiers who fall in and out of love with each other while rehearsing Marlene Dietrich tunes. When a firefight intrudes on a climactic performance for the troops, killing several of them, the mood darkens abruptly. If empire is a farce, Nichols suggests, it is a farce with a body count. "At least we are letting the empire go, leaving all these parts of the world where we've no business to be," one character observes in the play's final scene, before trailing off in a not-quite confession of guilt. "Oh, dear, the moral issues . . ."[15]

The capacity to reconstruct and reimagine exits from empire, circling back repeatedly to the moment when the curtain came down for good, made fictional narratives central to memory of colonial violence. By caricaturing the extremes of brutality, incorporating war stories in other genres, or mixing bloodshed with comedy and eroticism, creative writers found ways to make potentially unbearable histories of violence bearable, without disguising them beyond recognition or erasing them altogether. In other words, the promise of catharsis by reliving violence retained its allure long after the players in *Eleven Men Dead at Hola Camp* left the stage. As theorist Paul Ricoeur argued, the same troubling episodes that compel some to "flee with bad conscience" are cultivated by others "with morose delectation."[16] The British afterlife of colonial violence was not a return of the repressed but an endless repetition of the un-repressed, a series of ritualized performances that served as outlets for shame within limits.[17]

A 1970 episode of the ITV police drama *Special Branch* showed how easily memories of colonial violence could move from consciousness of guilt to empty but satisfying narratives of absolution. The episode opens on an upper-class woman, a customer in a Surrey antiques shop who learns that the shop's owner lived in Kenya during the counterinsurgency. "Did you fight them?" she asks, with a frisson of prurient excitement, as she fingers the long blade of a knife. "Must have been *frightful*." But the episode does not dwell on the perverse pleasure aroused by killing African insurgents. It is structured, instead, as a mystery: was a retired Special Branch man involved in a long-forgotten Emergency-era massacre? In the end, the retired officer (and the security forces he represents) are vindicated when the massacre turns out to have been a reprisal perpetrated by Mau Mau. The villain of the episode is not the police veteran, described as an "honest" public servant who did his duty under trying circumstances, but rather the scheming Whitehall mandarin who unearths old scandals for his own purposes.[18] What begins as an excavation of imperial skeletons concludes as a parable about the wisdom of leaving the past in peace. Too much memory, the episode implies, can be a dangerous thing.

Ironically, British culture throughout this period was saturated in memory of war—not colonial war but the Second World War. Even as half-guilty, half-exculpatory allusions to counterinsurgency recurred in literature, film, theater, and television, they did not come close to matching the volume or visibility of stories set in "the" war between 1939 and 1945. Only the Second World War provided a master narrative for national identity, one rooted in ideas of collective purpose and shared sacrifice, with something to offer both the left and the right.[19] Colonial war never had this unifying potential. While the political urgency of decolonization-era battles inevitably diminished over time, different communities maintained starkly different visions of the past, and the violence of the 1950s did not fit neatly into any of them.

After the battle for empire was lost, right-wing writers no longer had the same incentives to romanticize violence by British soldiers and settlers. Instead, they preferred to dwell on the instability and violence of postcolonial societies as a rebuke to the aspirations of decolonization. Retrospective narratives of colonial war were likelier to come from the left, loosely defined, but no agenda took shape around reckoning with the violence it inflicted. The Labour Party in the 1960s was heavily invested in the romance of the Commonwealth as a multiracial partnership, which in practice worked by prioritizing development projects and arms deals over the litigation of old grievances.[20] Neither the Malaysian state, which has steadfastly excluded Chinese Communist struggles from national commemorations, nor the

Kenyan state, which long maintained a "policy of amnesia" on Mau Mau, was likely to challenge these arrangements.[21] While black radicals in Britain sometimes described police brutality and other injustices as an inheritance from empire, West Indian slavery was cited as a precedent far more often than East African counterinsurgency. When militants did recall the Kenya Emergency, it was as an inspirational resistance struggle rather than a case study in oppression.[22] Then too, after the late 1960s, black Kenyans in Britain were vastly outnumbered by Kenyan Asians, who were not likely to identify with the Mau Mau at all.

For Cypriots in Britain, the strife on their home island in the 1960s and 1970s—culminating in the Greek coup d'état and Turkish invasion of 1974—cast doubt on the relevance of anticolonial narratives from the 1950s. Anglo-Cypriot director Michael Papas's film *The Private Right*, which debuted at the London Film Festival in 1966, showed a British interrogator presiding over the waterboarding of an EOKA fighter through an excruciating series of close-up shots.[23] But the bulk of the film concerns the insurgent's post-independence quest for revenge against another Greek Cypriot, the collaborator who betrayed him and carried out the torture with his own hands. As the EOKA veteran hunts his target through the Cypriot bars and cafés of North London, a fratricidal reckoning renders the British all but invisible in their own capital. Because colonial wars were also civil wars, their memory offered a precarious foundation for subaltern identities and national solidarities alike.[24]

When later generations in Britain acknowledged colonial violence, they did so with an undertone of resignation and without pressing for official recognition or reparation. Perhaps because so much was already known about violence, Britain saw few campaigns for access to archives and other mechanisms of "factual recovery" of the kind that mobilized French Algerian activists in the 1990s.[25] The memory politics that took shape around the wars in Malaya, Kenya, and Cyprus were not mainly concerned with establishing the truth about the past.[26] Rather, politicians, activists, and artists invoked them because they saw present-day crises as repetitions or patterns inscribed in an enduring culture of brutality. Since crises came and went, this kind of memory could be ephemeral. At the same time, its recurrence deepened the sense of colonial violence as somehow inescapable. A dark history that could not easily be integrated into national or subnational identities could not be fully repressed, either.

The American war in Vietnam revived uneasiness about the British war in Malaya because the parallels were so conspicuous. Both jungle conflicts in

Southeast Asia involved resettling populations on a massive scale, burning down huts, dumping defoliant chemicals from airplanes, and sometimes shooting unarmed civilians. As opinion in Britain began to turn against the Vietnam War, Labour politician George Brown—who had been a government minister during the Malayan Emergency—reminded the press that "there are an awful lot of specters in our cupboard, too."[27] He was even more forthcoming in private. At a boozy lunch with Kenneth Tynan in 1971, Brown blurted out: "We burned and tortured and maimed in Malaya.... Where war is concerned, in for a penny, in for a pound!"[28] Press coverage of the My Lai massacre perpetrated by American soldiers in 1968 provoked a reexamination of the most notorious British crime of the Malayan war: the 1948 massacre at Batang Kali. Recast as "Britain's My Lai," Batang Kali briefly featured in front-page newspaper stories, a BBC documentary, and a criminal investigation. Like most moments of postcolonial reckoning, this one produced no accountability for the perpetrators and no compensation for the victims. It was, instead, a fleeting drama of troubled conscience, a resurgence of irrepressible but also insoluble moral entanglements.

The Troubles in Northern Ireland inspired a more sustained moment of remembrance in the 1970s and 1980s. As IRA bombs targeted British cities and IRA assassination plots targeted British officials, the state wielded censorship powers more aggressively than in the 1950s. The casualties included a planned 1975 BBC broadcast of Irish dramatist Brian Phelan's *Article 5*, a play based on research in the Amnesty International archives, which showed British intelligence officers hooding, starving, electrocuting, and beating a prisoner.[29] Yet public controversy about the use of torture on IRA prisoners was not fully squelched. Though a series of government inquiries, lawsuits, press stories, books, and films, two facts became common knowledge. First, the British Army was relying on a torture protocol known as the "five techniques," which involved the use of sensory deprivation to disorient and disable victims. Second, these techniques originated in the colonial wars of 1950s. Official reports and muckraking journalists agreed on both points.[30] The wider repertoire of "emergency" tactics, from round-ups and indefinite detentions to movement controls and massacres, also resurfaced in Northern Ireland as counterinsurgency veterans including Frank Kitson took up positions at the top of the military-intelligence hierarchy.

The sense that Northern Ireland represented the latest and perhaps climactic chapter in a rearguard action of imperial collapse reawakened the ghosts of Malaya, Cyprus, and Kenya. A novel saturated in the bleak tones of decline, John Le Carré's *Tinker, Tailor, Soldier, Spy* (1974), made the backstory

of intelligence agent Ricki Tarr a journey through the dark side of decolonization: "He hung around Malaya and did a couple more jobs before being
called back to Brixton and refitted for special operations in Kenya—or, in less
sophisticated language, hunting Mau Mau for bounty."[31] Seven years later, the
BBC television film *Psy-Warriors*, directed by filmmaker Alan Clarke, developed the idea of colonial violence as imperial death rattle. Covering some of
the same ground as *Article Five*, *Psy-Warriors* offered a stark visual representation of torture, with prisoners forced into stress positions, subjected to noise
machines, and locked in cages against brightly lit white backdrops. A mon-
ologue by one of the military interrogators running the show suggested that
brutality was a symptom of empire's terminal decay:

> I spent the greater part of my working life watching British troops
> being pulled out of places they were never going to leave. A long
> hard line of colonial campaigns. And on every campaign the British
> used internment, concentration camps, and intense interrogation—
> torture . . . What you see in Ulster is the rear end of the cruelty and
> exploitation of over thirty colonial wars. The last colonial battlefield.
> The dog devouring its own tail . . . When there's nothing left to devour
> we'll devour ourselves.[32]

In an ironic twist, *Psy-Warriors* aired on the BBC on the same night that
IRA fighter Bobby Sands died of a hunger strike in a British prison. Like
the Notting Hill riots in the late 1950s, political terrorism, labor strife, and
other sources of unrest in the 1970s heightened anxieties about "feedback"
from a violent empire. Colonial violence was always most disturbing when it
threatened to come home or when it signified the loss of prestige and power.
The Troubles represented the confluence of these anxieties.

Even so, the violence of decolonization did not vanish as fears of instability receded in the 1980s and 1990s. The late imperial echoes of the 1982
Falklands War were not lost on protest singer Dave Rogers: "Once more the
old cry is for Queen and for country, / In Suez and Cyprus we've heard it
before / How long can the cling to this damp scrap of empire? / How many
young lives will be wasted in war?"[33] The BBC's landmark *End of Empire*
documentary (1985) showed interviews with Kikuyu detainees and Greek
Cypriot suspects who had been tortured and British officials who admitted
that brutality was pervasive. A 1998 BBC documentary, *Malaya: The
Undeclared War*, reproduced film of soldiers burning villages and the infamous *Daily Worker* photo of a soldier holding severed heads as trophies. As

FIGURE E.I Torture as symptom of late imperial decay: *Psy-Warriors*, directed by Alan Clarke for BBC's *Play for Today*, 1981. BBC Photo Library.

the National Service generation entered its golden years, their recollections grew more self-conscious about violence. A Kenya veteran spent ten pages of his 1999 memoir arguing that the shooting deaths of unarmed Africans met the legal definition of "excusable homicide."[34] A few veterans admitted that they should have been quicker to recognize the injustice of counterinsurgency tactics. "I would like to disown my younger self," wrote one Cyprus veteran looking back from 2015.[35]

If the official memory of memorials, textbooks, and museums remained largely immune from these intermittent bouts of atrocity consciousness, professional historians long displayed the same reticence. British imperial history, a field born in patriotic purpose, gave way in the second half of the twentieth century to the fragmentation of "area studies" and a collective disengagement from moral questions.[36] It was not until 2006 that pathbreaking books by historians David Anderson and Caroline Elkins on the Kenya Emergency moved colonial violence to the top of the scholarly agenda.[37] Here again, contemporary events made the late imperial past all but inescapable: the Anglo-American "war on terror" unleashed a familiar inventory of counterinsurgency tactics, some of them derived explicitly from the British campaigns of the 1950s. The fierce controversy generated by these new histories—especially Elkins's book, which documented the use of torture through dozens of recorded interviews with Kenyan survivors and witnesses—suggested that debates about the British Empire had become proxy battles over the American empire that succeeded it.[38]

Elkins's use of oral testimony, a standard practice in African history, represented a radical move in imperial history. Victims of colonial violence had not just been "given a voice"; a single narrative linked subjective experiences of suffering with decisions made by British officials in Nairobi and London. While breaking with the bloodlessness of earlier bureaucratic histories, Elkins established a connection between metropole and colony by tracing complicity through official chains of command. Historian Huw Bennett performed a similar feat, with a focus on military rather than civilian authorities, in his 2012 book on the British Army in Kenya.[39] Documenting the institutional dimensions of brutality proved decisive for the outcome of a lawsuit filed against the British government in 2009 by Kenyan victims of the counterinsurgency, in which Elkins, Anderson, and Bennett all served as expert witnesses. Once a long-reigning "code of silence" in the academy was broken, questions of colonial violence moved quickly to the High Court in London.[40]

Like the histories that helped to make it possible, the case of *Mutua and Others v. Foreign and Commonwealth Office* broke precedents. The elderly Kenyan plaintiffs were faced with daunting procedural hurdles that had thwarted many claims before them, including the expiration of the statute of limitations and the limits placed on employers' liability for wrongs committed by their employees. But Justice Richard McCombe, ruling for the plaintiffs on both counts, allowed the case to go forward. His decision was shaped by obvious revulsion at the torture described in the plaintiffs' testimony as well as the loosening of traditional tort rules in a recent series of cases on sexual abuse in the Catholic Church. Legal invulnerability for institutions accused of wrongdoing in the past was no longer assured.[41] The British government settled the suit soon afterward, establishing a nearly £20 million fund for the benefit of the survivors, financing a memorial in downtown Nairobi, and leading Foreign Secretary William Hague to acknowledge abuses by British authorities in the House of Commons in 2013.

An extraordinary and unlikely victory in many ways, the *Mutua* case also illustrates the limits of bringing colonial violence to court. Hague's statement of "regret" did not constitute the apology sought by many Kenyans; the monetary settlement, shared among more than 5,200 survivors, amounted to a modest £2,658 even for individuals who had been permanently disfigured. The significance of the case as precedent remains equally unclear. A lawsuit brought by Cypriot torture victims resulted in a 2019 settlement of £1 million, divided among thirty-three claimants, and another statement of regret from the British government.[42] But a lawsuit brought by a larger group of Kenyan survivors was dismissed by a judge in 2018 on the grounds that too much time had elapsed.[43] The High Court likewise rejected a 2012 suit that would have forced the British government to hold a public inquiry into the Batang Kali massacre.[44] Has the "juridification" of the past inaugurated a sustained process of memorialization in Britain or merely substituted for it? One thing, at least, is clear. The limits of the human lifespan mean that lawsuits brought by survivors of seven-decade-old wars do not represent a durable strategy for the future.

What George Brown called "the specters in our cupboard" can never be exorcised. No measure of reparation is ever fully reparative. The dead cannot be restored to life; the injured cannot be made whole; time cannot be regained. Then too, this particular history offers no promise of redemption through confrontation with long-suppressed truths. It is a history of consciously wrestling with complicity, as it happened and afterward, and of endless if questionably effective mechanisms for assuaging guilt. The distance between an imperial society and the violence it deployed elsewhere was always less stable than it appeared on the map. Even when it happened thousands of miles away, violence committed by British people, with British arms, in Britain's name, left its mark on Britain. Colonial violence was British violence.

In her foreword to *Mau Mau Detainee*, Margery Perham described the public reaction to brutality as "moral helplessness." It was a learned helplessness, not an innate condition, and some contemporaries resisted it. But many more recognized wrongdoing without seeking an end to it. From professional and ethical codes to racial ideologies and popular aesthetics, scripts for coexisting with violence were pervasive. While drawing in part on traditions of deference, these responses were shaped even more profoundly by the needs of the moment. Adapting to a world of crumbling empires meant shoring up some forms of authority while accepting powerlessness in other ways. The longing for sturdy institutions, clear chains of command, and cohesive communities reflected the uncertainties of decolonization as surely as fantasies of brutality. It was the individual's capacity to exercise moral agency that the end of empire seemed to diminish to the vanishing point. Living with violence at once remote and inescapable, existential and futile, unsettling and unstoppable, is no small part of the postcolonial condition.

Notes

ABBREVIATIONS

BBCWA   BBC Written Archives Centre, Reading
BC   Burns Library, Boston College
BI   Bishopsgate Institute, London
BLSA   British Library Sound Archive, London
BRCS   British Red Cross Society archive, London
BU   Howard Gotlieb Archival Research Center, Boston University
BY   Borthwick Institute for Archives, University of York
BO   Bodleian Library, Oxford University
CAC   Churchill Archives Centre, Cambridge University
CBMS   Conference of British Missionary Societies archive, SOAS
CCO   Christ Church, Oxford
CPGB   Communist Party of Great Britain archive, People's History Museum, Manchester
CUL   Cambridge University Library
DNB   Oxford *Dictionary of National Biography*
FCB   Fabian Colonial Bureau archive, Bodleian Library, Oxford
HHC   Hull History Centre, Kingston-on-Hull
IWM   Imperial War Museum, London
KCL   King's College, London
LHCMA   Liddell Hart Centre for Military Archives, King's College, London
LMA   London Metropolitan Archives
LPL   Lambeth Palace Library, London
LSE   London School of Economics Library
LSF   Library of the Society of Friends, Friends House, London
MGM   Manchester *Guardian* archive, Johns Rylands Library, Manchester
MO   Mass Observation archive, University of Sussex

MRC	Modern Records Centre, University of Warwick
NAM	National Army Museum, London
NYPL	New York Public Library
PA	Parliamentary Archives, London
PHM	People's History Museum, Manchester
PSU	Pennsylvania State University Libraries, State College, PA
PUL	Princeton University Library
SCRBC	Schomburg Center for Research in Black Culture, New York Public Library
SOAS	School of Oriental and African Studies, London
SRO	Staffordshire Record Office, Stafford
TNA	National Archives of the United Kingdom, London
UKDA	UK Data Archive
TPVA	Theatre and Performance Archive, Victoria & Albert Museum, London

INTRODUCTION

1. Diarist 5445 [M.C. Towler], entries for January 28, 1953, January 29, 1958, and September 22, 1958, Mass Observation archive, University of Sussex (hereafter MO).

2. Nick Hubble, *Mass-Observation and Everyday Life: Culture, History, Theory* (Houndmills: Palgrave Macmillan, 2005).

3. Graham Greene, *Ways of Escape* (New York: Simon & Schuster, 1980), 147–148.

4. Diarist 5353 [Nella Last], entry for February 29, 1948, MO.

5. Thelma Veness, *School Leavers: Their Aspirations and Expectations* (London: Methuen, 1962), 100–101.

6. Entry for December 3, 1952, in Marguerite Dupree, ed., *Lancashire and Whitehall: The Diary of Sir Raymond Streat*, vol. 2, *1939–57* (Manchester: Manchester University Press, 1987), 665.

7. Bob Edwards, *Goodbye Fleet Street* (London: Jonathan Cape, 1988), 81.

8. Summary of Reports on Public Opinion, February 16, 1952, and December 13, 1952, CCO 4/5/312; Summary of Reports on Public Opinion, November 12, 1955, CCO 4/6/336, BO.

9. Hugh Cudlipp, *Walking on the Water* (London: Bodley Head, 1976), 230. Conservative *Mirror* publisher Cecil Harmsworth King reached the same conclusion: see his *Strictly Personal: Some Memoirs of Cecil H. King* (London: Weidenfeld and Nicolson, 1969), 131.

10. George H. Gallup, ed., *The Gallup International Public Opinion Polls: Great Britain 1937-1975*, vol. 1, *1937-1964* (New York: Random House, 1976), 311.

11. Gallup, ed., *Public Opinion Polls*, 378; Summary of Reports on Public Opinion, no. 42, 8 June 1956, CCO 4/7/375, BO.

12. Jordanna Bailkin, "Where Did the Empire Go? Archives and Decolonization in Britain," *American Historical Review* 120, no. 3 (2015): 884–899, at 892; Emma Rothschild, *The Inner Life of Empires: An Eighteenth-Century History* (Princeton: Princeton University Press, 2011).

13. Summary of Reports on Public Opinion, January 1954, CCO 4/6/336, BO.

14. Summary of Reports on Public Opinion, February 1959, CCO 4/8/337, BO.

15. John Cowper Powys to Louis Wilkinson, December 28, 1955, *Letters of John Cowper Powys to Louis Wilkinson, 1935-1956* (London: Macdonald, 1958), 340.

16. Diary entry for August 27, 1959, in *Daring to Hope: The Diaries and Letters of Violet Bonham Carter, 1946-1969*, ed. Mark Pottle (London: Weidenfeld & Nicolson, 2000), 211.

17. Joshua Cole, "Massacres and Their Historians: Recent Histories of State Violence in France and Algeria in the Twentieth Century," *French Politics, Culture, and Society* 28, no. 1 (2010): 106–126, at 109.

18. Diary entry for June 30, 1959, Harold Nicolson, *Diaries and Letters, 1945-1962*, ed. Nigel Nicolson (London: Collins, 1968), 369.

19. Roger Chickering, "Total War: The Use and Abuse of a Concept," in *Anticipating Total War: The German and American Experiences, 1871-1914*, ed. Manfred F. Boemeke, Roger Chickering, and Stig Förster (Cambridge: Cambridge University Press, 1999), 21.

20. Put another way, "small wars" in terms of the resources expended by imperial powers could resemble "total wars" in terms of the disruption and destruction visited on colonized societies. See Erwin A. Schmidl, "Kolonialkriege: Zwischen grossem Krieg und kleinem Frieden," in *Formen des Krieges: Vom Mittelalter zum "Low-Intensity-Conflict,"* ed. Manfried Rauchensteiner and Erwin A. Schmidl (Graz: Verlag Styria, 1991); Dierk Walter, "Warum Kolonialkrieg?," in *Kolonialkriege: Militärische Gewalt im Zeichen des Imperialismus*, ed. Thoralf Klein and Frank Schumacher (Hamburg: HIS Verlag, 2006); Dierk Walter, *Colonial Violence: European Empires and the Use of Force*, trans. Peter Lewis (Oxford: Oxford University Press, 2017).

21. Antoinette Burton, *The Trouble with Empire: Challenges to Modern British Imperialism* (New York: Oxford University Press, 2015), 178.

22. Dane Kennedy, *Decolonization: A Very Short Introduction* (New York: Oxford University Press, 2016), 57.

23. John Darwin, *Britain and Decolonisation: The Retreat from Empire in the Post-War World* (London: Macmillan, 1988), 169.

24. Bernard Porter, *The Absent-Minded Imperialists: Empire, Society, and Culture in Britain* (Oxford: Oxford University Press, 2004), 2; John Darwin, "The Fear of Falling: British Politics and Imperial Decline since 1900," *Transactions of the Royal Historical Society* 36 (1986): 27–43, at 29; D. George Boyce, *Decolonisation*

and the British Empire, 1775-1997 (London: Macmillan, 1999), 270; Kenneth O. Morgan, "The Second World War and British Culture," in *From Reconstruction to Integration: Britain and Europe Since 1945*, ed. Brian Brivati and Harriet Jones (London: Leicester University Press, 1993), 40–41; David Cannadine, "Apocalypse When? British Politicians and 'Decline' in the Twentieth Century," in *Understanding Decline: Perceptions and Realities of British Economic Performance*, ed. Peter Clarke and Clive Trebilcock (Cambridge: Cambridge University Press, 1997), 261–262; Noel Annan, *Our Age: English Intellectuals Between the Wars— A Group Portrait* (New York: Random House, 1990), 357; Dominic Sandbrook, *Never Had It So Good: A History of Britain from Suez to the Beatles* (London: Little, Brown, 2005), 284–286. For a pioneering critique of the "minimal impact" thesis of decolonization, see Stuart Ward, ed., *British Culture and the End of Empire* (Manchester: Manchester University Press, 2001).

25. The prominent exceptions are two valuable studies of representations of counterinsurgency in British media: Susan L. Carruthers, *Winning Hearts and Minds: British Governments, the Media, and Colonial Counter-Insurgency, 1944-1960* (London: Leicester University Press, 1995), and Wendy Webster, *Englishness and Empire, 1939-1965* (Oxford: Oxford University Press, 2007), ch. 5. For recent studies that locate decolonization, though not warfare or violence, at the heart of post-1945 British history, see Jordanna Bailkin, *The Afterlife of Empire* (Berkeley: University of California Press, 2012); Sarah Stockwell, *The British End of the British Empire* (Cambridge: Cambridge University Press, 2018); Vanessa Ogle, "Archipelago Capitalism: Tax Havens, Offshore Money, and the State," *American Historical Review* 122, no. 5 (2017): 1431-1458; Ward, ed., *British Culture and the End of Empire*; Stuart Ward, *Untied Kingdom: A Global History of the End of Britain* (Cambridge: Cambridge University Press, 2022).

26. Robert Thompson, *Defeating Communist Insurgency: Experiences from Malaya and Vietnam* (London: Chatto & Windus, 1966); Richard L. Clutterbuck, *The Long Long War: Counterinsurgency in Malaya and Vietnam* (New York: Praeger, 1966); Julian Paget, *Counter-Insurgency Operations: Techniques of Guerilla Warfare* (New York: Walker, 1967), chs. 6–7; Andrew R. Molnar, et al., *Undergrounds in Insurgent, Revolutionary, and Resistance Warfare* (Washington: Special Operations Research Office, 1963), 170–173, 259–262; Richard Stubbs, *Hearts and Minds in Guerilla Warfare: The Malayan Emergency, 1948-1960* (Oxford: Oxford University Press, 1989); Thomas R. Mockaitis, *British Counterinsurgency, 1919-60* (London: Macmillan, 1990); John Nagl, *Learning to Eat Soup With a Knife: Counterinsurgency Lessons from Malaya and Vietnam* (Chicago: University of Chicago Press, 2005); Robert M. Cassidy, *Counterinsurgency and the Global War on Terror: Military Culture and Irregular War* (Stanford, CA: Stanford University Press, 2008).

27. *U.S. Army/Marine Corps Counterinsurgency Field Manual* (Chicago: University of Chicago Press, 2007).

28. Panoptic accounts of this reevaluation include John Newsinger, *British Counter-Insurgency: From Palestine to Northern Ireland* (New York: Palgrave Macmillan, 2002); David French, *The British Way in Counter-Insurgency, 1945-1967* (Oxford: Oxford University Press, 2011); Brian Drohan, *Brutality in an Age of Human Rights: Activism and Counterinsurgency at the End of the British Empire* (Ithaca, NY: Cornell University Press, 2018); Hew Strachan, "British Counter-Insurgency from Malaya to Iraq," *Journal of the Royal United Services Institute* 152 (2007): 8–11; Paul Dixon, "'Hearts and Minds'? British Counter-Insurgency from Malaya to Iraq," *Journal of Strategic Studies* 32, no. 3 (2009): 353–381.

29. From a growing body of case studies, see especially Caroline Elkins, *Imperial Reckoning: The Untold Story of Britain's Gulag in Kenya* (New York: Henry Holt, 2005); David Anderson, *Histories of the Hanged: The Dirty War in Kenya and the End of Empire* (New York: W.W. Norton, 2005); Huw Bennett, *Fighting the Mau Mau: The British Army and Counter-Insurgency in the Kenya Emergency* (Cambridge: Cambridge University Press, 2013); David French, *Fighting EOKA: The British Counter-Insurgency Campaign on Cyprus, 1955-59* (Oxford: Oxford University Press, 2011); Karl Hack, "Everyone Lived in Fear: Malaya and the British Way of Counter-Insurgency," *Small Wars & Insurgencies* 23, nos. 4–5 (2012): 671–699; Matthew Hughes, "The Banality of Brutality: British Armed Forces and the Repression of the Arab Revolt in Palestine, 1936-1939," *English Historical Review* no. 507 (2009): 313–354.

30. Stephen Howe, "When (If Ever) Did Empire End? 'Internal Decolonisation' in British Culture since the 1950s," in *The British Empire in the 1950s: Retreat or Revival?*, ed. Martin Lynn (Basingstoke: Macmillan, 2006), 225; Martin Thomas, *Fight or Flight: Britain, France, and Their Roads from Empire* (Oxford: Oxford University Press, 2014), 354. On the Algerian war in France, see especially Benjamin Stora, *La gangrène et l'oubli: La mémoire de la guerre d'Algérie* (Paris: La Découverte, 1991); Jim House and Neil MacMaster, *Paris 1961: Algerians, State Terror, and Memory* (Oxford: Oxford University Press, 2006); Todd Shepard, *The Invention of Decolonization: The Algerian War and the Remaking of France* (Ithaca, NY: Cornell University Press, 2006); James Le Sueur, *Uncivil War: Intellectuals and Identity Politics during the Decolonization of Algeria* (Philadelphia: University of Pennsylvania Press, 2001); Martin Evans, *The Memory of Resistance: French Opposition to the Algerian War, 1954-1962* (Oxford: Berg, 1997); Raphaëlle Branche and Sylvie Thénault, eds., *La France en guerre, 1954-1962: Expériences métropolitaines de la guerre d'indépendance algérienne* (Paris: Autrement, 2008); Linda Amiri, *La bataille de France: La guerre d'Algérie en France* (Paris: Robert Laffont, 2004).

31. Nicholas Owen, "Four Straws in the Wind: Metropolitan Anti-Imperialism, January-February 1960," in *The Wind of Change: Harold Macmillan and British Decolonization*, ed. L. J. Butler and Sarah Stockwell (Basingstoke: Palgrave Macmillan, 2013).

32. Stephen Howe, "Colonising and Exterminating? Memories of Imperial Violence in Britain and France," *Histoire@Politique* no. 11 (2010), online at https://www.cairn.info/revue-histoire-politique-2010-2-page-12.htm.

33. Compare Carruthers, *Winning Hearts and Minds*, and Webster, *Englishness and Empire*, on sympathetic imagery of British settlers, with Shepard, *Invention of Decolonization*, 192–204, 219–220, on the perception of *pieds noirs* in France.

34. Paul Gilroy, *After Empire: Melancholia or Convivial Culture?* (London: Routledge, 2004), 102.

35. Bernard Porter, *British Imperial: What the British Empire Wasn't* (London: I.B. Tauris, 2016), 183.

36. Ian Cobain, *The History Thieves: Secrets, Lies, and the Shaping of a Modern Nation* (London: Portobello Books, 2016); Thomas, *Fight or Flight*, 354. Some scholars have dissented from the narrative of colonial violence shrouded in secrecy. See Anderson, *Histories of the Hanged*, 309; Nicholas Owen, "'Facts are Sacred': the Manchester Guardian and Colonial Violence, 1930-32," *Journal of Modern History* 84, no. 3 (2012): 643–678, at 646.

37. David Anderson, "Mau Mau in the High Court and the 'Lost' British Empire Archives: Colonial Conspiracy or Bureaucratic Bungle?," *Journal of Imperial and Commonwealth History* 39, no. 5 (2011): 699–716; David M. Anderson, "Guilty Secrets: Deceit, Denial, and the Discovery of Kenya's 'Migrated' Archives," *History Workshop Journal* 80 (2015): 142–160; Caroline Elkins, "Looking beyond Mau Mau: Archiving Violence in the Era of Decolonization," *American Historical Review* 120, no. 3 (2015): 852–868; Mandy Banton, "Destroy? 'Migrate'? Conceal? British Strategies for the Disposal of Sensitive Records of Colonial Administrations at Independence," *Journal of Imperial and Commonwealth History* 40, no. 2 (2012): 321–335; Edward Hampshire, "'Apply the Flame More Searingly': The Destruction and Migration of the Archives of British Colonial Administration: A Southeast Asian Case Study," *Journal of Imperial and Commonwealth History* 41, no. 2 (2013): 334–352.

38. Stanley Cohen, *States of Denial: Knowing about Atrocity and Suffering* (Cambridge: Polity Press, 2001), 148.

39. Luise White, "Telling More: Lies, Secrets, and History," *History and Theory* 39, no. 4 (2000): 11–22.

40. Tom Crook, "Secrecy and Liberal Modernity in Victorian and Edwardian England," in *The Peculiarities of Liberal Modernity in Imperial Britain*, ed. Simon Gunn and James Vernon (Berkeley: University of California Press, 2011), 78–80.

41. Priya Satia, "Interwar Agnotology: Empire, Democracy, and the Production of Ignorance," in *Brave New World: Imperial and Democratic Nation-Building Between the Wars*, ed. Laura Beers and Geraint Thomas (London: Institute of Historical Research, 2012).

42. Michael Rogin, "'Make My Day!': Spectacle as Amnesia in Imperial Politics," *Representations* 29 (Winter 1990): 99–123.

43. Robert N. Proctor and Londa Schiebinger, eds., *Agnotology: The Making and Unmaking of Ignorance* (Stanford, CA: Stanford University Press, 2008); Niklas Luhmann, "The Ecology of Ignorance," in *Observations on Modernity*, trans. William Whobrey (Stanford, CA: Stanford University Press, 1998); Linsey McGoey, "On the Will to Ignorance in Bureaucracy," *Economy and Society* 36, no. 2 (2007): 212–235; Linsey McGoey, "The Logic of Strategic Ignorance," *British Journal of Sociology* 63, no. 3 (2012): 533–576.

44. Carol A. Heimer, "Inert Facts and the Illusion of Knowledge: Strategic Uses of Ignorance in HIV Clinics," *Economy and Society* 41, no. 1 (2012): 17–41.

45. Michael Smithson, "Toward a Social Theory of Ignorance," *Journal for the Theory of Social Behaviour* 15, no. 2 (1985): 151–172; Tore Bakken and Eric Lawrence Wiik, "Ignorance and Organization Studies," *Organization Studies* 39, no. 8 (2018): 1109–1120.

46. John Berger, "Photographs of Agony" (1972), in *Understanding a Photograph*, ed. Geoff Dyer (London: Penguin, 2013); Susan Sontag, *On Photography* (New York: Farar, Straus, and Giroux, 1977); Karen Haltunnen, "Humanitarianism and the Pornography of Pain in Anglo-American Culture," *American Historical Review* 100, no. 2 (1995): 303–334. Sontag famously softened her critique, to an extent, in *Regarding the Pain of Others* (New York: Farrar, Straus, and Giroux, 2003). A less ambivalent argument for the power of photography to "globalize our consciences" is Susie Linfield, *The Cruel Radiance: Photography and Political Violence* (Chicago: University of Chicago Press, 2010), here at 46.

47. James Dawes, *Evil Men* (Cambridge, MA: Harvard University Press, 2014), 54. See also the classic interpretation by Harold Perkin, *The Rise of Professional Society: England since 1880* (London: Routledge, 1989).

48. See especially Hannah Arendt, *Eichmann in Jerusalem: A Report on the Banality of Evil* (New York: Penguin, 1994 [1963]); Zygmunt Bauman, *Modernity and the Holocaust* (Ithaca, NY: Cornell University Press, 1989). Interpretations of late modern or postmodern warfare, characterized by a widening technological gap between adversaries and the increasing invulnerability of the aggressor, have stressed similar themes. See Zygmunt Bauman, "Wars of the Globalization Era," *European Journal of Social Theory* 4, no. 1 (2001): 11–28; Derek Gregory, "War and Peace," *Transactions of the Institute of British Geographers* 35 (2010): 154–186; Grégoire Chamayou, *A Theory of the Drone*, trans. Janet Lloyd (New York: New Press, 2015); John Kaag and Sarah Kreps, *Drone Warfare* (Cambridge: Polity Press, 2014); Hugh Gusterson, *Drone: Remote Control Warfare* (Cambridge, MA: MIT Press, 2016).

49. Cohen, *States of Denial*.

50. Catherine Hall and Daniel Pick, "Thinking About Denial," *History Workshop Journal* 84 (Autumn 2017): 1–23. Freud himself offered ambiguous and shifting definitions of disavowal, some of which implicated the failure to perceive reality and did not always clearly distinguish from denial. See Jean Laplanche and Jean-Bertrand Pontalis, *The Language of Psycho-Analysis*, trans. Donald Nicholson-Smith

(New York: W.W. Norton, 1973), 118–121. Although Bill Schwarz's history of settler colonialism in British culture invokes disavowal at several points, the argument ultimately relies on a kind of collective unconscious. "Memories of empire," Schwarz writes, "are carried into the post-imperial epoch by an acting out or unconscious repetition of prior racial assumptions and practices." See Bill Schwarz, *Memories of Empire*, vol. 1, *The White Man's World* (Oxford: Oxford University Press, 2011), 204–205.

51. Darius Rejali, *Torture and Democracy* (Princeton, NJ: Princeton University Press, 2007), 274–275, 291, 300.

52. S. B. Spies, *Methods of Barbarism? Roberts and Kitchener and Civilians in the Boer Republics, January 1900-May 1902* (Cape Town: Human & Rousseau, 1977); Aidan Forth, *Barbed-Wire Imperialism: Britain's Empire of Camps, 1876-1903* (Berkeley: University of California Press, 2017).

53. David E. Omissi, *British Air Power and Colonial Control: The Royal Air Force, 1919-1939* (Manchester: Manchester University Press, 1990); Priya Satia, "The Defense of Inhumanity: Air Control and the British Idea of Arabia," *American Historical Review* 111 (Februrary 2006): 16–51.

54. Kim Wagner, *Amritsar, 1919: An Empire of Fear and the Making of a Massacre* (New Haven, CT: Yale University Press, 2019).

55. See especially Caroline Elkins, *Legacy of Violence: A History of the British Empire* (London: Bodley Head, 2022).

56. This summary draws in particular on the indispensable history by Christopher Bayly and Tim Harper, *Forgotten Wars: Freedom and Revolution in Southeast Asia* (Cambridge, MA: Belknap Press of Harvard University Press, 2007).

57. French, *British Way*, 111.

58. My concise account here relies on the essential histories by Caroline Elkins, *Imperial Reckoning*, and David Anderson, *Histories of the Hanged*.

59. French, *British Way*, 120.

60. French, *British Way*, 133; John Blacker, "The Demography of Mau Mau: Fertility and Mortality in Kenya in the 1950s: A Demographer's Viewpoint," *African Affairs* 106 (April 2007): 205–227.

61. My summary here is indebted to Robert Holland, *Britain and the Revolt in Cyprus, 1954-1959* (Oxford: Clarendon Press, 1998).

62. French, *British Way in Counter-Insurgency*, 133.

63. Brian Drohan, "'A Litigious Island': Law, Rights, and Counterinsurgency during the Cyprus Emergency," in *Decolonization and Conflict: Colonial Comparisons and Legacies*, ed. Martin Thomas and Gareth Curless (London: Bloomsbury, 2017).

64. French, *Fighting EOKA*.

65. Mark Mazower, *No Enchanted Palace: The End of Empire and the Ideological Origins of the United Nations* (Princeton: Princeton University Press, 2009); Boyd van Dijk, *Preparing for War: The Making of the 1949 Geneva Conventions* (Oxford: Oxford University Press, 2022); Pieter Lagrou, "1945-1955: The Age of

Total War," in *Histories of the Aftermath: The Legacies of the Second World War in Europe*, ed. Frank Biess and Robert G. Moeller (New York: Berghahn, 2010), 289–291.

66. Howard Robinson, *Carrying British Mail Overseas* (New York: New York University Press, 1964), 317.

67. Marzia Maccaferri, "'A Splenetic Isolation': Il dibattito pubblico inglese di fronte all'Affair Suez," *Ventunesimo Secolo* 19, no. 2 (June 2009): 109–126.

68. Eliga H. Gould, "Zones of Law, Zones of Violence: The Legal Geography of the British Atlantic, circa 1772," *William and Mary Quarterly* 60, no. 3 (2003): 471–510.

CHAPTER I

1. Shusha Guppy, "Christopher Logue: The Art of Poetry LXVI," *Paris Review* no. 127 (Summer 1993): 238–264.

2. Christopher Logue to Charles [Fox], September 19, 1958, Logue papers, series 27, box 12, folder 4, Pennsylvania State University Libraries (hereafter PSU).

3. Logue to [Elisabeth] Hauptmann, June 2, 1956, series 27, box 11, folder 17, PSU.

4. Logue to [Marcel] Péju, April 10, 1957, Loge papers, series 27, box 11, folder 21, PSU.

5. Logue to Ian Carr, May 24, 1956, series 27, box 11, folder 17, PSU.

6. Logue to [Meary James Thurairajah Tambimuttu], January 21, 1957, series 27, box 11, folder 21, PSU.

7. George Ramsden, *Christopher Logue: A Bibliography, 1952-97* (Settrington: Stone Trough Books, 1997), 119.

8. Quoted in Kingsley Amis, *Socialism and the Intellectuals* ([London]: Fabian Society, 1957), 11.

9. Peter Worsley, "Imperial Retreat," in *Out of Apathy* (London: Stevens and Sons, 1960), 115–116.

10. E. P. Thompson, "Where Are We Now?," unpublished memorandum to the editorial board of *New Left Review* (1963), in *E.P. Thompson and the Making of the New Left: Essays and Polemics*, ed. Cal Winslow (New York: Monthly Review Press, 2014), 231–232.

11. On the anticolonial tradition in London, see especially Jonathan Schneer, *London 1900: The Imperial Metropolis* (New Haven: Yale University Press, 1999), chs. 7–9; Marc Matera, *Black London: The Imperial Metropolis and Decolonization in the Twentieth Century* (Berkeley: University of California Press, 2015); Minah Makalani, *In the Cause of Freedom: Radical Black Internationalism from Harlem to London, 1917-1939* (Chapel Hill: University of North Carolina Press, 2011); Penny von Eschen, *Race Against Empire: Black Americans and Anticolonialism, 1937-1957* (Ithaca, NY: Cornell University Press, 1997); Susan Pennybacker, *From Scottsboro to Munich: Race and Political Culture in 1930s Britain* (Princeton: Princeton University Press, 2009).

12. Nicholas Owen, "Critics of Empire in Britain," in *The Oxford History of the British Empire*, vol. 4, *The Twentieth Century*, ed. J. M. Brown and W. M. R. Louis (Oxford: Oxford University Press, 1999), 202.

13. Kennetta Hammond Perry, *London Is the Place for Me: Black Britons, Citizenship, and the Politics of Race* (New York: Oxford University Press, 2016); Rosalind Eleanor Wild, "'Black was the Colour of Our Fight': Black Power in Britain, 1955-1976" (PhD diss., University of Sheffield, 2008), ch. 1; Hakim Adi, "African Political Thinkers, Pan-Africanism, and the Politics of Exile, c. 1850-1970," in *Refugees and Cultural Transfer to Britain*, ed. Stefan Manz and Panikos Panayi (Abingdon: Routledge, 2013).

14. A. W. B. Simpson, *Human Rights and the End of Empire* (Oxford: Oxford University Press, 2001).

15. St. Clair Drake, "Mbiyu Koinange and the Pan-African Movement," in *Pan-African Biography*, ed. Robert A. Hall (Los Angeles: African Studies Center, University of California, Los Angeles, and Crossroads Press, 1987).

16. Stephen Howe, *Anticolonialism in British Politics: The Left and the End of Empire, 1918-1964* (Oxford: Clarendon Press, 1993), 205; Shiraz Durrani, *Never Be Silent: Publishing & Imperialism in Kenya, 1884-1963* (London: Vita Books, 2006), 223–225.

17. M. J. E. Bagot, Special Branch, to R. Lloyd-Thomas, Home Office, June 7, 1955, KV 2/2551, TNA.

18. Special Branch report no. 15/4564/4, November 3, 1955, KV 2/2552; Special Branch report no. 15/4286, September 2, 1954, TNA.

19. St. Clair Drake to E. Jefferson Murphy, June 13, 1957, box 73, Drake papers, Schomburg Center for Research in Black Culture, New York Public Library (hereafter SCRBC, NYPL).

20. Howe, *Anticolonialism*, 245.

21. Intelligence dossier on Joseph Zuzarte Murumbi, [1957?], FCO 141/6887, TNA.

22. Ismay Milford, "Harnessing the Wind: East and Central African Activists and Anticolonial Cultures in a Decolonising World, 1952-64" (PhD diss., European University Institute, 2019), 93–94, 120–121; Howe, *Anticolonialism*, 245.

23. Kenya Students' Adviser to Director of Education, October 1959, FCO 141/6702, TNA. On Koinange and Murumbi maintaining ties with Kenyan students, see St. Clair Drake to Mugo Gatheru, October 28, 1955, box 73, St. Clair Drake papers, MG 309, SCRBC, NYPL.

24. Hakim Adi, *West Africans in Britain, 1900-1960: Nationalism, Pan-Africanism, and Communism* London: Lawrence & Wishart, 1998), 169–170.

25. Wole Soyinka, *You Must Set Forth at Dawn: A Memoir* (New York: Random House, 2006), 36.

26. "View of Kenya African Students: Statement by Association in U.K.," *East Africa and Rhodesia* (May 23, 1957).

27. Howe, *Anticolonialism*, 214–217; Cheah Boon Kheng, *The Masked Comrades: A Study of the Communist United Front in Malaya, 1945-48* (Singapore: Times Books, 1979), 106–112.

28. A. J. Stockwell, "Leaders, Dissidents, and the Disappointed: Colonial Students in Britain as Empire Ended," *Journal of Imperial and Commonwealth History* 36, no. 3 (2008): 487–507, at 495–497; Howe, *Anticolonialism*, 216–217.

29. Stockwell, "Leaders, Dissidents, and the Disappointed," at 491; Yeo Kim Wah, "Joining the Communist Underground: The Conversion of English-Educated Radicals to Communism in Singapore," *Journal of the Malaysian Branch of the Royal Asiatic Society* 67, no. 1 (1994): 29–59, at 54–58; John Drysdale, *Singapore: Struggle for Success* (Singapore: Allen & Unwin, 1984), 135–138.

30. M. Baker, Ali Hassan, and Goh Keng Swee to National Council for Civil Liberties, March 29, 1951; M. Baker to Elizabeth Allen, n.d., U DCL 57/3, Hull History Centre (hereafter HHC).

31. Robin Oakley, "Cypriot Migration and Settlement in Britain" (DPhil diss., Oxford University, 1971).

32. Lena M. Jeger, "All for Enosis," *Spectator* (December 31, 1954); "3-Power Talks on Cyprus Start Today," *Dundee Courier* (August 29, 1955): 5.

33. Howe, *Anticolonialism*, 27–81; Geoff Eley, *Forging Democracy: The History of the Left in Europe, 1850-2000* (New York: Oxford University Press, 2002), 335; Nicholas Owen, *The British Left and India: Metropolitan Anti-Imperialism, 1885-1947* (Oxford: Oxford University Press, 2007).

34. On these ideological fault lines, see especially Christopher Moores, *Civil Liberties and Human Rights in Twentieth-Century Britain* (Cambridge: Cambridge University Press, 2017); Tom Buchanan, *Amnesty International and Human Rights Activism in Postwar Britain, 1945-1977* (Cambridge: Cambridge University Press, 2020), 82–83.

35. Amnesty, founded in 1961, represented an effort to bring these wings together. See Buchanan, *Amnesty International*, 119–123; James Loeffler, *Rooted Cosmopolitans: Jews and Human Rights in the Twentieth Century* (New Haven, CT: Yale University Press, 2018), 202–221.

36. Buchanan, *Amnesty International*, 57–59; Rob Skinner, "The Moral Foundations of Anti-Apartheid Activism, 1946-1960," *Journal of Southern African Studies* 35, no. 2 (2009): 399–416.

37. James Eaden and David Renton, *The Communist Party of Great Britain since 1920* (New York: Palgrave, 2002), 98–142; John Callaghan, *Cold War, Crisis, and Conflict: The CPGB, 1951-68* (London: Lawrence & Wishart, 2003), 17, 28, 130–135.

38. Raphael Samuel, *The Lost World of British Communism* (London: Verso, 2006), 48–49.

39. Peter Weiler, *British Labour and the Cold War* (Stanford: Stanford University Press, 1988).

40. *Report of Proceedings at the 85th Annual Trades Union Congress* (s.l.: Trades Union Congress, 1953), 464–466.

41. Ian Birchall, "'Vicarious Pleasure'? The British Far Left and the Third World, 1956-79," in *Against the Grain: The British Far Left from 1956*, ed. Evan Smith and Matthew Worley (Manchester: Manchester University Press, 2014); Evan Smith, *British Communism and the Politics of Race* (Leiden: Brill, 2018), 28–37.

42. Extract from Special Branch fortnightly summary no. 292, December 1952, HO 45/25579, TNA.

43. Extract from Special Branch fortnightly summary no. 293, January 1953, HO 45/25579, TNA. On Buckle, see Hakim Adi, "Forgotten Comrade? Desmond Buckle: An African Communist in Great Britain," *Science & Society* 70, no. 1 (2006): 22–45.

44. George Padmore, "The British Empire Is Worst Racket Yet Invented by Man," *New Leader* (December 15, 1939): 3.

45. William Gallacher, draft letter to *Daily Worker*, [1953], KV 2/1755, TNA; William Gallacher, *The Tyrants' Might is Passing* (London: Lawrence and Wishart, 1954), 36, 309.

46. Gallacher to the Political Committee, CPGB, February 19, 1953, KV 2/1755, TNA.

47. As early as 1952, MI5 wiretaps caught CPGB leaders complaining that Brockway was drawing African nationalists away from their party. See the report on a conversation between Idris Cox and Doris Lessing, November 6, 1952, KV 2/4055, TNA.

48. "Movement for Colonial Freedom Policy Statement," April 11, 1954, box 12, International League of Human Rights archive, NYPL; "Immediate Application of MCF Principles," March 1958, box 3, Movement for Colonial Freedom archive, School of Oriental and African Studies (hereafter MCF, SOAS.).

49. "Movement for Colonial Freedom," November 1955, CPGB archive, CP/CENT/INT/64/03, Communist Party of Great Britain archive, People's History Museum, Manchester (hereafter CPGB, PHM.).

50. Howe, *Anticolonialism*, ch. 6; P. S. Gupta, *Imperialism and the British Labour Movement, 1914-1964* (New York: Holmes and Meier, 1975), 359–362.

51. Howe, *Anticolonialism*, 237–238.

52. Central Council meeting minutes, September 25, 1957, box 3, MCF, SOAS.

53. Doris Lessing, *Walking in the Shade: Volume Two of My Autobiography, 1949-1962* (New York: Harper Collins, 1997), 207.

54. Rob Skinner, *The Foundations of Anti-Apartheid: Liberal Humanitarians and Transnational Activists in Britain and the United States, c. 1919-1964* (Basingstoke: Palgrave Macmillan, 2010), 178–182.

55. Gupta, *Imperialism and the British Labour Movement*, 385; Executive Committee minutes, October 22, 1959, box 1, MCF, SOAS.

56. Tony Benn, *Years of Hope: Diaries, Letters, and Papers, 1940-1962*, ed. Ruth Winstone (London: Hutchinson, 1994), 191, 257.

57. Fenner Brockway, *Towards Tomorrow* (London: Granada Publishing, 1977), 217; Benn, *Years of Hope*, 273–274; Josiah Brownell, "The Taint of Communism: The Movement for Colonial Freedom, the Labour Party, and the Communist Party of Great Britain, 1954-1970," *Canadian Journal of History/Annales canadiennes d'histoire* 42 (Autumn 2007): 235–258; Kenneth O. Morgan, "Imperialists at Bay: British Labour and Decolonization," *Journal of Imperial and Commonwealth History* 27, no. 2 (1999): 233–254.

58. Rodney Mace, *Trafalgar Square: Emblem of Empire* (London: Lawrence and Wishart, 1976), 308–310; "Our London Correspondence," *Manchester Guardian* (May 14, 1956); "Africans March in London," *Manchester Guardian* (April 19, 1959).

59. "Human Rights in the Colonies," MCF flyer, Henry Sara papers, MSS.15B/7/125; Fenner Brockway to Victor Gollancz, March 15, 1956, Gollancz papers, MSS.157/3/MC/1/3, MRC.Modern Records Centre, University of Warwick (hereafter MRC).

60. Extract from a Special Branch report on MCF meeting, June 28, 1956, KV 2/4389, TNA.

61. "Colonial Meeting," *Peace News* (October 1, 1954).

62. "Disturbances at London Meeting," Manchester Guardian (December 12, 1958); "Vicious Racial Campaign," *Manchester Guardian* (October 2, 1959); untitled photo, *Manchester Guardian* (May 12, 1958).

63. Ursula Grant Duff, Frida Laski, and Monica Whateley were members. See Kenya Committee, "National Deputation on Kenya," May 24, 1954, CP/CENT/INT/40/02, CPGB, PHM.

64. Stockwell, "Leaders, Dissidents, and the Disappointed."

65. Caroline Bamford, "The Politics of Commitment: The Early New Left in Britain, 1956-1962" (PhD diss., University of Edinburgh, 1983), 158–168; Stuart Hall, "Life and Times of the First New Left," *New Left Review* 61 (January–February 2010): 177–196.

66. "The Union," *The Isis* (November 14, 1956).

67. Ralph Samuel, "The Mind of British Imperialism," *Oxford Left* (Michaelmass 1954).

68. E. P. Thompson, "Through the Smoke of Budapest," *Reasoner* (November 1956).

69. Lin Chun, *The British New Left* (Edinburgh: Edinburgh University Press, 1993), 10–16; Stuart Hall, *Familiar Stranger: A Life Between Two Islands* (Durham, NC: Duke University Press, 2017), 243.

70. Carruthers, *Winning Hearts and Minds*, 33–35.

71. Fabian Klose, *Human Rights in the Shadow of Colonial Violence: The Wars of Independence in Kenya and Algeria* (Philadelphia: University of Pennsylvania Press, 2013).

72. *Malayan Monitor* (May–June 1949).

73. Kenya Committee, "Kenya Information Notes," [1952?].

74. Ralph Millner, *The Right to Live* (London: Falcon Press, 1955), 22–23.

75. George Orwell, "The Politics of the English Language," in *Essays* (New York: Everyman's Library, 2002), 963.

76. Alex Comfort, *How to Read the Newspapers (and Listen to the News Bulletins)* ([London]: Medical Association for the Prevention of War, [1955?]).

77. Eileen Fletcher, *Truth about Kenya: An Eye Witness Account* (London: Movement for Colonial Freedom, 1956).

78. Nicoletta F. Gullace, "War Crimes or Atrocity Stories? Anglo-American Narratives of Truth and Deception in the Aftermath of World War I," in *Sexual Violence in Conflict Zones: From the Ancient World to the Era of Human Rights*, ed. Elizabeth D. Heineman (Philadelphia: University of Pennsylvania Press, 2013).

79. George Orwell, *Diaries*, ed. Peter Davison (London: Penguin, 2009), 346.

80. Bernard Wasserstein, *Britain and the Jews of Europe 1939-1945* (London: Leicester University Press, 1999), 8, 148; John Taylor, *War Photography: Realism in the British Press* (London: Routledge, 1991), 64–71.

81. Kenya Committee, *Kenya Report* (1953), 11–12.

82. *Violation of Human Rights in Cyprus: A Factual Documentation* ([Nicosia?]: Ethnarchy of Cyprus, 1957).

83. "British Scorched Earth," *Malayan Monitor* (January 1949); "The Batang Kali Slaughter," *Malayan Monitor* (February 1949).

84. Kenya Committee, "Supplementary Speakers' Notes" (March 1955); Millner, *Right to Live*, 12–13.

85. *Malayan Monitor* (August 1948); Harry Pollitt, *Malaya: Stop the War!* (London: Communist Party of Great Britain, [1952?]).

86. Margaret Satterthwaite, "Finding, Verifying, and Curating Human Rights Facts," *Proceedings of the Annual Meeting of the American Society of International Law* 107 (2013): 62–65; Paul Gready, "'Responsibility to the Story,'" *Journal of Human Rights Practice* 2, no. 2 (2010): 177–190.

87. Annette Wieviorka, *The Era of the Witness*, trans. Jared Stark (Ithaca, NY: Cornell University Press, 2006).

88. *Violation of Human Rights in Cyprus*.

89. French, *Fighting EOKA*, 217–224.

90. Nicholas Owen, "Knowing and Not-Knowing: Complications in the Reporting of Colonial Violence," paper presented at Speaking Out workshop, University of Warwick, February 2021; Nicholas Owen, *Other People's Struggles: Outsiders in Social Movements* (New York: Oxford University Press, 2019), 53.

91. Fletcher, *Truth about Kenya*.

92. Fletcher, *Truth about Kenya*.

93. John Calder, *Pursuit* (London: Calder Publications, 2001), 143–149.

94. *Gangrene* (London: Calderbooks, 1959).

95. Ernest Law, "Five Months without Trial," in *Gangrene*.

96. Philip Maldon, "My Two Years in Kenya," *Peace News* (January 11, 1957): iv–v.

97. Peter Marris, "Accessory after the Fact," in *Conviction*, ed. Norman Mackenzie (London: MacGibbon & Kee, 1959).

98. In narratives of colonial war, critic Kristin Ross observes, "familiar objects appearing in a routine inventory can become metonymically ominous through their proximity" to violence. See Kristin Ross, *Fast Cars, Clean Bodies: Decolonization and the Reordering of French Culture* (Cambridge, MA: MIT Press, 1995), 112–113.

99. William Whitcombe and David Toon, "A Statement of Two Ex-Sergeant Warders Who Were Employed by the Cyprus Government and Resigned," February 16, 1957, U DJU 11/15, HHC; *Violation of Human Rights in Cyprus*, 67; "Cyprus: The Counter-Terror," *Time* (March 11, 1957). See also "Alleged Beatings in Cyprus: Complaints at a London Conference," *Times* (February 20, 1957).

100. "'I Do Not Wish To Kill Again'—C.O.," *Peace News* (April 23, 1954); David Larder, letter to *Guardian*, June 10, 2013; John Mortimer, interview with Arthur Scargill, in *In Character* (London: Allen Lane, 1983), 63.

101. Kenya Committee, *Kenya Report*.

102. *Cyprus—The Solution* (London: National Cypriot Committee and Movement for Colonial Freedom, [1958]).

103. Alison Light, *Forever England: Femininity, Literature, and Conservatism Between the Wars* (London: Routledge, 1991); Taylor, *War Photography*, 78–86; Webster, *Englishness and Empire*, 36–40.

104. Samuel Moyn, "In the Aftermath of Camps," in *Histories of the Aftermath: The Legacies of the Second World War in Europe*, ed. Frank Biess and Robert G. Moeller (New York: Berghahn Books, 2010).

105. Office of Director of Intelligence and Security, Nairobi, to Secretary of Defence, Nairobi, June 18, 1954, FCO 141/6887, TNA.

106. B. M. Kaggia et al., letter to *Observer* (June 8, 1958); *Violation of Human Rights in Cyprus*, 48.

107. John Rex, letter to editor, *Observer* (June 22, 1958): 6.

108. Fenner Brockway, *Why Mau Mau? An Analysis and a Remedy* (London: Congress of Peoples against Imperialism, 1953), 10.

109. Millner, *Right to Live*, 21; Kenya Committee, *Kenya Report*, 1.

110. John Saville and E. P. Thompson, "John Stuart Mill and EOKA," *New Reasoner* no. 7 (winter 1958-59): 1–11, at 7.

111. E. J. Hobsbawm, letter to editor, *Manchester Guardian* (January 28, 1954): 6.

112. John Calder, *Pursuit*, 143–144.

113. Peter Benenson, introduction to *Gangrene* (London: Calderbooks, 1959), 9, 19.

114. Worsley, "Imperial Retreat," 117.

115. "Algeria," *Universities & Left Review* (Summer 1957): 4; Saville and Thompson, "John Stuart Mill and EOKA," 7.

116. Worsley, "Imperial Retreat," 111.

117. Worlsey, "Imperial Retreat," 119.

118. Saville and Thompson, "John Stuart Mill and EOKA," 11.

119. Kathleen Lonsdale, letter to *Observer* (October 18, 1953).

120. Christopher Hilliard, *A Question of Obscenity: The Politics of Censorship in Modern England* (Princeton: Princeton University Press, 2021), 64–67.

121. Anthony Hugh Thompson, *Censorship in Public Libraries in the United Kingdom During the Twentieth Century*, (Epping: Bowker, 1975), 66, 95–96.

122. John Calder, letter to editor of the *Hastings and St. Leonards Obsever* (January 13, 1960); John Calder to Francis Williams, September 21, 1959, series I, box 9, Calder and Boyars Mss., Lilly Library, Indiana University, Bloomington.

123. For the legal reasoning on the Kenya Committee's 1953 pamphlet, see LO 2/231, TNA. For the non-prosecution decision on comments made by Donald Soper and others at an anti-Suez rally in 1956, including calls to defy conscription which were reproduced on a leaflet, see DPP 2/2603, TNA.

124. Calder, *Pursuit*, 149.

125. 529 *Parl. Deb.* H.C. (5th series) (1954) col. 203; *Manchester Guardian* (January 21, 1955).

126. Sheila Lynd, "The Kenya Terror They Call 'Screening,'" *Daily Worker* (February 14, 1955); "Journalist 'Tortured,'" *Daily Worker* (May 21, 1957); "Here's 'Law and Order' in Kenya," *Daily Worker* (November 13, 1952).

127. Carruthers, *Winning Hearts and Minds*, 110.

128. When the paper closed down in 1964, the cause was less the decline in circulation (which was comparable to that experienced by other major papers) than the solidly working-class readership which failed to attract advertisers. See James Curran, "Advertising and the Press," in *The British Press: A Manifesto*, ed. James Curran (London: Macmillan, 1978), 250–254.

129. "Malaya," *Daily Herald* (May 22, 1950).

130. Basil Davidson, "The Terrible Cost of a Little War," *Daily Herald* (January 24, 1955).

131. *Tribune* (May 31, 1957).

132. "Michael Foot Says . . . Save the Empire From Its 'Friends,'" *Daily Herald* (May 24, 1957).

133. "Kenya: Shocking Charges Made," *Tribune* (September 27, 1957).

134. *Tribune* (June 21, 1957).

135. "The Barbed-Wire Island," *Daily Herald* (July 2, 1958).

136. Frank Mort, *Capital Affairs: London and the Making of the Permissive Society* (New Haven, CT: Yale University Press, 2010).

137. "Tragedy," *Daily Mirror* (January 14, 1953); David Williams, "African Tragedy," *Daily Mirror* (June 22, 1953). See also Joanna Lewis, "Daddy Wouldn't Buy Me a Mau Mau: The British Popular Press and the Demoralization of Empire," in *Mau Mau and Nationhood: Arms, Authority and Narration*, ed. E. S. Atieno Odhiambo and John Lonsdale (Athens: Ohio University Press, 2003).

138. "Open Letter to Sir Evelyn," *Daily Mirror* (December 12, 1952).

139. "The Prisoner was Shouting Don't Burn Me," *Daily Mirror* (February 13, 1954); "The Old Man Who Said: I was Held Over Fire by Police," *Daily Mirror* (January

23, 1954); *Daily Mirror* (March 9, 1954); "And the White Men 'Grinned'" *Daily Mirror* (February 8, 1954).

140. "Makarios: Horrible Charges," *Daily Mirror* (June 20, 1957): 1.

141. Keith Waterhouse, "Are the British Cruel in Cyprus?" *Daily Mirror* (June 7, 1957).

142. "Stop This Bloodshed Now," *Daily Mirror* (December 17, 1955).

143. David Goldsworthy, *Colonial Issues in British Politics, 1945-1961: From "Colonial Development" to "Wind of Change"* (Oxford: Clarendon Press, 1971), 209–214.

144. Richard Vinen, *National Service: Conscription in Britain, 1945-1963* (London: Allen Lane, 2014), 361–362; Roger Broad, *Conscription in Britain, 1939-1964: The Militarisation of a Generation* (Abingdon: Routledge, 2006), 123; William P. Snyder, *The Politics of British Defense Policy, 1945-1962* (Columbus: Ohio State University Press, 1964), 54–55.

145. Camilla Schofield, *Enoch Powell and the Making of Postcolonial Britain* (Cambridge: Cambridge University Press, 2013), 110.

146. Vinen, *National Service*, 110–111; B. S. Johnson, ed., *All Bull: The National Servicemen* (London: Allison & Busby, 1973), 4.

147. *Questions to C.O.s from the Tribunals*, CBCO pamphlet, April 1951, Bishopsgate Institute (hereafter BI).

148. "Statement Showing the Orders of Conscientious Objectors Tribunals from 1 January 1949 to 30 June 1960," LAB 6/405, TNA; Vinen, *National Service*, 114–116.

149. "Conscientious Objector Ban Holds Up Plymouth Appointment," *Western Morning News* (April 22, 1949); "Protest Over Conscientious Objectors," *Warwickshire Advertiser* (May 29, 1953); secretary, Fellowship of Reconciliation, to town clerk, Bury, Lancashire, July 7, 1953, FOR 6/33, Fellowship of Reconciliation archive, London School of Economics Library (hereafter LSE).

150. The Ministry of Labour put the number of conscripts in those years at 1,718,884. See Vinen, *National Service*, 9.

151. CBCO annual reports.

152. Tobias Kelly, "Citizenship, Cowardice, and Freedom of Conscience: British Pacifists in the Second World War," *Comparative Studies in Society and History* 57, no. 3 (2015): 694–722.

153. Document "A," LAB 6/689, TNA.

154. "School-Teacher Will Not Fight in Colonial Wars," *Peace News* (November 19, 1954).

155. Olwen Battersby, "Belsen No Justification for Worse Evils," *Peace News* (December 10, 1954).

156. Add MS 88925/8/2 and Add MS 88925/8/3, BL.

157. Richard K. P. Pankhurst, *Kenya: The History of Two Nations* (London: Independent Publishing, [1954]), 83, 98.

158. Johnson, ed., *All Bull*, 243.

159. Bernard Crick, typescript [1956?], Crick papers 5/1/2, Birkbeck College, London.

160. LAB 6/628, TNA.

161. Thompson, introduction to *Out of Apathy*.

162. J. L. Austin, *How To Do Things with Words* (Oxford: Oxford University Press, 1962).

163. MEPO 3/1893, TNA.

164. Claire Langhamer, "'Who the Hell Are Ordinary People?' Ordinariness as a Category of Historical Analysis," *Transactions of the Royal Historical Society* 28 (2018): 175–195. On social science as both engine and mirror of this change, see Mike Savage, *Social Identities and Social Change in Britain Since 1940: The Politics of Method* (Oxford: Oxford University Press, 2010); Florence Sutcliffe-Braithwaite, *Class, Politics, and the Decline of Deference in England, 1968-2000* (Oxford: Oxford University Press, 2018); Jon Lawrence, *Me, Me, Me? The Search for Community in Post-War England* (Oxford: Oxford University Press, 2019).

165. George H. Gallup, ed., *The Gallup International Public Opinion Polls: Great Britain 1937-1975*, vol. 1, *1937-1964* (New York: Random House, 1976), 176.

166. Laura Beers, "Whose Opinion? Changing Attitudes Toward Opinion Polling in British Politics, 1937-1964," *Twentieth-Century British History* 17, no. 2 (2006): 177–205; Peter Richards, *Honourable Members: A Study of the British Backbencher* (London: Faber and Faber, 1959), 166–167.

167. K.E. Couzens, "A Minister's Correspondence," *Public Administration* 34, no. 3 (1956): 237–244, at 241–242.

168. Adrian Bingham, *Family Newspapers? Sex, Private Life, and the British Popular Press, 1981-1978* (Oxford: Oxford University Press, 2009), 9, 97.

169. Hugh Cudlipp, *Publish and Be Damned! The Astonishing Story of the* Daily Mirror (London: Andrew Dakers, 1953), 136.

170. Leonard C. Turner, letter to *Luton News* (November 19, 1953).

171. T. A. Hare, letter to *Shipley Times and Express* (June 3, 1953).

172. "Antaeus," letter to *Hartlepool Northern Daily Mail* (December 2, 1953). Other letters by the same writer reliably followed the Soviet line.

173. A. H. Newton, letter to *Daily Telegraph* (March 26, 1957); Charles Grosett, letter to *Daily Telegraph* (November 26, 1958). See also Thomas Anthem, letter to *Manchester Guardian* (October 15, 1956).

174. Ann Peasegood to Lyttelton, November 14, 1952, CO 967/254, TNA.

175. Sonya O. Rose, *Which People's War? National Identity and Citizenship in Britain, 1939-1945* (Oxford: Oxford University Press, 2003), 153–159.

176. Ralph Williams to Lyttelton, November 30, 1952, CO 968/260, TNA; Alison Haldane-Duncan to Noel-Baker, March 17, 1959, Noel-Baker papers, file 4/157, part 1, Churchill Archives Centre, Cambridge University (hereafter CAC).

177. Senior Bush to Castle, September 23, 1952; S.W. Davey to Castle, September 25, 1958; David R. Reid to Castle, November 2, 1958, MS Castle 252, Bodleian Library, Oxford (hereafter BO).

178. Jon Lawrence, "Forging a Peaceable Kingdom: War, Violence, and Fear of Brutalization in Post-First World War Britain," *Journal of Modern History* 75, no. 3 (2003): 557–589; Alan Allport, *Demobbed: Coming Home After the Second World War* (New Haven, CT: Yale University Press, 2009).

179. David Cesarani, "Lacking in Conviction: British War Crimes Policy and the National Memory of the Second World War," in *War and Memory in the Twentieth Century*, ed. Martin Evans and Ken Lunn (Oxford: Berg, 1997).

180. Trevor Dannatt and Patrick Heron, letter to *Manchester Guardian* (September 2, 1952); Gerald V. Tew, letter to *Manchester Guardian* (December 9, 1952).

181. Beatrice Wilson to Barbara Castle, October 6, 1958; Lilian Davis to Barbara Castle, October 5, 1958, MS Castle 252, BO.

182. Cesarani, "Lacking in Conviction"; Tony Kushner, *The Holocaust and the Liberal Imagination: A Social and Cultural History* (Oxford: Blackwell, 1994); Donald Bloxham, *Genocide on Trial: War Crimes Trials and the Formation of Holocaust History and Memory* (Oxford: Oxford University Press, 2001).

183. Eric Shafer, letter to *Times* (September 8, 1955).

184. C. T. Pertwee, letter to *Manchester Guardian* (May 31, 1956); Erich Fried, letter to *Manchester Guardian* (October 2, 1958).

185. W. C. Pettifer to Castle, October 14, 1958; A.F. Williams to Castle, October 10, 1958, MS Castle 252, BO; Rydell Wilson to Oliver Lyttelton, November 10, 1952, CO 967/260, TNA.

186. Arthur Robyns, letter to *Bedfordshire Times & Standard* (January 29, 1954); Williams to Lyttelton, November 30, 1952, CO 968/260, TNA; Stephen Crozier, letter to *Manchester Guardian* (December 4 1952).

187. Timothy Bewes, *The Event of Postcolonial Shame* (Princeton: Princeton University Press, 2010), 29–30.

CHAPTER 2

1. Ian Fleming, *Moonraker* (London: Jonathan Cape, 1955), 40.

2. On motives for reticence about violence, see Samuel Hynes, *The Soldiers' Tale: Bearing Witness to Modern War* (New York: Penguin, 1997), 116–119, 123–135; Alan Kramer, "The Sharp End, Witnessing, Perpetrating, and Suffering Violence in 20th Cenury Wars," in *A World at War, 1911-1949: Explorations in the Cultural History of War*, ed. Catriona Pennell and Filipe Ribeiro de Meneses (Leiden: Brill, 2019), 104–105; Catherine Lutz, "Making War at Home in the United States: Militarization and the Current Crisis," *American Anthropologist* 104, no. 3 (2002): 723–735; Bauman, "Wars of the Globalization Era," 27–28. On silences and the limitations of language, see James Dawes, *The Language of War: Literature and Culture in the U.S. from the Civil War through World War II* (Cambridge, MA: Harvard University Press, 2002); Kate McLoughlin, "War and Words," in *The Cambridge Companion to War Writing*, ed. Kate

McLoughlin (Cambridge: Cambridge University Press, 2009); Chris Daley, "The 'Atrocious Privilege': Bearing Witness to War and Atrocity in O'Brien, Levi, and Remarque," in *Arms and the Self: War, the Military, and Autobiographical Writing*, ed. Alex Vernon (Kent, OH: Kent State University Press, 2005); Klaus Latzel, "Vom Kriegserlebnis zur Kriegserfahrung: Theoretische und methodische Überlegungen zur erfahrungsgeschlichtlichen Untersuchung von Feldpostbriefen," *Militärgeschichlitche Mitteilungen* 56 (1997): 1–30.

3. Kim A. Wagner, *The Skull of Alum Bheg: The Life and Death of a Rebel of 1857* (New York: Oxford University Press, 2018), 149–160; Burton, *Trouble with Empire*, 42–45; Stephen M. Miller, "Duty or Crime? Defining Acceptable Behavior in the British Army in South Africa, 1899-1902," *Journal of British Studies* 49, no. 2 (2010): 311–331; Mo Moulton, *Ireland and the Irish in Interwar England* (Cambridge: Cambridge University Press, 2014), 34–38; Hughes, "Banality of Brutality."

4. Christopher Herbert, *War of No Pity: The Indian Mutiny and Victorian Trauma* (Princeton, NJ: Princeton University Press, 2008).

5. Cohen, *States of Denial*, 148.

6. *Semper Fidelis: Journal of the Devonshire Regiment* 1, no. 8 (November 1953): 351. The journal issue and original hand-drawn "scoreboard" are in WO 32/21721, TNA. For a Royal Marines "scoreboard" in Malaya, see *Jungle Journal* 2, no. 5 (May 1952), Imperial War Museum, London (hereafter IWM).

7. Simon Harrison, "The Colonial Manhunt and the Body Parts of Bandits: Hunting Schemas in British Counter-Insurgency," in *Dark Trophies: Hunting and the Enemy Body in Modern War* (New York: Berghahn Books, 2012).

8. Photograph album of Sgt. William Johnson, Coldstream Guards, 1946, catalogue no. 2003-03-627, National Army Museum, London (hereafter NAM); war diary, 1952-1953, catalogue no. GB554/B2/10, Suffolk Record Office, Bury St. Edmunds.

9. I. W. G. Martin letters, June 28, 1958 and July 31, 1958, Documents.1779, IWM.

10. French, *British Way*, 140–141; Bennett, *Fighting the Mau Mau*, 123–126; French, *Fighting EOKA*, 198, 204.

11. E. D. Jones to J. P. Ryan, September 28, 1958, SOC.Driberg C3, Driberg papers, Christ Church, Oxford (hereafter CCO). See also French, *British Way*, 171.

12. William Gerald Studdert-Kennedy to Rev. and Mrs. Studdert-Kennedy, September 21, 1953, item 206–11-8-47, NAM.

13. French, *British Way*, 151.

14. John Dewhurst, "Complicity," *British Medical Journal* 330 (January 22, 2005): 181.

15. French, *British Way*, 151–152.

16. E. M. Mahou to Barbara Castle, November 17, 1958, MS Castle 252, BO.

17. Peter Worsley, *An Academic Skating on Thin Ice* (New York: Berghahn Books, 2008), 120.

18. David R. Reid, November 2, 1958, MS Castle 252, BO.

19. Vinen, *National Service*, 20–21. On the politics of letter-writing in the Second World War, see Margaretta Jolly, "Between Ourselves: The Letter as Propaganda,"

in *Propaganda: Political Rhetoric and Identity, 1300-2000*, ed. Bertrand Taithe and Tim Thornton (Stroud: Sutton, 1999); Jenny Hartley, "'Letters are *Everything* These Days': Mothers and Letters in the Second World War," in *Epistolary Selves: Letters and Letter-Writers, 1600-1945*, ed. Rebecca Earle (Aldershot: Ashgate, 1999).

20. I am drawing here on a rich literature on soldiers' letters spanning national contexts. See Raphaëlle Branche, «*Papa, qu'as-tu fait en Algérie?*»: *Enquête sur un silence familial* (Paris: La Découverte, 2020); Clémentine Vidal-Naquet, "Écris-moi souvent," in *Une Histoire de la Guerre: Du XIXe siècle à nos jours*, ed. Bruno Cabanes (Paris: Seuil, 2018); Margaretta Jolly, "War Letters," in *Encyclopedia of Life Writing: Autobiographical and Biographical Forms*, vol. 2, ed. Margaretta Jolly (London: Fitzroy Dearborn, 2001); Angela Schwarz, "'Mit dem größtmöglichen Anstand weitermachen': Briefe britischer Kriegsteilnehmer und ihrer Angehörigen im Zweiten Weltkrieg," in *Andere Helme—andere Menschen? Heimaterfahrung und Frontalltag im Zweiten Weltkrieg*, ed. Detlef Vogel and Wolfram Wette (Essen: Klartext, 1995); Martin Humburg, "Deutsche Feldpostbriefe im Zweiten Weltkrieg: Ein Bestandsaufnahme," in *Andere Helme*, ed. Vogel and Wette.

21. 551 *Parl. Deb.* H.C. (5th ser.) (1956) col. 7.

22. Edward Wells, *Mailshot: A History of the Forces Postal Service* (s.l.: Defence Postal and Courier Services, 1987), 151, 167–169; Charles R. Entwistle, *The British Army Post Office in Conflict & Crisis Situations, 1946-1982* (Chavril: Abernethy, 2005).

23. Joint Intelligence Committee minutes, July 6, 1951, CAB 159/10, TNA.

24. Timothy Parsons, *The African Rank-and-File: Social Implications of Colonial Military Service in the King's African Rifles, 1902-1964* (Portsmouth, NH: Heinemann, 1999), 189–190; Sanjoy Bhattacharya, "British Military Information Management Techniques and the South Asian Soldier: Eastern India during the Second World War," *Modern Asian Studies* 34, no. 2 (2000): 483–510.

25. For a sample, see 159 *Parl. Deb.* H.L. (5th ser.) (1948) cols. 501–507; 518 *Parl. Deb.* H.C. (5th ser.) (1953) col. 28; 521 *Parl. Deb.* (5th ser.) (1953) cols. 182–183; 547 *Parl. Deb.* H.C. (5th ser.) (1955) col. 70.

26. Jonathan Fennell, *Fighting the People's War: The British and Commonwealth Armies and the Second World War* (Cambridge: Cambridge University Press, 2019), 698.

27. Sanjoy Bhattacharya, "British Military Information Management Techniques and the South Asian Soldier."

28. On the assumption that systematic postal censorship could only be justified in a rare "national emergency," see W. S. Herbert, Chairman, Standing Inter-Departmental Committee on Censorship, to Secretary, Joint Intelligence Committee, March 23, 1948, CAB 176/17, TNA. The French state, which censored the metropolitan press far more aggressively than Britain did in its colonial wars, nonetheless allowed soldiers in Algeria to write freely to their loved ones at home, for many of the same reasons. See Branche, *"Papa, qu'as-tu fait en Algérie?"*, 158–160, 176–179.

29. Janet Gurkin Altman, *Epistolarity: Approaches to a Form* (Columbus: Ohio State University Press, 1982), 13.

30. A. C. Worthington to William Gerald Studdert-Kennedy, May 13, 1952, item 2016–11-8–1, NAM.

31. P. J. Houghton-Brown, undated excerpts from letters, Brown papers, Documents.15316, IWM.

32. Quoted in Martin Bell, *The End of Empire: A Soldier's Story* (Barnsley: Pen & Sword Books, 2015), 59.

33. Schwarz, "'Mit dem größtmöglichen Anstand weitermachen,'" 210–211.

34. Peter Grant, *Letters from the Forest* (self-pub., East Lavant, Chichester, 2017), 74.

35. "A Policeman Looks at Kenya," *South London Press* (March 13, 1953).

36. "British Troops Disgusted," *Tribune* (March 4, 1955).

37. I. W. G. Martin letters, June 28, 1958, July 8, 1958, and July 24, 1958, Documents.1779, IWM.

38. I. W. G. Martin letters, July 8, 1958 and July 31, 1958, IWM.

39. Quoted in Bell, *End of Empire*, 65.

40. Arthur Helliwell, "An Elephant Put Me On This Trail!" *The People* (22 November 1953).

41. Worthington to Studdert-Kennedy, July 1, 1952, item 2016-11-8–11, NAM.

42. J. M. Roy to J. Henderson Stuart, [November 1956], CO 926/178, TNA.

43. Richard Unett to his parents, August 25, 1948, D3610/21/2/9, Staffordshire Record Office, Stafford (hereafter SRO).

44. Unett to his parents, October 2, 1948, D3610/21/2/21; August 26, 1948, D3610/21/2/13, SRO.

45. Unett to his parents, January 17, 1949, D3610/21/3/13; May 16, 1956, D3610/21/10/4, SRO.

46. Unett to his parents, August 9, 1956, D3610/21/10/25, SRO.

47. Unett to his parents, February 1, 1956, D3610/21/8/23, SRO.

48. Raymond Russell-Smith to Enid Russell-Smith, November 18, 1954, Russell-Smith papers, file 1/14, CAC.

49. Henry Barlow to Cecil and Joy Barlow, October 17, 1954 and February 6, 1955, Barlow papers, Borthwick Institute for Archives, University of York (hereafter BY).

50. Henry Barlow to Cecil and Joy Barlow, June 24, 1955, BY (emphasis added).

51. Henry Barlow to Cecil and Joy Barlow, July 10, 1955, BY.

52. Christopher Andrews, *The Defence of the Realm: The Authorized History of MI5* (London: Allen Lane, 2009), 336; Peter Wright, *Spycatcher: The Candid Autobiography of a Senior Intelligence Officer* (New York: Viking, 1987), 46.

53. Calder Walton, *Empire of Secrets: British Intelligence, the Cold War, and the Twilight of Empire* (New York: Overlook Press, 2013), 220, 263.

54. Graham Greene to Marie Newall, January 31, 1955, in *Graham Greene: A Life in Letters*, ed. Richard Greene (New York: Alfred A. Knopf, 2007), 213.

55. Stephen King-Hall, ed., *National News-Letter*, nos. 661–662 (March 24, 1949), Liddell Hart Centre for Military Archives, King's College London (hereafter LCHMA, KCL).

56. John Larkman to Hilda Selwyn-Clarke, May 24, 1956, box 175, file 1, Fabian Colonial Bureau archive (hereafter FCB), BO.

57. [John Larkman] to Hilda-Selwyn Clarke, typed excerpt, October, 11, 1958, box 175, file 1, FCB, BO.

58. Elspeth Huxley to Gervas Huxley, October 1953, in *Nellie: Letters from Africa*, ed. Elspeth Huxley (London: Weidenfeld and Nicolson, 1980), 194.

59. Nellie Huxley to Elspeth Huxley, July 25, 1954, in *Nellie*, ed. Elspeth Huxley, 204.

60. E. Montgomery Campbell to her mother, n.d. [1952], Documents.16541, IWM.

61. Malcolm Barnes, reader's report on *Jungle Green* by Arthur Campbell, January 19, 1953, AURR 21/1/99, Allen & Unwin archive, University of Reading.

62. K. John, "Notes for the Novel-Reader," *Illustrated London News* (October 6, 1956).

63. Sue Bradley, ed., *The British Book Trade: An Oral History* (London: British Library, 2008), 141.

64. Paula Rabinowitz, *American Pulp: How Paperbacks Brought Modernism to Main Street* (Princeton, NJ: Princeton University Press, 2014).

65. Michael Paris, *Warrior Nation: Images of War in British Popular Culture, 1850-2000* (London: Reaktion Books, 2000), 164–167.

66. Woody Haut, *Pulp Culture: Hardboiled Fiction and the Cold War* (London: Serpent's Tail, 1995); Bill Osgerby, "Muscular Manhood and Salacious Sleaze: The Singular World of the 1950s Macho Pulps," in *Containing America: Cultural Production and Consumption in Fifties America*, ed. Nathan Abrams and Julie Hughes (Birmingham: University of Birmingham Press, 2000); Gregory A. Daddis, *Pulp Vietnam: War and Gender in Cold War Men's Adventure Magazines* (Cambridge: Cambridge University Press, 2020), 48–52, 108–119.

67. Bradford Wright, *Comic Book Nation: The Transformation of Youth Culture in America* (Baltimore: Johns Hopkins University Press, 2001), 149–156; Michael Goodrum and Philip Smith, *Printing Terror: American Horror Comics as Cold War Commentary and Critique* (Manchester: Manchester University Press, 2021), 41–72.

68. Martin Barker, *A Haunt of Fears: The Strange History of the British Horror Comics Campaign* (Jackson: University Press of Mississippi, 2006).

69. James Campbell, "Combat Gnosticism: The Ideology of First World War Poetry Criticism," *New Literary History* 30, no. 1 (1999): 203–215. See also Alex Adams, *How to Justify Torture: Inside the Ticking Bomb Scenario* (London: Repeater, 2019), 59; Yuval Noah Harari, *The Ultimate Experience: Battlefield Revelations and the Making of Modern War Culture, 1450-2000* (New York: Palgrave Macmillan, 2008).

70. J. W. G. Moran, *Spearhead in Malaya* (London: Peter Davies, 1959), 37, 80–83.

71. Erwin, "Britain's Small Wars," 182; John Newsinger, "The Military Memoir in British Imperial Culture: The Case of Malaya," *Race & Class* 35, no. 3 (1994): 47–62, at

58–59; James A. Mangan and Callum McKenzie, "Martial Conditioning, Military Exemplars, and Moral Certainties: Imperial Hunting as Preparation for War," *International Journal of the History of Sport* 25, no. 9 (2008): 1132–1167.

72. Richard Miers, *Shoot to Kill* (London: Faber and Faber, 1959), 170; James Macdonald, *My Two Jungles* (London: George G. Harrap, 1957), 191; Katharine Sim, *The Moon At My Feet* (London: Hodder and Stoughton, 1959), 149.

73. Robert Ruark, *Something of Value* (London: Transworld, 1980 [1955]), 438.

74. Arthur Campbell, *Jungle Green* (Boston: Little Brown, 1954), 56, 138, 232.

75. Newsinger, "Military Memoir in British Imperial Culture," 60. Especially lurid examples include Frank Kitson, *Gangs and Counter-Gangs* (London: Barrie and Rockliff, 1960), 142, 176; Campbell, *Jungle Green*, 233–234; Macdonald, *My Two Jungles*, 191.

76. Macdonald, *My Two Jungles*, 191, 243.

77. [Geoffrey Bownas], "Jungle War," *Times Literary Supplement* (3 June 1959).

78. See the sales figures in AUC 584/19, Allen & Unwin archive, University of Reading.

79. John Squire, "British Soldier in Malaya," *Illustrated London News* (August 22, 1953); Harold Nicolson, "War of Nerves," *Observer* (July 19, 1953).

80. "Jungle War," *Yorkshire Post* (July 21, 1953); Derrick Sington, "War in Malaya," *Manchester Guardian* (August 7, 1953).

81. Anne McClintock, *Imperial Leather: Race, Gender, and Sexuality in the Colonial Conquest* (New York: Routledge, 1995), 147.

82. Daniel Nash [W. R. Loader], *Not Yours the Island* (London: Jonathan Cape, 1956), 130.

83. Oswald Wynd, *The Gentle Pirate: An Entertainment* (Garden City, NY: Doubleday, 1951), 94–95.

84. Diana Buttenshaw, *Violence in Paradise* (London: Hodder & Stoughton, 1957), 74, 82, 139–143.

85. M. M. Kaye, *Death in Kenya* (New York: St. Martin's, 1983), 89–90. Later editions of the book were retitled from the original publication of *Later Than You Think* (London: Longmans, Green, 1958).

86. Gordon Landsborough, *The Violent People* (London: Cassell, 1960), 39–41.

87. Landsborough, *Violent People*, 131, 175.

88. Buttenshaw, *Violence in Paradise*, 45, 51, 71, 126; John Appleby, *The Bad Summer* (London: Hodder & Staughton, 1958), 19, 74; C.T. Stoneham, *Kenya Mystery* (London: Museum Press, 1954), 67; Lavender Lloyd, *The Verandah Room* (London: Eyre & Spottiswoode, 1955), 149.

89. Moran, *Spearhead in Malaya*, 186.

90. Stoneham, *Kenya Mystery*, 67.

91. Peter J. Kalliney, *Commonwealth of Letters: British Literary Culture and the Emergence of Postcolonial Aesthetics* (New York: Oxford University Press, 2013); Gail Low, *Publishing the Postcolonial: Anglophone West African and Caribbean Writing in the UK, 1948-1968* (Abingdon: Routledge, 2011).

92. Victor Stafford Reid, *The Leopard* (Chatham, New Jersey: Chatham Bookseller, 1972), 12, 19, 50, 81.

93. George W. Target, "The Face of Violence," *Liberty* (February 1, 1972): 2–7.

94. David Maughan-Brown, *Land, Freedom, and Fiction: History and Ideology in Kenya* (London: Zed Books, 1985), 157–182.

95. G. W. Target, *The Missionaries* (London: Gerald Duckworth, 1961), 101–110.

96. Target, *Missionaries*, 101.

97. Target, *Missionaries*, 110–111.

98. Michael Cornish, *An Introduction to Violence* (London: Cassell, 1960), 91–93.

99. Michael Taussig, "Culture of Terror—Space of Death: Roger Casement's Putumayo Report and the Explanation of Torture," *Comparative Studies in Society and History* 26, no. 3 (1984): 467–497, at 471.

100. Cornish, *Introduction to Violence*, 92.

101. T. W. Hutton, "Tales of Action," *Birmingham Post* (February 16, 1960); [Anthony Cronin], "After the Gospels," *Times Literary Supplement* (July 21, 1961); Roy Perrott, "Rio to Rhondda," *Guardian* (January 29, 1960).

102. Cornish, *Introduction to Violence*, 112.

103. W. B. Thomas, *The Touch of Pitch: A Story of Mau Mau* (London: Allan Wingate, 1956), 90, 116, 191–195.

104. Anthony Burgess, *The Long Day Wanes: A Malayan Trilogy* (New York: W. W. Norton, 1992), 64.

105. Burgess, *Long Day Wanes*, 36. On "ironic absolution" as a bulwark against moral outrage, see Cheryl B. Welch, "Colonial Violence and the Rhetoric of Evasion: Tocqueville on Algeria," *Political Theory* 31, no. 2 (2003): 235–264, at 248–251.

106. Andrew Biswell, *The Real Life of Anthony Burgess* (London: Picador, 2006), 169. See also Lee Erwin, "Britain's Small Wars: Domesticating 'Emergency,'" in *The Edinburgh Companion to Twentieth-Century British and American War Literature*, ed. Adam Piette and Mark Rawlinson (Edinburgh: Edinburgh University Press, 2012).

107. On Sillitoe's politics, see Matthew Whittle, *Post-War British Literature and the "End of Empire"* (London: Palgrave Macmillan, 2016), 57–60.

108. Ned Stafford, "Han Suyin" (obituary), *British Medical Journal* 246 (January 12, 2013): 29.

109. Han Suyin, *My House Has Two Doors* (New York: Putnam, 1980), 57.

110. Han, *My House Has Two Doors*, 60.

111. "Malaya: The Emergency in its Seventh Year," typescript draft, 1954, Han Suyin papers, box 11, Howard Gotlieb Archival Research Center, Boston University (hereafter BU).

112. "Malaya: The Emergency in its Seventh Year," *The Reporter* (December 16, 1954): 23–27.

113. Elizabeth Comber to Edward Weeks, June 3, 1952, Edward Weeks papers, box 55.3, Harry Ransom Center, University of Texas, Austin.

114. The novel has generated surprisingly little literary criticism. A useful introduction is Fiona Lee, "Epistemological Checkpoint: Reading Fiction as a Translation of History," *Postcolonial Text* 9, no. 1 (2014): 1–21.

115. [David Tylden-Wright], "Fear and Frustration," *Times Literary Supplement* (August 3, 1956); Elizabeth Bowen, "Testing Ground for Schoolmasters," *Tatler* (August 29, 1956); John Wain, "New Novels," *Observer* (July 29, 1956); Peter St. John, "New Novels," *New Statesman* (July 21, 1956).

116. Han, *And the Rain My Drink*, 112–113.

117. Han, *And the Rain My Drink*, 30.

118. Han, *And the Rain My Drink*, 213.

119. Victor Purcell to Han Suyin, July 18, 1956, Han Suyin papers, box 89, BU.

120. Nicola Wilson, "Middlemen, Middlebrow, Broadbrow," in *British Literature in Transition, 1920-1940: Futility and Anarchy*, ed. Charles Ferrall and Dougal McNeill (Cambridge: Cambridge University Press, 2018).

121. Bowen, "Testing Ground for Schoolmasters"; R.C. Churchill, "New Novels," *Birmingham Daily Post* (July 31, 1956); K. John, "Notes for the Novel-Reader," *Illustrated London News* (October 6, 1956).

122. Richard Steadman-Jones, "Colonial Fiction for Liberal Readers: John Masters and the Savage Family Saga," in *End of Empire and the English Novel Since 1945*, ed. Rachel Gilmour and Bill Schwarz (Manchester: Manchester University Press, 2011).

CHAPTER 3

1. For a concise overview of official "cover-ups" in the wars of decolonization, see French, *British Way*, 166–172.

2. For instance, the outpouring of rhetoric on settler colonialism in the late nineteenth century treated its violence in "perfunctory and evasive" ways. See Duncan Bell, *The Idea of Greater Britain: Empire and the Future of World Order, 1860-1900* (Princeton, NJ: Princeton University Press, 2007), 115–116.

3. David Edgerton, "Liberal Militarism and the British State," *New Left Review*, no. 185 (1991): 138–169; David Edgerton, *Warfare State: Britain 1920-1970* (Cambridge: Cambridge University Press, 2006). Classic accounts of militarism either neglected Britain or treated it as an exception to the European pattern. See, e.g., Alfred Vagts, *A History of Militarism* (Westport, CT: Greenwood Press, 1981 [1937]).

4. Bernard Semmel, *Jamaican Blood and Victorian Conscience: The Governor Eyre Controversy* (Westport, CT: Greenwood Press, 1976); Helen Fein, *Imperial Crime and Punishment: The Massacre at Jallianwala Bagh and British Judgment, 1919-1920* (Honolulu: University Press of Hawaii, 1977); Derek Sayer, "British Reaction to the Amritsar Massacre, 1919-1920," *Past & Present* 131 (1991): 130–164.

5. W. Fitzhugh Brundage, *Civilizing Torture: An American Tradition* (Cambridge, MA: Belknap Press of Harvard University Press, 2018), 5.

6. "Sir Hugh Foot Defends 'Angry' Soldiers," *Birmingham Post* (September 22, 1958); Keith Waterhouse, "Are the British Cruel in Cyprus?" *Daily Mirror* (June 7, 1957): 9.

7. "New Assessment in Kenya," *Times* (January 26, 1954).

8. "Politics of Violence" transcript, November 27, 1963, reel T73, BBC Written Archives Centre, Reading (hereafter BBCWA).

9. "Opinion," *Daily Express* (December 22, 1953).

10. "The Best We Can Do," *Spectator* (October 1, 1959): 3–5.

11. Stanley Mayes, *Cyprus and Makarios* (London: Putnam, 1960), 136.

12. Peter Paris [pseud.], *The Impartial Knife: A Doctor in Cyprus* (New York: David McKay, 1961), 198–199.

13. "Terrorism and the Answer," *Daily Telegraph* (November 22, 1955).

14. "No Peace with Mau Mau," *Western Mail* (March 4, 1954).

15. "Rules for Kenya War," *Dundee Courier and Advertiser* (December 11, 1953).

16. Howard Williams, *Paradise Precarious* (London: Welcome Press, [1959?]), 134, 140.

17. *Tonight* transcript, September 23, 1958, reel 48, BBCWA.

18. Nancy Crawshaw, *The Cyprus Revolt: An Account of the Struggle for Union with Greece* (London: Allen & Unwin, 1978), 245.

19. "Ex-Serviceman," letter to *Newcastle Evening Chronicle* (October 7, 1958).

20. Kitson, *Gangs and Counter-Gangs*, 46.

21. "Malaya Bandits: 'End Not Yet in Sight,'" *Coventry Evening Telegraph* (January 27, 1950).

22. "Red Sickle is Moving Through East Asia," *Coventry Evening Telegraph* (March 31, 1950).

23. "Mau Mau Thugs Should Be Exterminated": Kenya Settler's Talk to Evesham Rotarians," *Evesham Standard* (May 7, 1954); James W. Stapleton, *The Gate Hangs Well* (London: Hammond, Hammond, [1957]), 209.

24. Richard Overy, "'Why We Bomb You': Liberal War-Making and Moral Relativism in the RAF Bomber Offensive, 1940-45," in *Liberal Wars: Anglo-American Strategy, Ideology, and Practice*, ed. Alan Cromartie (Abingdon: Routledge, 2015). On openness about reprisals against German civilians, see also Mark Connelly, "The British People, the Press, and the Strategic Air Campaign Against Germany, 1939-45," *Contemporary British History* 16, no. 2 (2002): 39–58; Brett Holman, "'Bomb Back, and Bomb Hard': Debating Reprisals During the Blitz," *Australian Journal of Politics and History* 58, no. 3 (2012): 394–407.

25. Richard Overy, "Constructing a Space for Dissent in War: The Bombing Restriction Committee, 1941-1945," *English Historical Review*, no. 550 (2016): 596–622, at 616–617.

26. "The Price of Mau Mau," *Sunderland Daily Echo* (December 21, 1953).

27. "Rules for Kenya War," *Dundee Courier and Advertiser* (December 11, 1953).

28. George W. Dymond to Tom Driberg, April 12, 1952, SOC.Driberg A8, COO.

29. R. H. S. Crossman, "London Diary," *New Statesman* (November 22, 1958): 715–716.

30. Harold Soref, quoted in National Union of Conservative and Unionist Associations, *73rd Annual Conference: Margate, 8–10th October, 1953* (London: s.n., n.d.), 61.

31. Benenson, introduction to *Gangrene*, 37.

32. E. J. Hobsbawm, letter to *Manchester Guardian* (January 28, 1954).

33. Daniel Ussishkin, *Morale: A Modern British History* (New York: Oxford University Press, 2017).

34. Nancy Crawhaw to John Reddaway, June 17, 1956, Crawshaw papers, box 1, folder 6, Princeton University Library (hereafter PUL).

35. M. H. Ratton to Graham Greene, October 6, 1953, Greene papers, box 73, folder 36, Burns Library, Boston College (hereafter BC).

36. Worsley, "Imperial Retreat," 117.

37. R. H. S. Crossman, "London Diary," *New Statesman* (November 22, 1958): 715–716.

38. Benenson, introduction to *Gangrene*, 37.

39. Diarist 5445, entry for September 22, 1958, MO.

40. "Babs' Boob!" *Daily Sketch* (September 23, 1958).

41. Cassandra, "Are They Different Abroad?" *Daily Mirror* (September 24, 1958).

42. *Tonight* transcript, September 23, 1958, reel 48, BBCWA. The interviewer was Geoffrey Johnson-Smith, a Conservative who would go on to win a seat in Parliament in 1959 by defeating Lena Jeger in the Holborn and St. Pancras constituency.

43. Goldsworthy, *Colonial Issues in British Politics*, 356.

44. Tellex report, October 3, 1959, "General Election 1959: Election Addresses, Conservative Leaflets and Guides," PHM.

45. Mrs. E. Whitehead to Morgan Phillips, June 8, 1961; Miss A. James to Morgan Phillips, June 8, 1961; anonymous letter to Morgan Phillips, n.d., London Labour Party archive, ACC/2417/L/013/002, London Metropolitan Archives (hereafter LMA).

46. Schwarz, *White Man's World*; Liam J. Liburd, "Beyond the Pale: Whiteness, Masculinity, and Empire in the British Union of Fascists, 1932-1940," *Fascism: Journal of Comparative Fascist Studies* 7 (2018): 275–296.

47. Barbara Bush, "Gender and Empire: The Twentieth Century," in *Gender and Empire*, ed. Philippa Levine (Oxford: Oxford University Press, 2004); Joanna Lewis, *Empire State-Building: War and Welfare in Kenya, 1925-1952* (James Currey: Oxford, 2000). On the rhetoric and the reality of the shift from coercion to community, see also Erik Linstrum, *Ruling Minds: Psychology in the British Empire* (Cambridge, MA: Harvard University Press, 2016), ch. 5.

48. *Tonight* transcript, September 23, 1958, reel 48, BBCWA.

49. "Babs' Boob!" *Daily Sketch* (September 23, 1958); Cassandra [William Connor], "Women of Westminster," *Daily Mirror* (September 25, 1958).

50. Anne Edwards, "The Doctor's Downfall," *Daily Express* (October 1, 1958).

51. Liam J. Liburd, "Thinking Imperially: The British Fascisti and the Politics of Empire, 1923-1925," *Twentieth Century British History* 32, no. 1 (2021): 46–67.

52. Hugh Trevaskis, letter to *Daily Telegraph* (November 12, 1958).

53. Elmo Murray, letter to *Wiltshire Times* (April 21, 1956).

54. E. H. Baxter, letter to *Yorkshire Post* (September 30, 1955).

55. Quoted in Goldsworthy, *Colonial Issues*, 303.

56. Aubrey Wilson, "Are We Too 'Kid Glove' with Mau Mau?" *Lancashire Evening Post* (January 25, 1954).

57. Norman Hallett, letter to *Western Mail* (October 11, 1958).

58. H. Minchin, letter to *Daily Mail* (September 21, 1955).

59. D. F. Gurran, letter to *Daily Mail* (November 13, 1958); A.F.T. Ord, letter to *Daily Mail* (September 22, 1955).

60. Edward Pearce, ed., *The Golden Talking-Shop: The Oxford Union Debates Empire, World War, Revolution, and Women* (Oxford: Oxford University Press, 2016), 533–534.

61. Major James Friend, quoted in Nigel Nicolson, *Long Life* (London: Weidenfeld & Nicolson, 1997), 170.

62. Excerpts from interviews with Mrs. H. and "Batten," Stevenage study, RS 1/301, BI.

63. Interviews 050 and 291 in "Angels in Marble: Working-Class Conservatives in Urban England, 1958-1960," Study Number 7429, UK Data Archive (hereafter UKDA), online at https://beta.ukdataservice.ac.uk/datacatalogue/studies/study?id=7429 (registration required). The survey analysis published by two social scientists in the late 1960s had little to say about empire while focusing on attitudes about class, hierarchy, and deference. See Robert McKenzie and Allan Silver, *Angels in Marble: Working Class Conservatives in Urban England* (Chicago: University of Chicago Press, 1968).

64. Interview with Elsie B., December 17, 1959, Stevenage study, RS 1/302, BI.

65. Interviews 443, 685, 269, "Angels in Marble," UKDA.

66. D. E. Butler, *The British General Election of 1951* (London: Macmillan, 1952), 118–128; Leon D. Epstein, *British Politics in the Suez Crisis* (Urbana: University of Illinois Press, 1964).

67. Gallup (ed.), *Gallup International Public Opinion Polls: Great Britain*, vol. 1, 282–283, 308, 361, 394, 602.

68. Interview with David P., n.d., Bethnal Green Youth Survey, RS 1/314, BI.

69. Quoted in Philip Murphy, *Party Politics and Decolonization: The Conservative Party and British Colonial Policy in Tropical Africa, 1951-1964* (Oxford: Clarendon Press, 1995), 133.

70. "John Bull," letter to *Newcastle Evening Chronicle* (October 7, 1958).

71. T. Paddy, letter to *Daily Mail* (March 30, 1959).

72. Audrey Hilton, *This England: Selections from the* New Statesman *This England Column, 1953-57* (London: Statesman and Nation, 1957), 15.

73. Interview with David A. and Bert B., Bethnal Green Youth Survey, RS 1/311, BI; interview with Vera H., n.d., Stevenage study, RS 1/302, BI.

74. "Dealing with Terrorism," *The Sphere* (December 3, 1955).

75. "Mau Mau Defiance," *Dundee Courier* (November 26, 1952)

76. Lawrence Durrell to Richard Aldington, c. September 14–24, 1958, in *Literary Lifelines: The Richard Aldington-Lawrence Durrell Correspondence*, ed. Ian S. MacNiven and Harry T. Moore (New York: Viking Press, 1981), 54.

77. Hugh Trevor-Roper to Bernard Berenson, November 25, 1956, in *Letters from Oxford: Hugh Trevor-Roper to Bernard Berenson*, ed. Richard Davenport-Hines (London: Phoenix, 2007), 209.

78. Pugh, *"Hurrah for the Blackshirts!"*; Martin Pugh, "Britain and Its Empire," in *The Oxford Handbook of Fascism*, ed. R. J. B. Bosworth (Oxford University Press, 2010); Dan Stone, "The English Mistery, the BUF, and the Dilemmas of British Fascism," *Journal of Modern History* 75 (2003): 336–358.

79. Philip Murphy, *Alan Lennox-Boyd: A Biography* (London: I.B. Tauris, 1999).

80. On the social geography of interwar fascism, see G. C. Webber, "Patterns of Membership and Support for the British Union of Fascists," *Journal of Contemporary History* 19, no. 4 (1984): 575–606. For suggestive similarities in the geographic distribution of Popular Front support in the 1970s, see Richard C. Thurlow, *Fascism in Britain: A History, 1918-1985* (Oxford: Basil Blackwell, 1987), 289; Christopher T. Husbands, *Racial Exclusionism and the City: The Urban Support of the National Front* (London: Allen & Unwin, 1983).

81. Paul Stocker, "The Postwar British Extreme Right and Empire, 1945-1967," *Religion Compass* 9, no. 5 (2015): 162–172; cf. Joe Mulhall, "From Apathy to Obsession: The Reactions of A.K. Chesterton and the British Far Right to Imperial Decline," *Patterns of Prejudice* 50, no. 4–5 (2016): 458–477, which usefully explores the role of anti-Semitism in fascist responses to decolonization but downplays the significance of empire to post-1945 fascism.

82. Kushner, *Holocaust and the Liberal Imagination*; David Cesarani, "Great Britain," in *The World Reacts to the Holocaust*, ed. David S. Wyman (Baltimore: Johns Hopkins University Press, 1996).

83. David Leitch, "Explosion at the King David Hotel," in *The Age of Austerity*, ed. Michael Sissons and Philip French (London: Hodder and Stoughton, 1963); Paul Bagon, "The Impact of the Jewish Underground Upon Anglo Jewry: 1945-1947" (MPhil thesis, University of Oxford, 2003), 126–29.

84. [James Caunt], *An Editor on Trial: Rex v. Caunt* (Morecambe: Morecambe Press, 1947).

85. Bagon, "Impact of the Jewish Underground," 127; Metropolitan Police Telegrams, January 1, 1947, March 11, 1948, and May 25, 1948, MEPO 3/1893, TNA; Graham Macklin, *Very Deeply Dyed in Black: Sir Oswald Mosley and the Resurrection of British Fascism after 1945* (London: I.B. Tauris, 2007), 46.

86. A. K. Chesterton, *Empire or Eclipse: Grim Realities of the Mid-Twentieth Century* (London: Candour Publishing, [1965?]), BL. See also Stocker, "Postwar British Extreme Right"; Mulhall, "From Apathy to Obsession."

87. A. K. Chesterton, *Sound the Alarm! A Warning to the British Nations* (Croydon: Candour Publishing, [1954?]), BL.

88. A. K. Chesterton, untitled manuscript, n.d., folder C11, A. K. Chesterton papers, University of Bath archives.

89. Chesterton, *Sound the Alarm!*, 9.

90. Chesterton, untitled manuscript, n.d., folder C11, A. K. Chesterton papers, University of Bath archives.

91. Thurlow, *Fascism in Britain*, 250.

92. John Larkman, "African Nationalism," *Combat*, no. 3 (April–June 1959).

93. "National Labour Activities," *Combat*, no. 2 (January–March 1959); "Atrocity Fiends Whitewashed," *Combat*, no. 4 (autumn 1959); "News Round-Up: Kenya Sell-Out," *Combat*, no. 6 (May–June 1960).

94. Chesterton, *Empire or Eclipse*, 7.

95. "5,000 at National Labour Rally," *Combat*, no. 4 (autumn 1959).

96. "Blacks Go Berserk," *Combat*, no. 3 (April–June 1959).

97. Peter Ling, "Atrocity Fiends Whitewashed," *Combat* (autumn 1959).

98. Cf. John E. Richardson, "Racial Populism in British Fascist Discourse: The Case of *Combat* and the British National Party," in *Analysing Fascist Discourse: European Fascism in Talk and Text*, ed. Ruth Wodak and John E. Richardson (Abingdon: Routledge, 2013).

99. Darwin, "Fear of Falling," 41.

100. Quoted in Paul Stocker, *Lost Imperium: Far Right Visions of the British Empire, c. 1920-1980* (Abingdon: Routledge, 2021), 183.

101. Richard Hilton, *Imperial Obituary: The Mysterious Death of the British Empire* (Devon: Britons Publishing Company, 1968), 100 (emphasis in original).

102. Stuart Hall, "The Great Moving Right Show," in *Selected Political Writings: The Great Moving Right Show and Other Essays*, ed. Sally Davison, David Fatherstone, Michael Rustin, and Bill Schwarz (London: Lawrence and Wishart, 2017).

103. Thurlow, *Fascism in Britain*, 223–259; Neill Nugent, "Post-War Fascism?," in *British Fascism: Essays on the Radical Right in Inter-War Britain*, ed. Kenneth Lunn and Richard C. Thurlow (London: Croom Helm, 1980); Nicholas Hillman, "'Tell Me Chum, In Case I Got It Wrong. What Was It We Were Fighting During the War?' The Re-Emergence of British Fascism, 1945-58," *Contemporary British History* 15, no. 4 (2001): 1–34.

104. Mort, *Capital Affairs*; Stuart Hall et al., *Policing the Crisis: Mugging, the State, and Law and Order* (London: Macmillan, 1978), 235. The idea of "the Establishment" was popularized by journalist Henry Fairlie in a 1955 article about the Cambridge spy ring.

105. Quoted in Liam Liburd, "The Eternal Imperialists: Empire, Race, and Gender on the British Radical Right, 1918-1968" (PhD thesis, University of Sheffield, 2019), 250.

106. Lord Salisbury to Roy Welensky, October 24, 1962, Welensky papers 665/4, BO.

107. C. Northcote Parkinson, *A Law Unto Themselves: Twelve Portraits* (Boston: Houghton Mifflin, 1966).

108. "Proposed dialogue script for a filmed discussion with Field Marshal Sir Gerald Templer," March 30, 1977, catalogue no. 8011-132-2, NAM; Frank Kitson, *Low Intensity Operations: Subversion, Insurgency, and Peacekeeping* (London: Faber and Faber, 1971), 24–25.

109. The honors conferred in the 1960s and 1970s sent an especially strong signal at a time when the imperial connections of the royal honors system were coming under attack. See Tobias Harper, *From Servants of the Empire to Everyday Heroes: The British Honours System in the Twentieth Century* (Oxford: Oxford University Press, 2020).

110. Amy Whipple, "Revisiting the 'Rivers of Blood' Controversy: Letters to Enoch Powell," *Journal of British Studies* 28, no. 3 (2009): 717–735.

111. Bill Schwarz, "'The Only White Man in There': The Re-Racialisation of England, 1956-1968," *Race & Class* 38, no. 1 (1996): 65–78.

112. Quoted in Webster, *Englishness and Empire*, 123.

113. Kathleen Sloan Chickman to Mark Abrams, January 13, 1959; anonymous Handsworth resident to Mark Abrams, [December 1958], ABRMS 6/4/6, CAC.

114. R. Humphries to Mark Abrams, [December 1958], ABRMS 6/4/6, CAC.

115. T. R. Fyvel, *Troublemakers: Rebellious Youth in an Affluent Society* (New York: Schocken Books, 1962), 40, 139.

116. Lord Salisbury to Patrick Wall, September 17, 1963, quoted in Mark Joseph Pitchford, "The Conservative Party and the Extreme Right, 1945-1975" (PhD thesis, Cardiff University, 2009), 167. On the rivalry between the two men, see S. J. Ball, "Banquo's Ghost: Lord Salisbury, Harold Macmillan, and the High Politics of Decolonization, 1957-1963," *Twentieth Century British History* 16, no. 1 (2005): 74–102.

117. Goldsworthy, *Colonial Issues*, 286–304; John Ramsden, *The Age of Churchill and Eden, 1940-1957* (London: Longman, 1995), 262–263.

118. Harold Nicolson to Vita Sackville-West, May 15, 1958, in Nicolson, *Diaries and Letters, 1945-1962*, ed. Nicolson, 349.

119. Quoted in Pitchford, "The Conservative Party and the Extreme Right," 113.

120. Schwarz, *White Man's World*, 429–433; Lisa Mason, "The Development of the Monday Club and Its Contribution to the Conservative Party and the Modern British Right, 1961 to 1990" (PhD thesis, University of Wolverhampton, 2004).

121. Patrick Seyd, "Factionalism within the Conservative Party: The Monday Club," *Government and Opposition* 7, no. 2 (1972): 464–487; Martin Walker, *The National Front* (London: Fontana, 1977), 108–132. On Conservative support

for Rhodesia, see Schwarz, *White Man's World*, 427–428. For the removal of immigrants, see Daniel Renshaw, *The Discourse of Repatriation in Britain, 1845-2016: A Political and Social History* (London: Routledge, 2021), 163–165.

122. Murphy, *Party Politics and Decolonization*, 9.

123. E. H. Baxter, letter to *Yorkshire Post* (September 30, 1955).

124. Wyndham Lewis to Henry Regnery, June 17, 1953, in *The Letters of Wyndham Lewis*, ed. W. K. Rose (Norfolk, CT: New Directions, 1963), 549–550.

125. Quoted in Victor Bailey, *The Rise and Fall of the Rehabilitative Idea, 1895-1970* (London: Routledge, 2019), 364.

126. Epstein, *British Politics in the Suez Crisis*, 137–138.

CHAPTER 4

1. Thomas and Curless, eds., *Decolonization and Conflict*; Linstrum, *Ruling Minds*, ch. 5; Emily Baughan, "Rehabilitating an Empire: Humanitarian Collusion with the Colonial State during the Kenyan Emergency, c. 1954-1960," *Journal of British Studies* 59, no. 1 (2020): 57–79; Muriam Haleh Davis, "'The Transformation of Man' in French Algeria: Economic Planning and the Postwar Social Sciences, 1958-1962," *Journal of Contemporary History* 52, no. 1 (2017): 73–94. A valuable account of these tensions in the late Victorian British Empire is Forth, *Barbed-Wire Imperialism*.

2. Fein, *Imperial Crime and Punishment*.

3. Even committed pacifists bent their principles sufficiently to participate in the national mobilization of the Second World War, thereby retaining a voice in debates about how the war against Germany was waged. See Richard Overy, "Pacifism and the Blitz," *Past & Present* 219 (May 2013): 201–236.

4. On the 1960s as the turning point for British secularization, see Callum G. Brown, *The Death of Christian Britain: Understanding Secularization, 1800-2000* (London: Routledge, 2001); Hugh McLeod, *The Religious Crisis of the 1960s* (Oxford: Oxford University Press, 2007).

5. Brown, *Death of Christian Britain*; Adrian Hastings, *A History of English Christianity, 1920-1985* (London: Collins, 1986), 443–447, 458.

6. On the limitations of the postwar "religious revival," see S. J. D. Green, *The Passing of Protestant England: Secularization and Social Change, c. 1920-1960* (Cambridge: Cambridge University Press, 2011), 242–272.

7. Alister Chapman, "The International Context of Secularization in England: The End of Empire, Immigration, and the Decline of Christian National Identity, 1945-1970," *Journal of British Studies* 54 (2015): 163–189, at 166–169.

8. Brown, *Passing of Protestant England*, 255–256.

9. Daniel S. Loss, "The Institutional Afterlife of Christian England," *Journal of Modern History* 89, no. 2 (2017): 282–313.

10. Keith Robbins, *England, Ireland, Scotland, Wales: The Christian Church, 1900-2000* (Oxford: Oxford University Press, 2008), 234–241.

11. David Ayers, "Hewlett Johnson: Britain's Red Dean and the Cold War," in *Religion and the Cold War: A Global Perspective*, ed. Philip Muehlenbeck (Nashville: Vanderbilt University Press, 2012); Kenneth Leech, "Stanley George Evans," *Oxford Dictionary of National Biography* (hereafter *DNB*). Evans, unlike Johnson, lost his enthusiasm for Soviet Communism after 1956.

12. Rob Skinner, "Facing the Challenge of 'Young Africa': Apartheid, South Africa, and British Decolonisation," *South African Historical Journal* 54, no. 1 (2005): 54–71.

13. Huddleston sermon, [1957-1959], MS Huddleston 367, BO; L. John Collins, *Faith under Fire* (London: Leslie Frewin, 1966), 158, 162. On Collins and the peace movement, see also Petra Goedde, *The Politics of Peace: A Global Cold War History* (New York: Oxford University Press, 2019), 102–110.

14. Sermon at St. Paul's Cathedral, January 12, 1957, Collins papers, vol. 3302, Lambeth Palace Library (hereafter LPL).

15. Sermon at St. Paul's Cathedral, September 24, 1950, Collins papers, vol. 3302, LPL.

16. Sermon at St. Paul's Cathedral, September 7, 1958, Collins papers, vol. 3302, LPL; "Hangings in Cyprus Criticized by Canon: 'Offence Against Christian Way of Life,'" *Birmingham Post* (September 10, 1956); "Canon L.J. Collins Says: People Are Not Tools," *Birmingham Post* (March 2, 1957).

17. "Sermon Preached in Canterbury Cathedral," October 19, 1958, Stanley Evans papers, ref. U DEV 6/6, HHC; Leslie D. Weatherhead, "Mau Mau and Missions," *Methodist Recorder* (11 February 1954); Frank Bouverie, "Mau Maus and Christians: A Personal Experience," *Modern Churchman* 44, no. 2 (1954): 86–90.

18. John Marsh, "Cyprus: A Matter of Conscience," *The Christian World* (March 8, 1956); "Which First—Politics or Religion?" *Western Mail* (December 9, 1958).

19. "Berwick Man in Kenya Protests," *Berwickshire News* (February 24, 1958); "Dr. Soper Talks on Communism, Mau Mau, T.V., and Strike Threat," *Berwick Advertiser* (December 17, 1953).

20. John Mailley to Archbishop of York, November 27, 1952, Stansgate papers, 224/3–14, Parliamentary Archives (hereafter PA).

21. Ann Peasegood to Lyttelton, November 14, 1952, CO 967/254, TNA.

22. Philip Radley to Geoffrey Fisher, November 28, 1953, Fisher papers, vol. 127, LPL.

23. K. J. M. Boggs to Fisher, December 12, 1953, Fisher papers, vol. 127, LPL.

24. Transcript of MRA conference, Mackinac Island, Michigan, September 23, 1959; "Cyprus: The Way the Nations Are Meant to Live," MRA press release, September 15, 1959, MS Oxford Movement 3/38, BO.

25. David Anthem to R. A. B. Butler, December 7, 1956, CO 926/178, TNA.

26. John Stuart, *British Missionaries and the End of Empire: East, Central, and Southern Africa, 1939-64* (Grand Rapids: William B. Eerdmans, 2011), 151.

27. John Anderson, "The Tory Party at Prayer? The Church of England and British Politics in the 1950s," *Journal of Church and State* 58, no. 3 (2015): 417–439; Sarah Stockwell, "'Improper and Even Unconstitutional': The Involvement of the Church of England in the Politics of the End of Empire in Cyprus," in *From*

the Reformation to the Permissive Society: A Miscellany in Celebration of the 400th Anniversary of Lambeth Palace Library*, ed. Melanie Barber and Stephen Taylor with Gabriel Sewell (Woodbridge, UK: Boydell Press, 2010).

28. C.M.S. Executive Committee Resolution, January 14, 1953, Fisher papers, vol. 120, LPL; "Reward Killings in Kenya," *Church Times* (December 11, 1953); Walter Low to Fisher, February 20, 1954, Fisher papers, vol. 143, LPL.

29. "Kenya—Time for Action!" (London: Church Missionary Society, [1955]).

30. Olive Anderson, "The Growth of Christian Militarism in Mid-Victorian Britain," *English Historical Review* no. 338 (1971): 46–72; Edward Berenson, *Heroes of Empire: Five Charismatic Men and the Conquest of Africa* (Berkeley: University of California Press, 2011); John M. MacKenzie, introduction to *Popular Imperialism and the Military, 1850-1950* (Manchester: Manchester University Press, 1992).

31. Leslie Hunter, *The Seed and the Fruit: Christian Morality in a Time of Transition* (London: SCM Press, 1953), 50.

32. Cuthbert Bardsley, *Sundry Times, Sundry Places* (London: A.R. Mowbray, 1962), 46.

33. A.W. Hopkins, "President's Visit to 'Forward Areas' in Malaya," *Methodist Recorder* (March 10, 1955).

34. Dianne Kirby, *Church, State, and Propaganda: The Archbishop of York and International Relations* (Hull: University of Hull Press, 1999), 183–185.

35. Kenya Colony, *The Archbishop of Canterbury's Tour of Kenya* (London: Pitkin Pictorials, 1955).

36. David Lloyd Owen diary, entry for May 30, 1952, no. 1998-06-176, NAM.

37. Oliver Lyttelton, *The Memoirs of Lord Chandos: An Unexpected View from the Summit* (New York: New American Library, 1963), 394–395.

38. Campbell, *Jungle Green*, 122.

39. Gordon C. Zahn, *The Military Chaplaincy: A Study of Role Tension in the Royal Air Force* (University of Toronto Press, 1969), 146–148.

40. Lee Kam Hing, "A Neglected Story: Christian Missionaries, Chinese New Villagers, and Communists in the Battle for 'Hearts and Minds' in Malaya, 1948-1960," *Modern Asian Studies* 47, no. 6 (2013): 1977–2006.

41. Inter-Church Aid and Refugee Service, "Report on the Rehabilitation Programme of the Christian Council of Kenya," n.d., Christian Aid papers, CA/A/2/6, School of Oriental and African Studies (hereafter SOAS); John Casson, "Missionaries, Mau Mau, and the Christian Frontier," in *Missions and Missionaries*, ed. Pieter N. Holtrop and Hugh McLeod (Woodbridge: Boydell Press, 2000).

42. T.N. Harper, *The End of Empire and the Making of Malaya* (Cambridge: Cambridge University Press, 1999), 183–187; Clemens Six, *Secularism, Decolonisation, and the Cold War in South and Southeast Asia* (New York: Routledge, 2018), ch. 4; Philip Boobbyer, "Moral Re-Armament in Africa in the Era of Decolonization," in *Missions, Nationalism, and the End of Empire*, ed. Brian Stanley (Grand Rapids: William B. Eerdmans, 2003).

43. *Week of Prayer: October 12–18, 1952* (London: Church Missionary Society, 1952), in P. G. Bostock papers, GB 0162 Micr.Afr.642, reel 1, BO; Ethel Izzard, *New Friends: A Story of Malaya* (London: Highway Press, 1955).

44. "Mau Mau—and Ourselves," *Methodist Recorder* (September 22, 1955); Stephen Foot, "Africa: Choice for a Continent," *Methodist Recorder* (October 7, 1954).

45. Inter-Church Aid and Refugee Service, *Legions of the Lost*, n.d.; Stuart, "Anglican Mission," 160.

46. Craig Calhoun, "A World of Emergencies: Fear, Intervention, and the Limits of the Cosmopolitan Order," *Canadian Review of Sociology and Anthropology* 41, no. 4 (2004): 373–395.

47. "Pilgrimage to St. Paul's," *Times* (December 28, 1951); "Call for Dismissal of Dean of Canterbury," *Times* (July 20, 1951)

48. Fisher to Carey, February 27, 1953, Fishers papers, vol. 120, LPL.

49. Lee, "Neglected Story," 1986–1989; Six, *Secularism, Decolonisation, and the Cold War*, 133–134.

50. Norman Goodall, "The Limits of Co-Operation," *International Review of Missions* no. 176 (October 1955): 447–454.

51. "What Friends Hope to Do in Kenya," *Wayfarer* 33, no. 10 (October 1954): 149–150; Eric Cleaver to editor of *Friend* (draft), June 8, 1956, FSC/KEN/6, LSF.

52. H. A. Wittenbach, *Eastern Horizons* (London: Highway Press, 1954), 85–86.

53. Letter to Frank Buchman, November 21, 1959, box 137, Moral Rearmament Movement archive, Library of Congress.

54. T. A. Morrison to Max Warren, April 27, 1955, box 279, "CMS and Colonial Secretary" folder, Conference of British Missionary Societies archive (hereafter CBMS), SOAS.

55. P. G. Bostock, circular letter, August 27, 1955, box 279, "Memoranda, 1954-56" folder, CBMS, SOAS.

56. [Carey Francis], circular letter, December 29, 1954, box 279, "Memoranda, 1954-56" folder, CBMS, SOAS.

57. C.M.S. Executive Committee Resolution, January 14, 1953; M. A. C. Warren to Bishop Carey, January 14, 1953, Fisher papers, vol. 120, LPL. On the Bewes mission, see also Stuart, *British Missionaries and the End of Empire*, 141–144.

58. Bewes to Baring, January 28, 1953, Fisher papers, vol. 127, LPL.

59. Bewes to Baring, January 28, 1953, Fisher papers, vol. 127, LPL.

60. Bewes to Fisher, February 25, 1953, Fisher papers, vol. 127, LPL.

61. Elkins, *Imperial Reckoning*, 94.

62. "Alleged Death Under Beating of Mau Mau Suspect," *Manchester Guardian* (February 10, 1953): 12.

63. Bewes to Fisher, February 25, 1953, Fisher papers, vol. 127, LPL.

64. "Memorandum on Police Methods in Kenya," [February 1953], Fisher papers, vol. 127, LPL.

65. Fisher to Bewes, February 27, 1953, Fisher papers, vol. 127, LPL.

66. Fisher to I. G. Hobart-Hampden, September 15, 1953, Fisher papers, vol. 127, LPL.

67. Bewes, "Memorandum on Police Methods in Kenya," [February 1953], Fisher papers, vol. 127, LPL.

68. Bewes to Fisher, September 17, 1953, Fisher papers, vol. 127, LPL.

69. George Bell to Jim Little, September 17, 1953, Bell papers, vol. 98, LPL.

70. Baring to Bewes, October 14, 1953, Fisher papers, vol. 127, LPL.

71. G. C. [George Chichester], "Memorandum on Conversation with Evelyn Baring," December 9, 1953, vol. 127, LPL.

72. Baring to Bewes, October 14, 1953, Fisher papers, vol. 127, LPL.

73. Fisher to Radley, December 3, 1953, Fisher papers, vol. 127, LPL.

74. Fisher to Walter Carey, February 27, 1953, Fisher papers, vol. 120, LPL; Fisher to Bell, November 27, 1953, Fisher papers, vol. 127, LPL.

75. P. G. Bostock to Max Warren, November 30, 1953, Bostock papers, reel 1, BO.

76. T. F. C. Bewes, *Kikuyu Conflict: Mau Mau and the Christian Witness* (London: Highway Press, 1954), 68.

77. Walter Low to Fisher, February 20, 1954, Fisher papers, vol. 143, LPL.

78. Fisher to Beecher, January 6, 1954, Fisher papers, vol. 158, LPL; David Steel, letter to *East African Standard* (February 22, 1954); Beecher to Fisher, April 16, 1955, Fisher papers, vol. 158, LPL.

79. "Copy of Reuters message," May 29, 1956, FSC/KEN/6, LSF; Eric D. Cleaver, letter to *Times* (June 1, 1956): 11.

80. Mark Freeman, "Muscular Quakerism? The Society of Friends and Youth Organisations in Britain, c. 1900-1950," *English Historical Review* 125, no. 514 (2010): 642–669.

81. Maude Brayshaw to Eric Cleaver, September 2, 1956, FSC/KEN/6, file 10; Eric Cleaver to Roderick Ede, May 10, 1956, FSC/KEN/6, file 4, LSF.

82. Robert Landor to Ede and Cleaver, June 18, 1956, FSC/KEN/6, file 7, LSF.

83. Ede to Cleaver, June 1, 1956, FSC/KEN/6, file 4; [Cleaver] to Stanley A. Morrison, June 22, 1956, FSC/KEN/6, file 4, LSF.

84. Landor to Ede and Cleaver, June 18, 1956; Cleaver to editor of *Friend* (draft), June 8, 1956, FSC/KEN/6, file 1, LSF.

85. Landor to Ede and Cleaver, June 18, 1956; John Starke to Leslie Smith, June 11, 1956, FSC/KEN/6, file 1, LSF.

86. Cleaver to Sturge, May 21, 1956, FSC/KEN/6, file 4; Sturge to Cleaver, May 14, 1956, LSF.

87. Cleaver to editor of *Friend* (draft), June 8, 1956, LSF.

88. Stanley Sweet to Sturge, June 13, 1956, box FSC/KEN/6, file 7; Margaret V. Fox to Sturge, July 2, 1956, box FSC/KEN/6, file 7; Edgar Bowes to Cleaver, [June 1956], box FSC/KEN/6, file 9; Maurice Hussey to Cleaver, June 2, 1956, box FSC/KEN/6, file 9; "Meeting for Sufferings" [National Quaker body] to Alan Lennox-Boyd, July 14, 1956, box FSC/KEN/5, file 4, FSC.

89. Sophia Rosenfeld, *Common Sense: A Political History* (Cambridge, MA: Harvard University Press, 2011), 36–38.

90. Keith Thomas, "Cases of Conscience in Seventeenth-Century England," in *Public Duty and Private Conscience in Seventeenth-Century England*, ed. John Morrill, Paul Slack, and Daniel Woolf (Oxford: Oxford University Press, 1993); Edward Vallance, "The Kingdom's Case: The Use of Casuistry as a Political Language, 1640-1692," *Albion* 34, no. 4 (2002): 557–583.

91. James Tully, "Governing Conduct," in *Conscience and Casuistry in Early Modern Europe*, ed. Edmund Leites (Cambridge: Cambridge University Press, 1988); Margaret Sampson, "Laxity and Liberty in Seventeenth-Century Political Thought," in *Conscience and Casuistry*, ed. Leites; Edmund Leites, "Casuistry and Character," in *Conscience and Casuistry*, ed. Leites; Albert R. Jonsen and Stephen Toulmin, *The Abuse of Casuistry: A History of Moral Reasoning* (Berkeley: University of California Press, 1989), 163–164.

92. Leites, "Casuistry and Character," in *Conscience and Casuistry*, ed. Leites.

93. Lindsay Dewar, *A Short Introduction to Moral Theology* (London: A.R. Mowbray, 1956), 33.

94. Lindsay Dewar and Cyril E. Hudson, *Christian Morals: A Study in First Principles* (London: University of London Press, 1956 [1945]); R. C. Mortimer, *Christian Ethics* (London: Hutchinson's University Library, 1950), 71.

95. Martin Thornton, "Re-Review: Kenneth Kirk's *Some Principles of Moral Theology*," *Modern Churchman* 29, no. 2 (1987): 54–57, at 54.

96. Kenneth Kirk, *Some Principles of Moral Theology and Their Application* (London: Longmans, 1952 [1920]), 186; Mortimer, *Christian Ethics*, 70.

97. "Missionary Study," n.d., Kenneth Kirk MS 4354, LPL. Although the sermon is undated, Kirk's treatment of "shirker," "slacker," and "war baby" as novel terms suggests that he wrote shortly after the First World War.

98. Sermon on Mark 5:9, n.d., Kenneth Kirk MS 4354, LPL.

99. Kirk, *Some Principles of Moral Theology*, 189.

100. Stanley G. Evans, "Morals and Immorals," in *Return to Reality: Some Essays on Contemporary Christianity*, ed. Stanley G. Evans (London: Zeno, [1954]), 283–290.

101. Loss, "Institutional Afterlife of Christian England."

102. *Dual Standards of Morality: A Symposium* (London: Friends Home Service Committee, 1960), 7–8.

103. Richard K. Ullmann, "The Christian Faith in Relation to the State," in *The Society of Friends, the Church, and the State* (London: Friends' Book Centre, [1953]), 36.

104. C. S. Lewis, *Christian Behaviour: A Further Series of Broadcast Talks* (New York: Macmillan, 1943), 15.

105. G. W. Bromiley, *Reasonable Service: A Study in Christian Conduct* (London: Inter-Varsity Fellowship, 1948), 64; John Murray, *The Daily Life of the Christian* (London: SCM Press, 1955), 110–111.

106. K.N. Phillips, *From Mau Mau to Christ* ([Stirling]: Stirling Tract Enterprise, 1958), 7, 24, 60.

107. Caroline Moorehead, *Dunant's Dream: War, Switzerland, and the History of the Red Cross* (New York: Carroll & Graf, 1999); David P. Forsythe, *The Humanitarians: The International Committee of the Red Cross* (Cambridge: Cambridge University Press, 2005); John F. Hutchinson, *Champions of Charity: War and the Rise of the Red Cross* (Boulder, CO: Westview Press, 1996); Thomas G. Weiss, "Principles, Politics, and Humanitarian Action," *Ethics & International Affairs* 13, no. 1 (1999): 1–22.

108. Michael Barnett and Janice Stein, eds., *Sacred Aid: Faith and Humanitarianism* (New York: Oxford University Press, 2012); Hans Joas, *The Sacredness of the Person: A New Genealogy of Human Rights*, trans. Alex Skinner (Washington: Georgetown University Press, 2013); Forsythe, *Humanitarians*, 27–28; Gerald Steinacher, *Humanitarians at War: The Red Cross in the Shadow of the Holocaust* (Oxford: Oxford University Press, 2017), 11.

109. Hutchinson, *Champions of Charity*; Steinacher, *Humanitarians at War*; Forsythe, *Humanitarians*, 44–50.

110. Klose, *Human Rights in the Shadow of Colonial Violence*; Yolana Pringle, "Humanitarianism, Race, and Denial: The International Committee of the Red Cross and Kenya's Mau Mau Rebellion, 1952-60," *History Workshop Journal* no. 84 (2017): 89–107, at 94.

111. "British Red Cross Work in the Malayan New Villages," press release, August 25, 1955, RCC/1/12/4/234, British Red Cross Society archive, London (hereafter BRCS).

112. "Activités de la Croix-Rouge Britannique au Kenya," *Revue internationale de la Croix-Rouge* no. 455 (November 1956): 669–672.

113. W. Clifford, "The Red Cross in Cyprus, 1956-1958," RCC/1/12/1/35, BRCS.

114. Angela Limerick diary, Acc. 1594/18, BRCS; "Our London Correspondence," *Manchester Guardian* (May 1, 1954); Noel Barber, *The War of the Running Dogs: How Malaya Defeated the Communist Guerrillas* (London: Collins, 1971), 106–107.

115. Pegeen Hill, interview with Louise Brodie, October 3–4, 2013, C1155/19, British Library Sound Archive (hereafter BLSA); Angela Limerick, Red Cross Appeal script, April 18, 1956, BBCWA; Alan Burgess, "'Symbol of Humanity': The Story of the Work of the British Red Cross," *London Calling* (July 12, 1951): 9.

116. "Wednesday Talk" script, April 10, 1957, reel A4/A5, BBCWA.

117. Rosemary Wall and Anne Marie Rafferty, "Nursing and the 'Hearts and Minds' Campaign, 1948-1958: The Malayan Emergency," in the *Routledge Handbook on the Global History of Nursing*, ed. Patricia D'Antonio, Julie A. Fairman, and Jean C. Whelan (New York: Routledge, 2013); F. Lees to Secretary, British Red Cross Society, June 1, 1954, RCC/1/12/4/234, BRCS.

118. Lady Grey, "Report on Red Cross Work in Kenya after Visiting Reserves," [1955], RCC/1/12/1/37, BRCS.

119. Pegeen Hill, interviewed by Louise Brodie, 2013-10-03, catalogue no. C1155X0019XX-0004, BLSA.

120. Woolton memorandum, November 11, 1955, RCC/1/12/1/35, BRCS.

121. Tehila Sasson, "In the Name of Humanity: Britain and the Rise of Global Humanitarianism" (PhD diss., University of California, Berkeley, 2015); Matthew Hilton, "Ken Loach and the Save the Children Film: Humanitarianism, Imperialism, and the Changing Role of Charity in Postwar Britain," *Journal of Modern History* 87, no. 2 (2015): 357–394.

122. "Extracts from Miss Whittington's Diary—1954," Acc. 13337/1, BRCS.

123. Report by Joan Whittington, March 1954[?], RCC/1/12/1/8; "Extracts from Minutes of a Meeting of the Executive Committee, Kenya Branch," 28 July 1955, RCC/1/12/1/37; Teresa Spens to Whittington (extract), September 14, 1953 RCC/1/12/1/8, BRCS.

124. Spens to Whittington, September 14, 1953 RCC/1/12/1/8.

125. Helga [Hoppé] to Limerick, January 4, 1958, RCC/1/12/1/84, BRCS.

126. A.L. Bullivant to secretary, BRCSS, March 2, 1953, RCC/1/12/1/8.

127. Michael Scott, Africa Bureau, to BRCSS, February 10, 1953, RCC/1/12/1/8, BRCS.

128. Klose, *Human Rights in the Shadow of Colonial Violence*, 130–132; "Reports on the Visits Made During the Second Mission of the International Committee of the Red Cross to Kenya," June-July 1959, RCC/1/12/1/83, BRCS.

129. "Activités de la Croix-Rouge Britannique au Kenya," 671.

130. Joan Whittington, "The Emergency in Kenya," *British Red Cross Society Quarterly Review* 41, no. 3 (July 1954): 100–103; Joan Whittington memorandum, "ICRC and Kenya," January 9, 1957, RCC/1/12/1/83, BRCS.

131. Joan Whittington, "Comments on ICRC Kenya Report," May 29, 1957, RCC/1/12/1/83, BRCS.

132. F.H.D. Pritchard, "Kenya Emergency and ICRC," December 13, 1956, RCC/1/12/1/83, BRCS.

133. Pritchard, "Kenya—ICRC," December 19, 1956, and Angela Limerick to Leopold Boissier, August 9, 1955, RCC/1/12/1/83; Angela Limerick to W.A.C. Mathison, January 11, 1957, and "Notes of Meeting at Foreign Office," July 4, 1956, RCC/1/12/5/12, BRCS.

134. Limerick to Paul Ruegger, August 24, 1953, RCC/1/12/5/12, BRCS.

135. For a sample of the domestic criticism, see "Britain Has Barred Red Cross in Kenya," *Reynold's News* (November 16, 1956).

136. Angela Limerick to Marcel Junod, August 11, 1955, RCC/1/12/1/83, BRCS.

137. Pritchard, "Kenya Emergency and ICRC," December 13, 1956, and "Notes on Letter from ICRC to HMG Concerning Visits to Detention Camps in Kenya," January 8, 1957, RCC/1/12/1/83, BRCS.

138. F.H.D. Pritchard to Roger Gallopin, July 11, 1958, RCC/1/12/1/83, BRCS.

139. Whittington to [FHD Pritchard], January 9. 1957, RCC/1/12/1/84; Spens to Whittington, September 14, 1953, RCC/1/12/1/8; Helga [Hoppé] to Limerick, January 4, 1958, RCC/1/12/1/84, BRCS.

140. Joan Whittington, quoted in "Red Cross Work in Kenya," *Times* (May 1, 1954); Whittington memorandum, "ICRC and Kenya," January 9, 1957, and Whittington diary (extracts), 1954, RCC/1/12/1/83, BRCS.

141. [Hoppé] to Limerick, January 4, 1958, BRCS.

142. Limerick diary, entries for January 13, 1957, and January 29, 1957, Acc. 1594/25, BRCS.

143. Limerick to Hoppé, January 15, 1958, RCC/1/12/1/84, BRCS.

144. David de Traz, "Pyla Detention Camp," report of visit on March 24, 1957; David de Traz, "Pyla Camp," report of visit on December 16, 1958, RCC/1/12/1/84, BRCS; James Avery Joyce, *Red Cross International and the Strategy of Peace* (New York: Oceana, 1959), 187.

145. Penelope Tremayne, *Below the Tide* (Boston: Houghton Mifflin, 1959), 7, 154.

146. "Notes for File of Vice-Chairman's Conversation with Mr. Borsinger," June 26, 1958; Limerick to Léopold Boissier, January 21, 1959, RCC/1/12/1/84.

147. Woolton to F. H. D. Pritchard, June 7, 1958, and Woolton to Limerick, June 7, 1958, MS Woolton 50/1, BO.

148. Geoffrey Cassian Senn, quoted in Pringle, "Humanitarianism, Race, and Denial," 94.

149. Jonathan Moore, ed., *Hard Choices: Moral Dilemmas in Humanitarian Intervention* (Lanham, MD: Rowan & Littlefield, 1998).

150. Michael N. Barnett, *Empire of Humanity: A History of Humanitarianism* (Ithaca, NY: Cornell University Press, 2011), 136.

151. Jakob Kellenberger, "Speaking Out or Remaining Silent in Humanitarian Work," *Revue internationale de la Croix-Rouge* no. 855 (September 2004): 593–609. Doctors Without Borders is, of course, the Red Cross rival best known for disdaining silence in the name of neutrality, although the difference between their institutional cultures can be overstated. See Marie-Luce Desgrandschamps, "Revenir sur le mythe fondateur de Médecins Sans Frontières: les relations entre les médecins français et le CICR pendant la guerre du Biafra (1967–1970)," *Relations internationales* no. 146 (2011): 95–108; Rony Brauman, "Les liaisons dangereuses du témoignage humanitaire et de la propagande politique," in *Crises extrêmes: Face aux massacres, aux guerres civiles et aux genocides,* ed. Marc Le Pape, Johanna Siméant and Claudine Vidal (Paris: Éditions La Découverte, 2006); Rony Brauman, "Médecins Sans Frontières and the ICRC: matters of principle," *International Review of the Red Cross* 94 (Winter 2012): 1523–1535.

152. For a cognate argument about the antebellum United States, see Joyce E. Chaplin, "Slavery and the Principle of Humanity: A Modern Idea in the Early Lower South," *Journal of Social History* 24, no. 2 (1990): 299–315.

CHAPTER 5

1. D. G. Bridson, "Africa—Presenting a Continent to the World," *Radio Times* (April 15, 1955).

2. Philip Knightley, *The First Casualty: From the Crimea to Vietnam: The War Correspondent as Hero, Propagandist, and Myth Maker* (New York: Harcourt Brace Jovanovich, 1975); Philip Knightley, "The Cheerleaders of World War II," *British Journalism Review* 6, no. 2 (1995): 40–45; R. J. Wilkinson-Latham, *From Our Special Correspondent: Victorian War Correspondents and Their Campaigns* (London: Hodder and Stoughton, 1979); Roger T. Stearn, "War Correspondents and Colonial War, c. 1870-1900," in *Popular Imperialism and the Military, 1850-1950*, ed. John M. MacKenzie (Manchester: Manchester University Press, 1992); Paul L. Moorcraft and Philip M. Taylor, *Shooting the Messenger: The Political Impact of War Reporting* (Washington, DC: Potomac Books, 2008); Susan L. Carruthers, *The Media at War* (London: Palgrave Macmillan, 2011).

3. For a recent critique of the standard narrative, see Kevin Williams, *A New History of War Reporting* (New York: Routledge, 2020).

4. Carruthers, *Winning Hearts and Minds*; Weber, *Englishness and Empire*. But see Lewis, "Daddy Wouldn't Buy Me a Mau Mau," for a contrasting view.

5. For a roughly parallel interpretation of US press coverage of the persecution of Jews in the Third Reich, see Deborah Lipstadt, *Beyond Belief: The American Press and the Coming of the Holocaust, 1933-1945* (New York: Free Press, 1986).

6. Ann Laura Stoler, "'In Cold Blood': Hierarchies of Credibility and the Politics of Colonial Narratives," *Representations* 37 (Winter 1992): 151–189. See also the excellent analysis by Owen, "'Facts are Sacred.'"

7. Frantz Fanon, *The Wretched of the Earth*, trans. Constance Farrington (London: Penguin, 2001), 61.

8. In its original usage in media studies, the "media event" was a planned spectacle, often with ritualistic and solidaristic overtones, such as the Olympic Games, a coronation, or a presidential debate. See Daniel Dayan and Elihu Katz, *Media Events: The Live Broadcasting of History* (Cambridge, MA: Harvard University Press, 1992), and for the precursor concept of the "pseudo-event," Daniel Boorstin, *The Image or What Happened to the American Dream* (New York: Atheneum, 1961). Increasingly, however, the term has been expanded to wars, natural disasters, and other violent disruptions. See Nick Couldry, Andreas Hepp, and Friedrich Krotz, eds., *Media Events in a Global Age* (London: Routledge, 2010).

9. Slavoj Zizek, *Violence: Six Sideways Reflections* (New York: Picador, 2008).

10. Matthew Farish, "Modern Witnesses: Foreign Correspondents, Geopolitical Vision, and the First World War," *Transactions of the Institute of British Geographers* 26, no. 3 (2001): 273–287.

11. Colin Seymour-Ure, *The British Press and Broadcasting since 1945* (Oxford: Basil Blackwell, 1991), 131. Figures are for the period 1947–1965.

12. Martin Harrison, *Young Meteors: British Journalism, 1957-1965* (London: Jonathan Cape, 1998), 16–18.

13. Grace Wyndham Goldie, *Facing the Nation: Television and Politics, 1936-1976* (London: Bodley Head, 1977), 45, 194–195; Geoffrey Cox, *Pioneering Television News: A First Hand Report on a Revolution in Journalism* (London: John Libbey, 1995), 117.

14. Asa Briggs, *The History of Broadcasting in the United Kingdom*, vol. 4, *Sound and Vision* (Oxford: Oxford University Press, 1979), 574–577, 581–586; Briggs, *History of Broadcasting*, vol. 5, *Competition* (Oxford: Oxford University Press, 1995), 62; Martin Conboy, *Journalism: A Critical History* (Thousand Oaks, CA: Sage, 2004).

15. Cox, *Pioneering Television News*, 69.

16. James Chapman, *British Comics: A Cultural History* (London: Reaktion, 2011), 60–63, 87–90.

17. "Aspects of the Anti-Bandit 'War': Army, R.A.F., and Police Action in Malaya," *Illustrated London News* (May 20, 1950); "Searching a Forest for Terrorists: British Troops in a Cyprus Drive," *Illustrated London News* (January 14, 1956); "Mau Mau Terrorism in Kenya; Some Arrests and a Murdered Chief," *Illustrated London News* (November 1, 1952).

18. Cyril Ramsay Jones, "New Broom in Malaya," *Picture Post* (May 3, 1952); "Tim Raison, "Terrorist Hunt in Cyprus," *Picture Post* (April 7, 1956); "MAU MAU: 'Get Out Get Out,'" *Picture Post* (November 29, 1952).

19. "Malayan Operation: Patrols Through the Jungle," March 24, 1952, online at http://www.aparchive.com/metadata/MALAYAN-OPERATION-PATROLS-THRO UGH-JUNGLE/985c57b3bf9740dba64ea1b71f86a3f4; "Commando Patrol in Cyprus," October 17, 1955, online at http://www.aparchive.com/metadata/ COMMANDO-PATROL-IN-CYPRUS/c5aace157e9347cf866cb7ed69844214.

20. "Devons in Action in Malaya," April 4, 1949, online at https://www.britishpathe. com/video/devons-in-action-in-malaya/.

21. "Operation 'Black Mac,'" January 31, 1957, online at http://www.aparchive.com/ metadata/OPERATION-BLACK-MAC-/34e0641d03924ec6ad0dd7c64 d684149.

22. Briefing by Regimental Commander, March 23, 1953, shelfmark 9cloo15424, BLSA.

23. Sidney Wavell commentary, March 23, 1953, shelfmark 9cloo15424, BLSA.

24. Wavell commentary, BLSA.

25. "What is Mau Mau?" *Picture Post* (March 27, 1954); "Fresh Rioting in Nicosia: Stone-Throwing Countered by Tear-Gas and Baton Charges," *Illustrated London News* (November 5, 1955).

26. "In Malaya It's a War Between Two Ideologies and Two Armies," *Picture Post* (June 20, 1953); "Washing the Soul of Mau Mau" (October 22, 1956).

27. *The Road to Embu* script, June 8, 1955, BBCWA.

28. "Mau Mau Victims Funeral," February 16, 1953, online at https://www.briti shpathe.com/video/mau-mau-victims-funeral/; "Cyprus Outrage," September

10, 1958, online at http://www.movietone.com/N_myResearch_view.cfm? ItemID = 241003.

29. Webster, *Englishness and Empire*.

30. "Fighting the Bandits in Malaya," narrated by Edward Ward, March 8, 1952, shelfmark sx 26150/5, BLSA.

31. 1pm bulletin, January 3, 1953, reel 349/350, BL; "Three Against Mau Mau," *Illustrated London News* (January 17, 1953).

32. Ronnie Noble, *Shoot First! Assignments of a Newsreel Cameraman* (London: George G. Harrap, 1955), 248–250.

33. Claire Mauss-Coupeaux, *A travers le viseur: images d'appelés en Algérie, 1955-1962* (Lyon: Aedelsa, 2003), 97.

34. "Commando Patrol in Cyprus," October 17, 1955, online at http://www.moviet one.com/N_myResearch_view.cfm?ItemID=241000.

35. "Assignment Mau Mau," May 7, 1953, online at https://www.britishpathe.com/ video/assignment-mau-mau-exclusive/.

36. "Cyprus Outrage," September 10, 1958, online at http://www.movietone.com/N_ myResearch_view.cfm? ItemID = 241003.

37. "MAU MAU: 'Get Out Get Out.'"

38. "What is Mau Mau?"

39. "A Journey in Malaya," February 3, 1953.

40. 6pm bulletin, April 20, 1952, reel 329/330; 6pm bulletin, June 14, 1953, reel 363/364; 6pm bulletin, December 14, 1952, reel 347/348, BL.

41. John Freeman, *Panorama*, January 22, 1958, reel 31, BBCWA.

42. "Jungle is Barrier in Rebel Round-Up," April 4, 1949, online at http://www.moviet one.com/N_myResearch_view.cfm?ItemID=241004; "The Fight in Malaya," episode of *This Modern Age*, December 5, 1950, online at https://www.itvarchive. com/Production/CFD1368/0001/ (registration required).

43. Patrick O'Donovan, "Malayan Remedy Still Lacking," *Observer* (September 19, 1948); Patrick O'Donovan, *For Fear of Weeping* (London: Macgibbon and Kee, 1950), 36.

44. Marjorie [Banks] Ward, script for "Journey in Kenya," R19/596, BBCWA. It appears that the only surviving script in the BBC archives is for the Overseas Service broadcast scheduled for July 1955 rather than the Home Service broadcast, which took place three months earlier. Judging by criticisms received after the Home Service broadcast, it seems that the two scripts did not differ greatly.

45. The stories are too numerous to cite comprehensively. For a sampling, see "Alleged Death Under Beating of Mau Mau Suspect," *Manchester Guardian* (February 10, 1953); "Kenya Security Methods," *Times* (April 18, 1953); "'Prizes' For Shooting Mau Mau," *Manchester Guradian* (November 30, 1953); "Nairobi 'Burning' Charges," *Times* (February 13, 1954); "M.P.s Call for Big Changes in Kenya," *Times* (February 24, 1954); "Treatment of Mau Mau Suspect," *Times* (April 5, 1954); "Soldier Accused of Torture," *Manchester Guardian* (November 30, 1954);

"Kikuyu Woman's Interrogation," *Times* (December 4, 1954); "Kenya Police Sentenced," *Times* (September 2, 1955); "Allegation of Ill Treatment of Cypriots at Interrogation," *Times* (April 4, 1956); "Cyprus Interrogation," *Times* (May 30, 1957); "African Kept in Detention Since 1954," *Manchester Guardian* (June 6, 1954); "Cypriots' Stories of Ill-Treatment," *Times* (July 30, 1957); "Unexpected Turn in Nicosia Trial," *Times* (September 9, 1958); "Reopened Inquest on Detained Cypriot," *Times* (May 28, 1959); "Mau Mau Beaten Continuously," *Manchester Guardian* (April 2, 1959).

46. "Police Methods in Malaya," *Manchester Guardian* (August 27, 1951).

47. "Severing of an Ear: Officer's Evidence at Nairobi Trial," *Times* (March 10, 1954); "Askari Obeyed Alleged Order to Cut Off Kikuyu's Ear," *Manchester Guardian* (March 9, 1954); "A Nation's Conscience," *Times* (November 28, 1953).

48. "Darkest Africa," *Yorkshire Post and Leeds Mercury* (December 4, 1953).

49. 9pm bulletin, April 17, 1953, reel 357/358, BL.

50. *At Home and Abroad*, December 4, 1956, reel T19, BBCWA.

51. 9am bulletin, December 24, 1954, reel 409/410; 1pm bulletin, April 5, 1956, reel 451/452, BL.

52. 6pm bulletin, April 2, 1952, reel 329/330; 6pm bulletin, April 23, 1952, reel 331/332, BL.

53. "Today in Parliament," December 15, 1954, reel 409/410; "Yesterday in Parliament," December 22, 1956, reel 473/474, BL.

54. *At Home and Abroad*, April 26, 1955, reel T18, BBCWA.

55. Extract from *Tonight*, September 23, 1958, reel 48, BBCWA.

56. J.B. Perry Robinson, "Form and Tactics of Post War Terrorism," October 13, 1955, reel T441, BBCWA.

57. Louis Heren, *Growing Up on* The Times (London: Hamish Hamilton, 1978), 136–142, 152–153.

58. James Cameron, *Point of Departure: An Attempt at Autobiography* (New York: McGraw Hill, 1967), 82; Michael Davidson, *The World, The Flesh, and Myself* (Swaffham: Gay Men's Press, 1997), 324.

59. Davidson, *The World, The Flesh, and Myself*, 296.

60. Michael Davidson to Tom Driberg, April 24, 1952, SOC.Driberg S3, CCO.

61. Charles Foley, *Island in Revolt* (London: Longmans, 1962), 37.

62. Jonathan Stubbs, "Making Headlines in a State of Emergency: The Case of the *Times of Cyprus*, 1955-1960," *Journal of Imperial & Commonwealth History* 45, no. 1 (2017): 70–92.

63. Oliver Woods, confidential memorandum on "Brutality in Kenya," January 28, 1954, News UK archive, Enfield (hereafter News UK).

64. Lewis, "Daddy Wouldn't Buy Me a Mau Mau"; French, *British Way in Counter-Insurgency*, 171.

65. Eric Downton, *Wars without End* (Toronto: Stoddard, 1987), 235–237.

66. Edward Ward, *I've Lived Like a Lord* (London: Joseph, 1970), 203.

67. Alexander Campbell, *The Heart of Africa* (New York: Knopf, 1954), 256–257; Sandy Gall, *Don't Worry About the Money Now* (London: Hamish Hamilton, 1983), 33; "'Truth About Kenya' Committee has Four-Year Plan," *East African Standard* [1954], Hutt papers, folder C/8, Cambridge University Library (hereafter CUL).

68. P.J. Monkhouse to Vernon Bartlett, April 17, 1956; Alan Lennox-Boyd to P. J. Monkhouse, April 21, 1956, B B73, Manchester Guardian archive, John Rylands Library, University of Manchester (hereafter MGM).

69. Nancy Crawshaw to Leslie Glass, July 9, 1956; Crawshaw to Glass, September 16, 1956, Crawshaw papers, box 1, folder 6, PUL.

70. Fred Majdalany, *State of Emergency: The Full Story of Mau Mau* (Boston: Houghton Mifflin, 1963), 187.

71. Iverach McDonald, *History of the Times*, vol. 5, *Struggles in War and Peace, 1939-1966* (London: Macmillan 1984), 280.

72. McDonald, *Struggles in War and Peace*, 406–407.

73. Simon Elmes, *Hello Again . . . Nine Decades of Radio Voices* (London: Arrow Books, 2012), 25.

74. Cox, *Pioneering Television News*, 117–119.

75. Donald Read, *The Power of News: The History of Reuters, 1849-1989* (Oxford: Oxford University Press, 1992), 232–234; James Curran and Jean Seaton, *Power without Responsibility: The Press and Broadcasting in Britain* (London: Routledge, 1997), 141, 147.

76. The *Times* followed in 1966. See McDonald, *Struggles in War and Peace*, 400.

77. Stephen E. Koss, *The Rise and Fall of the Political Press in Britain*, vol. 2, *The Twentieth Century* (Chapel Hill: University of North Carolina Press, 1981); Curran and Seaton, *Power without Responsibility*, 44, 72; Kevin Williams, *Read All About It! A History of the British Newspaper* (London: Routledge, 2010), 188–189, 192–193; Ralph Negrine, *Politics and the Mass Media in Britain* (London: Routledge, 1989), 59.

78. Philip Elliott, "Professional Ideology and Organizational Change: The Journalist since 1800," in *Newspaper History from the Seventeenth Century to the Present Day*, ed. George Boyce, James Curran, and Pauline Wingate (London: Sage, 1978); Conboy, *Journalism*, 200.

79. Charles Rigby, *The Staff Journalist* (London: Pitman, 1950), 38–41; Clement J. Bundock, *The National Union of Journalists: A Jubilee History, 1907-1957* (Oxford: Oxford University Press, 1957), 230–231; Denis Hamilton, *Editor-in-Chief: The Fleet Street Memoirs of Sir Denis Hamilton* (London: Hamish Hamilton, 1989), 67–70; John Dryburgh Wright, "The National Council for the Training of Journalists: Twenty-Five Years of Progress and Problems" (PhD diss., University of Texas at Austin, 1979).

80. Koss, *Rise and Fall of the Political Press*.

81. Robert Sinclair, *The British Press: The Journalist and His Conscience* (London: Home and Van Thal, 1949), 239.

82. Frank Illingworth, *Questions Answered About Journalism* (London: Jordan and Sons, 1946), 34–35; Rigby, *Staff Journalist*, 42–43.

83. Illingworth, *Questions Answered About Journalism*, 32.

84. Rigby, *Staff Journalist*, 1.

85. Sinclair, *The British Press*, 81.

86. Lorraine Daston and Peter Galison, *Objectivity* (New York: Zone Books, 2007).

87. Stephen J. A. Ward, *The Invention of Journalism Ethics: The Path to Objectivity and Beyond* (Montreal: McGill-Queen's University Press, 2015), 219.

88. Deakin to Quilliam, October 24, 1945, News UK.

89. Quoted in McDonald, *Struggles in War and Peace*, 246.

90. Woods memoranda, December 8, 1952, December 23, 1952, and January 28, 1954, Confidential Memorandum file on Kenya, News UK.

91. "Our Special Correspondent," "Limited Results of Campaign against Mau Mau," *The Times* (November 19, 1952).

92. Cf. Thomas W. Laqueur, "Bodies, Details, and the Humanitarian Narrative," in *The New Cultural History*, ed. Lynn Hunt (Berkeley: University of California Press, 1989).

93. Woods to McDonald, January 29, 1953, file IMC/1/ Woods correspondence, News UK.

94. Woods memorandum, January 28, 1954, Confidential Memorandum file on Kenya, News UK.

95. Ian McDougall, *Foreign Correspondent* (London: Frederick Muller, 1980), 59; Alastair Matheson, *States of Emergency: Reporting Africa for Half a Century* (Nairobi: Media Matters, 1992), 47.

96. Gall, *Don't Worry about the Money Now*, 35–36.

97. Woods memorandum, December 8, 1952, Confidential Memorandum file on Kenya, News UK.

98. Matheson, *States of Emergency*, 40.

99. Woods memorandum, January 28, 1954, Confidential Memorandum file on Kenya, News UK.

100. Maria Newall to Graham Greene, October 15, 1953, Greene papers, box 73, folder 35, BC.

101. Graham Greene, "Mau Mau—The Terror by Night," *Sunday Times* (September 27, 1953); "Mau Mau, the Black God," *Sunday Times* (October 4, 1953).

102. Greene to Catherine Walston, August 28, 1953, Greene papers, box 16, folder 27, Georgetown University Library; Norman Sherry, *The Life of Graham Greene*, vol. 2, *1939-1955* (New York: Penguin, 1994), 462.

103. Graham Greene, "A Nation's Conscience," letter to the *Times* (December 4, 1953).

104. Greene to Peter Anstruther, December 7, 1953, and Greene to Barclay Nihill, December 14, 1953, Greene papers, box 73, folder 36, BC.

105. Graham Greene, *A Burnt-Out Case* (London: Penguin, 1977 [1960]), 43.

106. Jeremy Lewis, *David Astor: A Life in Print* (London: Jonathan Cape, 2016).

107. Cyril Dunn to David Astor, October 31, 1954, Dingle Foot papers, file 5/7, CAC.

108. Cyril Dunn, "Justice in Kenya," *Observer* (December 12, 1954).

109. Colin Legum, "Memo re: Letter from Mariira Detainees" [1958]; Colin Legum to Kenneth [Obank?], July 4, 1958, OBS/6/1/1/1/1/1/15, Guardian News and Media Archive, London; "Kenya Frees 1,000 Each Month," *Observer*, August 17, 1958, 4.

110. Worsley, *Skating on Thin Ice*, 120.

111. "We Need Facts," *Daily Herald* (September 22, 1953).

112. C. H. Rolph, *Kingsley: The Life, Letters, and Diaries of Kingsley Martin* (London: Gollancz, 1973).

113. "Terror and Counter–Terror," *New Statesman* (May 16, 1953): 567.

114. Kingsley Martin to L. A. Cooke, April 20, 1953, file 18/1, New Statesman archive, University of Sussex Library, Brighton.

115. Foley, *Island in Revolt*, 131.

116. Davidson, *The World, The Flesh, and Myself*, 339.

117. [John Rowley?], "The Famagusta Reprisals," n.d., C4/B9/44/1, MGM; Nancy Crawshaw to Alastair Hetherington, February 19, 1956, Crawshaw papers, box 1, folder 6, PUL.

118. Lawrence Durrell to Richard Aldington, November 23–26, 1958, in *Literary Lifelines*, ed. MacNiven and Moore, 68.

119. "High Court of Justice: Queen's Bench Division," *Times* (December 19, 1958); "The Observer: Libel Settlement," *Observer* (December 21, 1958).

120. Nancy Crawshaw, "Justice in Cyprus I—An Inquiry Needed," *Manchester Guardian* (July 1, 1957).

121. Kenneth Mackenzie to Eric Baker, October 1, 1958, Eric Baker papers, file 1/E, University of Bradford.

122. French, *Fighting EOKA*.

123. [Norman Macdonald], "Use by Talks Department of BBC Foreign Correspondents," January 19, 1956, file R28/311, BBCWA.

124. A. H. Wigan to Ian McCulloch, July 21, 1955, file R28/312/1, BBCWA.

125. Leonard Miall, *Inside the BBC: British Broadcasting Characters* (London: Weidenfeld & Nicolson, 1994), 125–126; Michael Tracey, *The Decline and Fall of Public Service Broadcasting* (Oxford: Oxford University Press, 1998), 94.

126. Miall, *Inside the BBC*, 100.

127. Tony Shaw, "Eden and the BBC During the 1956 Suez Crisis: A Myth Re-Examined," *Twentieth Century British History* 6, no. 3 (1995): 320–343.

128. A. H. Wigan to Director of News and Current Affairs, July 27, 1959, and Director of External Broadcasting [Beresford Clark] to Director General [Ian Jacob], April 29, 1959, R28/311, BBCWA.

129. Lennox-Boyd to Jacob, July 8, 1955, R19/596, BBCWA.

130. Tangye Lean to Jacob, July 6, 1955, R19/596, BBCWA.

131. O. J. Whitley to Controller of Overseas Services [Hugh Carleton Greene], June 20, 1955, R19/596, BBCWA.

132. Jacob to Lennox-Boyd, July 13, 1955, R19/596, BBCWA.

133. *Panorama* script, December 8, 1958, reel 31, BBCWA.

134. *At Home and Abroad* script, August 28, 1956, reel T19, BBCWA.

135. Barbara J. Shapiro, *A Culture of Fact: England, 1550-1720* (Ithaca, NY: Cornell University Press, 2000). See also Michael Schudson, *Origins of the Ideal of Objectivity in the Professions: Studies in the History of American Journalism and American Law, 1830-1940* (New York: Garland, 1990).

136. Elizabeth Kolsky, *Colonial Justice in British India: White Violence and the Rule of Law* (Cambridge: Cambridge University Press, 2010); Catherine L. Evans, *Unsound Empire: Civilization and Madness in Late-Victorian Law* (New Haven, CT: Yale University Press, 2021), 158–161.

137. Howe, *Anticolonialism in British Politics*, 256–60.

138. BBC Home Service news bulletin, December 5, 1951, reel 320, BBCWA.

139. Thomas Fox-Pitt to Anthony Sampson, July 24, 1954, file G539, Anti-Slavery Society papers, BO.

CHAPTER 6

1. Dylan Cave, "Empire's Twilight," *Sight & Sound* 21, no. 12 (December 2011): 12–13.

2. David Anderson, "Mau Mau at the Movies: Contemporary Representations of an Anti-Colonial War," *South African Historical Journal* 48, no. 1 (2003): 71–89.

3. On the traditional of imperial cinema and its revival in the 1950s, see James Chapman, "Action, Spectacle, and the *Boy's Own Tradition* in British Cinema," in *The British Cinema Book*, ed. Robert Murphy (London: Palgrave Macmillan for the British Film Institute, 2008); James Chapman and Nicholas J. Cull, *Projecting Empire: Imperialism and Popular Culture* (London: I.B. Tauris, 2009), 1–15.

4. Chapman and Cull, *Projecting Empire*, 8–9; Susan Carruthers, "Two Faces of 1950s Terrorism: The Film Presentation of Mau Mau and the Malayan Emergency," *Small Wars & Insurgencies* 6, no. 1 (1995): 17–43.

5. Christine Geraghty, *British Cinema in the Fifties: Gender, Genre, and the 'New Look'* (London: Routledge, 2000), 120–132; Paul B. Rich, *Cinema and Unconventional Warfare in the Twentieth Century: Insurgency, Terrorism, and Special Operations* (London: Bloomsbury, 2018), 34–38; Tony Shaw, *British Cinema and the Cold War: The State, Propaganda, and Consensus* (London: I.B. Tauris, 2006), 54–56; Jon Cowans, *Empire Films and the Crisis of Colonialism, 1946-1959* (Baltimore: Johns Hopkins University Press, 2015), 158–166; Marcia Landy, *British Genres: Cinema and Society, 1930-1960* (Princeton: Princeton University Press, 1991), 115–117; Richard Dyer, "White," *Screen* 29, no. 4 (1988): 44–65. Despite its limitations, *Windom's Way* was the most progressive of this group: the clearest in its condemnation of colonial violence and the most skeptical about the continuation of empire

in anything like its traditional form. See Cowans, *Empire Films*, 148; Raymond Durgnat, *A Mirror for England: British Movies from Austerity to Affluence* (London: Palgrave Macmillan for the British Film Institute, 2011 [1970]), 96.

6. Sarah Street, *Colour Films in Britain: The Negotiation of Innovation 1900-55* (Basingstoke: Palgrave Macmillan, 2012); Lydia Nead, *The Tiger in the Smoke: Art and Culture in Post-War Britain* (New Haven, CT: Yale University Press, 2017), 181–182.

7. Raymond Williams, "Drama in a Dramatised Society," in *Raymond Williams on Television: Selected Writings*, ed. Alan O'Connor (London: Routledge, 1989).

8. Carruthers, "Two Faces of 1950s Terrorism," 35–36.

9. Minute, DO 191/92, TNA.

10. David Cairns and Shaun Richards, "No Good Brave Causes? The Alienated Intellectual and the End of Empire," *Literature and History* 14, no. 2 (1988): 194–206.

11. Kenneth Tynan, "The Voice of the Young," in *Plays in Review, 1956-1980: British Drama and the Critics*, ed. Gareth Lloyd Evans and Barbara Lloyd Evans (London: Batsford Academic and Educational, 1985), 53.

12. Cairns and Richards, "No Good Brave Causes?"; Alistair Davies and Peter Saunders, "Literature, Politics, and Society," in *Society and Literature 1945-1970*, ed. Alan Sinfield (London: Methuen, 1983); Dan Rebellato, "Look Back at Empire: British Theatre and Imperial Decline," in *British Culture and the End of Empire*, ed. Ward.

13. Steve Nicholson, *The Censorship of British Drama, 1900-1968*, vol. 3, *The Fifties* (Exeter: University of Exeter Press, 2020), 168.

14. Entry for July 1, 1959, in *Daring to Hope*, ed. Pottle, 209.

15. Entries for November 2, 1956 and July 8, 1962, in *The Kenneth Williams Diaries*, ed. Russell Davies (London: HarperCollins, 1993), 127, 194.

16. Lindsay Anderson, "Court Style," in *At the Royal Court: 25 Years of the English Stage Company*, ed. Richard Findlater (Ambergate: Amber Lane Press, 1981), 145; Bill Gaskill, "My Apprenticeship," in *At the Royal Court*, ed. Findlater, 60.

17. John Elsom, *Post-War British Theatre* (London: Routledge and Kegan Paul, 1976), 7–9; Stephen Lacey, *British Realist Theatre: The New Wave in Its Context, 1956-1965* (London: Routledge, 1995), 40–41.

18. Dan Rebellato, *1956 and All That: The Making of Modern British Drama* (London: Routledge, 1999), 62–63.

19. Philip Roberts, *The Royal Court Theatre and the Modern Stage* (Cambridge: Cambridge University Press, 1999), 62, 70.

20. Nicholson, *Censorship of British Drama*, vol. 3.

21. Nicholson, *Censorship of British Drama*, vol. 3, 11–13, 164–168, 172–173, 217–219.

22. Colin Chambers, *The Story of Unity Theatre* (London: Lawrence & Wishart, 1989); Andrew Davies, *Other Theatres: The Development of Alternative and Experimental Theatre in Britain* (Basingstoke: Macmillan, 1987), 141, 149–150.

23. Claire Warden, *British Avant-Garde Theatre* (Basingstoke: Palgrave Macmillan, 2012), 25–31.

24. Mona Brand, *Enough Blue Sky: The Autobiography of Mona Brand, An Unknown Well-Known Playwright* (Sydney: Tawny Pipit Press, 1995), 147; "The Unity: 'Strangers in the Land,'" *The Stage* (November 27, 1952).

25. Mona Brand, *Strangers in the Land*, in *Two Plays About Malaya* (London: Lawrence and Wishart, 1954), 21, 30.

26. Brand, *Strangers in the Land*, 47.

27. Brand, *Enough Blue Sky*, 147–148; Brand, *Strangers in the Land*, 29.

28. Brand, *Strangers in the Land*, 31–33.

29. Brand, *Enough Blue Sky*, 150.

30. Davies, *Other Theatres*, 152–155.

31. Joan Littlewood, *Joan's Book: The Autobiography of Joan Littlewood* (London: Methuen, 2003), 285–289.

32. Howard Goorney, *The Theatre Workshop Story* (London: Eyre Methuen, 1981), 61–62.

33. Robert Leach, *Theatre Workshop: Joan Littlewood and the Making of Modern Theatre* (Exeter: University of Exeter Press, 2006), 141.

34. Brendan Behan, *The Hostage*, in *The Complete Plays* (London: Methuen, 1978), 192–193.

35. Behan, *The Hostage*, 206 (my expurgation).

36. Behan, *The Hostage*, 180, 223.

37. Behan, *The Hostage*, 163, 179.

38. Behan, *The Hostage*, 186, 202, 223.

39. Brendan Behan, *An Giall* and *The Hostage*, trans. and ed. Richard Wall (Washington, DC: Catholic University of America Press, 1987).

40. Ulrick O'Connor, *Brendan Behan* (London: Hamish Hamilton, 1970), 203–206.

41. Nicholson, *Censorship of British Drama*, vol. 3, 158–159.

42. "Chit Chat," *The Stage* (October 2, 1958).

43. Harold Hobson, review of *The Hostage*, *Sunday Times* (October 19, 1958); *Encore* TK.

44. Rebellato, *1956 and All That*, 10–18.

45. Lacey, *British Realist Theatre*, 54–58; Leach, *Theatre Workshop*, 140; Rebellato, *1956 and All That*, 66–69.

46. Michael Patterson, *Strategies of Political Theatre: Post-War British Playwrights* (Cambridge: Cambridge University Press, 2003), 16–17.

47. John Osborne, *The Entertainer*, in *Plays Two* (London: Faber and Faber, 1998), 13, 24–27.

48. Cf. Rebellato, *1956 and All That*, 139–141.

49. Lloyd Evans and Lloyd Evans, eds., *Plays in Review*, 59.

50. Charles A. Carpenter, *Dramatists and the Bomb: American and British Playwrights Confront the Nuclear Age, 1945-1964* (Westport, CT: Greenwood Press, 1999), 103–106; Jonathan Key, "The Atomic Drama," in *Acts of War: The Representation*

of Military Conflict on the British Stage and Television since 1945, ed. Tony Howard and John Stokes (Aldershot: Scolar Press, 1996).

51. Doris Lessing, *Each His Own Wilderness*, in *New English Dramatists: Three Plays*, ed. E. Martin Browne (Harmondsworth: Penguin, 1960), 15.

52. Lessing, *Each His Own Wilderness*, 67.

53. "Always Uniform," *Record Mirror* (September 5, 1959), Theatre and Performance Archive, Victoria & Albert Museum (hereafter TPVA).

54. THM/273/7/2/29, English State Company/Royal Court Theatre archive, TPVA.

55. John Russell Taylor, *Anger and After: A Guide to the New British Drama* (London: Methuen, 1962), 266–267; Tony Howard and John Stokes, introduction to *Acts of War*, 14.

56. Willis Hall, *The Long and the Short and the Tall: A Play in Two Acts* (London: Heinemann, 1959), 102.

57. Hall, *Long and the Short and the Tall*, 52, 102.

58. Hall, *Long and the Short and the Tall*, 56.

59. Hall, *Long and the Short and the Tall*, 69.

60. "'Rep.' Breaks New Ground," *Birmingham Weekly Post* (September 18, 1959); "Cardiff Shows Next," *Western Mail* (October 31, 1959); Angus Wilson, "Reluctant Killers," *Observer* (January 11, 1959); "Pacifist Play Has No Clichés," *Kensington Post* (January 16, 1959).

61. Rebellato, *1956 and All That*, 142.

62. Rebellato, *1956 And All That*, 148–149.

63. William Gaskill, *A Sense of Direction* (London: Faber and Faber, 1988), 35–40.

64. Bertolt Brecht, "A Necessary Observation on the Struggle Against Barbarism" (1935), in *Brecht on Art and Politics*, ed. Steve Giles and Tom Kuhn (London: Bloomsbury, 2005), 157.

65. Lacey, *British Realist Theatre*, 156; Raymond Williams, *Politics and Letters: Interviews with* New Left Review (London: Verso, 2015), 216–217.

66. John Willett, *The Theatre of Bertolt Brecht: A Study from Eight Aspects* (London: Methuen, 1959), 66.

67. Williams, *Politics and Letters*, 217–218.

68. John Arden, untitled essay, in Johnson, *All Bull*, ed., 234.

69. John Arden, *Serjeant Musgrave's Dance: An Un-historical Parable*, in *Plays: One* (London: Methuen, 1987), 36, 89, 93.

70. Quoted in Charles Marowitz and Simon Trussler, eds., *Theatre at Work: Playwrights and Productions in the Modern British Theatre* (New York: Hill and Wang, 1968), 44. There is confusion about the death toll in the Famagusta reprisals. While Arden understood that four adults and one child died and used those figures for the play, recent histories suggest that two or three people died. See French, *Fighting EOKA*, 209; Holland, *Britain and the Revolt in Cyprus*, 287; Drohan, *Brutality in an Age of Human Rights*, 74.

71. Arden, *Serjeant Musgrave's Ghost*, 100, 105.

72. Philip Hope-Wallace in *Plays in Review*, ed. Lloyd Evans and Lloyd Evans, 88; Arden, introduction to *Serjeant Musgrave's Ghost*, 13.

73. Arden, *Serjeant Musgrave's Ghost*, 28, 85.

74. Stuart Hall, "Serjeant Musgrave's Dance," *New Left Review*, no. 1 (January-February 1960): 50–51.

75. This account is reconstructed from the press reviews in THM/273/7/2/36, English Stage Company/Royal Court Theatre archive, TPVA.

76. Wole Soyinka, "The Past Must Address Its Present," Nobel Lecture, December 8, 1986, online at https://www.nobelprize.org/prizes/literature/1986/soyinka/lecture/.

77. Gaskill, *Sense of Direction*, 37; Gordon Maxwell Bolar, "The Sunday Productions Without Décor at the Royal Court Theatre, 1957-1975" (PhD diss., Louisiana State University, 1984), 76; Theresa Robbins Dudeck, *Keith Johnstone: A Critical Biography* (London: Bloomsbury Methuen Drama, 2013), 46.

78. Soyinka, "The Past Must Address Its Present."

79. Soyinka, "The Past Must Address Its Present."

80. Tony Garnett, "Contexts," in *British Television Drama: Past, Present, and Future*, ed. Johnathan Bignell, Stephen Lacey, and Madeleine Macmurraugh-Kavanagh (Basingstoke: Palgrave, 2000); Don Taylor, *Days of Vision: Working with David Mercer: Television Drama Then and Now* (London: Methuen, 1990), 32–33.

81. Irene Shubik, "Television Drama Series: A Producer's View," in *British Television Drama*, ed. Bignell, Lacey, and Macmurraugh-Kavanagh, 42.

82. John Caughie, "Progressive Television and Documentary Drama," in *Popular Television and Film: A Reader*, ed. Tony Bennett (London: British Film Institute, 1981), at 333.

83. George W. Brandt, *British Television Drama* (Cambridge: Cambridge University Press, 1981), 8–13.

84. Laura Mulvey, "Melodrama In and Out of the Home," in *High Theory/Low Culture: Analysing Popular Television and Film*, ed. Colin MacCabe (Manchester: Manchester University Press, 1986), 95; Thomas Elsaesser, "Tales of Sound and Fury: Observations on the Family Melodrama," in *Imitations of Life: A Reader on Film and Television Melodrama*, ed. Marcia Landy (Detroit: Wayne State University Press, 1991).

85. Lez Cooke, *British Television Drama: A History* (London: BFI, 2003), 9; Malcolm Page, "Television Drama in Britain," *Quarterly Journal of Speech* 57, no. 2 (1971): 214–220, at 220. Jason Jacobs, *The Intimate Screen: Early British Television Drama* (Oxford: Oxford University Press, 2000), stresses innovations that broke free from the theatrical paradigm, especially after 1955, but also demonstrates that contemporaries saw lingering, close-up shots of actors as the hallmark of the form.

86. Troy Kennedy Martin, "Nats Go Home," *Encore* 48 (1964): 21–33.

87. "Minister Is Playwright," *The Stage* (May 17, 1956).

88. Cecil J. Davey, *Flame in the Forest* script, airdate May 22, 1956, BBCWA.

89. Audience Research Report, *Flame in the Forest*, June 12, 1956, BBCWA.

90. Steve Nicholson, "Africa on the British Stage, 1955-1966," in *Africa on the Contemporary London Stage*, ed. Tiziana Morosetti (Basingstoke: Palgrave Macmillan, 2018), 46–47.

91. Willis Hall, *Airmail from Cyprus*, in *The Television Playwright: Ten Plays for BBC Television* (New York: Hill and Wang, 1960). The airdate was November 11, 1958.

92. Audience Research Report, *Airmail from Cyprus*, November 24, 1958, BBCWA.

93. Hugh Vaughan Williams, *The Terrorists* script, airdate November 2, 1961, BBCWA.

94. Ronald Harwood and Caspar Wrede, *Private Potter* script, airdate April 6, 1961, Ronald Harwood papers, Add. MS 88881/2/4, BL. A big-screen remake of *Private Potter*, again starring Courtenay, was released by MGM in 1962.

95. Unfortunately, no script or film of *The Night of the Apes* survives. My summary here draws on the following reviews: Mary Crozier, "300 Per Cent Television," *Guardian* (August 28, 1961); "Telecrit," *Liverpool Echo* (August 28, 1961); "Programme Reviews," *The Stage* (August 31, 1961); "Last Night . . . And To-Night . . . On TV and Radio," *Belfast Telegraph* (August 28, 1961); "Shaky Plot Provides Exciting Drama," *Leicester Evening Mail* (August 28, 1961).

96. Troy Kennedy Martin, *Incident at Echo Six* script, airdate December 9, 1958, BBCWA.

97. Troy Kennedy Martin, *The Interrogator* script, airdate December 4, 1961, BBCWA.

98. John Newsinger, "A Counter-Insurgency Tale: Frank Kitson in Kenya," *Race & Class* 31, no. 4 (1990): 62–72.

99. Iain MacCormick, *One Morning Near Troodos* script, airdate September 10, 1956, BBCWA.

100. "Arrow in the Air," *Times* (October 10, 1957).

101. E.D.S. Corner, *Negative Evidence* script, airdate February 7, 1961, Associated Rediffusion collection, ITM-11452, British Film Institute.

102. Ronald Barthes, "Grammaire africaine," in *Mythologies* (Paris: Seuil, 2005 [1997]), 129.

EPILOGUE

1. Maurice Edelman, *Minister of State* [U.S. edition of *The Minister*] (Philadelphia: J.B. Lippincott, 1962), 89, 156–158.

2. Edelman, *Minister of State*, 128, 153, 182.

3. Edelman, *Minister of State*, 194.

4. Sasson, "In the Name of Humanity."

5. The only memorials dedicated exclusively to post-1945 wars appear to be plaques in regimental chapels. See the Imperial War Museum's War Memorials register at https://www.iwm.org.uk/memorials.

6. Cf. Bill Schwarz, "Ways of Seeing," in *Visual Culture and Decolonisation in Britain*, ed. Simon Faulkner and Anandi Ramamurthy (Milton: Routledge, 2019).

7. There is a contrast here with Henry Rousso's classic, psychoanalytically informed narrative of French memory of the Occupation, which distinguishes an initial period of repressive taboos from a later period of obsessive reenactment. See Henry Rousso, *The Vichy Syndrome: History and Memory in France since 1944*, trans. Arthur Goldhammer (Cambridge, MA: Harvard University Press, 1991).

8. Rodis Roufos, *The Age of Bronze* (London: Heinemann, 1960).

9. Marshall S. Clough, *Mau Mau Memoirs: History, Memory, and Politics* (Boulder, CO: Lynn Rienner, 1998).

10. Margery Perham, foreword to J. M. Kariuki, *Mau Mau Detainee: The Account by a Kenya African of His Experience in Detention Camps, 1953-1960* (Oxford: Oxford University Press, 1963), xi.

11. Peter Barnes, *Sclerosis* (typescript), GEN MSS 625, series II, Bernard Frank Dukore Collection of Peter Barnes, Beinecke Library, Yale University. The gruesome display may have been inspired in part by Antonin Arnaud's 1958 "Theater of Cruelty" manifesto and its call for terrifying effects to shock audiences.

12. "The 'V' Men," episode of *Gideon's Way*, airdate October 17, 1964, online at https://www.youtube.com/watch?v=JT2kbsHk3Hg.

13. Delphine Robic-Diaz, *La guerre d'Indochine dans le cinema français: Images d'un trou de memoire* (Rennes: Presses Universitaires de Rennes, 2015), 308.

14. C. P. Taylor, *Bandits!* (Cullercoats: Iron Press, 1977), 17.

15. Peter Nichols, *Privates on Parade*, in *Plays: 2* (London: Bloomsbury, 1991), 202.

16. Paul Ricoeur, *Memory, History, Forgetting*, trans. Kathleen Blamey and David Pellauer (Chicago: University of Chicago Press, 2004), 79.

17. For "repetition of the repressed," see Stora, *La gangrène et l'oubli*, 320.

18. "Depart in Peace," episode of *Special Branch*, airdate August 25, 1970, online at https://www.dailymotion.com/video/x7bqzyk.

19. This is true even if, since the 1980s, right-wing patriotic nostalgia has eclipsed collectivist and welfarist representations of the war. See Geoff Eley, "Finding the People's War: Film, British Collective Memory, and World War II," *American Historical Review* 106, no. 3 (2001): 818–838.

20. Robert Saunders, "Brexit and Empire: 'Global Britain' and the Myth of Imperial Nostalgia," *Journal of Imperial and Commonwealth History* 48, no. 6 (2020): 1140–1174, at 1151; Poppy Cullen, "'Playing Cold War Politics': The Cold War in Anglo-Kenyan Relations in the 1960s," *Cold War History* 18, no. 1 (2018): 37–54.

21. On Malaysia, see Karl Hack and Kevin Blackburn, *War Memory and the Making of Modern Malaysia and Singapore* (Singapore: NUS Press, 2012). For the "policy of amnesia," see Marshall S. Clough, "Mau Mau and the Contest for Memory," in *Mau Mau and Nationhood*, ed. Odhiambo and Lonsdale. A useful recent assessment is Lotte Hughes, "Memorialization and Mau Mau: A Critical Review," in *Dedan Kimathi on Trial: Colonial Justice and Popular Memory in Kenya's Mau Mau Rebellion*, ed. Julie Macarthur (Athens: Ohio University Press, 2017).

22. Rob Waters, *Thinking Black: Britain, 1964-1985* (Berkeley: University of California Press, 2019), 76, 105–107.

23. Prints of the film are held by the Film Study Center, Museum of Modern Art, New York, and the British Film Institute, London.

24. Henry Rousso distinguishes these functions in *The Haunting Past: History, Memory, and Justice in Contemporary France*, trans. Ralph Schoolcraft (Philadelphia: University of Pennsylvania Press, 1998), 12–13.

25. House and MacMaster, *Paris 1961*, 296–297. For "factual recovery," see Mark Osiel, *Mass Atrocity, Collective Memory, and the Law* (New Brunswick, NJ: Transaction Publishers, 2000), 270.

26. This is a striking contrast with Northern Ireland, where the politics of memory since the 1970s have been largely concerned with truth claims. A fuller comparative study is needed, but three particularities of the Troubles stand out. First, the British government was even more committed to strategies of secrecy, denial, and shielding the military from accountability than in the 1950s. Second, memories of the conflict have been thoroughly integrated into the identities of the two major communities in Northern Ireland. Finally, the constitutional questions underlying the conflict remain unresolved. See Graham Dawson, "Trauma, Place, and the Politics of Memory: Bloody Sunday, Derry, 1972-2004," *History Workshop Journal* no. 59 (2005): 151–178; Thomas Leahy, "The Politics of Troubles Memories in Northern Ireland and the Republic of Ireland, 1998 to 2018," *Innovation: The European Journal of Social Science Research* 32, no. 3 (2019): 293–314.

27. Bayly and Harper, *Forgotten Wars*, 450.

28. Entry for May 6, 1971, in *The Diaries of Kenneth Tynan*, ed. John Lahr (London: Bloomsbury, 2001), 47.

29. Brian Phelan, *Article 5* shooting script, box 1, folder 8, Phelan papers, MSS 0681, University of Delaware Library.

30. United Kingdom, *Report of the Committee of Privy Counselors Appointed to Consider Authorised Procedures for the Interrogation of Persons Suspected of Terrorism*, Cmnd. 4901 (London: HMSO, 1972); Peter Taylor, *Beating the Terrorists? Interrogation in Omagh, Gough, and Castlereach* (Harmondsworth: Penguin, 1980), 20.

31. John Le Carré, *Tinker, Tailor, Soldier, Spy* (New York: Alfred A. Knopf, 1974), 34.

32. Alan Clarke, dir., *Psy-Warriors* (1981).

33. "Malvinas" (1982) in *Peace Songs: WMA Anniversary Collection*, ed. John Jordan (London: Kahn & Averill for the Worker's Music Association, 1989).

34. Peter Hewitt, *Kenya Cowboy: A Police Officer's Account of the Mau Mau Emergency* (Johannesburg: 30° South, 2008 [1999]), 191–201.

35. Bell, *End of Empire*, 64.

36. Richard Drayton, "Where Does the World Historian Write From? Objectivity, Moral Conscience, and the Past and Present of Imperialism," *Journal of Contemporary History* 46, no. 3 (2011): 671–685.

37. Anderson, *Histories of the Hanged*; Elkins, *Imperial Reckoning*.

38. Dane Kennedy, *The Imperial History Wars: Debating the British Empire* (London: Bloomsbury, 2018), 108.

39. Bennett, *Fighting the Mau Mau.*

40. Richard Drayton, "Where Does the World Historian Write From?" 680.

41. Mayo Moran, "The Problem of the Past: How Historic Wrongs Become Legal Problems," *University of Toronto Law Review* 69, no. 4 (2019): 421–472.

42. *Athanasios Sophocleous and Others v. Secretary of State for the Foreign and Commonwealth Office and Another.*

43. *Kimathi and Others v. Foreign and Commonwealth Office.*

44. *Chong Nyok Keyu and Others v. Foreign and Commonwealth Office and Another.*

Bibliography

Newspaper articles and letters to the editor are omitted.

Adams, Alex. *How to Justify Torture: Inside the Ticking Bomb Scenario*. London: Repeater, 2019.

Adi, Hakim. "Forgotten Comrade? Desmond Buckle: An African Communist in Great Britain." *Science & Society* 70, no. 1 (2006): 22–45.

Adi, Hakim. *West Africans in Britain, 1900-1960: Nationalism, Pan-Africanism, and Communism*. London: Lawrence & Wishart, 1998.

Adi, Hakim, and Anandi Ramamurthy. "Fragments in the History of the Visual Culture of Anti-Colonial Struggle." In *Visual Culture and Decolonisation in Britain*, edited by Simon Faulkner and Anandi Ramamurthy, 237–262. Milton: Routledge, 2019.

Allport, Alan. *Demobbed: Coming Home After the Second World War*. New Haven, CT: Yale University Press, 2009.

Altman, Janet Gurkin. *Epistolarity: Approaches to a Form*. Columbus: Ohio State University Press, 1982.

Amiri, Linda. *La bataille de France: La guerre d'Algérie en France*. Paris: Robert Laffont, 2004.

Amis, Kingsley. *Socialism and the Intellectuals*. [London]: Fabian Society, 1957.

Anderson, David. "Guilty Secrets: Deceit, Denial, and the Discovery of Kenya's 'Migrated' Archives." *History Workshop Journal* 80 (2015): 142–160.

Anderson, David. *Histories of the Hanged: The Dirty War in Kenya and the End of Empire*. New York: W.W. Norton, 2005.

Anderson, David. "Mau Mau at the Movies: Contemporary Representations of an Anti-Colonial War." *South African Historical Journal* 48, no. 1 (2003): 71–89.

Anderson, David. "Mau Mau in the High Court and the 'Lost' British Empire Archives: Colonial Conspiracy or Bureaucratic Bungle?" *Journal of Imperial and Commonwealth History* 39, no. 5 (2011): 699–716.

Anderson, John. "'On Very Slippery Ground': The British Churches, Archbishop Fisher and the Suez Crisis." *Contemporary British History* 29, no. 3 (2015): 341–358.

Anderson, John. "The Tory Party at Prayer? The Church of England and British Politics in the 1950s." *Journal of Church and State* 58, no. 3 (2015): 417–439.

Anderson, Lindsay. "Court Style." In *At the Royal Court: 25 Years of the English Stage Company*, edited by Richard Findlater, 143–148. Ambergate: Amber Lane Press, 1981.

Anderson, Olive. "The Growth of Christian Militarism in Mid-Victorian Britain." *English Historical Review*, no. 338 (1971): 46–72.

Andrews, Christopher. *The Defence of the Realm: The Authorized History of MI5*. London: Allen Lane, 2009.

Annan, Noel. *Our Age: English Intellectuals Between the Wars—A Group Portrait*. New York: Random House, 1990.

Appleby, John. *The Bad Summer*. London: Hodder & Staughton, 1958.

Arden, John. *Serjeant Musgrave's Dance: An Un-historical Parable*. In *Plays: One*. London: Methuen, 1987.

Arendt, Hannah. *Eichmann in Jerusalem: A Report on the Banality of Evil*. New York: Penguin, 1994.

Austin, J. L. *How To Do Things with Words*. Oxford: Oxford University Press, 1962.

Ayers, David. "Hewlett Johnson: Britain's Red Dean and the Cold War." In *Religion and the Cold War: A Global Perspective*, edited by Philip Muehlenbeck, 65–87. Nashville: Vanderbilt University Press, 2012.

Bagon, Paul. "The Impact of the Jewish Underground Upon Anglo Jewry: 1945-1947." MPhil thesis, University of Oxford, 2003.

Bailey, Victor. *The Rise and Fall of the Rehabilitative Idea, 1895-1970*. London Routledge, 2019.

Bailkin, Jordanna. *The Afterlife of Empire*. Berkeley: University of California Press, 2012.

Bailkin, Jordanna. "Where Did the Empire Go? Archives and Decolonization in Britain." *American Historical Review* 120, no. 3 (2015): 884–899.

Bakken, Tore, and Eric Lawrence Wiik. "Ignorance and Organization Studies." *Organization Studies* 39, no. 8 (2018): 1109–1120.

Bamford, Caroline. "The Politics of Commitment: The Early New Left in Britain, 1956-1962." PhD dissertation, University of Edinburgh, 1983.

Banton, Mandy. "Destroy? 'Migrate'? Conceal? British Strategies for the Disposal of Sensitive Records of Colonial Administrations at Independence." *Journal of Imperial and Commonwealth History* 40, no. 2 (2012): 321–35.

Barber, Noel. *The War of the Running Dogs: How Malaya Defeated the Communist Guerrillas*. London: Collins, 1971.

Bardsley, Cuthbert. *Sundry Times, Sundry Places*. London: A.R. Mowbray, 1962.

Barker, Martin. *A Haunt of Fears: The Strange History of the British Horror Comics Campaign*. Jackson: University Press of Mississippi, 2006.

Barnes, Geoffrey. *With the Dirty Half-Hundred in Malaya: Memories of National Service, 1951-52*. Royston: Mulu Press, 2001.

Barnett, Michael, and Janice Stein, eds. *Sacred Aid: Faith and Humanitarianism*. New York: Oxford University Press, 2012.

Barthes, Roland. *Mythologies*. Paris: Seuil, 2005.

Bauman, Zygmunt. *Modernity and the Holocaust*. Ithaca, NY: Cornell University Press, 1989.

Bauman, Zygmunt. "Wars of the Globalization Era." *European Journal of Social Theory* 4, no. 1 (2001): 11–28.

Bayly, Christopher. *Empire and Information: Intelligence Gathering and Social Communication in India, 1780-1870*. Cambridge: Cambridge University Press, 1996.

Bayly, Christopher, and Tim Harper. *Forgotten Wars: Freedom and Revolution in Southeast Asia*. Cambridge, MA: Belknap Press of Harvard University Press, 2007.

Beers, Laura. "Whose Opinion? Changing Attitudes Toward Opinion Polling in British Politics, 1937-1964." *Twentieth-Century British History* 17, no. 2 (2006): 177–205.

Behan, Brendan. *An Giall* and *The Hostage*. Translated and edited by Richard Wall. Washington, DC: Catholic University of America Press, 1987.

Behan, Brendan. *The Hostage*. In *The Complete Plays*. London: Methuen, 1978.

Bell, Duncan. *Dreamworlds of Race: Empire and the Utopian Destiny of Anglo-America*. Princeton, NJ: Princeton University Press, 2020.

Bell, Duncan. *The Idea of Greater Britain: Empire and the Future of World Order, 1860-1900*. Princeton, NJ: Princeton University Press, 2007.

Bell, Martin. *The End of Empire: A Soldier's Story*. Barnsley: Pen & Sword Books, 2015.

Benn, Tony. *Years of Hope: Diaries, Letters, and Papers, 1940-1962*. Edited by Ruth Winstone. London: Hutchinson, 1994.

Bennett, Huw. "The British Army and Controlling Barbarization during the Kenya Emergency." In *Warrior's Dishonour: Barbarity, Morality, and Torture in Modern Warfare*, edited by George Kassimeris, 59–80. Aldershot: Ashgate, 2006.

Bennett, Huw. *Fighting the Mau Mau: The British Army and Counter-Insurgency in the Kenya Emergency*. Cambridge: Cambridge University Press, 2013.

Berenson, Edward. *Heroes of Empire: Five Charismatic Men and the Conquest of Africa*. Berkeley: University of California Press, 2011.

Berger, John. "Photographs of Agony." In *Understanding a Photograph*, edited by Geoff Dyer, 30–34. London: Penguin, 2013.

Bewes, Timothy. *The Event of Postcolonial Shame*. Princeton: Princeton University Press, 2010.

Bewes, T. F. C. *Kikuyu Conflict: Mau Mau and the Christian Witness*. London: Highway Press, 1954.

Bhattacharya, Sanjoy. "British Military Information Management Techniques and the South Asian Soldier: Eastern India during the Second World War." *Modern Asian Studies* 34, no. 2 (2000): 483–510.

Bignell, Jonathan, Stephen Lacey, and Madeleine Macmurraugh-Kavanagh, eds. *British Television Drama: Past, Present, and Future*. Basingstoke: Palgrave, 2000.

Birchall, Ian. "'Vicarious Pleasure'? The British Far Left and the Third World, 1956-79." In *Against the Grain: The British Far Left from 1956*, edited by Evan Smith and Matthew Worley, 190–208. Manchester: Manchester University Press, 2014.

Bingham, Adrian. *Family Newspapers? Sex, Private Life, and the British Popular Press, 1981-1978*. Oxford: Oxford University Press, 2009.

Blacker, John. "The Demography of Mau Mau: Fertility and Mortality in Kenya in the 1950s: A Demographer's Viewpoint." *African Affairs* 106 (April 2007): 205–227.

Bloxham, Donald. *Genocide on Trial: War Crimes Trials and the Formation of Holocaust History and Memory*. Oxford: Oxford University Press, 2001.

Bolar, Gordon Maxwell. "The Sunday Productions Without Décor at the Royal Court Theatre, 1957-1975." PhD dissertation. Louisiana State University, 1984.

Boobbyer, Philip. "Moral Re-Armament in Africa in the Era of Decolonization." In *Missions, Nationalism, and the End of Empire*, edited by Brian Stanley, 212–236. Grand Rapids: William B. Eerdmans, 2003.

Boon Kheng, Cheah. *The Masked Comrades: A Study of the Communist United Front in Malaya, 1945-48*. Singapore: Times Books, 1979.

Boorstin, Daniel. *The Image or What Happened to the American Dream*. New York: Atheneum, 1961.

Bourke, Joanna. *An Intimate History of Killing: Face-to-Face Killing in Twentieth-Century Warfare*. New York: Basic Books, 1999.

Boyce, George D. *Decolonisation and the British Empire, 1775-1997*. London: Macmillan, 1999.

Bradley, Sue, ed. *The British Book Trade: An Oral History*. London: British Library, 2008.

Branche, Raphael. *"Papa, qu'as-tu fait en Algérie?": Enquête sur un silence familial*. Paris: La Découverte, 2020.

Branche, Raphaëlle, and Sylvie Thénault, eds. *La France en guerre, 1954-1962: Expériences métropolitaines de la guerre d'indépendance algérienne*. Paris: Autrement, 2008.

Brand, Mona. *Enough Blue Sky: The Autobiography of Mona Brand, An Unknown Well-Known Playwright*. Sydney: Tawny Pipit Press, 1995.

Brand, Mona. *Strangers in the Land*. In *Two Plays About Malaya*. London: Lawrence and Wishart, 1954.

Brandt, George W. *British Television Drama*. Cambridge: Cambridge University Press, 1981.

Brauman, Rony. "Les liaisons dangereuses du témoignage humanitaire et de la propagande politique." In *Crises extrêmes: Face aux massacres, aux guerres civiles et aux genocides*, edited by Marc Le Pape, Johanna Siméant and Claudine Vidal, 188–204. Paris: Éditions La Découverte, 2006.

Brauman, Rony. "Médecins Sans Frontières and the ICRC: Matters of Principle." *International Review of the Red Cross* 94 (Winter 2012): 1523–1535.

Briggs, Asa. *The History of Broadcasting in the United Kingdom*. 5 vols. Oxford: Oxford University Press, 1961-1994.

Broad, Roger. *Conscription in Britain, 1939-1964: The Militarisation of a Generation*. Abingdon: Routledge, 2006.

Brockway, Fenner. *Towards Tomorrow*. London: Granada Publishing, 1977.

Brockway, Fenner. *Why Mau Mau? An Analysis and a Remedy*. London: Congress of Peoples against Imperialism, 1953.

Bromiley, G.W. *Reasonable Service: A Study in Christian Conduct*. London: Inter-Varsity Fellowship, 1948.

Brothers, Caroline. *War and Photography: A Cultural History*. London: Routledge, 1998.

Brown, Callum G. *The Death of Christian Britain: Understanding Secularization, 1800-2000*. London: Routledge, 2001.

Brownell, Josiah. "The Taint of Communism: The Movement for Colonial Freedom, the Labour Party, and the Communist Party of Great Britain, 1954-1970." *Canadian Journal of History/Annales canadiennes d'histoire* 42, no. 2 (Autumn 2007): 235–258.

Brundage, W. Fitzhugh. *Civilizing Torture: An American Tradition*. Cambridge, MA: Belknap Press of Harvard University Press, 2018.

Buchanan, Tom. *Amnesty International and Human Rights Activism in Postwar Britain, 1945-1977*. Cambridge: Cambridge University Press, 2020.

Buettner, Elizabeth. *Europe after Empire: Decolonization, Society, and Culture*. Cambridge: Cambridge University Press, 2016.

Bundock, Clement J. *The National Union of Journalists: A Jubilee History, 1907-1957*. Oxford: Oxford University Press, 1957.

Burgess, Anthony. *The Long Day Wanes: A Malayan Trilogy*. New York: W. W. Norton, 1992.

Burton, Antoinette. *The Trouble with Empire: Challenges to Modern British Imperialism*. New York: Oxford University Press, 2015.

Bush, Barbara. "Gender and Empire: The Twentieth Century." In *Gender and Empire*, edited by Philippa Levine, 77–111. Oxford: Oxford University Press, 2004.

Butler, D. E. *The British General Election of 1951*. London: Macmillan, 1952.

Butler, D. E., and Richard Rose. *The British General Election of 1959*. London: Macmillan, 1960.

Buttenshaw, Diana. *Violence in Paradise*. London: Hodder & Stoughton, 1957.

Cairns, David, and Shaun Richards. "No Good Brave Causes? The Alienated Intellectual and the End of Empire." *Literature and History* 14, no. 2 (1988): 194–206.

Calder, John. *Pursuit*. London: Calder Publications, 2001.

Calhoun, Craig. "A World of Emergencies: Fear, Intervention, and the Limits of the Cosmopolitan Order." *Canadian Review of Sociology and Anthropology* 41, no. 4 (2004): 373–395.

Callaghan, John. *Cold War, Crisis, and Conflict: The CPGB, 1951-68*. London: Lawrence & Wishart, 2003.

Cameron, James. *Point of Departure: An Attempt at Autobiography*. New York: McGraw Hill, 1967.

Campbell, Alexander. *The Heart of Africa*. New York: Knopf, 1954.

Campbell, Arthur. *Jungle Green*. Boston: Little Brown, 1954.

Campbell, James. "Combat Gnosticism: The Ideology of First World War Poetry Criticism." *New Literary History* 30, no. 1 (1999): 203–215.

Cannadine, David. "Apocalypse When? British Politicians and 'Decline' in the Twentieth Century." In *Understanding Decline: Perceptions and Realities of British Economic Performance*, edited by Peter Clarke and Clive Trebilcock, 261–284. Cambridge: Cambridge University Press, 1997.

Carpenter, Charles A. *Dramatists and the Bomb: American and British Playwrights Confront the Nuclear Age, 1945-1964*. Westport, CT: Greenwood Press, 1999.

Carruthers, Susan. *The Media at War*. London: Palgrave Macmillan, 2011.

Carruthers, Susan. "Two Faces of 1950s Terrorism: The Film Presentation of Mau Mau and the Malayan Emergency." *Small Wars & Insurgencies* 6, no. 1 (1995): 17–43.

Carruthers, Susan. *Winning Hearts and Minds: British Governments, the Media, and Colonial Counter-Insurgency, 1944-1960*. London: Leicester University Press, 1995.

Cassidy, Robert M. *Counterinsurgency and the Global War on Terror: Military Culture and Irregular War*. Stanford, CA: Stanford University Press, 2008.

Casson, John. "Missionaries, Mau Mau, and the Christian Frontier." In *Missions and Missionaries*, edited by Pieter N. Holtrop and Hugh McLeod, 200–215. Woodbridge: Boydell Press, 2000.

[Caunt, James]. *An Editor on Trial:* Rex v. Caunt. Morecambe: Morecambe Press, 1947.

Cave, Dylan. "Empire's Twilight." *Sight & Sound* 21, no. 12 (December 2011): 12–13.

Cesarani, David. "Great Britain." In *The World Reacts to the Holocaust*, edited by David S. Wyman, 599–641. Baltimore: Johns Hopkins University Press, 1996.

Cesarani, David. "Lacking in Conviction: British War Crimes Policy and the National Memory of the Second World War." In *War and Memory in the Twentieth Century*, edited by Martin Evans and Ken Lunn, 27–36. Oxford: Berg, 1997.

Chamayou, Grégoire. *A Theory of the Drone*. Translated by Janet Lloyd. New York: New Press, 2015.

Chambers, Colin. *The Story of Unity Theatre*. London: Lawrence & Wishart, 1989.

Chaplin, Joyce E. "Slavery and the Principle of Humanity: A Modern Idea in the Early Lower South." *Journal of Social History* 24, no. 2 (1990): 299–315.

Chapman, Alister. "The International Context of Secularization in England: The End of Empire, Immigration, and the Decline of Christian National Identity, 1945-1970." *Journal of British Studies* 54 (2015): 163–189.

Chapman, James. "Action, Spectacle, and the *Boy's Own Tradition* in British Cinema." In *The British Cinema Book*, edited by Robert Murphy, 217–225. London: Palgrave Macmillan for the British Film Institute, 2008.

Chapman, James. *British Comics: A Cultural History*. London: Reaktion, 2011.

Chapman, James, and Nicholas J. Cull. *Projecting Empire: Imperialism and Popular Culture*. London: I.B. Tauris, 2009.

Chesterton, A. K. *Empire or Eclipse: Grim Realities of the Mid-Twentieth Century*. London: Candour Publishing, [1965?].

Chesterton, A. K. *Sound the Alarm! A Warning to the British Nations*. Croydon: Candour Publishing, [1954?].

Chickering, Roger. "Total War: The Use and Abuse of a Concept." In *Anticipating Total War: The German and American Experiences, 1871-1914*, edited by Manfred F. Boemeke, Roger Chickering, and Stig Förster, 13–28. Cambridge: Cambridge University Press, 1999.

Chun, Lin. *The British New Left*. Edinburgh: Edinburgh University Press, 1993.

Clough, Marshall S. "Mau Mau and the Contest for Memory." In *Mau Mau and Nationhood: Arms, Authority and Narration*, edited by E.S. Atieno Odhiambo and John Lonsdale, 252–267. Athens: Ohio University Press, 2003.

Clough, Marshall S. *Mau Mau Memoirs: History, Memory, and Politics*. Boulder, CO: Lynn Rienner, 1998.

Clutterbuck, Richard L. *The Long Long War: Counterinsurgency in Malaya and Vietnam*. New York: Praeger, 1966.

Cobain, Ian. *The History Thieves: Secrets, Lies, and the Shaping of a Modern Nation*. London: Portobello Books, 2016.

Cohen, Stanley. *States of Denial: Knowing about Atrocity and Suffering*. Cambridge: Polity Press, 2001.

Cole, Joshua. "Massacres and Their Historians: Recent Histories of State Violence in France and Algeria in the Twentieth Century." *French Politics, Culture, and Society* 28, no. 1 (2010): 106–126.

Collins, L. John. *Faith under Fire*. London: Leslie Frewin, 1966.

Comfort, Alex. *How to Read the Newspapers (and Listen to the News Bulletins)*. [London]: Medical Association for the Prevention of War, [1955?].

Conboy, Martin. *Journalism: A Critical History*. Thousand Oaks, CA: Sage, 2004.

Connelly, Mark. "The British People, the Press, and the Strategic Air Campaign Against Germany, 1939-45." *Contemporary British History* 16, no. 2 (2002): 39–58.

Cooke, Lez. *British Television Drama: A History*. London: BFI, 2003.

Cornish, Michael. *An Introduction to Violence*. London: Cassell, 1960.

Couldry, Nick, Andreas Hepp, and Friedrich Krotz, eds. *Media Events in a Global Age*. London: Routledge, 2010.

Couzens, K. E. "A Minister's Correspondence." *Public Administration* 34, no. 3 (1956): 237–244.

Cowans, Jon. *Empire Films and the Crisis of Colonialism, 1946-1959*. Baltimore: Johns Hopkins University Press, 2015.

Cox, Geoffrey. *Pioneering Television News: A First Hand Report on a Revolution in Journalism*. London: John Libbey, 1995.

Crawshaw, Nancy. *The Cyprus Revolt: An Account of the Struggle for Union with Greece*. London: Allen & Unwin, 1978.

Crook, Tom. "Secrecy and Liberal Modernity in Victorian and Edwardian England." In *The Peculiarities of Liberal Modernity in Imperial Britain*, edited by Simon Gunn and James Vernon, 72–90. Berkeley: University of California Press, 2011.

Cullen, Poppy. "'Playing Cold War Politics': The Cold War in Anglo-Kenyan Relations in the 1960s." *Cold War History* 18, no. 1 (2018): 37–54.

Curran, James, ed. *The British Press: A Manifesto*. London: Macmillan, 1978.

Curran, James, and Jean Seaton. *Power without Responsibility: The Press and Broadcasting in Britain*. London: Routledge, 1997.

Cudlipp, Hugh. *Publish and Be Damned! The Astonishing Story of the* Daily Mirror. London: Andrew Dakers, 1953.

Cudlipp, Hugh. *Walking on the Water*. London: Bodley Head, 1976.

Cyprus — The Solution. London: National Cypriot Committee and Movement for Colonial Freedom, [1958].

Daddis, Gregory A. *Pulp Vietnam: War and Gender in Cold War Men's Adventure Magazines*. Cambridge: Cambridge University Press, 2020.

Daley, Chris. "The 'Atrocious Privilege': Bearing Witness to War and Atrocity in O'Brien, Levi, and Remarque." In *Arms and the Self: War, the Military, and Autobiographical Writing*, edited by Alex Vernon, 182–201. Kent, OH: Kent State University Press, 2005.

Darnton, Robert. "Journalism: All the News That Fits We Print." In *The Kiss of Lamourette: Reflections in Cultural History*, 60–93. New York: Norton, 1991.

Darwin, John. "The Fear of Falling: British Politics and Imperial Decline since 1900." *Transactions of the Royal Historical Society* 36 (1986): 27–43.

Daston, Lorraine, and Peter Galison. *Objectivity*. New York: Zone Books, 2007.

Davenport-Hines, Richard, ed. *Letters from Oxford: Hugh Trevor-Roper to Bernard Berenson*. London: Phoenix, 2007.

Davidson, Michael. *The World, The Flesh, and Myself*. Swaffham: Gay Men's Press, 1997.

Davies, Alistair, and Peter Saunders. "Literature, Politics, and Society." In *Society and Literature 1945-1970*, edited by Alan Sinfield, 13–50. London: Methuen, 1983.

Davies, Andrew. *Other Theatres: The Development of Alternative and Experimental Theatre in Britain*. Basingstoke: Macmillan, 1987.

Davies, Russell, ed. *The Kenneth Williams Diaries*. London: HarperCollins, 1993.

Davis, Muriam Haleh. "'The Transformation of Man' in French Algeria: Economic Planning and the Postwar Social Sciences, 1958-1962." *Journal of Contemporary History* 52, no. 1 (2017): 73–94.

Dawes, James. *Evil Men*. Cambridge, MA: Harvard University Press, 2014.

Dawes, James. *The Language of War: Literature and Culture in the U.S. from the Civil War through World War II*. Cambridge, MA: Harvard University Press, 2002.

Dawson, Graham. "Trauma, Place, and the Politics of Memory: Bloody Sunday, Derry, 1972-2004." *History Workshop Journal* no. 59 (2005): 151–178.

Dayan, Daniel, and Elihu Katz. *Media* Events: The Live Broadcasting of History. Cambridge, MA: Harvard University Press, 1992.

de Cruz, Gerald. *Facing Facts in Malaya*. London: Union of Democratic Control, 1952.

Desgrandchamps, Marie-Luce. "Revenir sur le mythe fondateur de Médecins Sans Frontières: les relations entre les médecins français et le CICR pendant la guerre du Biafra (1967–1970)." *Relations internationales* no. 146 (2011): 95–108.

Dewar, Lindsay. *A Short Introduction to Moral Theology*. London: A.R. Mowbray, 1956.

Dewar, Lindsay, and Cyril E. Hudson. *Christian* Morals: A Study in First Principles. London: University of London Press, 1956.

Dewhurst, John. "Complicity." *British Medical Journal* 330 (January 22, 2005): 181.

Dixon, Paul. "'Hearts and Minds'? British Counter-Insurgency from Malaya to Iraq," *Journal of Strategic Studies* 32, no. 3 (2009): 353–381.

Downton, Eric. *Wars without End.* Toronto: Stoddard, 1987.

Drake, St. Clair. "Mbiyu Koinange and the Pan-African Movement." In *Pan-African Biography*, edited by Robert A. Hall, 161–170. Los Angeles: African Studies Center, University of California, Los Angeles, and Crossroads Press, 1987.

Drayton, Richard. "Where Does the World Historian Write From? Objectivity, Moral Conscience, and the Past and Present of Imperialism." *Journal of Contemporary History* 46, no. 3 (2011): 671–685.

Drohan, Brian. *Brutality in an Age of Human Rights: Activism and Counterinsurgency at the End of the British Empire.* Ithaca, NY: Cornell University Press, 2018.

Drohan, Brian. "'A Litigious Island': Law, Rights, and Counterinsurgency during the Cyprus Emergency." In *Decolonization and Conflict: Colonial Comparisons and Legacies*, edited by Martin Thomas and Gareth Curless, 99–114. London: Bloomsbury, 2017.

Drysdale, John. *Singapore: Struggle for Success.* Singapore: Allen & Unwin, 1984.

Dual Standards of Morality: A Symposium. London: Friends Home Service Committee, 1960.

Dudeck, Theresa Robbins. *Keith Johnstone: A Critical Biography.* London: Bloomsbury Methuen Drama, 2013.

Dupree, Marguerite, ed. *Lancashire and Whitehall: The Diary of Sir Raymond Streat.* 2 vols. Manchester: Manchester University Press, 1987.

Durgnat, Raymond. *A Mirror for England: British Movies from Austerity to Affluence.* London: Palgrave Macmillan for the British Film Institute, 2011.

Durrani, Shiraz. *Never Be Silent: Publishing & Imperialism in Kenya, 1884-1963.* London: Vita Books, 2006.

Dyer, Richard. "White." *Screen* 29, no. 4 (1988): 44–65.

Eaden, James, and David Renton. *The Communist Party of Great Britain since 1920.* New York: Palgrave, 2002.

Edelman, Maurice. *Minister of State.* [U.S. edition of *The Minister*.]. Philadelphia: J.B. Lippincott, 1962.

Edgerton, David. "Liberal Militarism and the British State." *New Left Review* no. 185 (1991): 138–169.

Edwards, Bob. *Goodbye Fleet Street.* London: Jonathan Cape, 1988.

Eley, Geoff. "Finding the People's War: Film, British Collective Memory, and World War II." *American Historical Review* 106, no. 3 (2001): 818–838.

Eley, Geoff. *Forging Democracy: The History of the Left in Europe, 1850-2000.* New York: Oxford University Press, 2002.

Elkins, Caroline. *Imperial Reckoning: The Untold Story of Britain's Gulag in Kenya.* New York: Henry Holt, 2005.

Elkins, Caroline. *Legacy of Violence: A History of the British Empire*. London: Bodley Head, 2022.

Elkins, Caroline. "Looking beyond Mau Mau: Archiving Violence in the Era of Decolonization." *American Historical Review* 120, no. 3 (2015): 852–868.

Elliott, Philip. "Professional Ideology and Organizational Change: The Journalist since 1800." In *Newspaper History from the Seventeenth Century to the Present Day*, edited by George Boyce, James Curran, and Pauline Wingate, 172–191. London: Sage, 1978.

Ellis, John. *The Sharp End: The Fighting Man in World War II*. New York: Scribner, 1980.

Elmes, Simon. *Hello Again . . . Nine Decades of Radio Voices*. London: Arrow Books, 2012.

Elsaesser, Thomas. "Tales of Sound and Fury: Observations on the Family Melodrama." In *Imitations of Life: A Reader on Film and Television Melodrama*, edited by Marcia Landy, 68–91. Detroit: Wayne State University Press, 1991.

Elsom, John. *Post-War British Theatre*. London: Routledge and Kegan Paul, 1976.

Entwistle, Charles R. *The British Army Post Office in Conflict & Crisis Situations, 1946-1982*. Chavril: Abernethy, 2005.

Epstein, Leon D. *British Politics in the Suez Crisis*. Urbana: University of Illinois Press, 1964.

Erwin, Lee. "Britain's Small Wars: Domesticating 'Emergency.'" In *The Edinburgh Companion to Twentieth-Century British and American War Literature*, edited by Adam Piette and Mark Rawlinson, 181–189. Edinburgh: Edinburgh University Press, 2012.

Evans, Catherine L. *Unsound Empire: Civilization and Madness in Late-Victorian Law*. New Haven, CT: Yale University Press, 2021.

Evans, Martin. *The Memory of Resistance: French Opposition to the Algerian War, 1954-1962*. Oxford: Berg, 1997.

Evans, Stanley G. "Morals and Immorals." In *Return to Reality: Some Essays on Contemporary Christianity*, edited by Stanley G. Evans, 272–300. London: Zeno, [1954].

Fanon, Frantz. *The Wretched of the Earth*. Translated by Constance Farrington. London: Penguin, 2001.

Farish, Matthew. "Modern Witnesses: Foreign Correspondents, Geopolitical Vision, and the First World War." *Transactions of the Institute of British Geographers* 26, no. 3 (2001): 273–287.

Fein, Helen. *Imperial Crime and Punishment: The Massacre at Jallianwala Bagh and British Judgment, 1919-1920*. Honolulu: University Press of Hawaii, 1977.

Fennell, Jonathan. *Fighting the People's War: The British and Commonwealth Armies and the Second World War*. Cambridge: Cambridge University Press, 2019.

Findlater, Richard, ed. *At the Royal Court: 25 Years of the English Stage Company*. Ambergate: Amber Lane Press, 1981.

Fleming, Ian. *Moonraker*. London: Jonathan Cape, 1955.

Fletcher, Eileen. *Truth about Kenya: An Eye Witness Account*. London: Movement for Colonial Freedom, 1956.

Foley, Charles. *Island in Revolt*. London: Longmans, 1962.

Forsythe, David P. *The Humanitarians: The International Committee of the Red Cross*. Cambridge: Cambridge University Press, 2005.

Forth, Aidan. *Barbed-Wire Imperialism: Britain's Empire of Camps, 1876-1903*. Berkeley: University of California Press, 2017.

Freeman, Mark. "Muscular Quakerism? The Society of Friends and Youth Organisations in Britain, c. 1900-1950." *English Historical Review* 125, no. 514 (2010): 642–669.

French, David. *The British Way in Counter-Insurgency, 1945–1967*. Oxford: Oxford University Press, 2011.

French, David. *Fighting EOKA: The British Counter-Insurgency Campaign on Cyprus, 1955-59*. Oxford: Oxford University Press, 2011.

Fussell, Paul. *The Great War and Modern Memory*. New York: Oxford University Press, 2000.

Fyvel, T. R. *Troublemakers: Rebellious Youth in an Affluent Society*. New York: Schocken Books, 1962.

Gall, Sandy. *Don't Worry About the Money Now*. London: Hamish Hamilton, 1983.

Gallacher, William. *The Tyrants' Might Is Passing*. London: Lawrence and Wishart, 1954.

Gallup, George H., ed. *The Gallup International Public Opinion Polls: Great Britain 1937-1975*. 2 vols. New York: Random House, 1976.

Gangrene. London: Calderbooks, 1959.

Garnett, Tony. "Contexts." In *British Television Drama: Past, Present, and Future*, edited by Johnathan Bignell, Stephen Lacey, and Madeleine Macmurraugh-Kavanagh, 16–29. Basingstoke: Palgrave, 2000.

Gaskill, [William]. "My Apprenticeship." In *At the Royal Court: 25 Years of the English Stage Company*, edited by Richard Findlater, 57–61. Ambergate: Amber Lane Press, 1981.

Gaskill, William. *A Sense of Direction*. London: Faber and Faber, 1988.

Geraghty, Christine. *British Cinema in the Fifties: Gender, Genre, and the "New Look."* London: Routledge, 2000.

Gilroy, Paul. *After Empire: Melancholia or Convivial Culture?* London: Routledge, 2004.

Goedde, Petra. *The Politics of Peace: A Global Cold War History*. New York: Oxford University Press, 2019.

Goldie, Grace Wyndham. *Facing the Nation: Television and Politics, 1936-1976*. London: Bodley Head, 1977.

Goldsworthy, David. *Colonial Issues in British Politics, 1945-1961: From "Colonial Development" to "Wind of Change."* Oxford: Clarendon Press, 1971.

Goodrum, Michael, and Philip Smith. *Printing Terror: American Horror Comics as Cold War Commentary and Critique*. Manchester: Manchester University Press, 2021.

Goorney, Howard. *The Theatre Workshop Story*. London: Eyre Methuen, 1981.

Gopal, Priyamvada. *Insurgent Empire: Anticolonial Resistance and British Dissent*. London: Verso, 2019.

Gould, Eliga H. "Zones of Law, Zones of Violence: The Legal Geography of the British Atlantic, circa 1772." *William and Mary Quarterly* 60, no. 3 (2003): 471–510.

Grant, Peter. *Letters from the Forest*. Self-published, East Lavant, Chichester, 2017.

Gready, Paul. "'Responsibility to the Story.'" *Journal of Human Rights Practice* 2, no. 2 (2010): 177–190.

Green, S. J. D. *The Passing of Protestant England: Secularization and Social Change, c. 1920-1960*. Cambridge: Cambridge University Press, 2011.

Greene, Graham. *A Burnt-Out Case*. London: Penguin, 1977.

Greene, Richard, ed. *Graham Greene: A Life in Letters*. New York: Knopf, 2007.

Gullace, Nicoletta F. "War Crimes or Atrocity Stories? Anglo-American Narratives of Truth and Deception in the Aftermath of World War I." In *Sexual Violence in Conflict Zones: From the Ancient World to the Era of Human Rights*, edited by Elizabeth D. Heineman, 105–121. Philadelphia: University of Pennsylvania Press, 2013.

Guppy, Shusha. "Christopher Logue: The Art of Poetry LXVI." *Paris Review* no. 127 (Summer 1993): 238–264.

Gupta, P. S. *Imperialism and the British Labour Movement, 1914-1964*. New York: Holmes and Meier, 1975.

Gready, Paul. "'Responsibility to the Story.'" *Journal of Human Rights Practice* 2, no. 2 (2010): 177–190.

Greene, Graham. *Ways of Escape*. New York: Simon & Schuster, 1980.

Gregory, Derek. "'The Rush to the Intimate': Counterinsurgency and the Cultural Turn." *Radical Philosophy* 150 (July–August 2008): 8–23.

Gregory, Derek. "War and Peace." *Transactions of the Institute of British Geographers* 35 (2010): 154–186.

Gusterson, Hugh. *Drone: Remote Control Warfare*. Cambridge, MA: MIT Press, 2016.

Hack, Karl. "Everyone Lived in Fear: Malaya and the British Way of Counter-Insurgency." *Small Wars & Insurgencies* 23, nos. 4–5 (2012): 671–699.

Hack, Karl, and Kevin Blackburn. *War Memory and the Making of Modern Malaysia and Singapore*. Singapore: NUS Press, 2012.

Hall, Catherine, and Daniel Pick. "Thinking About Denial." *History Workshop Journal* no. 84 (Autumn 2017): 1–23.

Hall, Stuart. *Familiar Stranger: A Life Between Two Islands*. Durham, NC: Duke University Press, 2017.

Hall, Stuart. "The Great Moving Right Show." In *Selected Political Writings: The Great Moving Right Show and Other Essays*, edited by Sally Davison, David Featherstone, Michael Rustin, and Bill Schwarz, 172–186. Durham, NC: Duke University Press, 2017.

Hall, Stuart. "Serjeant Musgrave's Dance." *New Left Review* no. 1 (January–February 1960): 50–51.

Hall, Stuart, Chas Critcher, Tony Jefferson, John Clarke, and Brian Roberts. *Policing the Crisis: Mugging, the State, and Law and Order*. London: Macmillan, 1978.

Hall, Willis. *The Long and the Short and the Tall: A Play in Two Acts.* London: Heinemann, 1959.

Haltunnen, Karen. "Humanitarianism and the Pornography of Pain in Anglo-American Culture." *American Historical Review* 100, no. 2 (1995): 303–334.

Hamilton, Denis. *Editor-in-Chief: The Fleet Street Memoirs of Sir Denis Hamilton.* London: Hamish Hamilton, 1989.

Hampshire, Edward. "'Apply the Flame More Searingly': The Destruction and Migration of the Archives of British Colonial Administration: A Southeast Asian Case Study." *Journal of Imperial and Commonwealth History* 41, no. 2 (2013): 334–352.

Harari, Yuval Noah. *The Ultimate Experience: Battlefield Revelations and the Making of Modern War Culture, 1450-2000.* New York: Palgrave Macmillan, 2008.

Harper, T. N. *The End of Empire and the Making of Malaya.* Cambridge: Cambridge University Press, 1999.

Harper, Tobias. *From Servants of the Empire to Everyday Heroes: The British Honours System in the Twentieth Century.* Oxford: Oxford University Press, 2020.

Harrison, Martin. *Young Meteors: British Journalism, 1957-1965.* London: Jonathan Cape, 1998.

Harrison, Simon. *Dark Trophies: Hunting and the Enemy Body in Modern War.* New York: Berghahn Books, 2012.

Harrison, Simon. "Skulls and Scientific Collecting in the Victorian Military: Keeping the Enemy Dead in British Frontier Warfare." *Comparative Studies in Society and History* 50, no. 1 (2008): 285–303.

Hartley, Jenny. "'Letters are *Everything* These Days': Mothers and Letters in the Second World War." In *Epistolary Selves: Letters and Letter-Writers, 1600-1945,* edited by Rebecca Earle, 152–182. Aldershot: Ashgate, 1999.

Hastings, Adrian. *A History of English Christianity, 1920-1985.* London: Collins, 1986.

Haut, Woody. *Pulp Culture: Hardboiled Fiction and the Cold War.* London: Serpent's Tail, 1995.

Heimer, Carol A. "Inert Facts and the Illusion of Knowledge: Strategic Uses of Ignorance in HIV Clinics." *Economy and Society* 41, no. 1 (2012): 17–41.

Herbert, Christopher. *War of No Pity: The Indian Mutiny and Victorian Trauma.* Princeton, NJ: Princeton University Press, 2008.

Heren, Louis. *Growing Up on The Times.* London: Hamish Hamilton, 1978.

Hewitt, Peter. *Kenya Cowboy: A Police Officer's Account of the Mau Mau Emergency.* Johannesburg: 30° South, 2008.

Hilliard, Christopher. *A Question of Obscenity: The Politics of Censorship in Modern England.* Princeton: Princeton University Press, 2021.

Hillman, Nicholas. "'Tell Me Chum, In Case I Got It Wrong. What Was It We Were Fighting During the War?' The Re-Emergence of British Fascism, 1945-58." *Contemporary British History* 15, no. 4 (2001): 1–34.

Hilton, Audrey. *This England: Selections from the* New Statesman *This England Column, 1953-57.* London: Statesman and Nation, 1957.

Hilton, Matthew. "Ken Loach and the Save the Children Film: Humanitarianism, Imperialism, and the Changing Role of Charity in Postwar Britain." *Journal of Modern History* 87, no. 2 (2015): 357–394.

Hilton, Richard. *Imperial Obituary: The Mysterious Death of the British Empire.* Devon: Britons Publishing Company, 1968.

Holland, Robert. *Britain and the Revolt in Cyprus, 1954-1959.* Oxford: Clarendon Press, 1998.

Holman, Brett. "'Bomb Back, and Bomb Hard': Debating Reprisals During the Blitz." *Australian Journal of Politics and History* 58, no. 3 (2012): 394–407.

Houghton, Frances. *The Veterans' Tale: British Military Memoirs of the Second World War.* Cambridge: Cambridge University Press, 2019.

House, Jim, and Neil MacMaster. *Paris 1961: Algerians, State Terror, and Memory.* Oxford: Oxford University Press, 2006.

Howard, Tony, and John Stokes, eds. *Acts of War: The Representation of Military Conflict on the British Stage and Television since 1945.* Aldershot: Scolar Press, 1996.

Howe, Stephen. *Anticolonialism in British Politics: The Left and the End of Empire, 1918-1964.* Oxford: Clarendon Press, 1993.

Howe, Stephen. "Colonising and Exterminating? Memories of Imperial Violence in Britain and France." *Histoire@Politique* no. 11 (2010). Online at https://www.cairn.info/revue-histoire-politique-2010-2-page-12.htm.

Howe, Stephen. "When (If Ever) Did Empire End? 'Internal Decolonisation' in British Culture since the 1950s." In *The British Empire in the 1950s: Retreat or Revival?*, edited by Martin Lynn, 214–237. Basingstoke: Macmillan, 2006.

Hubble, Nick. *Mass-Observation and Everyday Life: Culture, History, Theory.* Houndmills: Palgrave Macmillan, 2005.

Hughes, Geraint. "Guerrillas in Our Midst: Reflections on the British Experience of Counter-Insurgency in Popular Fiction." *Small Wars & Insurgencies* (2022). Advance online publication.

Hughes, Lotte. "Memorialization and Mau Mau: A Critical Review." In *Dedan Kimathi on Trial: Colonial Justice and Popular Memory in Kenya's Mau Mau Rebellion*, edited by Julie Macarthur, 339–374. Athens: Ohio University Press, 2017.

Hughes, Matthew. "The Banality of Brutality: British Armed Forces and the Repression of the Arab Revolt in Palestine, 1936-1939." *English Historical Review* no. 507 (2009): 313–354.

Humburg, Martin. "Deutsche Feldpostbriefe im Zweiten Weltkrieg: Ein Bestandsaufnahme." In *Andere Helme—andere Menschen? Heimaterfahrung und Frontalltag im Zweiten Weltkrieg*, edited by Detlef Vogel and Wolfram Wette, 13–35. Essen: Klartext, 1995.

Hunter, Leslie. *The Seed and the Fruit: Christian Morality in a Time of Transition.* London: SCM Press, 1953.

Husbands, Christopher T. *Racial Exclusionism and the City: The Urban Support of the National Front.* London: Allen & Unwin, 1983.

Hutchinson, John F. *Champions of Charity: War and the Rise of the Red Cross*. Boulder, CO: Westview Press, 1996.

Huxley, Elspeth, ed. *Nellie: Letters from Africa*. London: Weidenfeld and Nicolson, 1980.

Hynes, Samuel. *The Soldiers' Tale: Bearing Witness to Modern War*. New York: Penguin, 1997.

Illingworth, Frank. *Questions Answered About Journalism*. London: Jordan and Sons, 1946.

Innes, Christopher. *Modern British Drama: The Twentieth Century*. Cambridge: Cambridge University Press, 2002.

Izzard, Ethel. *New Friends: A Story of Malaya*. London: Highway Press, 1955.

Jacobs, Jason. *The Intimate Screen: Early British Television Drama* (Oxford: Oxford University Press, 2000.

Joas, Hans. *The Sacredness of the Person: A New Genealogy of Human Rights*. Translated by Alex Skinner. Washington: Georgetown University Press, 2013.

Johnson, B. S., ed. *All Bull: The National Servicemen*. London: Allison & Busby, 1973.

Jolly, Margaretta. "Between Ourselves: The Letter as Propaganda." In *Propaganda: Political Rhetoric and Identity, 1300-2000*, edited by Bertrand Taithe and Tim Thornton, 239–261. Stroud: Sutton, 1999.

Jolly, Margaretta. "War Letters." In *Encyclopedia of Life Writing: Autobiographical and Biographical Forms*, vol. 2, edited by Margaretta Jolly, 927–930. London: Fitzroy Dearborn, 2001.

Jonsen, Albert R., and Stephen Toulmin. *The Abuse of Casuistry: A History of Moral Reasoning*. Berkeley: University of California Press, 1989.

Jordan, John, ed. *Peace Songs: WMA Anniversary Collection*. London: Kahn & Averill for the Worker's Music Association, 1989.

Joyce, James Avery. *Red Cross International and the Strategy of Peace*. New York: Oceana, 1959.

Kaag, John, and Sarah Kreps. *Drone Warfare*. Cambridge: Polity Press, 2014.

Kalliney, Peter J. *Commonwealth of Letters: British Literary Culture and the Emergence of Postcolonial Aesthetics*. New York: Oxford University Press, 2013.

Kariuki, J. M. *Mau Mau Detainee: The Account by a Kenya African of His Experience in Detention Camps, 1953-1960*. Oxford: Oxford University Press, 1963.

Kaye, M. M. *Death in Kenya*. New York: St. Martin's, 1983. First published as *Later Than You Think*. London: Longmans, Green, 1958.

Kellenberger, Jakob. "Speaking Out or Remaining Silent in Humanitarian Work." *Revue internationale de la Croix-Rouge* no. 855 (September 2004): 593–609.

Kelly, Tobias. "Citizenship, Cowardice, and Freedom of Conscience: British Pacifists in the Second World War." *Comparative Studies in Society and History* 57, no. 3 (2015): 694–722.

Kelly, Tobias. *This Side of Silence: Human Rights, Torture, and the Recognition of Cruelty*. Philadelphia: University of Pennsylvania Press, 2012.

Kennedy, Dane. *Decolonization: A Very Short Introduction*. New York: Oxford University Press, 2016.

Kennedy, Dane. *The Imperial History Wars: Debating the British Empire*. London: Bloomsbury, 2018.

Key, Jonathan. "The Atomic Drama." In *Acts of War: The Representation of Military Conflict on the British Stage and Television since 1945*, edited by Tony Howard and John Stokes, 110–126. Aldershot: Scolar Press, 1996.

Government of Kenya. *The Archbishop of Canterbury's Tour of Kenya*. London: Pitkin Pictorials, 1955.

Kenya—Time for Action! London: Church Missionary Society, [1955].

King, Cecil Harmsworth. *Strictly Personal: Some Memoirs of Cecil H. King*. London: Weidenfeld and Nicolson, 1969.

Kirk, Kenneth. *Conscience and Its Problems: An Introduction to Casuistry*. London: Longmans, 1948.

Kirk, Kenneth. *Some Principles of Moral Theology and Their Application*. London: Longmans, 1952.

Kitson, Frank. *Gangs and Counter-Gangs*. London: Barrie and Rockliff, 1960.

Kitson, Frank. *Low Intensity Operations: Subversion, Insurgency, and Peacekeeping*. London: Faber and Faber, 1971.

Klose, Fabian. *Human Rights in the Shadow of Colonial Violence: The Wars of Independence in Kenya and Algeria*. Philadelphia: University of Pennsylvania Press, 2013.

Knightley, Philip. "The Cheerleaders of World War II." *British Journalism Review* 6, no. 2 (1995): 40–45.

Knightley, Philip. *The First Casualty: From the Crimea to Vietnam: The War Correspondent as Hero, Propagandist, and Myth Maker*. New York: Harcourt Brace Jovanovich, 1975.

Kolsky, Elizabeth. *Colonial Justice in British India: White Violence and the Rule of Law*. Cambridge: Cambridge University Press, 2010.

Koss, Stephen E. *The Rise and Fall of the Political Press in Britain*. Vol. 2, *The Twentieth Century*. Chapel Hill: University of North Carolina Press, 1981.

Kramer, Alan. "The Sharp End, Witnessing, Perpetrating, and Suffering Violence in 20th Century Wars." In *A World at War, 1911-1949: Explorations in the Cultural History of War*, edited by Catriona Pennell and Filipe Ribeiro de Meneses, 83–107. Leiden: Brill, 2019.

Kushner, Tony. *The Holocaust and the Liberal Imagination: A Social and Cultural History*. Oxford: Blackwell, 1994.

LaCapra, Dominick. *Writing History, Writing Trauma*. Baltimore: Johns Hopkins University Press, 2001.

Lacey, Stephen. *British Realist Theatre: The New Wave in Its Context, 1956-1965*. London: Routledge, 1995.

Lagrou, Pieter. "1945-1955: The Age of Total War." In *Histories of the Aftermath: The Legacies of the Second World War in Europe*, edited by Frank Biess and Robert G. Moeller, 287–296. New York: Berghahn, 2010.

Lahr, John, ed. *The Diaries of Kenneth Tynan*. London: Bloomsbury, 2001.

Landsborough, Gordon. *The Violent People*. London: Cassell, 1960.

Landy, Marcia. *British Genres: Cinema and Society, 1930-1960*. Princeton: Princeton University Press, 1991.

Langhamer, Claire. "'Who the Hell are Ordinary People?' Ordinariness as a Category of Historical Analysis." *Transactions of the Royal Historical Society* 28 (2018): 175–195.

Laplanche, Jean, and Jean-Bertrand Pontalis. *The Language of Psycho-Analysis*. Translated by Donald Nicholson-Smith. New York: W.W. Norton, 1973.

Laqueur, Thomas W. "Bodies, Details, and the Humanitarian Narrative." In *The New Cultural History*, edited by Lynn Hunt, 176–204. Berkeley: University of California Press, 1989.

Latzel, Klaus. "Vom Kriegserlebnis zur Kriegserfahrung: Theoretische und methodische Überlegungen zur erfahrungsgeschlichtlichen Untersuchung von Feldpostbriefen." *Militärgeschichtlitche Mitteilungen* 56 (1997): 1–30.

Lawrence, Jon. "Forging a Peaceable Kingdom: War, Violence, and Fear of Brutalization in Post-First World War Britain." *Journal of Modern History* 75, no. 3 (2003): 557–589.

Lawrence, Jon. *Me, Me, Me? The Search for Community in Post-War England*. Oxford: Oxford University Press, 2019.

Le Carré, John [David Cornwell]. *Tinker, Tailor, Soldier, Spy*. New York: Alfred A. Knopf, 1974.

Le Sueur, James. *Uncivil War: Intellectuals and Identity Politics during the Decolonization of Algeria*. Philadelphia: University of Pennsylvania Press, 2001.

Leach, Robert. *Theatre Workshop: Joan Littlewood and the Making of Modern Theatre*. Exeter: University of Exeter Press, 2006.

Leahy, Thomas. "The Politics of Troubles Memories in Northern Ireland and the Republic of Ireland, 1998 to 2018." *Innovation: The European Journal of Social Science Research* 32, no. 3 (2019): 293–314.

Lee, Fiona. "Epistemological Checkpoint: Reading Fiction as a Translation of History." *Postcolonial Text* 9, no. 1 (2014): 1–21.

Lee, Kam Hing. "A Neglected Story: Christian Missionaries, Chinese New Villagers, and Communists in the Battle for 'Hearts and Minds' in Malaya, 1948-1960." *Modern Asian Studies* 47, no. 6 (2013): 1977–2006.

Leitch, David. "Explosion at the King David Hotel." In *The Age of Austerity*, edited by Michael Sissons and Philip French, 58–85. London: Hodder and Stoughton, 1963.

Leites, Edmund, ed. *Conscience and Casuistry in Early Modern Europe*. Cambridge: Cambridge University Press, 1988.

Lessing, Doris. *Each His Own Wilderness*. In *New English Dramatists: Three Plays*. Edited by E. Martin Browne. Harmondsworth: Penguin, 1960.

Lessing, Doris. *Walking in the Shade: Volume Two of My Autobiography, 1949-1962.* New York: Harper Collins, 1997.

Lewis, C. S. *Christian Behaviour: A Further Series of Broadcast Talks.* New York: Macmillan, 1943.

Lewis, Jeremy. *David Astor: A Life in Print.* London: Jonathan Cape, 2016.

Lewis, Joanna. "Daddy Wouldn't Buy Me a Mau Mau: The British Popular Press and the Demoralization of Empire." In *Mau Mau and Nationhood: Arms, Authority and Narration*, edited by E. S. Atieno Odhiambo and John Lonsdale, 227–250. Athens: Ohio University Press, 2003.

Lewis, Joanna. *Empire State-Building: War & Welfare in Kenya, 1925-1952.* Oxford: James Currey, 2000.

Leys, Ruth. *Trauma: A Genealogy.* Chicago: University of Chicago Press, 2000.

Liburd, Liam J. "Beyond the Pale: Whiteness, Masculinity, and Empire in the British Union of Fascists, 1932-1940." *Fascism: Journal of Comparative Fascist Studies* 7 (2018): 275–296.

Liburd, Liam J. "The Eternal Imperialists: Empire, Race, and Gender on the British Radical Right, 1918-1968." PhD dissertation. University of Sheffield, 2019.

Liburd, Liam J. "Thinking Imperially: The British Fascisti and the Politics of Empire, 1923-1925." *Twentieth Century British History* 32, no. 1 (2021): 46–67.

Light, Alison. *Forever England: Femininity, Literature, and Conservatism Between the Wars.* London: Routledge, 1991.

Linfield, Susie. *The Cruel Radiance: Photography and Political Violence.* Chicago: University of Chicago Press, 2010.

Linstrum, Erik. "Domesticating Chemical Weapons: Tear Gas and the Militarization of Policing in the British Imperial World, 1919-1981." *Journal of Modern History* 91, no. 3 (2019): 557–585.

Linstrum, Erik. "Facts about Atrocity: Reporting Colonial Violence in Postwar Britain." *History Workshop Journal* 84 (Autumn 2017): 108–127.

Linstrum, Erik. *Ruling Minds: Psychology in the British Empire.* Cambridge, MA: Harvard University Press, 2016.

Lipstadt, Deborah. *Beyond Belief: The American Press and the Coming of the Holocaust, 1933-1945.* New York: Free Press, 1986.

Littlewood, Joan. *Joan's Book: The Autobiography of Joan Littlewood.* London: Methuen, 2003.

Lloyd, Lavender. *The Verandah Room.* London: Eyre & Spottiswoode, 1955.

Lloyd Evans, Gareth and Lloyd Evans, Barbara, eds. *Plays in Review, 1956-1980: British Drama and the Critics.* London: Batsford Academic and Educational, 1985.

Loeffler, James. *Rooted Cosmopolitans: Jews and Human Rights in the Twentieth Century.* New Haven, CT: Yale University Press, 2018.

Loss, Daniel S. "The Institutional Afterlife of Christian England," *Journal of Modern History* 89, no. 2 (2017): 282–313.

Low, Gail. *Publishing the Postcolonial: Anglophone West African and Caribbean Writing in the UK, 1948-1968.* Abingdon: Routledge, 2011.

Lutz, Catherine. "Making War at Home in the United States: Militarization and the Current Crisis." *American Anthropologist* 104, no. 3 (2002): 723–735.

Luhmann, Niklas. "The Ecology of Ignorance." In *Observations on Modernity*, translated by William Whobrey, 75–111. Stanford, CA: Stanford University Press, 1998.

Lyttelton, Oliver. *The Memoirs of Lord Chandos: An Unexpected View from the Summit.* New York: New American Library, 1963.

Maccaferri, Marzia. "'A Splenetic Isolation': Il dibattito pubblico inglese di fronte all'Affair Suez." *Ventunesimo Secolo* 19, no. 2 (June 2009): 109–126.

Macdonald, James. *My Two Jungles.* London: George G. Harrap, 1957.

Mace, Rodney. *Trafalgar Square: Emblem of Empire.* London: Lawrence and Wishart, 1976.

MacKenzie, John M., ed. *Popular Imperialism and the Military, 1850-1950.* Manchester: Manchester University Press, 1992).

Macklin, Graham. *Very Deeply Dyed in Black: Sir Oswald Mosley and the Resurrection of British Fascism after 1945.* London: I.B. Tauris, 2007.

MacNiven, Ian S., and Harry T. Moore, eds. *Literary Lifelines: The Richard Aldington-Lawrence Durrell Correspondence.* New York: Viking Press, 1981.

Majdalany, Fred. *State of Emergency: The Full Story of Mau Mau.* Boston: Houghton Mifflin, 1963.

Makalani, Minah. *In the Cause of Freedom: Radical Black Internationalism from Harlem to London, 1917-1939.* Chapel Hill: University of North Carolina Press, 2011.

Mangan, James A., and Callum McKenzie. "Martial Conditioning, Military Exemplars, and Moral Certainties: Imperial Hunting as Preparation for War." *International Journal of the History of Sport* 25, no. 9 (2008): 1132–1167.

Mann, Michael. "Authoritarian and Liberal Militarism: A Contribution from Comparative and Historical Sociology." In *International Theory: Positivism and Beyond*, edited by Steve Smith, Ken Booth, and Marysia Zalewski, 221–239. Cambridge: Cambridge University Press, 2010.

Martin, Troy Kennedy. "Nats Go Home." *Encore* no. 48 (1964): 21–33.

Marowitz, Charles, and Simon Trussler, eds. *Theatre at Work: Playwrights and Productions in the Modern British Theatre.* New York: Hill and Wang, 1968.

Marris, Peter. "Accessory after the Fact." In *Conviction*, edited by Norman Mackenzie, 171–182. London: MacGibbon & Kee, 1959.

Mason, Lisa. "The Development of the Monday Club and Its Contribution to the Conservative Party and the Modern British Right, 1961 to 1990." PhD dissertation, University of Wolverhampton, 2004.

Matheson, Alastair. *States of Emergency: Reporting Africa for Half a Century.* Nairobi: Media Matters, 1992.

Maughan-Brown, David. *Land, Freedom, and Fiction: History and Ideology in Kenya.* London: Zed Books, 1985.

Mauss-Coupeaux, Claire. *A travers le viseur: images d'appelés en Algérie, 1955-1962.* Lyon: Aedelsa, 2003.

Mayes, Stanley. *Cyprus and Makarios.* London: Putnam, 1960.

Mazower, Mark. *No Enchanted Palace: The End of Empire and the Ideological Origins of the United Nations*. Princeton: Princeton University Press, 2009.

McClintock, Anne. *Imperial Leather: Race, Gender, and Sexuality in the Colonial Conquest*. New York: Routledge, 1995.

McDonald, Iverach. *History of the* Times. Vol. 5, *Struggles in War and Peace, 1939-1966*. London: Macmillan 1984.

McDougall, Ian. *Foreign Correspondent*. London: Frederick Muller, 1980.

McGoey, Linsey. "The Logic of Strategic Ignorance." *British Journal of Sociology* 63, no. 3 (2012): 533–576.

McGoey, Linsey. "On the Will to Ignorance in Bureaucracy." *Economy and Society* 36, no. 2 (2007): 212–235.

McKenzie, Robert, and Allan Silver. *Angels in Marble: Working Class Conservatives in Urban England*. Chicago: University of Chicago Press, 1968.

McLeod, Hugh. *The Religious Crisis of the 1960s*. Oxford: Oxford University Press, 2007.

McLoughlin, Kate. "War and Words." In *The Cambridge Companion to War Writing*, edited by Kate McLoughlin, 15–24. Cambridge: Cambridge University Press, 2009.

Miall, Leonard. *Inside the BBC: British Broadcasting Characters*. London: Weidenfeld & Nicolson, 1994.

Miers, Richard. *Shoot to Kill*. London: Faber and Faber, 1959.

Milford, Ismay. "Harnessing the Wind: East and Central African Activists and Anticolonial Cultures in a Decolonising World, 1952–64." PhD dissertation. European University Institute, 2019.

Miller, Stephen M. "Duty or Crime? Defining Acceptable Behavior in the British Army in South Africa, 1899-1902." *Journal of British Studies* 49, no. 2 (2010): 311–333.

Millner, Ralph. *The Right to Live*. London: Falcon Press, 1955.

Mockaitis, Thomas R. *British Counterinsurgency, 1919–60*. London: Macmillan, 1990.

Moeller, Susan D. *Compassion Fatigue: How the Media Sell Disease, Famine, War, and Death*. New York: Routledge, 1999.

Molnar, Andrew R., et al. *Undergrounds in Insurgent, Revolutionary, and Resistance Warfare*. Washington: Special Operations Research Office, 1963.

Moore, Jonathan, ed. *Hard Choices: Moral Dilemmas in Humanitarian Intervention*. Lanham, MD: Rowan & Littlefield, 1998.

Moorcraft, Paul L., and Philip M. Taylor. *Shooting the Messenger: The Political Impact of War Reporting*. Washington, DC: Potomac Books, 2008.

Moorehead, Caroline. *Dunant's Dream: War, Switzerland, and the History of the Red Cross*. New York: Carroll & Graf, 1999.

Moores, Christopher. *Civil Liberties and Human Rights in Twentieth-Century Britain*. Cambridge: Cambridge University Press, 2017.

Moran, J. W. G. *Spearhead in Malaya*. London: Peter Davies, 1959.

Moran, Mayo. "The Problem of the Past: How Historic Wrongs Become Legal Problems." *University of Toronto Law Review* 69, no. 4 (2019): 421–472.

Morgan, Kenneth O. "Imperialists at Bay: British Labour and Decolonization." *Journal of Imperial and Commonwealth History* 27, no. 2 (1999): 233–254.

Morgan, Kenneth O. "The Second World War and British Culture." In *From Reconstruction to Integration: Britain and Europe Since 1945*, edited by Brian Brivati and Harriet Jones, 33–46. London: Leicester University Press, 1993.

Mort, Frank. *Capital Affairs: London and the Making of the Permissive Society*. New Haven, CT: Yale University Press, 2010.

Mortimer, John. *In Character*. London: Allen Lane, 1983.

Mortimer, R.C. *Christian Ethics*. London: Hutchinson's University Library, 1950.

Moulton, Mo. *Ireland and the Irish in Interwar England*. Cambridge: Cambridge University Press, 2014.

Moyn, Samuel. "In the Aftermath of Camps." In *Histories of the Aftermath: The Legacies of the Second World War in Europe*, edited by Frank Biess and Robert G. Moeller, 49–64. New York: Berghahn Books, 2010.

Moyn, Samuel. *Human Rights and the Uses of History*. New York: Verso, 2014.

Moyn, Samuel. *The Last Utopia: Human Rights in History*. Cambridge, MA: Harvard University Press, 2010.

Mulhall, Joe. "From Apathy to Obsession: The Reactions of A.K. Chesterton and the British Far Right to Imperial Decline." *Patterns of Prejudice* 50, nos. 4–5 (2016): 458–477.

Mulvey, Laura. "Melodrama In and Out of the Home." In *High Theory/Low Culture: Analysing Popular Television and Film*, edited by Colin MacCabe, 80–100. Manchester: Manchester University Press, 1986.

Murphy, Philip. *Alan Lennox-Boyd: A Biography*. London: I.B. Tauris, 1999.

Murphy, Philip. *Party Politics and Decolonization: The Conservative Party and British Colonial Policy in Tropical Africa, 1951-1964*. Oxford: Clarendon Press, 1995.

Murray, John. *The Daily Life of the Christian*. London: SCM Press, 1955.

Nagl, John. *Learning to Eat Soup With a Knife: Counterinsurgency Lessons from Malaya and Vietnam*. Chicago: University of Chicago Press, 2005.

Nash, Daniel [W.R. Loader]. *Not Yours the Island*. London: Jonathan Cape, 1956.

Nead, Lydia. *The Tiger in the Smoke: Art and Culture in Post-War Britain*. New Haven, CT: Yale University Press, 2017.

Negrine, Ralph. *Politics and the Mass Media in Britain*. London: Routledge, 1989.

Newsinger, John. *British Counter-Insurgency: From Palestine to Northern Ireland*. New York: Palgrave Macmillan, 2002.

Newsinger, John. "A Counter-Insurgency Tale: Frank Kitson in Kenya," *Race & Class* 31, no. 4 (1990): 62–72.

Newsinger, John. "The Military Memoir in British Imperial Culture: The Case of Malaya." *Race & Class* 35, no. 3 (1994): 47–62.

Nicolson, Harold. *Diaries and Letters, 1945-1962*. Edited by Nigel Nicolson. London: Collins, 1968.

Nicolson, Nigel. *Long Life*. London: Weidenfeld & Nicolson, 1997.

Nichols, Peter. *Privates on Parade*. In *Plays: 2*. London: Bloomsbury, 1991.

Nicholson, Steve. "Africa on the British Stage, 1955-1966." In *Africa on the Contemporary London Stage*, edited by Tiziana Morosetti, 45–64. Basingstoke: Palgrave Macmillan, 2018.

Nicholson, Steve. *The Censorship of British Drama, 1900-1968*. Vol. 3, *The Fifties*. Exeter: University of Exeter Press, 2020.

Noble, Ronnie. *Shoot First! Assignments of a Newsreel Cameraman*. London: George G. Harrap, 1955.

Nugent, Neill. "Post-War Fascism?" In *British Fascism: Essays on the Radical Right in Inter-War Britain*, edited by Kenneth Lunn and Richard C. Thurlow, 205–226. London: Croom Helm, 1980.

O'Connor, Ulrick. *Brendan Behan*. London: Hamish Hamilton, 1970.

O'Donovan, Patrick. *For Fear of Weeping*. London: Macgibbon and Kee, 1950.

Oakley, Robin. "Cypriot Migration and Settlement in Britain." DPhil dissertation, Oxford University, 1971.

Ogle, Vanessa. "Archipelago Capitalism: Tax Havens, Offshore Money, and the State." *American Historical Review* 122, no. 5 (2017): 1431–1458.

Omissi, David E. *British Air Power and Colonial Control: The Royal Air Force, 1919-1939*. Manchester: Manchester University Press, 1990.

Orwell, George. *Diaries*. Edited by Peter Davison. London: Penguin, 2009.

Orwell, George. "The Politics of the English Language." In *Essays*, edited by John Carey, 954–966. New York: Everyman's Library, 2002.

Osborne, John. *The Entertainer*. In *Plays: Two*. London: Faber and Faber, 1998.

Osgerby, Bill. "Muscular Manhood and Salacious Sleaze: The Singular World of the 1950s Macho Pulps." In *Containing America: Cultural Production and Consumption in Fifties America*, edited by Nathan Abrams and Julie Hughes, 125–150. Birmingham: University of Birmingham Press, 2000.

Osiel, Mark. *Mass Atrocity, Collective Memory, and the Law*. New Brunswick, NJ: Transaction Publishers, 2000.

Overy, Richard. "Constructing a Space for Dissent in War: The Bombing Restriction Committee, 1941-1945," *English Historical Review* no. 550 (2016): 596–622.

Overy, Richard. "Pacifism and the Blitz." *Past & Present* 219 (May 2013): 201–236.

Overy, Richard. "'Why We Bomb You': Liberal War-Making and Moral Relativism in the RAF Bomber Offensive, 1940–45." In *Liberal Wars: Anglo-American Strategy, Ideology, and Practice*, edited by Alan Cromartie, 22–37. Abingdon: Routledge, 2015.

Owen, Nicholas. "'Facts are Sacred': the Manchester Guardian and Colonial Violence, 1930-32." *Journal of Modern History* 84, no. 3 (2012): 643–78.

Owen, Nicholas. *The British Left and India: Metropolitan Anti-Imperialism, 1885-1947*. Oxford: Oxford University Press, 2007.

Owen, Nicholas. "Critics of Empire in Britain." In *The Oxford History of the British Empire*, vol. 4, *The Twentieth Century*, edited by Judith M. Brown and Wm. Roger Louis, 188–211. Oxford: Oxford University Press, 1999.

Owen, Nicholas. "Four Straws in the Wind: Metropolitan Anti-Imperialism, January-February 1960." In *The Wind of Change: Harold Macmillan and British Decolonization*, edited by L. J. Butler and Sarah Stockwell, 116–139. Basingstoke: Palgrave Macmillan, 2013.

Owen, Nicholas. "Knowing and Not-Knowing: Complications in the Reporting of Colonial Violence." Paper presented at Speaking Out workshop, University of Warwick, February 2021.

Owen, Nicholas. *Other People's Struggles: Outsiders in Social Movements*. New York: Oxford University Press, 2019.

Page, Malcolm. "Television Drama in Britain." *Quarterly Journal of Speech* 57, no. 2 (1971): 214–220.

Paget, Julian. *Counter-Insurgency Operations: Techniques of Guerilla Warfare*. New York: Walker, 1967.

Pankhurst, Richard K. P. *Kenya: The History of Two Nations*. London: Independent Publishing, [1954].

Paris, Michael. *Warrior Nation: Images of War in British Popular Culture, 1850-2000*. London: Reaktion Books, 2000.

Paris, Peter [pseud.]. *The Impartial Knife: A Doctor in Cyprus*. New York: David McKay, 1961.

Parkinson, C. Northcote. *A Law Unto Themselves: Twelve Portraits*. Boston: Houghton Mifflin, 1966.

Parsons, Timothy. *The African Rank-and-File: Social Implications of Colonial Military Service in the King's African Rifles, 1902-1964*. Portsmouth, NH: Heinemann, 1999.

Patterson, Michael. *Strategies of Political Theatre: Post-War British Playwrights*. Cambridge: Cambridge University Press, 2003.

Pearce, Edward, ed. *The Golden Talking-Shop: The Oxford Union Debates Empire, World War, Revolution, and Women*. Oxford: Oxford University Press, 2016.

Perkin, Harold. *The Rise of Professional Society: England since 1880*. London: Routledge, 1989.

Phillips, K. N. *From Mau Mau to Christ* [Stirling]: Stirling Tract Enterprise, 1958.

Pissas, Michael N. *The Truth about Concentration Camps in Cyprus*. New York: s.n., 1957.

Pitchford, Mark Joseph. "The Conservative Party and the Extreme Right, 1945-1975." PhD dissertation, Cardiff University, 2009.

Pollitt, Harry. *Malaya: Stop the War!* London: Communist Party of Great Britain, [1952].

Porter, Bernard. *The Absent-Minded Imperialists: Empire, Society, and Culture in Britain*. Oxford: Oxford University Press, 2004.

Porter, Bernard. *British Imperial: What the British Empire Wasn't*. London: I.B. Tauris, 2016.

Pottle, Mark, ed. *Daring to Hope: The Diaries and Letters of Violet Bonham Carter, 1946-1969*. London: Weidenfeld & Nicolson, 2000.

Powys, John Cowper. *Letters of John Cowper Powys to Louis Wilkinson, 1935-1956*. London: Macdonald, 1958.

Pringle, Yolana. "Humanitarianism, Race, and Denial: The International Committee of the Red Cross and Kenya's Mau Mau Rebellion, 1952-60." *History Workshop Journal* no. 84 (2017): 89–107.

Proctor, Robert N., and Londa Schiebinger, eds. *Agnotology: The Making and Unmaking of Ignorance*. Stanford, CA: Stanford University Press, 2008.

Pugh, Martin. "Britain and Its Empire." In *The Oxford Handbook of Fascism*, edited by R. J. B. Bosworth, 489–506. Oxford University Press, 2010.

Pugh, Martin. *"Hurrah for the Blackshirts!": Fascists and Fascism in Britain Between the Wars*. London: Pimlico, 2006.

Rabinowitz, Paula. *American Pulp: How Paperbacks Brought Modernism to Main Street*. Princeton, NJ: Princeton University Press, 2014.

Ramsden, George. *Christopher Logue: A Bibliography, 1952-97*. Settrington: Stone Trough Books, 1997.

Ramsden, John. *The Age of Churchill and Eden, 1940-1957*. London: Longman, 1995.

Read, Donald. *The Power of News: The History of Reuters, 1849-1989*. Oxford: Oxford University Press, 1992.

Rebellato, Dan. *1956 and All That: The Making of Modern British Drama*. London: Routledge, 1999.

Reid, Victor Stafford. *The Leopard*. Chatham, New Jersey: Chatham Bookseller, 1972.

Rejali, Darius. *Torture and Democracy*. Princeton, NJ: Princeton University Press, 2007.

Renshaw, Daniel. *The Discourse of Repatriation in Britain, 1845-2016: A Political and Social History*. London: Routledge, 2021.

Rich, Paul B. *Cinema and Unconventional Warfare in the Twentieth Century: Insurgency, Terrorism, and Special Operations*. London: Bloomsbury, 2018.

Richards, Peter. *Honourable Members: A Study of the British Backbencher*. London: Faber and Faber, 1959.

Richardson, John E. "Racial Populism in British Fascist Discourse: The Case of *Combat* and the British National Party." In *Analysing Fascist Discourse: European Fascism in Talk and Text*, edited by Ruth Wodak and John E. Richardson, 181–202. Abingdon, Routledge, 2013.

Ricoeur, Paul. *Memory, History, Forgetting*. Translated by Kathleen Blamey and David Pellauer. Chicago: University of Chicago Press, 2004.

Rigby, Charles. *The Staff Journalist*. London: Pitman, 1950.

Robbins, Keith. *England, Ireland, Scotland, Wales: The Christian Church, 1900-2000*. Oxford: Oxford University Press, 2008.

Roberts, Philip. *The Royal Court Theatre and the Modern Stage*. Cambridge: Cambridge University Press, 1999.

Robic-Diaz, Delphine. *La guerre d'Indochine dans le cinema français: Images d'un trou de mémoire*. Rennes: Presses Universitaires de Rennes, 2015.

Robinson, Howard. *Carrying British Mail Overseas*. New York: New York University Press, 1964.

Rogin, Michael. "'Make My Day!': Spectacle as Amnesia in Imperial Politics." *Representations* 29 (Winter 1990): 99–123.

Rolph, C.H. *Kingsley: The Life, Letters, and Diaries of Kingsley Martin*. London: Gollancz, 1973.

Rose, Sonya O. *Which People's War? National Identity and Citizenship in Britain, 1939–1945*. Oxford: Oxford University Press, 2003.

Rose, W. K., ed. *The Letters of Wyndham Lewis*. Norfolk, CT: New Directions, 1963.

Rosenfeld, Sophia. *Common Sense: A Political History*. Cambridge, MA: Harvard University Press, 2011.

Ross, Kristin. *Fast Cars, Clean Bodies: Decolonization and the Reordering of French Culture*. Cambridge, MA: MIT Press, 1995.

Rothberg, Michael. *Multidirectional Memory: Remembering the Holocaust in the Age of Decolonization*. Stanford, CA: Stanford University Press, 2009.

Rothschild, Emma. *The Inner Life of Empires: An Eighteenth-Century History*. Princeton: Princeton University Press, 2011.

Roufos, Rodis. *The Age of Bronze*. London: Heinemann, 1960.

Rousso, Henry. *The Haunting Past: History, Memory, and Justice in Contemporary France*. Translated by Ralph Schoolcraft. Philadelphia: University of Pennsylvania Press, 1998.

Rousso, Henry. *The Vichy Syndrome: History and Memory in France since 1944*. Translated by Arthur Goldhammer. Cambridge, MA: Harvard University Press, 1991.

Ruark, Robert. *Something of Value*. London: Transworld, 1980.

Samuel, Raphael. *The Lost World of British Communism*. London: Verso, 2006.

Sandbrook, Dominic. *Never Had It So Good: A History of Britain from Suez to the Beatles*. London: Little, Brown, 2005.

Sasson, Tehila. "In the Name of Humanity: Britain and the Rise of Global Humanitarianism." PhD dissertation, University of California, Berkeley, 2015.

Satia, Priya. "The Defense of Inhumanity: Air Control and the British Idea of Arabia." *American Historical Review* 111 (February 2006): 16–51.

Satia, Priya. "Interwar Agnotology: Empire, Democracy, and the Production of Ignorance." In *Brave New World: Imperial and Democratic Nation-Building Between the Wars*, edited by Laura Beers and Geraint Thomas, 209–225. London: Institute of Historical Research, 2012.

Satia, Priya. *Time's Monster: How History Makes History*. Cambridge, MA: Belknap Press of Harvard University Press, 2020.

Satterthwaite, Margaret. "Finding, Verifying, and Curating Human Rights Facts." *Proceedings of the Annual Meeting of the American Society of International Law* 107 (2013): 62–65.

Saunders, Robert. "Brexit and Empire: 'Global Britain' and the Myth of Imperial Nostalgia." *Journal of Imperial and Commonwealth History* 48, no. 6 (2020): 1140–1174.

Savage, Mike. *Social Identities and Social Change in Britain Since 1940: The Politics of Method*. Oxford: Oxford University Press, 2010.

Scarry, Elaine. *The Body in Pain: The Making and Unmaking of the World.* New York: Oxford University Press, 1987.

Schmidl, Erwin A. "Kolonialkriege: Zwischen grossem Krieg and kleinem Frieden." In *Formen des Krieges: Vom Mittelalter zum "Low-Intensity-Conflict,"* edited by Manfried Rauchensteiner and Erwin A. Schmidl, 111–138. Graz: Verlag Styria, 1991.

Schofield, Camilla. *Enoch Powell and the Making of Colonial Britain.* Cambridge: Cambridge University Press, 2013.

Schudson, Michael. *Origins of the Ideal of Objectivity in the Professions: Studies in the History of American Journalism and American Law, 1830-1940.* New York: Garland, 1990.

Schwarz, Angela. "'Mit dem größtmöglichen Anstand weitermachen': Briefe britischer Kriegsteilnehmer und ihrer Angehörigen im Zweiten Weltkrieg." In *Andere Helme—andere Menschen? Heimaterfahrung und Frontalltag im Zweiten Weltkrieg,* edited by Detlef Vogel and Wolfram Wette, 205–236. Essen: Klartext, 1995.

Schwarz, Bill. *Memories of Empire.* Vol. 1, *The White Man's World.* Oxford: Oxford University Press, 2011.

Schwarz, Bill. "'The Only White Man in There': The Re-Racialisation of England, 1956-1968." *Race & Class* 38, no. 1 (1996): 65–78.

Schwarz, Bill. "Ways of Seeing." In *Visual Culture and Decolonisation in Britain,* edited by Simon Faulkner and Anandi Ramamurthy, 263–270. Milton: Routledge, 2019.

Semmel, Bernard. *Jamaican Blood and Victorian Conscience: The Governor Eyre Controversy.* Westport, CT: Greenwood Press, 1976.

Seyd, Patrick. "Factionalism within the Conservative Party: The Monday Club." *Government and Opposition* 7, no. 2 (1972): 464–487.

Seymour-Ure, Colin. *The British Press and Broadcasting since 1945.* Oxford: Basil Blackwell, 1991.

Shapiro, Barbara J. *A Culture of Fact: England, 1550-1720.* Ithaca, NY: Cornell University Press, 2000.

Shaw, Tony. *British Cinema and the Cold War: The State, Propaganda, and Consensus.* London: I.B. Tauris, 2006.

Shaw, Tony. "Eden and the BBC During the 1956 Suez Crisis: A Myth Re-Examined." *Twentieth Century British History* 6, no. 3 (1995): 320–343.

Sim, Katharine. *The Moon At My Feet.* London: Hodder and Stoughton, 1959.

Seal, Lizzie. "Sources of Public Response to the Death Penalty in Britain, 1930-65." *Legal Information Management* 16, no. 2 (2016): 91–94.

Shepard, Todd. *The Invention of Decolonization: The Algerian War and the Remaking of France.* Ithaca, NY: Cornell University Press, 2006.

Sherry, Norman. *The Life of Graham Greene.* Vol. 2, *1939-1955.* New York: Penguin, 1994.

Shubik, Irene. "Television Drama Series: A Producer's View." In *British Television Drama,* edited by Johnathan Bignell, Stephen Lacey, and Madeleine Macmurraugh-Kavanagh, 45–51. Basingstoke: Palgrave, 2000.

Sillitoe, Alan. *Key to the Door.* New York: Alfred A. Knopf, 1962.

Simpson, A.W.B. *Human Rights and the End of Empire: Britain and the Genesis of the European Convention*. Oxford: Oxford University Press, 2001.

Sinclair, Robert. *The British Press: The Journalist and His Conscience*. London: Home and Van Thal, 1949.

Six, Clemens. *Secularism, Decolonisation, and the Cold War in South and Southeast Asia*. New York: Routledge, 2018.

Skinner, Rob. "Facing the Challenge of 'Young Africa': Apartheid, South Africa, and British Decolonisation." *South African Historical Journal* 54, no. 1 (2005): 54–71.

Skinner, Rob. *The Foundations of Anti-Apartheid: Liberal Humanitarians and Transnational Activists in Britain and the United States, c. 1919-1964*. Basingstoke: Palgrave Macmillan, 2010.

Skinner, Rob. "The Moral Foundations of Anti-Apartheid Activism, 1946-1960." *Journal of Southern African Studies* 35, no. 2 (2009): 399–416.

Smith, Evan. *British Communism and the Politics of Race*. Leiden: Brill, 2018.

Smithson, Michael. "Toward a Social Theory of Ignorance." *Journal for the Theory of Social Behaviour* 15, no. 2 (1985): 151–172.

Snyder, William P. *The Politics of British Defense Policy, 1945-1962*. Columbus: Ohio State University Press, 1964.

Sontag, Susan. *On Photography*. New York: Farar, Straus, and Giroux, 1977.

Sontag, Susan. *Regarding the Pain of Others*. New York: Farar, Straus, and Giroux, 2003.

Soyinka, Wole. "The Past Must Address Its Present." Nobel Lecture, December 8, 1986. Online at https://www.nobelprize.org/prizes/literature/1986/soyinka/lecture/.

Soyinka, Wole. *You Must Set Forth at Dawn: A Memoir*. New York: Random House, 2006.

Spender, Stephen. *World Within World*. New York: Modern Library, 2001.

Spies, S.B. *Methods of Barbarism? Roberts and Kitchener and Civilians in the Boer Republics, January 1900-May 1902*. Cape Town: Human & Rousseau, 1977.

Stapleton, James W. *The Gate Hangs Well*. London: Hammond, Hammond, [1957].

Steadman-Jones, Richard. "Colonial Fiction for Liberal Readers: John Masters and the Savage Family Saga." In *End of Empire and the English Novel Since 1945*, edited by Rachel Gilmour and Bill Schwarz, 74–91. Manchester: Manchester University Press, 2011.

Stearn, Roger T. "War Correspondents and Colonial War, c. 1870-1900." In *Popular Imperialism and the Military, 1850-1950*, edited by John M. MacKenzie, 139–161. Manchester: Manchester University Press, 1992.

Steinacher, Gerald. *Humanitarians at War: The Red Cross in the Shadow of the Holocaust*. Oxford: Oxford University Press, 2017.

Stocker, Paul. *Lost Imperium: Far Right Visions of the British Empire, c. 1920-1980*. Abingdon: Routledge, 2021.

Stocker, Paul. "The Postwar British Extreme Right and Empire, 1945-1967." *Religion Compass* 9, no. 5 (2015): 162–172.

Stockwell, Sarah. *The British End of the British Empire*. Cambridge: Cambridge University Press, 2018.

Stockwell, Sarah. "'Improper and Even Unconstitutional': The Involvement of the Church of England in the Politics of the End of Empire in Cyprus." In *From the Reformation to the Permissive Society: A Miscellany in Celebration of the 400th Anniversary of Lambeth Palace* Library, edited by Melanie Barber and Stephen Taylor with Gabriel Sewell, 583–656. Woodbridge, UK: Boydell Press, 2010.

Stoler, Ann Laura. "'In Cold Blood': Hierarchies of Credibility and the Politics of Colonial Narratives." *Representations* 37 (Winter 1992): 151–189.

Stone, Dan. "The English Mistery, the BUF, and the Dilemmas of British Fascism." *Journal of Modern History* 75 (2003): 336–358.

Stoneham, C. T. *Kenya Mystery*. London: Museum Press, 1954.

Strachan, Hew. "British Counter-Insurgency from Malaya to Iraq." *Journal of the Royal United Services Institute* 152 (2007): 8–11.

Strachan, Hew. "The British Way in Warfare Revisited." *Historical Journal* 26, no. 2 (1983): 447–461.

Street, Sarah. *Colour Films in Britain: The Negotiation of Innovation 1900-55*. Basingstoke: Palgrave Macmillan, 2012.

Stuart, John. *British Missionaries and the End of Empire: East, Central, and Southern Africa, 1939-64*. Grand Rapids: William B. Eerdmans, 2011.

Stubbs, Jonathan. "Making Headlines in a State of Emergency: The Case of the *Times of Cyprus*, 1955-1960." *Journal of Imperial & Commonwealth History* 45, no. 1 (2017): 70–92.

Stubbs, Richard. *Hearts and Minds in Guerilla Warfare: The Malayan Emergency, 1948-1960*. Oxford: Oxford University Press, 1989.

Sutcliffe-Braithwaite, Florence. *Class, Politics, and the Decline of Deference in England, 1968-2000*. Oxford: Oxford University Press, 2018.

Suyin, Han. *And the Rain My Drink*. Boston: Little, Brown, 1956.

Suyin, Han. *My House Has Two Doors*. New York: Putnam, 1980.

Target, G.W. *The Missionaries*. London: Gerald Duckworth, 1961.

Taylor, C.P. *Bandits!* Cullercoats: Iron Press, 1977.

Taylor, Don. *Days of Vision: Working with David Mercer: Television Drama Then and Now*. London: Methuen, 1990.

Taylor, John. *War Photography: Realism in the British Press*. London: Routledge, 1991.

Taylor, John Russell. *Anger and After: A Guide to the New British Drama*. London: Methuen, 1962.

Taussig, Michael. "Culture of Terror—Space of Death: Roger Casement's Putumayo Report and the Explanation of Torture." *Comparative Studies in Society and History* 26, no. 3 (1984): 467–497.

Thomas, Keith. "Cases of Conscience in Seventeenth-Century England." In *Public Duty and Private Conscience in Seventeenth-Century England*, edited by John Morrill, Paul Slack, and Daniel Woolf, 29–56. Oxford: Oxford University Press, 1993.

Thomas, Martin. *Fight or Flight: Britain, France, and Their Roads from Empire.* Oxford: Oxford University Press, 2014.

Thomas, Martin, and Gareth Curless, eds. *Decolonization and Conflict: Colonial Comparisons and Legacies.* London: Bloomsbury, 2017.

Thomas, W. B. *The Touch of Pitch: A Story of Mau Mau.* London: Allan Wingate, 1956.

Thompson, Anthony Hugh. *Censorship in Public Libraries in the United Kingdom During the Twentieth Century.* Epping: Bowker, 1975.

Thompson, E. P. "Where Are We Now ?" In *E.P. Thompson and the Making of the New Left: Essays and Polemics,* edited by Cal Winslow, 215–247. New York: Monthly Review Press, 2014.

Thompson, Robert. *Defeating Communist Insurgency: Experiences from Malaya and Vietnam.* London: Chatto & Windus, 1966.

Thurlow, Richard. *Fascism in Britain: A History, 1918-1985.* Oxford: Basil Blackwell, 1987.

Thurlow, Richard. *Fascism in Modern Britain.* Phoenix Mill, England: Sutton, 2000.

Tracey, Michael. *The Decline and Fall of Public Service Broadcasting.* Oxford: Oxford University Press, 1998.

Tremayne, Penelope. *Below the Tide.* Boston: Houghton Mifflin, 1959.

Ullmann, Richard K. "The Christian Faith in Relation to the State." In *The Society of Friends, the Church, and the State,* 24–38. London: Friends' Book Centre, [1953].

United Kingdom. *Report of the Committee of Privy Counselors Appointed to Consider Authorised Procedures for the Interrogation of Persons Suspected of Terrorism.* Cmnd. 4901. London: HMSO, 1972.

U.S. Army/Marine Corps Counterinsurgency Field Manual. Chicago: University of Chicago Press, 2007.

Ussishkin, Daniel. *Morale: A Modern British History.* New York: Oxford University Press, 2017.

Vagts, Alfred. *A History of Militarism.* Westport, CT: Greenwood Press, 1981.

Vallance, Edward. "The Kingdom's Case: The Use of Casuistry as a Political Language, 1640-1692." *Albion* 34, no. 4 (2002): 557–583.

van Dijk, Boyd. *Preparing for War: The Making of the 1949 Geneva Conventions.* Oxford: Oxford University Press, 2022.

Veness, Thelma. *School Leavers: Their Aspirations and Expectations.* London: Methuen, 1962.

Vidal-Naquet, Clémentine. "Écris-Moi Souvent." In *Une Histoire de la Guerre: Du XIXe siècle à nos jours,* edited by Bruno Cabanes, 391–396. Paris: Seuil, 2018.

Violation of Human Rights in Cyprus: A Factual Documentation. [Nicosia]: Ethnarchy of Cyprus, 1957.

Wagner, Kim. *Amritsar, 1919: An Empire of Fear and the Making of a Massacre.* New Haven, CT: Yale University Press, 2019.

Wagner, Kim. *The Skull of Alum Bheg: The Life and Death of a Rebel of 1857.* New York: Oxford University Press, 2018.

Walker, Martin. *The National Front.* London: Fontana, 1977.

Wall, Rosemary, and Anne Marie Rafferty. "Nursing and the 'Hearts and Minds' Campaign, 1948-1958: The Malayan Emergency." In the *Routledge Handbook on the Global History of* Nursing, edited by Patricia D'Antonio, Julie A. Fairman, and Jean C. Whelan, 218–236. New York: Routledge, 2013.

Walter, Dierk. *Colonial Violence: European Empires and the Use of Force.* Translated by Peter Lewis. Oxford: Oxford University Press, 2017.

Walter, Dierk. "Warum Kolonialkrieg?" In *Kolonialkriege: Militärische Gewalt im Zeichen des Imperialismus*, edited by Thoralf Klein and Frank Schumacher, 14–43. Hamburg: HIS Verlag, 2006.

Walton, Calder. *Empire of Secrets: British Intelligence, the Cold War, and the Twilight of Empire.* New York: Overlook Press, 2013.

Ward, Edward. *I've Lived Like a Lord.* London: Joseph, 1970.

Ward, Stephen J.A. *The Invention of Journalism Ethics: The Path to Objectivity and Beyond.* Montreal: McGill-Queen's University Press, 2015.

Ward, Stuart, ed. *British Culture and the End of Empire.* Manchester: Manchester University Press, 2001.

Warden, Claire. *British Avant-Garde Theatre.* Basingstoke: Palgrave Macmillan, 2012.

Wasserstein, Bernard. *Britain and the Jews of Europe 1939-1945.* London: Leicester University Press, 1999.

Waters, Rob. *Thinking Black: Britain, 1964-1985.* Berkeley: University of California Press, 2019.

Webber, G. C. "Patterns of Membership and Support for the British Union of Fascists." *Journal of Contemporary History* 19, no. 4 (1984): 575–606.

Webster, Wendy. *Englishness and Empire, 1939-1965.* Oxford: Oxford University Press, 2007.

Weiler, Peter. *British Labour and the Cold War.* Stanford: Stanford University Press, 1988.

Weiss, Thomas G. "Principles, Politics, and Humanitarian Action." *Ethics & International Affairs* 13, no. 1 (1999): 1–22.

Welch, Cheryl B. "Colonial Violence and the Rhetoric of Evasion: Tocqueville on Algeria." *Political Theory* 31, no. 2 (2003): 235–264.

Wells, Edward. *Mailshot: A History of the Forces Postal Service.* s.l.: Defence Postal and Courier Services, 1987.

Whipple, Amy. "Revisiting the 'Rivers of Blood' Controversy: Letters to Enoch Powell." *Journal of British Studies* 28, no. 3 (2009): 717–735.

White, Luise. *Fighting and Writing: The Rhodesian Army at War and Postwar.* Durham, NC: Duke University Press, 2021.

White, Luise. "Telling More: Lies, Secrets, and History," *History and Theory* 39, no. 4 (2000): 11–22.

Whittle, Matthew. *Post-War British Literature and the "End of Empire."* London: Palgrave Macmillan, 2016.

Wieviorka, Annette. *The Era of the Witness*. Translated by Jared Stark. Ithaca, NY: Cornell University Press, 2006.

Wilkinson-Latham, R.J. *From Our Special Correspondent: Victorian War Correspondents and Their Campaigns*. London: Hodder and Stoughton, 1979.

Willett, John. *The Theatre of Bertolt Brecht: A Study from Eight Aspects*. London: Methuen, 1959.

Williams, Francis. *Dangerous Estate: The Anatomy of Newspapers*. London: Longmans, 1957.

Williams, Howard. *Paradise Precarious*. London: Welcome Press, [1959?].

Williams, Kevin. *A New History of War Reporting*. New York: Routledge, 2020.

Williams, Kevin. *Read All About It! A History of the British Newspaper*. London: Routledge, 2010.

Williams, Raymond. "Drama in a Dramatised Society." In *Raymond Williams on Television: Selected Writings*, edited by Alan O'Connor, 3–13. London: Routledge, 1989.

Williams, Raymond. *Politics and Letters: Interviews with* New Left Review. London: Verso, 2015.

Wilson, Nicola. "Middlemen, Middlebrow, Broadbrow." In *British Literature in Transition*, 1920-1940: *Futility and Anarchy*, edited by Charles Ferrall and Dougal McNeill, 315–330. Cambridge: Cambridge University Press, 2018.

Wittenbach, H.A. *Eastern Horizons*. London: Highway Press, 1954.

Worsley, Peter. *An Academic Skating on Thin Ice*. New York: Berghahn Books, 2008.

Worsley, Peter. "Imperial Retreat." In *Out of Apathy*, edited by E.P. Thompson, 101–140. London: Stevens and Sons, 1960.

Wright, Bradford. *Comic Book Nation: The Transformation of Youth Culture in America*. Baltimore: Johns Hopkins University Press, 2001.

Wright, John Dryburgh. "The National Council for the Training of Journalists: Twenty-Five Years of Progress and Problems." PhD dissertation, University of Texas at Austin, 1979.

Wright, Peter. *Spycatcher: The Candid Autobiography of a Senior Intelligence Officer*. New York: Viking, 1987.

Wynd, Oswald. *The Gentle Pirate: An Entertainment*. Garden City, NY: Doubleday, 1951.

Yeo, Kim Wah. "Joining the Communist Underground: The Conversion of English-Educated Radicals to Communism in Singapore." *Journal of the Malaysian Branch of the Royal Asiatic Society* 67, no. 1 (1994): 29–59.

Zahn, Gordon C. *The Military Chaplaincy: A Study of Role Tension in the Royal Air Force*. University of Toronto Press, 1969.

Zizek, Slavoj. *Violence: Six Sideways Reflections*. New York: Picador, 2008.

Index

For the benefit of digital users, indexed terms that span two pages (e.g., 52–53) may, on occasion, appear on only one of those pages.